WEYERHAEUSER ENVIRONMENTAL BOOKS

William Cronon, Editor

Weyerhaeuser Environmental Books explore human relationships with natural environments in all their variety and complexity. They seek to cast new light on the ways that natural systems affect human communities, the ways that people affect the environments of which they are a part, and the ways that different cultural conceptions of nature profoundly shape our sense of the world around us. A complete list of the books in the series appears at the end of this book.

DAVID BIGGS FOREWORD BY WILLIAM CRONON

QUAGMIRE

NATION-BUILDING AND NATURE IN THE MEKONG DELTA

UNIVERSITY OF WASHINGTON PRESS SEATTLE AND LONDON

Quagmire: Nation-Building and Nature in the Mekong Delta is published
with the assistance of a grant from the Weyerhaeuser Environmental Books
Endowment, established by the Weyerhaeuser Company Foundation,
members of the Weyerhaeuser family, and Janet and Jack Creighton.

University of Washington Press
PO Box 50096, Seattle, WA 98145, USA
www.washington.edu/uwpress

Designed and composed by Pamela Canell. Typeset in Minion, a font created
by Robert Slimbach in 1991, and Scala, a font created by Martin Majoor in 1990.
Printed and bound by Thomson-Shore, Inc., in Chelsea, Michigan, on 50#
Natures Natural paper.

Library of Congress Cataloging-in-Publication Data
Biggs, David A.
Quagmire : nation-building and nature in the Mekong Delta / David Biggs.
p. cm. — (Weyerhaeuser environmental books)
Includes bibliographical references and index.
ISBN 978-0-295-99199-3 (pbk. : alk. paper)
1. Mekong River Delta (Vietnam and Cambodia)—Environmental conditions.
2. Water resources development—Mekong River Delta (Vietnam and Cambodia)
3. Nation-building—Vietnam. I. Title.
GE160.V5B54 2010   959.7'8—dc22   2010019727

The paper used in this publication is acid-free and 90 percent recycled from at
least 50 percent post-consumer waste. It meets the minimum requirements of
American National Standard for Information Sciences—Permanence of Paper for
Printed Library Materials, ANSI z39.48–1984.

For Hồng Anh, Xuân Anh, and Kiên

CONTENTS

Foreword: Nation-Making in the Mekong Mire by William Cronon ix

Acknowledgments xv

Introduction 3

1   Water's Edge 23

2   Water Grid 53

3   Hydroagricultural Crisis 91

4   Balkanization 127

5   Modernization 153

6   American War 197

Epilogue 227

Notes 237

Bibliography 271

Index 289

FOREWORD Nation-Making in the Mekong Mire

by William Cronon

I n 1962, a relatively unknown reporter named David Halberstam arrived
in South Vietnam. For the next two years, he wrote a series of articles for
the *New York Times* depicting the failings and corruptions of a regime
that the United States was seeking to defend, using aid and advisors, from
what Washington perceived as a growing Communist threat. President
John F. Kennedy was angry enough about Halberstam's coverage to urge
the *Times* to send its young reporter home. The paper's publisher refused,
and when Halberstam finally left Southeast Asia two years later, his work
was awarded a Pulitzer Prize. Although he is today best known for what
many regard as the finest book ever written about the American debacle
in Vietnam — *The Best and the Brightest*, published in 1972 — Halberstam
also published a remarkably prescient volume seven years earlier that more
or less predicted the military and political disaster that had yet to unfold.
That book is not much remembered today, but its title, *The Making of a*

Quagmire, has ever since provided the single most influential metaphor for the war it depicted.

Quagmire. It is a curious word in English, and its use in this unexpected context suggests Halberstam's special gifts as a writer. *Quag* was used in sixteenth-century England to describe marshy or boggy ground, especially if covered with a layer of turf that shakes or quakes when one walks across it (quag and quake are in fact nearly the same word). *Mire* (derived in Middle English from an Old Norse word for bog) conveys a nearly identical meaning—wet spongy earth, as in a bog or marsh, or heavy water-saturated mud. When the two combine into a single word, the result almost seems redundant, multiplying the muckiness of the marshy, swampy, watery ground. All these boggy associations led in turn to the symbolic meaning the word acquired within a couple centuries of first entering the language: a circumstance one sinks into from which it proves ever more difficult to extricate oneself. This was the meaning Halberstam had most in mind when he chose *quagmire* to label the American situation in Vietnam: a difficult, confusing, engulfing position that despite the best efforts of seemingly competent people only became worse the more they struggled to slog on. Halberstam's quagmire was military, political, and above all moral. Without comprehending the consequences of their own actions, the best and brightest of the nation's leaders found themselves mired in the jungles of Southeast Asia—bogged down, rudderless, entangled, entrapped. The marshy metaphors pile up to convey the sense of confused hopelessness that eventually became a dominant American interpretation of Vietnam and all that it stood for.

As compelling as such language might seem as a way to understand Vietnam in the 1960s, it nonetheless lays a few traps of its own for unwary readers. This is especially true in the United States, where the symbolic quagmire can all too easily tempt Americans to turn a blind eye toward the lived realities of the Vietnam War. Failure to notice the realities of Vietnam's places and people, let alone understand them, was among the most important reasons the war happened as it did. This is in fact one of Halberstam's chief insights. By accepting the Cold War conflict with the Soviet Union as their chief interpretive framework, American leaders overlooked the extent to which they were projecting onto Vietnam an imagined geography that resided far more in their own minds than in the actual landscapes of Southeast Asia. This could be just as true for those who opposed the war as for those who supported it. When in his inaugural address John Kennedy called on his fellow Americans to "bear the burden of a long twilight struggle," he was unwittingly framing the narrative that pointed toward the war ahead. And when Francis Ford Coppola borrowed the central character and story from Joseph Conrad's most famous novella for his film *Apocalypse Now*, he recast Kennedy's symbolism as the heart of darkness for a nation that had lost its soul. Although such images say a great deal about the United States in the 1960s and 1970s, neither Kennedy's twilight struggle nor Coppola's heart of darkness is of much use when seeking an understanding of Vietnam itself.

To gain such understanding, there are few better places to turn than the book you hold in your hands. *Quagmire: Nation Building and Nature in the Mekong Delta* uses the seemingly unlikely tools of environmental history to reinterpret the full sweep of the Vietnamese past, from precolonial times through the French and American eras to the postwar present. Although there is intentional irony in David Biggs's decision to adopt Halberstam's famous word for the title of his own book, that irony points toward a much deeper truth. Beneath the metaphysical symbolism of the stories that the French and Americans told to explain their activities in Vietnam was an actual physical quagmire whose material and environmental realities can tell us far more about the Vietnamese past than do the colonial narratives that have been fashioned from its muck.

Biggs's focus is not on all of Vietnam but on the southernmost portion of that nation, where the Mekong River flows into the South China Sea. Although the Mekong is one of the world's great watercourses, surpassing in length all U.S. rivers save for the combined Mississippi-Missouri, most Americans would be hard-pressed to place it on a map, let alone describe its centrality to the geography of Southeast Asia and the wars that have been fought there. Twenty-seven hundred miles in length, the Mekong River drains more than 300,000 square miles as it makes its journey from Tibet through China's Yunnan Province southeast to Myanmar, Laos, Thailand, Cambodia, and Vietnam. There, before it reaches the ocean, it spreads out in countless channels or distributaries across a vast plain occupying more than 15,000 square miles. Much of the terrain varies no more than a meter in height, making this one of the flattest delta landscapes anywhere on the planet. Tidal pulses can reach as much as a hundred kilometers upstream from the sea, and the seasonal monsoon rains regularly bring floodwaters that inundate thousands of square miles. Human beings seeking to make homes for themselves in such a place quickly come to understand meanings for "quagmire"—no matter what words they use for it—that are richer and subtler, damper and earthier, than the moral metaphors of failed colonial wars.

David Biggs's brilliance in *Quagmire* is to explore the myriad ways in which the intermingled elements of land and water profoundly shaped efforts to build a nation in the challenging and ever-shifting geographies of the Mekong Delta. Centuries prior to the coming of the French in the 1860s, the Khmer Empire established and maintained settlements in the rocky uplands above the river. Among Biggs's most important contributions is his insistence that there is more continuity between the pre-colonial and colonial periods in Southeast Asia than recent scholarly interpretations have sometimes suggested. He is equally insistent that neither the colonizer nor the colonized can be understood if we fail to explore their relationships with the landscapes on which they strove to create state structures and national identities. He goes further than almost any other scholar before him in demonstrating how essential it is to take environment seriously even if one's primary goal is to understand the political histories of colonies, empires, and nations.

To name just one striking example, among the first projects the French pursued in consolidating their colonial occupation of Indochina in the second half of the nineteenth century was to build new canals to redirect the river's flow, establish new access to the Gulf of Thailand, and make the serpentine waterways of the delta more accessible to boats capable of carrying commodities and fighting wars. Among their most ambitious achievements was the Chợ Gạo, or Duperré Canal, which connected the colonial capital of Sài Gòn (now Hồ Chí Minh City) with the nearest delta port. Opened with great celebrations in 1877, the canal silted to the point of becoming unnavigable just two years later. Carried by complex tidal currents emanating from both sides of the newly created waterways, silt accumulated in the middle of such canals to form sandbars, which the French called "dead points" because ships could not travel across them for several months of the year. Although the French engineers had failed to anticipate these navigational barriers, local canal builders had long been familiar with them—and viewed them more positively than did their colonial counterparts. What the French saw as "dead points" native residents of the delta saw as "meeting points," places where travelers from opposite sides of a canal corridor could beach their boats to meet and exchange goods. What the colonizers saw as problems needing to be fixed were seen by the colonized as opportunities to be welcomed. In much the same way, the shifting channels and islands that colonial armies found so confusing provided perfect cover for the local rebels and guerrilla soldiers who opposed them.

Travel with David Biggs to the Mekong Delta, and you will find yourself paying unexpectedly close attention to the flatness of the ground, the slow flow of the water, the tangle of the vegetation, the seasonality of the rainfall, the heights of the tides, and the ever-changing topography of the river and its channels. Fascinating in and of themselves, these in turn supply the contexts in which you will come to new understandings of the interactions among Khmer, Chinese, and Vietnamese residents with the engineers, diplomats, advisors, traders, and soldiers sent first by the French and eventually by the Americans. *Quagmire* is not mainly a revisionist history of the Vietnam War—the United States military is present only in the final chapter—but readers will surely find themselves rethinking their views of that war long before they approach the end of this superb book. By asking us to take the river and its peoples seriously, by showing us how much we can learn by looking beyond metaphors to see real water and real mud, real people and real history, David Biggs points the way toward deepened understandings of nature and nation that reach far beyond the place where the Mekong finally pours its waters into the sea.

ACKNOWLEDGMENTS

B ooks are only partial reflections of the many conversations, experiences, and supportive relationships that nurture them to life. From 1993 to 1996, Volunteers in Asia, a nonprofit organization that sends college graduates to teach English in several Asian countries, including Vietnam, afforded me my first opportunities to explore Vietnamese landscapes and culture, before it dawned on me that this might turn into a career. I extend my thanks to friends such as Lan Thảo, Cô Mai, and Ân, who joined me on some of these early, formative adventures. As a graduate student at the University of Washington, I benefited tremendously from the attentions of Professors Laurie Sears, Richard White, Christoph Giebel, Nicholas Chrisman, Keith Benson, Charles Keyes, and others associated with the Department of History and the Southeast Asia Center. I owe particular thanks to Laurie Sears as an academic adviser and life coach who helped me wade through the quagmires of academic life with

ACKNOWLEDGMENTS

constant admonitions to slow down and enjoy the ride while applying for every grant imaginable. Her diligence paid off in Foreign Language and Area Studies (FLAS) grants (1998–2000, 2003) and a Visiting Committee grant (1996–97) that permitted me to improve my Vietnamese to a passable level. My University of Washington experience was also deeply enriched by the many graduate students and friends I met along the way. Richard White's seminar introduced me to such characters as Matt Klingle, Connie Chiang, and Coll Thrush, who not only made these seminars fun but also greatly informed my study of environmental history with constant allusions to the American West. Along those lines, I am also especially grateful to Richard for his incisive and dedicated readings of many paper and chapter drafts. Sarah Van Fleet and others at the Southeast Asia Center were instrumental in building a dynamic community of Vietnamese and Vietnamese studies doctoral students at the university. Thanks especially to Hạnh and Alex, Sanh, Câm, Judith, Brad, Đức, Ngọc, Harriet, George, Jamie, Michele, Rie, Woonkyung, Joe, and the many visitors to the Big Time Friday Seminars on "the Ave." These friendships I carried with me over the Pacific to Vietnam and beyond.

I could not have pursued field research in Vietnam without support from many institutions over the years. I studied at the Southeast Asia Summer Studies Institute (ASU '97) and followed this with study at Cần Thơ University in 1999 with Thầy Nở and Cô Thủy of the Department of Literature thanks to a Blakemore Foundation Grant. An IIE Fulbright Travel Grant (2000) and a Fulbright Hayes Fellowship (2001–2) gave me time to live in the delta and make good use of stretches of time in between document pulls at the Vietnam National Archives. The staff at the Institute of Social Sciences and the Humanities and the Vietnam National Archives Center #2 in Hồ Chí Minh City and Drs. Chiếm, Ni, and Bé of the Department of Natural Resources and Environmental Management at Cần Thơ University were consistently patient and tolerant, and they were instrumental as sponsors in getting letters stamped and doors opened.

Expansion of this project into a book continued in the United States as I embarked on several stints of research at the U.S. National Archives in College Park and began teaching at the University of California, Riverside, in 2004. Thanks especially to Archivist Richard Boylan for helping me navigate the immense collections of the U.S. Armed Forces records, where the signal-to-noise ratio is often faint at best. Later chapters of this book benefited immensely from the input of my colleagues. Thanks especially to Henk Maier, Justin McDaniel, and Michael Feener for reading sections during a UCR Center for Ideas and Society seminar, and my appreciation extends to a fabulously congenial, creative Department of History and College of Humanities, Arts, and Social Sciences. I was fortunate enough to receive a UC Presidential Research Fellowship in the Humanities and a National Endowment for the Humanities Summer Stipend that afforded me time off from teaching to expand the later chapters and complete the book. Later sections of this book also benefited from a series of paper presentations and conferences involving Nancy Peluso and Ken MacLean. A special thanks goes to Edward Miller for his limitless generosity with sources and deep knowledge of the Diệm era.

At the University of Washington Press, Marianne Keddington-Lang and Bill Cronon took up the manuscript and were immensely supportive in the review and editing process. Thanks to them and especially to the anonymous readers for straightening out tortuous prose and for copious, thoughtful notes.

Research and writing can be enormously taxing on one's personal life, so I reserve final acknowledgments for the many friends and family along the way who supported me in less tangible but no less important ways. Thanks to Peter Thorin and the rotating members of the Sài Gòn posse for making archival trips to "the city" (*thành phố*) not only productive but oftentimes ridiculously fun. Thanks to the six uncles in Cần Thơ for introducing me to such things as death anniversaries and Christmas masses in Vietnamese. Uncle Minh has passed, but I thank his family for being my Cần Thơ family away from home. Thanks also to Uncle Thủy for the many provocative discussions and insights into Cần Thơ life. Thanks especially to my neighbors on Alley 123 in Cần Thơ and to Walter, Katie, Katherine, Peggy, and especially Thơ for her friendship and Huỳnh for additional laughs and translation and transcription of the interviews. In Seattle, thanks to Amir, Dave, Harvey, and the Puppet Lab for much-needed short-term employment and advice on maps. Along those lines, thanks to Stephanie Toothman, Jesse Kennedy, and the Klondike gang for their support and for showing me what an incredible return we get out of the few tax dollars that support the National Park Service.

Warm thanks to my extended family for remaining supportive throughout. Thanks to Thầy Ba and Mẹ Hiệp and especially Lan Thảo for adopting me in 1994 and helping me learn a bit more about the meaning of family. I thank Ba Tô and Mẹ Nguyện for openhearted support from our first meeting at the engagement ceremony in 2000. Thanks to my father and mother, William and Susan Biggs, for their steadfast encouragement for me to do as country singer Garth Brooks once said and "follow my river." I don't know that they meant for me to take it so literally, but none-theless they were there when I needed them and I am eternally grateful.

Finally, the person to whom I owe the deepest gratitude, for her con-stant support and delicious food, is my wife, Hồng Anh. Since our meeting at the Army Pool in 2000, my quality of life has improved exponentially. Thank you for keeping me light, sharing the journey, and believing in this project.

ACKNOWLEDGMENTS

QUAGMIRE

FIG. 1. *Tidal Creek in the Mekong Delta. The small boats in the center of this image are three-sided canoes* (ghe tam bàn). *The domed structures on the right are brick kilns and in the distance is a coconut grove.* Source: *Emile Gsell; albumen photo on paper, presented to Governor Le Myre de Vilers by the Colonial Council in 1882. Donated to the Foreign Affairs Library in 1894. Ministry of Foreign Affairs Archives, Paris, "Le Myre de Vilers," no. A000776.*

Mountains are the bones of the land and water the blood,

animating traffic from which rise settled lands. —*Trịnh Hoài Đức*[1]

INTRODUCTION

I n October 1879, just after the peak of the Mekong River's annual floods, a French gunboat entered a deteriorated canal on a survey mission to chart a waterway that once linked river traffic on the Mekong to sea traffic in the Gulf of Siam. Since 1867, the Vĩnh Tế Canal had formed part of French Cochinchina's border with Cambodia, and for another decade, France's brown-water fleet in Indochina—armor-plated steamers with gun platforms built atop steel towers—fought various local groups to maintain control of the Mekong Delta. Since 1859, the admiral-governors had been busy expanding Sài Gòn's ports and its emerging downtown, the rue Catinat; but out in the western borderlands, there was little, if any, evidence of the French presence save a few tricolors planted on militia posts, telegraph wires strung up on straggly, cajeput stumps, and the occasional white steamship plying the shallow, muddy water. From 1859 to 1879, a motley parade of junior officers, some staying on in the colony after their tours of duty, engaged in the various military and civilian activities required to maintain order and administer key services.

It was only after the January 1879 election in France, a sweeping victory for left-leaning Republicans, that the admiral-governors left and a new, civilian administration began to implement a host of reforms and construction projects that resembled what today might be recognized as nation-building. These projects were designed not only to realize profits and facilitate exploitation of Cochinchina's natural resources but also to transform the lives of colonial subjects and the landscapes they inhabited. Colonial governors and public-works engineers submitted all manner of proposals for government and private investment—railroads, public schools, canals, and roads—to realize *la mission civilisatrice*. Paternalistic and chauvinistic by design, *la mission civilisatrice* was also situated squarely within the Center Left of French politics; it was a progressive venture.

Naval hydrographer Jacques Rénaud was likely one of these progressives. Working aboard the gunboat *Hache* on the Vĩnh Tế Canal in 1879, he used soil core drills, depth gauges, and other instruments to measure water flow and bottom features along the seventy-kilometer path of the Vĩnh Tế Canal. Excerpts from his report, published in a popular colonial journal, described his sixteen-day journey and gave a precise picture of the ecological and social conditions on this waterway far from the villas, cafés, and macadam-paved streets of Sài Gòn. In some stretches, the canal's banks disappeared below giant shallow lakes of muddy water fed by the Mekong's autumn monsoon floods. In other sections, *lục bình* (water hyacinth, *Eichhornia crassipes*), a different sort of Western invasive, clogged the canal in a dense floating mat of vegetation that threatened to stop the propeller-driven ship dead in its path. On guard against potential ambushes from Khmer or Vietnamese insurgents who might be lurking on the banks, the gunboat's crew jumped into the canal with machetes and hacked a path through the *lục bình*.

In general, Rénaud's prognosis for economic development in the region was not good. Soil corings revealed a hard-packed marine clay with colorful bands ranging from white to a dark ferrous red that, to any farmer, signaled severely acidic conditions unfavorable for riziculture (rice cultivation). Repeated blows with a sledgehammer sank an iron coring drill just a meter deep, and the crew used a ship-mounted hoist to pull it out. Ending his journey at Hà Tiên in a bay opening to the blue waters of the Gulf of Siam, Rénaud encountered more bad news. With the French development of modern facilities at Sài Gòn, commercial trade at the once-prosperous port of Hà Tiên had diminished to a trickle of domestic commodities such as rice, dried fish, and pepper.[2]

Rénaud's report is interesting historically for the ways it situated the painstaking work of surveying into a more colorful account of nearby landmarks and the surrounding landscape, a colonial travelogue. As was common among engineers in his day, Rénaud published his account in a popular journal, *Excursions et reconnaissances,* intended for a French audience fascinated with exploration and opportunities for investment overseas. He offered readers not only a glimpse of the canal but a deeper historical gaze into its surroundings. He revealed to readers that the original canal was the result of an arduous, five-year Vietnamese public-works campaign begun in 1820 that required tens of thousands of conscripted laborers. The work killed several hundred via drought and disease; and in 1822 Vietnamese troops had to put down a Khmer workers' revolt sparked by the working conditions and Vietnamese incursions into formerly Khmer territory. Midway along the canal's course, Rénaud and the crew stopped to visit a group of tombs and temples located at the base of Sam Mountain. The interpreter on board translated for Rénaud a commemorative text in Chinese characters carved on a stone tablet, the Vietnamese royal government's memorial to the fallen workers. It listed the achievements of the military governor who oversaw the construction of the canal and promoted new settlements in the western frontier. Rénaud included the full translation of the text in his essay and added his own observations, comparing the Vietnamese governor's struggle to suppress Khmer revolts with French struggles in the 1870s to put down local revolts led by Vietnamese and Khmer groups from the area. Like many young men of his day, Rénaud appreciated that nation-building involved constant negotiation among the demands of new projects, native people, and the environment. To Rénaud, the Vietnamese canal and settlements represented a "work in progress," and he lamented that nothing had been done to restore the waterway or to "continue the work [*l'oeuvre*] of civilization started by the Vietnamese" since the French conquest had ended in 1867.[3]

Like Rénaud's investigation of nature and history along the Vĩnh Tế Canal, this book is motivated by a similar interest in how the activities and politics of nation-building were connected to the historically and environmentally complex places where they occurred. Whether imperialist or nationalist in design, public works such as roads and canals incorporated many overlapping layers of negotiations between different groups of people and the environments they inhabited. Technology also figured centrally in these struggles as newer, laborsaving machines such as steam-powered dredges reconfigured the costs and benefits involved in construction. The winding maze of rivers and permeable soils of the Mekong Delta offer rich vantage points for such an investigation. Its relatively sparsely inhabited floodplains and riverbanks were subjected to waves of intensive settlement and engineering in the nineteenth and twentieth centuries that, despite some of the most violent warfare in the modern era, have continued unabated to the present day.

The Mekong Delta today is one of Vietnam's most productive regions because of its industrial and agricultural exports destined for the global economy. Just as in 1822 and 1879, however, political debates over the use of the delta's water landscapes continue. Farmers seek compensation for lands lost to public works and urban expansion, while constituencies across the nation debate new development schemes. Often, new projects are sited directly atop the ruins of earlier, abandoned ones. Present-day industrial zones, for example, often cover the abandoned runways and bases left by Americans; and new constructions such as the Mỹ Thuận Bridge, completed in 2000, have realized plans to span the Mekong's main branches first drafted by a Japanese firm in 1963. Since the 1990s, provincial and national authorities have even returned to Vĩnh Tế Canal to raise levees and extend a new highway destined to bring more commerce across the international border.

Because of these multiple, overlapping layers of constructed spaces and the delta's amorphous, amphibious nature, it serves as an ideal environment for a history of modernization oriented to physical examples of slippage, erasure, and rupture. The delta's unsolid surfaces, where it is often difficult to reach solid ground, repeatedly challenge human efforts to build permanent spaces. Every September and October, monsoon rains bring sweeping floods that cover much of the flatlands and threaten to erase the dense array of fields and levees and the fragile network of roads and bridges. Almost every inch of the delta's surfaces are cultivated by human hands (including water surfaces), but the Mekong, a Lao word meaning "mother of rivers," can in a matter of days erase every trace of such work. The Vietnamese term for the river delta, "Nine Dragons" (Cửu Long), likewise suggests a geomantic, serpentine force that on occasion wriggles beyond its courses. Besides the river, ocean tides pulsing into one of the world's flattest deltas present challenges to irrigation, often threatening to cover fields in saltwater; and the delta's sticky clay and high waterline require heavy construction to float atop dozens of piers sunk several meters below the delta floor. Success for nation builders—military commanders, public-works engineers, and settlers—in such a fluid, volatile environment requires careful consideration of not only the economics and politics involved in funding projects but also siting. Especially during the Indochina Wars and earlier colonial struggles, schemes to extend the state's infrastructure often failed due to both military or political resistance and forces of natural resistance. Even during the most intensive years of American military intervention before 1975, American know-how and technology were often pitted against a rural society and an aquatic environment that were poorly understood. One American journalist, observing a host of counterinsurgency programs in 1968, wrote: "To the Americans, Vietnam is a counterinsurgency laboratory, alive with new projects and new ideas. But to the people in the hamlets, Vietnam is a counterinsurgency graveyard overgrown with weeds and speckled with monuments: abandoned model settlements, forts, and refugee camps."[4]

This graveyard perspective gets at one of the dangers of nation-building in such a fluid place. Burst dikes, collapsed bridges, and ruined crops often redirect public attention to the state in such visceral ways that various forms of popular protest follow. Such political effects stemming from the failure of levees, dikes, and settlement schemes are not limited to Vietnam but are common around the world and are likely to worsen as the climate warms and sea levels rise.

With nature playing a more prominent role in the modern history of nation-building, the old metaphor of foreign military intervention in Vietnam as a (political) quagmire gives rise to another question: what of *real* quagmires? American readers first encountered the political use of the term "quagmire" in *New York Times* journalist David Halberstam's 1964 Pulitzer Prize–winning account of the Kennedy administration's policies in Vietnam; as the war escalated, repeating images on television screens of soldiers wading through flooded fields or fording muddy canals provided a potent visual cue that American machines and troops had become literally bogged down.[5] Americans, however, were not the first foreigners in the delta to sink, metaphorically or physically. By exploring the quagmire as both a natural and a political place, this book challenges a prevailing tendency among writers to stretch Vietnam's history across an invisible national map that ignores its variable, complex terrains.[6]

Considering the fates of both the nation and nature in this history of a quagmire, I have set out to recast the colonial and postcolonial history

7

of nation-building in Vietnam by leaving behind the smoke-filled, air-conditioned spaces of downtown government offices and foreign agencies in Sài Gòn, Hà Nội, Washington, Moscow, Beijing, and Paris for the immense, watery surfaces of the Mekong Delta. Like Rénaud's journey on the Vĩnh Tế Canal, this book follows several generations of mapmakers, engineers, soldiers, scientists, farmers, and revolutionaries from such urban centers to remote project sites, where they contacted local inhabitants and specific natural features. It examines their attempts to bring the abstract designs of nation-building into reality amid the buzzing, moving surfaces that surrounded them.

The environmental history that results is thus one oriented to an array of contact sites, places such as the Vĩnh Tế Canal, where agents of nation-building engaged in complex technical and historical dialogues with the surrounding environment and local inhabitants. These encounters generated a significant paper trail in Vietnamese, French, and American archives, where surveys and reports were often accompanied by letters, court disputes, and other artifacts collected and filed along the way. The history that follows is less a critique of the modern philosophy of nation-building or state-centered development than a study of the ways that nature figured into these designs.[7] I examine how technology, landscape, nature, and ideas produced the historically complicated, densely occupied environments in the present. I draw ideas from environmental history and from science and technology studies that over the past few decades have extended consideration of the permeable boundaries separating things of man-made and nature-made origins.[8] Were one to visit the delta today, a glimpse of rusting American hardware turned into household building supplies or a former air base tarmac now operating as an industrial zone might convince readers of the potential for hybridity in nation-building. I also suggest that the twin projects of war making and nation-building did not cause the quagmire; rather, the quagmire—both the physical place and the political complexities associated with it—existed long before and continues long after. Despite a tendency in postcolonial studies to represent colonial and postcolonial state actions as distinct ruptures from the precolonial past, a closer study of such sites as the Vĩnh Tế Canal frequently indicates continuities where earlier, native designs and later, foreign designs overlap. Quagmires were not just threatening, volatile places; they were also graveyards littered with older projects that often challenged newcomers.

8   Besides the delta environment, there are two communities of human

actors involved in this history: the nation builders, who brought new technologies, investment capital, and plans, and the many local inhabitants who were involved in these projects. Whether opposed to them or not, the masses of farmers, laborers, and settlers played an important, though often undocumented, role in nation-building. As with many other public-works campaigns initiated around the world in the nineteenth and twentieth centuries, nation-building in the Mekong Delta required large groups of laborers and succeeded only if settlers invested the new infrastructure with labor to clear trees and establish fields in the soft clay. Thus, the supervisory roles of engineers, politicians, and mapmakers have to be juxtaposed to the collective power of settlers, laborers, and, at times, insurgents. In Southeast Asia especially, such topics as peasant complicity or resistance to various state schemes have received a good deal of attention.[9] Nowhere was this process of resistance more articulated than in the Mekong Delta, where peasants not only resisted or sabotaged government projects but also joined revolutionary guerrilla movements and often killed foreign engineers.[10] Idealizing peasant resistance to state authority in the Mekong Delta may in some ways reflect yet another foreign stereotype, but a careful reading of the experiences of local people at these frontiers of nation-building is important for yielding more nuanced perspectives of the long-term effects of such activity.[11]

In Vietnamese popular works and imagination, the Mekong Delta has long been an important water frontier for the nation's economic and political expansion. Popular writers such as Sơn Nam describe the delta frontier as a riverine civilization (*văn minh sông nước*) and contrast it with the more stable, terrestrial landscapes of the northern (Hà Nội) and central (Huế) plains. Blending skills as a fiction writer and popular historian, Sơn Nam has described the delta to Vietnamese readers as a rough, colorful frontier reminiscent of Mark Twain's Mississippi River (fig. 1). For Vietnamese and other migrants, life on the Mekong offered freedom from the conventions of traditional society in more historic centers such as Hà Nội or Huế. Like the Mississippi and the American West, the Mekong Delta in the nineteenth century was subjected to the political and economic forces of an expanding state—first the Vietnamese and then, after 1859, the French. As Leo Marx observed of Twain's Mississippi in the late 1800s, and as Sơn Nam also notes of the Mekong, collisions between individuals and the rapidly expanding machinery of a modernizing state were pivotal, representative events that delineated broader ideological and environmental shifts in history.[12] Also like Twain, Sơn Nam embroiders his accounts of such collisions with colorful anecdotes about settlers, colonial scandals, and the monstrous capacities of machines such as steam dredges and gunboats to alter the existing pastoral landscape.[13]

Another native-born writer of the delta, the Vietnamese-French historian Pierre Brocheux, has similarly explored the delta as a modern frontier subject to French colonial designs. He describes in detail how the arrival of the French made an already-heterodox social milieu even more complex. The delta of the 1920s was, like many settler frontiers, a socially ambiguous society (it served as the backdrop for Marguerite Duras's best-selling 1984 novel *L'Amant*). French *colons* frequently married Vietnamese women, and Chinese merchants managed many of the largest commercial enterprises. Colonial frontier society differed from older frontier life both in the politics of French rule and in the scale of settlement encouraged by new technologies for land reclamation. By the 1890s, it was common to see thousands of poor migrants following the path of steam dredges in sampans (*ghe tam bản*) loaded with tools, supplies, and building materials. They built huts, burned down sections of the forest, and began the back-breaking work of clearing stumps and forming fields. Once land was cleared, however, the settlers often found that they had been swindled out of their land by absentee landlords, and they either left for new lands elsewhere or worked out some arrangement.[14]

In this book I explore the quagmire-as-frontier in a number of ways. First, I extend the discussion beyond the colonial experience described in Brocheux's work and the nationalist, anticolonial experiences described in Sơn Nam's books. In the last three chapters I consider postcolonial legacies: What happened to nation-building programs after 1945 and especially during the volatile, violent decades of cold-war military conflict from 1945 to 1975. I am neither the first to consider colonial struggles in the Mekong Delta nor the first to study American experiences there after 1954; however, I am one of the first to consider continuities and overlaps between precolonial, colonial, and postcolonial eras of nation-building. Recent works on the American War reflect the increasing attention paid by foreign scholars to the ways that revolutionary and peasant experiences during the war were connected with specific places.[15] Few studies on the war, however, consider how the environment—both natural and built—played into these struggles. As a new addition to the genres of both frontier and war literature, this book employs a different approach, one that considers the delta's colonial and postcolonial pasts as continuous pasts inscribed into the landscape.

This modern, quagmire history is also set within a large genre of historical literature on colonial expansion and its effects on subject environments. It may surprise some readers to learn that Sơn Nam likened Vietnamese settlement of the Mekong Delta in the nineteenth century to American conquests west of the Mississippi. Although Sơn Nam admits that his comparison of the Vietnamese "southward march" (*nam tiến*) to Manifest Destiny was influenced by the imagery of wagon trains in Hollywood Westerns playing in Sài Gòn cinemas in the 1960s, his comparison of these two frontier histories is instructive.[16] First, the modern commercial networks established in the Mekong Delta (as in the American West) relied in part on immigrants, especially Chinese, who filled important niches in new labor and commodity markets. Though they played very different roles in the Mekong Delta and in California, the Chinese presence was as important to nation-building in the delta as it was in Southern California's citrus groves, San Francisco's Chinatown, and Nevada's silver mines. Second, the existence of large, sparsely settled areas in the Mekong Delta encouraged banditry, with river pirates assuming the role played by outlaw horsemen in Hollywood Westerns. Third, in the hinterlands beyond the relatively thin networks of Vietnamese garrisons and settlements strung along the main waterways was an ethnically and culturally heterogeneous world where families were ethnically mixed and one might hear any mix of languages spoken at a market or work site, including Chinese, Vietnamese, Khmer, French, English, Malay, and Thai.

Under colonial rule, the Mekong Delta soon also resembled other rapidly urbanizing frontiers circa 1900 in the sense that it was transforming into a modern hydraulic landscape. Although Karl Wittfogel's controversial book *Oriental Despotism* (1957) argued that the large hydraulic infrastructures needed to sustain societies in Asia reflected a kind of uniquely Asian, hydraulic politics, many of the most densely populated irrigated landscapes in modern Asia were recent creations, often established under European colonial rule in the late nineteenth century.[17] The Mekong Delta, despite its proximity to ancient irrigated landscapes such as Angkor Wat upstream and some remains of ancient hydraulic infrastructure around Long Xuyên, had less in common with traditional irrigated landscapes in Asia and more with newly reclaimed lands under the control of *modern* hydraulic bureaucracies such as those described in Donald Worster's *Rivers of Empire* or Michael Adas's *The Burma Delta*.[18] While control over most of these colonial landscapes had by 1960 reverted to postcolonial, national governments, the fate of the Mekong was somewhat unique in that French colonial engineers were replaced not only by Vietnamese state engineers but by a large contingent of American advisers and contractors. On loan from the U.S. Bureau of Reclamation and the Army Corps of Engineers, American technical advisers left such places as the Colorado River for the Mekong to work for the United Nations–sponsored Mekong River Commission. In the 1950s and 1960s, they drafted dozens of feasibility studies for water control schemes, often drawing upon prior experiences in such places as the Florida Everglades and the San Joaquin Delta. This more international dimension of reclamation and nation-building in the Mekong Delta offers fertile ground for comparative study of the ways that nation-building and nature commingled in other places.

Navigating the Delta

For most readers, the Mekong Delta may connote a distant horizon of green paddy fields tended by people wearing conical hats (*nón lá*) or scenes of old ladies rowing narrow boats filled with goods destined for a floating market. Fortunately, a booming tourist industry in the region has gone a long way to replace older ideas of the delta as a treacherous swamp hiding guerrillas dressed in black pajamas and carrying AK-47's. Today, a popular Vietnamese tourist board slogan touts it as a "destination for the new millennium." Beyond these popular images and slogans, however, most readers likely have little in the way of a mental map by which to appreciate the delta as a more complex space comprising many smaller hydroecological regions and important landmarks by which most locals navigate.

In thinking about the kinds of mental maps readers may use to aid their navigation through the following pages, it is worth considering the kinds of maps that historical figures used. Roughly, they can be divided into two general types: the bird's-eye view and the surface, or experiential, view. The inventions of remote sensing and aerial photography in the twentieth century changed the way that most nation builders and those who read their studies understood and represented the delta. Until the popularization of maps in textbooks and other works, this bird's-eye view of the delta was largely unavailable to the millions of people who lived and traveled across its surfaces every day. There was (and still largely is) a difference in perspective that reflected deeper differences in people's education, class, and mobility. Any foreign visitor who has flown across the delta's dense web of canals on the southern approach into Hồ Chí Minh City's airport and then headed out by car or boat into the delta can readily appreciate the stark differences when the bird's-eye view gives way to the surface view. One leaves the elevated, air-conditioned window at ten thousand feet for a seat in a vehicle engulfed in the sights, smells, and traffic on the canals or roadways of the delta's surface. Very quickly, the villages and fields start to look the same; and it is only after several months that bridge-canal intersections, towns, or other sites become familiar landmarks. Schooling, especially in social studies and geography classes, teaches us how to read the bird's-eye maps; and orienteering by way of Cartesian coordinates, maps, compasses, and now GPS navigation systems is a fundamental skill for foreign tourists, colonial surveyors, and militaries.

Although this approach conveys interesting data about an environment, it fails to capture episodes of creation or destruction, any sense of dynamic change—the ebb and flow of tides, the surging floods of the river in autumn, or the ripening of rice before the harvest. The assault on a tourist's senses—blaring horns, crowded boat traffic, people balanced precariously on motorbikes, mosquitoes biting, or drenching monsoon showers—is a reminder that survival in such a place demands movement, negotiation, and experience. Scholars, urban planners, and tourists have all to varying degrees had to accept the importance of incorporating this surface knowledge into their analyses; for tourists, that is perhaps the joy and the challenge of travel. J. B. Jackson's call for valuing the "vernacular landscape" reminds us that foreign readers and visitors are entering places known in very different ways by locals, who navigate by all manner of formal and colloquial landmarks.[19]

While scholars have argued that the shift to a bird's-eye perspective represents a shift toward a more modern, globalizing perspective, in practice the shifts between one environmental view and the other are more complex. Many historical actors, especially before the advent of airplanes, learned from both perspectives, complementing knowledge gained from maps with knowledge gained from the surface. Rénaud's survey is a case in point; and colonial surveyors until the 1920s traveled across Indochina on foot, by carriage, or by boat using trigonometric calculations and simple tools to produce planimetric maps. The borders of late-nineteenth-century maps are often filled with anecdotal text commentary; and large blank spaces attest to surveyors' limited access in earlier eras. Also, once soldiers or colonial administrators settled into a province, they soon became attuned to the shifting surfaces of water and mud through which they traveled. As many American soldier memoirs attest, knowing the terrain was often more important than knowing what could be seen from above.

Given my emphasis on nation-building, perhaps the first boundaries worth considering are the delta's hydrologic boundaries. As in many places, the national boundary separating Vietnam and Cambodia follows, not the delta's hydraulic lines, but imaginary, straight lines running across blank surfaces. The delta extends well into Cambodia and covers about one million hectares of marshland around the main branches of the Mekong River below Phnom Penh (map 1).[20] In this book I will concentrate for the most part on events happening in the lower four-fifths of the delta in Vietnam; however, the porous border region with Cambodia played (and still plays) a major role in the history of the region. To the southwest and the southeast, the delta environment gives way to the Gulf of Thailand (Siam) and the South China Sea; both of these water bodies play important roles in shaping the delta. Tidal pulses from these two water basins vary, creating an extremely complex hydrological matrix with shifting currents in the canals and arroyos. This daily ebb and flow of water reaches up to one hundred kilometers upstream; and it is an important force for both irrigation and transport. These two tidal influences are largely responsible for the delta's extreme flatness; its average elevation rises just one meter per one hundred kilometers, thus amplifying the vulnerability of settlements to floods and high tides.

Besides the tides, the formative feature is the Mekong River. The river originates in the Tibetan Plateau and travels some six thousand kilometers through Yunnan Province (China), Laos, Thailand, and Cambodia before reaching the delta. In geologic terms, the valley formed over two million years ago in the late Tertiary period, and the first delta formed in what is now an arc of red-clay hills stretching from Hồ Chí Minh City to Tây Ninh and Phnom Penh. Even as late as 6000 BCE, well after the end of the last ice age, large areas of the modern delta area were still routinely inundated with seawater. Areas over sixty kilometers inland today contain traces of underlying coral reefs and sand dunes from the ancient coastline.[21] The Mekong Delta is thus a relatively young area that has expanded rapidly seaward due to high loads of silt carried from upstream. Within the last two thousand years, the delta has expanded such that ancient seaports from 400 CE now lie twenty kilometers or more inland.

In response to the hydraulic environment, the region's most densely occupied places are located on elevated land called *miệt vườn* (garden strips).[22] The alluvial banks along rivers and canals as well as more ancient

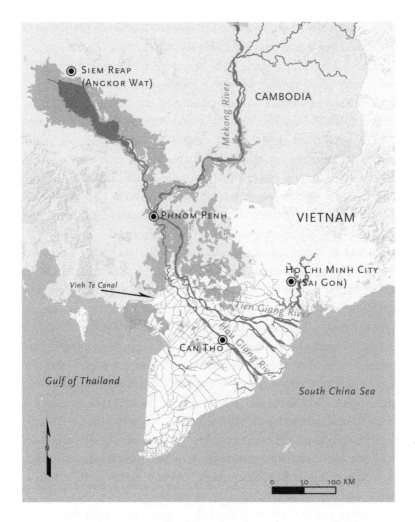

MAP 1. *Mekong River and Delta. This map shows areas susceptible to seasonal flooding (shaded) as well as the main courses of the Mekong River through Cambodia and Vietnam.* Source: Author.

sand hills (*gò*) make up most of the high ground (two to three meters above sea level) in the delta. One of the delta's key defining features (as seen on the surface) is the juxtaposition of these narrow settlements on the water's edge and the immense interiors of forests, plains, and mangroves. From these narrow strips and islandlike hills, a mixed society of Khmer, Chinese, and Vietnamese settlers slowly expanded orchards, fields, roads, and canals outward into the submerged terrain beyond. It was in these

15

same thin strips that French soldiers and colonial planters later worked to build colonial institutions and expand yet further.

The only other elevated lands in the delta are a few groups of islandlike granitic mountains in the upstream reaches on both sides of the Cambodian border (map 2). These mountains not only play important ecological roles but are also important sites for ancient history. It was only after aerial photographs of the delta were widely available in the late 1920s that amateur researchers drew attention to crop markings and traces of ancient canals. Pierre Paris, a provincial administrator in Long Xuyên, suggested that these remnants might be linked to Chinese records describing Funan.[23] Beginning with Louis Malleret's 1943 campaign at the base of Ba Thê Mountain, archaeological digs confirmed the association. The ancient waterways passed settlements and pilgrimage sites associated with a pre-Khmer civilization called Funan (ca. 300 BCE–600 CE) after a name in Chinese texts or Oc Eo Culture after this first dig site. Subsequent research suggests that these mountains and hills formed nodes for an ancient network of maritime canals and adjacent settlements associated with a warehousing center that supplied goods for a once-thriving sea-based trade route between China and India.[24] Material traces from this human culture include wooden piers, gold jewelry, Buddhist and Hindu statues, brick foundations, and traces of major canals. Despite a new wave of research and archaeological digs that have resumed since the 1990s, relatively little is known of the extent of Funan since almost all traces of its wooden piers and perishable goods have vanished in the delta's soft, acidic mud. Chinese records from the polity's tribute missions to the Chinese emperor note that Funan included major settlements at Oc Eo/Ba Thê, at Angkor Borei, and in the present-day Đồng Tháp (Plain of Reeds).[25]

Since the 1500s, European and other visitors to the delta have regarded it as a volatile frontier between a divided Cambodian kingdom and an expanding southern Vietnamese state with its center at Huế. Vietnamese, Khmer, Chinese, and European accounts from the 1700s on describe it in terms similar to those of more ancient visitors: a swampy wilderness with small trading posts located along the riverbanks. By the 1750s, newer Chinese and Vietnamese villages were established close to older, Khmer centers. The delta in the eighteenth and nineteenth centuries remained a violently contested frontier settled by Vietnamese migrants, Chinese émigrés, Khmer inhabitants, and all manner of rebels.[26] Chinese migrants, part of a South Seas network of Ming loyalist (*Minh hương*) merchants, were largely responsible for establishing or expanding new river ports at

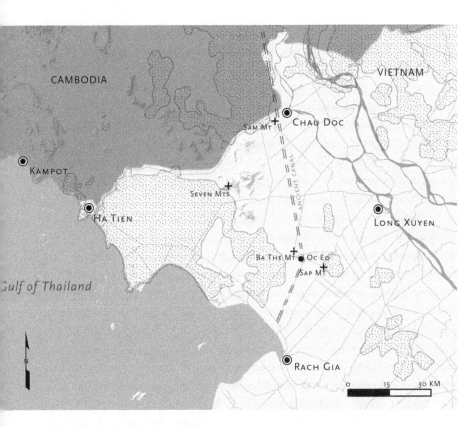

MAP 2. *The Long Xuyên Quadrangle. The dashed line indicates the path of an ancient canal, and the label Oc Eo indicates the largest collection of sites of the Oc Eo Culture, named after an existing, ethnic-Khmer village in the area at the time of excavations in the 1940s. Source: Author.*

such places as Sài Gòn, Mỹ Tho, and Hà Tiên. In the 1700s, leaders of these Chinese groups received concessions from the Vietnamese and Cambodian kingdoms to operate these ports as semi-independent city-states. By the 1770s, the city-states became enveloped in major battles involving Chinese-Vietnamese forces at Hà Tiên and Chinese-Thai forces at Chantaburi. These battles then gave way to a civil war between dueling Vietnamese factions in the 1780s that lasted until 1802.

It was only after 1802, with the reunification of Vietnam under the Nguyễn dynasty in Huế, that an early-modern Vietnamese state committed significant funds and manpower to building an extensive administrative and physical infrastructure throughout the kingdom. Because of the delta's economic importance to the kingdom, military governors and surveyors invested considerable efforts in the six military provinces (*trấn*) of the delta and in Sài Gòn. By the time of the French conquest, much of the delta region beyond the alluvial strips and adjacent fields remained sparsely settled, but provincial and district officials nevertheless managed to survey and describe these areas in land registers, a few planimetric maps, and provincial gazetteers (*địa chí*). The delta's remote mountains such as the Seven Mountains (Thất Sơn) received considerable attention, as they remained refuges for rebels, mystics, and various wild animals, including elephants and tigers.

While the differentiation between *miệt vườn* and interior is one of the major visual and ecological defining features of the delta, the vast flatlands are also distinguished by their susceptibility to flooding, their proximity to saltwater, and their associated plant communities. Two areas that caused the most angst for nation-building were the two seasonally inundated floodplains straddling the Cambodian border: the Long Xuyên Quadrangle and Đồng Tháp (the latter better known during the Vietnam War as the Plain of Reeds). Both of these basins (map 3) act as sinks every September and October, when monsoon rains cause the Mekong to rise several meters above its normal levels. The hydrologic extent of the Long Xuyên Quadrangle extends into Cambodia, and the corners include two river ports, Châu Đốc and Long Xuyên, and two coastal ports, Hà Tiên and Rạch Giá.

On the Mekong's northern side is the other major catchment basin, the Đồng Tháp floodplain. The term "Plain of Reeds" is from the French Plaine des Jonqs, so named for the tall, waving fields of reeds (*sậy*) that grew there. Roughly ten feet high, they covered many narrow creeks and arroyos, making the area an ideal hiding place for rebels. The French term reflects a colonial, military association of the low-lying lands with the threat of ambush, and it is not a translation of the Vietnamese name. "Đồng Tháp Mười" refers to the central historic feature of the plain (*đồng*), a ten-story brick tower (*tháp*) once located on a slight hill (ancient sand dune) (*gò*) in the center of the area (present-day Đồng Tháp). Because of its slightly elevated vantage point and central location, Vietnamese royal forces, expanding into the area in the 1750s, likely maintained similar watchtowers at the site over succeeding decades.[27]

The Eastern Coastal Zone forms another distinctive region, this one defined by alternating rows of sand ridges and backswamps that parallel the coastline. During the dry season, saltwater from the coast penetrates

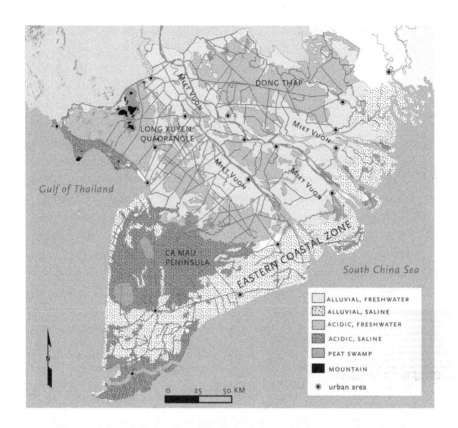

MAP 3. *Ecoregions of the Mekong Delta. Note that most of the urban areas in the delta are located within the freshwater alluvial zone known locally as the* miệt vườn *(garden strips), which follow the major banks of the main rivers and arroyos.* Source: *Author.*

inland via creeks and canals, preventing year-round rice cultivation unless dikes and irrigation are available. Besides sheltering pirates and enduring occasional typhoons, the Eastern Coastal Zone has always been important culturally for the production of fermented fish sauce (*nước mắm*) and other seafood products that form a staple in the Vietnamese diet to the present day. Villagers fish, harvest shellfish, and engage in salt production and other maritime activities and live in elevated huts situated over broad tidelands covered by water during high tide. In Vietnam as elsewhere, these coastal communities had a reputation for being rough places where pirates hid out and many fishermen doubled as smugglers. The Rừng Sát mangrove forest north of this area, where the Mekong and Sài Gòn Rivers meet, was notorious as a haven for guerrillas throughout the Indochina Wars.

The Eastern Coastal Zone gives way in the far south to the Cà Mau Peninsula, which is geologically the youngest area of the delta and was formed by broad layers of silt pushed southward by ocean currents from the river's mouths. The peninsula's name comes from the Khmer term for "black water" (*tuk khmau*). The water's blackish color is produced by high levels of tannins that leach out of the peat soil. This area remains ecologically important because it contains the last vestiges of the old peat swamp that once may have covered most of the peninsula (see map 3).[28] Like the brackish waters of the Eastern Coastal Zone, the water in much of the Cà Mau Peninsula runs salty half the year. Given the peninsula's severely acidic environment, its inaccessibility, and its proximity to the sea, it has remained one of the most important rebel landscapes in times of war.

Another important human element in the delta, especially since the mid-nineteenth century, has been a pattern of ever-increasing human immigration. Vietnamese immigration was closely linked with Chinese immigration to the delta beginning in the seventeenth century. Until 1802, the Nguyễn Lords governed the southern frontier in collaboration with a divided Cambodian kingdom, relying on a mix of force and diplomacy to establish posts in former Khmer centers such as Mesar (Mỹ Tho), Kampong Reussey (Bến Tre), Koh Gong (Gò Công), and Peam Ba-rach (Long Xuyên).[29] In 1757, in return for promoting a Cambodian pretender to the throne, the Nguyễn gained additional concessions—to Phsar Dek (Sa Dec), Long Ho (Vĩnh Long), and Mot Chrouk (Châu Đốc)—thus extending the nominal domain of the Vietnamese kingdom to its present-day boundaries (map 4).[30] It was not until the mid-1800s, however, that the delta population was majority Vietnamese; and only after the 1890s did Vietnamese immigration produce a significantly Vietnamese majority throughout the region.

Also important to the delta's environmental history are the plant and animal species that were part of these human migrations, notably rice, various fish species, and a Western invasive species called *lục bình* (water hyacinth, *Eichornia crassipes*). Humans both nurtured and battled against various plant and animal species in this incredibly fertile frontier as they forged their settlements. Rice cultivation was of course the primary attraction for settlers interested in creating homesteads in the area, and the following chapters consider various aspects of its cultivation in relation to nation-building. Water hyacinth remained a persistent threat to movement

MAP 4. *Delta Towns and Roads. The darker lines show most two-lane paved roads in the delta region. The fainter lines indicate canals.* Source: *Author.*

in the canals, regularly threatening to clog unattended waterways and stop boats in their paths. This floating vegetation native to the Amazon spread rapidly each year in huge, floating mats as floods penetrated low-lying areas. The mats slow water movement, creating ideal places for mosquitoes to breed. In the 1800s, the plant began appearing at exhibitions and in botanical gardens around the world. Vietnamese botanist Phạm Hoàng Hộ notes that *Eichhornia crassipes* was first documented in Vietnam in 1902, when it was introduced to the colonial botanical garden in Sài Gòn.[31] Such colonizing, hardy plants are matched by equally hardy, if not voracious, fish and aquatic species. The delta has supported a diverse array of migratory freshwater and saltwater species; however, native and introduced catfish as well as snakehead fish (*Channidae, cá lóc*) make up the bulk of species raised in ponds and caught in flooded fields.[32]

21

Besides orienting the reader to the delta's basic geography and the two ways of navigating it—from above and from the surface—this brief introduction to the delta's precolonial past should also dispel any notion that the environment subjected to various nation-building campaigns in the nineteenth and twentieth centuries was tamed or tranquil. It was precisely the delta's wildness, its volatile nature, and its vulnerable settlements in the *miệt vườn* that made it most accessible to the fleet of French gunboats that entered its waters in the 1860s.

I followed the call to arms as a young boy,

Drawing sharpened sword to confront the hardships of these times.

A hero meets adversity not looking at the ground,

For an enemy's scorching hatred can never burn the sky.

—*Nguyễn Trung Trực, October 27, 1868*[1]

1 WATER'S EDGE

French colonial rule in Indochina began in 1859 after a series of violent engagements on the water. After their show of gunboat diplomacy near the Vietnamese capital in Đà Nẵng Bay unraveled into a near defeat, the French fleet retreated from the heavily protected central Vietnamese coast. On February 17, 1859, the French fleet recorded its first victory over the Vietnamese at their southern fortress Gia Định (Sài Gòn) (map 5). Two frigates, three steam-powered gunboats, three transport ships, and one steamer began the assault at dawn with round after round of cannon fire. French and Spanish forces, together with a locally recruited band of mercenaries, launched an attack on the citadel walls that by midafternoon ended with the capture of the fortress and the raising of the tricolor.[2] Despite this relatively quick, shock-and-awe victory on the shoreline, fighting continued for two more years just kilometers inland from the riverbank with no major French advances. Nguyễn Tri

FIG. 2. *Waterfront along Bảo Định Canal (Arroyo de la Poste), Mỹ Tho, 1898. The view looks south to where the canal empties into the upper branch of the Mekong River, or Tiền Giang.* Source: *J. C. Baurac,* La Cochinchine et ses habitants: Provinces de l'est *(Saigon: Imprimerie commerciale Rey, 1899), 16.*

Phương, southern commander of Vietnam's royal army, blocked access to upstream areas beyond the French docks at Sài Gòn and Chợ Lớn. While French entrepreneurs and military units built a modern wharf in the city, the Vietnamese camps outside Sài Gòn grew to twenty-one thousand troops forming a line of forts with a new headquarters at Chí Hoà (near present-day Hồ Chí Minh City Airport). As fighting across the blockade lines increased, French commanders finally organized a major ground offensive on February 24, 1861, with three thousand troops plus reinforcements coming from French and Spanish ships anchored in the river. Over three hundred European soldiers died in two days of fighting, along with an estimated one thousand Vietnamese. Two years after the initial battle at Gia Định, France had won its first military victory against the Vietnamese on terra firma.[3]

The victory, however, did not signal a turning point in the conquest nor an abandonment of the protection afforded by the waters. Paulin Vial, a frigate captain who served during the conquest and wrote a history of it in

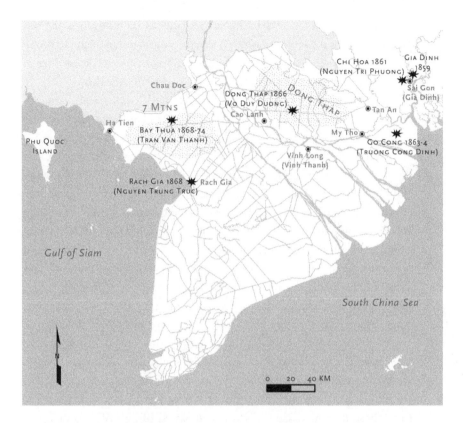

MAP 5. *Major Battles during the French Conquest of the Delta. The anticolonial resistance followed a general trend westward from the first battles in Gia Định in 1859 and around Soai Rạp Inlet and Gò Công in 1863 to Đồng Tháp in 1866 and the Long Xuyên Quadrangle from 1866 to 1874.* Source: *Author.*

1874, reported that after the victory at Chí Hoà Admiral Bonard withdrew officers from forts built on the Mekong River to consolidate control of the Sài Gòn waterfront. Vietnamese military commanders fleeing Sài Gòn thus took the opportunity to seize the French forts and camps on the Mekong, especially the property of colonial collaborators.[4] For another year and a half, the French focused on building the port and city around Sài Gòn while Vietnamese commanders such as Trương Công Định built new camps in such Mekong towns as Gò Công and at the Nguyễn-era barracks (*dinh*) at Vĩnh Long (map 5). A peace treaty unexpectedly proffered by King Tự Đức in June 1862 suddenly halted this new reorganization of authority and splintered the Vietnamese resistance. Phan Thanh Giản, the highest-ranking Nguyễn official in the delta, left for France to continue negotiations on the treaty for the king, but Nguyễn military commanders such as Trương Công Định rejected it outright and organized guerrilla attacks on French outposts on Sài Gòn's southern frontier at Tân An and Mỹ Tho.

The next five years of colonial conquest and Vietnamese resistance repeatedly tested the limits of French authority in battles fought at watery border zones where deep, navigable streams gave way to shallow creeks and swamps. The swamps around Sài Gòn, the immense Đồng Tháp, and the eastern coastal regions around Gò Công absorbed rebel factions of the Nguyễn army that launched repeated assaults on colonial forts built at the edges of navigable waterways and roads. One unit under Định attacked a French fort at Nhiêu Thuộc near Mỹ Tho. While only a handful of colonial troops were killed, French fears about more attacks set off a massive naval operation against Định. On February 25, 1863, about twenty French and Spanish ships blocked the deeper creeks and rivers draining from Gò Công, where Định was believed to have his headquarters. A floating hospital was anchored in one of the creeks while earthen batteries were built across others to support additional artillery besides that on board the vessels. The Spanish corvette *Circé* waited in Soai Rạp Inlet while eight French gunboats anchored in other tidal creeks as far inland as they could travel without running aground. The ground forces that carried out the attack from these floating assault platforms consisted of half of a battalion of Algerian *tirailleurs* (light infantry) garrisoned at Shanghai and a battalion of Filipino soldiers raised by the Spanish (still partners with the French in the colonial conquest) from Manila. In the onslaught of this invasion, Định's forces scattered, abandoning uniforms and regrouping in other marshes.[5] Admiral Bonard used the victory to pressure King Tự Đức to honor the terms of the 1862 treaty when the signed version returned from Paris. Trương Công Định escaped and continued to lead small ambushes until 1864, when a junior lieutenant betrayed him to the French.

Other Vietnamese continued to fight, retreating ever deeper into the delta's wild interiors as French forces tightened their control on waterways close to Sài Gòn. Some of the most notable include Võ Duy Dương, who led operations in the Đồng Tháp until 1866; Nguyễn Trung Trực, who had a base of support in the lower delta region around Rạch Giá until 1868; and Trần Văn Thành, who led a millenarian Buddhist sect and organized a network of separatist communities along the Vĩnh Tế Canal from 1868 to 1874.[6] Each rebel movement differed, but they all followed a similar logic with regard to the water environment, retreating far from navigable channels into the swamps. Võ Duy Dương, a wealthy landlord before 1862, led over a thousand soldiers from among his tenants and built a base on Tower Hill (Gò Tháp), the ancient sand hill in the center of Đồng Tháp (see map 5).[7] Two overland tracks, navigable for a month or two at the end of the dry season, connected the fort to distant villages; most people reached it by *sampan*. Dương's forces hid there, and by night they solicited money and food from communities on the edge of the marsh. During the rainy season from April to November 1865, they raided more French forts on the edge of the swamps in attempts to foment a general insurrection. The French waited for the water to recede in the winter before launching a ground-based assault in April. This time Europeans fought alongside a newly trained force of several hundred Vietnamese soldiers who followed an ambitious local collaborator, Trần Bá Lộc. Not only the close combat but the mud, leeches, mosquitoes, and sun took a heavy toll on the Europeans, leaving over one hundred dead. After seven days, however, the native militia finally captured Tower Hill, scoring an important victory over the rebels in the delta's largest swamp.[8]

Nguyễn Trung Trực's campaigns from 1862 to 1868 moved the center of anticolonialism farther south into the lower delta (Hậu Giang) as the French expanded naval operations there after 1862. Trực, a locally born fisherman, masterminded an attack that blew up a three-mast French warship anchored on the Bến Lức River some twenty kilometers from Sài Gòn at an important water junction with the Arroyo de la Poste (Bảo Định Canal), which was the only inland waterway at the time conveying boat traffic from Sài Gòn to the delta.[9] Trực's destruction of the warship brought him immediate fame as a popular hero. King Tự Đức bestowed upon him the honorific title sergeant major (*quản cơ*), and he and several hundred followers fled from the fighting to establish bases in the lower delta region near Rạch Giá. After six years of evading French troops and watching the French gain control over former Vietnamese outposts in the lower delta, he led a last-ditch attack in June 1868 on the newly completed colonial provincial headquarters in Rạch Giá (map 5). After killing the Europeans sleeping inside, the group fled to Phú Quốc Island. French units caught up with them there, captured Trực, and brought him to the Central Prison in Sài Gòn, where he was executed on October 27, 1868.[10]

Dương's defeat and Trực's execution caused another leader of the era, Trần Văn Thành, to build a base in the remote border area around Vĩnh Tế Canal. Thành was a priest who led a millenarian Buddhist sect that had grown up in the region since 1847. A charismatic monk, Đoàn Minh

Huyền, preached here and offered healing amulets during a devastating cholera epidemic in 1849, gained a strong local following, and declared himself an incarnation of the Buddha. His millenarian interpretation of Buddhist folk religion blended Khmer and Vietnamese practices with magical incantations and folk interpretations of Buddhist scripture. Thành, a sergeant major serving in the Nguyễn army, converted to the religion after staying at the Temple of Western Peace with Huyền and quickly rose to prominence in the sect.[11] Following Huyền's death in 1856, Thành and his wife led the sect, founding new settlements in the interior region east of Vĩnh Tế Canal in the years before the French conquest began. In later fighting with French forces, Thành served under Định until 1864 and under Dương until 1866 before attempting to contact Trực in 1867. After Trực's capture in 1868, he returned to the settlements he and his wife had founded and led the sect's followers into a dense, swampy forest called Bảy Thưa (map 5). There they built a new community that was both anticolonial and religious in its inception. They dug canals to bring in freshwater and allow communication with outside settlements. In her study of Hòa Hảo Buddhism and millenarian politics, Huê Tâm Hồ Tai explains that, unlike other rebels, Thành's successful evasion of French authorities for six more years was largely due to his appeal as a sect leader, and that it was he who joined the cause of millenarianism with anticolonialism in the region.[12]

The appeal of the millenarian tradition in this region, however, was due not only to frontier politics but also to the devastation that another recent arrival, cholera, brought by water. Canal projects and new settlements involved thousands of people working in muddy basins with stagnant pools of wastewater. Cholera epidemics swept the region repeatedly in the nineteenth century and killed up to half of all people exposed to it. Just one infected body, if it touched the water, could infect thousands. During the colonial conquest, the carnage of military engagements was combined with the even greater devastation wrought by cholera. Tens of thousands of corpses lined the dry roads, stacked up to be cremated in huge pyres, given the shortage of dry land. Such sights must have caused many peasants to believe that the final days were at hand and that a Buddhist *maitreya* would soon arrive as had been prophesied. Even after Thành's death in 1873, his followers continued to attract new adepts, especially the laborers conscripted to excavate French waterways such as Chợ Gạo Canal (1876–77).[13] They wore amulets inscribed with the four characters "Bửu Sơn Kỳ Hương" and recited secret incantations to receive magical protection from epidemics.

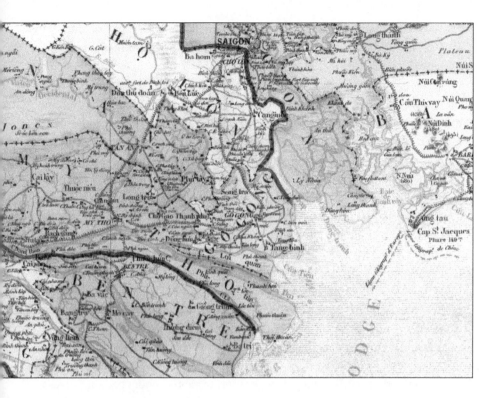

FIG. 3. *Waterways and Telegraph Lines. This excerpt from an 1883 map shows a marked contrast in the level of detail between the newer administrative boundaries and the waterways, as well as the French forts and posts scattered along major roads and riverbanks. The crosshatched lines indicate telegraph wires strung along roads and waterways to connect the posts. In 1871 the colony's telegraph network was linked to the Singapore–Hong Kong deep-sea cables at Cap St. Jacques (Vũng Tàu), shown here in the middle right.* Source: *Insert map titled "Cochinchine en 1883" produced by Captain M. Bigrel, in A. Boüinais and A. Paulus,* La Cochinchine contemporaine *(Paris: Librairie algérienne et coloniale, 1884).*

The French conquest of Cochinchina was intensely oriented to movement on the water. The first maps published widely for European audiences in the 1880s reflect this; in one such map, the outlines of the new colony are represented by hatched lines that flow in broad curves across blank terrain, while the branching network of creeks, rivers, and canals is drawn in fine detail (fig. 3). Based on his work on maps in Siam, Thongchai Winichakul suggests that maps facilitated modern imaginings of colonial-era states as *geo-bodies* formed from the outline of political borders. If we imagine such a geo-body for Cochinchina, we see that Cochinchina followed a very different trajectory from most places in Southeast Asia. Surveys of Cochinchina's political boundary and the tedious work of placing boundary markers on territory often submerged under floods began several decades after the initial mapping of its underwater terrain. Even well into the twentieth century, *miền tây* (Cochinchina's western, or delta, region) was not typically represented as a sovereign region but as a sovereign topology, one measured by hydrographic engineers such as Jacques Rénaud and then patrolled by gunboats and police.[14]

Colonial maps of Cochinchina in the 1880s included another interesting set of lines: a network of lines with crosshatchings indicating about one thousand kilometers of low-grade telegraph wires strung along the waterways to connect Sài Gòn to the forts and administrative centers established in the delta (see fig. 3). French naval units attached the wires to trees and poles beginning in 1863, and across the immense branches of the Mekong they used more expensive underwater cable, insulated with gutta-percha, an important colonial commodity first discovered in island Southeast Asia. Telegraph lines rapidly compressed the space of this frequently inundated, impassable colonial topology, allowing telegraph operators to send warnings from one fort to another about pending attacks or other events.[15] One line led out to sea at Cap St. Jacques (Vũng Tầu), where in 1871 it joined the Hong Kong and Singapore trunk lines operated by Sir John Pender's Cable and Wireless Company. This connection further extended France's administrative reach by allowing rapid communication between Paris and the colony.[16]

Colonial Alterations to the Water Landscape

While telegraphs may have compressed the space of communication between the delta and Sài Gòn, Cochinchina's early governors neverthe-less focused on the need to build new inland waterways that would allow their gunboats to respond more quickly to uprisings in the swamps. In 1875 Admiral Victor-Auguste Duperré set out to build a new network of inland waterways that would convey deep-draft French ships to major river ports without requiring them to navigate the delta's shoal-ridden inlets. The only existing routes from Sài Gòn to the delta were several waterways first established in the 1700s that reached east from Chợ Lớn via the Bến Lức River to the Bà Bèo Canal or to the Bảo Định Canal

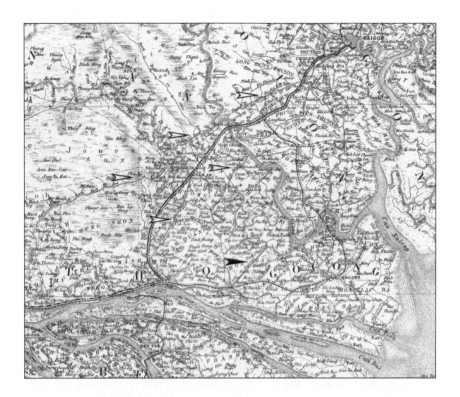

FIG. 4. *Early Colonial Canals in the Eastern Coastal Zone. This excerpt from a republished 1880s military map of Cochinchina shows the major road and telegraph line connecting Sài Gòn with Mỹ Tho. The white arrows, added for reference, show precolonial routes for inland transport of rice to the kingdom's central granaries at Chợ Lớn before 1860. The top-center white arrow shows the* giáp nước *at Thủ Thừa. After the French conquest, the admiral-governors sought to bypass this Chinese-controlled inland waterway by traveling into Soai Rạp Inlet and then traveling up the Vàm Cỏ River to the new shipping canal (denoted with a black arrow). Also, note Đồng Tháp to the west of the older canals.* Source: Carte de la Cochinchine française *(Paris: Augustin Challamel, 1901).*

(ca. 1816). However, these shallow, crowded waterways were thronged with boats transporting rice to Chợ Lớn, and they did not permit even the smallest gunboats to pass in all conditions (fig. 4). With new funds from Paris and an army of conscripted laborers, the Department of Public Works (DPW) commenced digging (by hand) seven new projects intended to facilitate ship traffic through the Eastern Coastal Zone.[17] Each was roughly one hundred meters wide and five or six meters deep. French engineers such as Rénaud, educated at the elite École des ponts et chaussées, planned these canals much the same way that they planned roads. The large projects were to form a backbone for navigation from which narrower, secondary canals would then branch off. From these secondary canals, tertiary canals just wide enough for two boats to pass would connect individual hamlets.

Of the colonial projects, Chợ Gạo, or Duperré, Canal was by far the most important and expensive for the colony. It connected Sài Gòn to the nearest delta port, Mỹ Tho. Mỹ Tho was the largest town in the delta at the time, expanded largely via the commerce generated from ethnic-Chinese enterprises. From this embarkation point, steamboats carried passengers, mail, and cargo across the rivers to other delta towns and upstream to Phnom Penh. Once completed, Chợ Gạo Canal reduced travel times between Sài Gòn and the delta from a sixteen-hour trip over open seas to an eight-hour trip in protected waters.[18] The project required over twenty-five thousand laborers, each working under a corvée (conscripted labor) system for about one month (fig. 5). The channel was only eleven kilometers long, but work dragged on for more than a year due to another outbreak of cholera and various hydrological problems associated with linking two separate river systems.

The finished canal was initially a success, and Governor Duperré along with a coterie of his officials inaugurated it with great fanfare in 1877; but in several months, the canal was no longer navigable. Bars of silt formed across the main channel and reduced its depth at low tide to less than a meter. All of the waterways except one were soon choked off by what engineers called *dos d'âne*, bars of silt that formed where opposing water currents met and silt fell from stilled water.[19] Because the delta was so flat, tides caused water flowing in the tidal creeks and canals to reverse their currents daily. With this diurnal action "dead points" formed where water flowing into the canal from both openings met in the middle and released sediment to form wide bars, some a few hundred meters long. Because of the Mekong Delta's extreme flatness, this tidal effect could be found more than one hundred kilometers inland.[20]

Colonial engineers and local residents understood the delta environment differently; for instance, what colonial engineers considered "dead points" locals understood as "meeting points" (*giáp nước*). The village of Thủ Thừa, located on an older canal between the East and West Vàm Cỏ Rivers,

FIG. 5. *Duperré/Chợ Gạo Canal Project. This photograph taken by Emile Gsell (ca. 1876-77) shows digging at an early stage of the project. Such projects were labor intensive and required lines of people to convey clay from the bottom of the channel to the top. The harsh working conditions put the relatively few French overseers at risk of insurrection. On the far left, one of the few French representatives overseeing the work is seated on horseback and surrounded by a platoon of native militiamen. Source: Emile Gsell; albumen photo on paper, presented to Governor Le Myre de Vilers by the Colonial Council in 1882. Donated to the Foreign Affairs Library in 1894. Ministry of Foreign Affairs Archives, Paris, "Le Myre de Vilers," no. A000760.*

became a popular stopover for interregional commerce (see fig. 4).[21] People coming from one end of the canal traveled to the *giáp nước* to buy and sell goods produced in the Mekong Delta—areca, coconut, oranges, sugar, and rice—while people coming from the other end brought goods from Sài Gòn. Sellers traveling by oar used the shift in currents to and from the *giáp nước* to time their trips. After high tide peaked and the current reversed, they returned home with the current. For longer trips, a person might rest at the *giáp nước* before continuing on with the current. People in the delta adapted to the tides rather than working to eliminate them; *giáp nước* punctuated their journeys from one province to another, coinciding with the daily ebb and flow of tides.

Such tidal fluctuations in creeks and canals were also beneficial for rice fields planted beyond the banks. Water levels in the arroyos (*rạch*) and ditches (*mương*) rose and fell a few meters, often exposing a bare, exposed channel bed at low tide. This tidal ebb and flow provided clean water for irrigation, carried fertilizer in the form of silt, and evacuated wastewater let out from the fields. In the paddy, water slowly leached hydrogen sulfate (H_2SO_4), a weak acid that forms in aerated clays. If allowed to sit for too long, sulfuric acid dissolved aluminum and iron ions, stunting or poisoning the growing rice. To prevent alum (*đất phèn*) from building up, farmers periodically drained their paddies by opening up the field dikes to drain water out with the falling tide. When the tide rose again, they let freshwater in and then closed the paddies. The most highly prized farmland was located in the natural alluvial region of the eastern delta, where fields were subject to tidal effects.

Colonial Machines

The same tides that irrigated fields and rendered French canals impassable might have ended colonial expansion into the Mekong Delta had it not been for a major shift in French politics and technologies used in the colonial building programs under the Third Republic.[22] After the popular elections in 1879 brought reform-minded politicians into power, a pro-republican admiral, Jean Bernard Jauréguiberry, became head of the Ministry of the Navy and Colonies and immediately set out to reform conditions in the French navy and naval colonies. Of particular importance to Cochinchina was his decision to appoint a civilian, rather than a naval, officer as governor. He lauded the colony's transition to civilian rule, declaring: "The moment has finally arrived to affirm our sovereignty through creations of public utility, proving to the Annamites [Vietnamese] that we are, above all, their benefactors. In this point of view, the maintenance of canals, creation of roads, construction of bridges, study of railroads, and establishment of hospitals and schools will be the object of our preoccupation."[23] Governor Charles Le Myre de Vilers arrived as Cochinchina's first civilian governor and initiated new investigations, including Rénaud's survey of Vĩnh Tế Canal. Rénaud's comment about continuing "the work [*l'oeuvre*] of civilization started by the Vietnamese" was indicative of a secular *mission civilisatrice*, an ideology of modernization pushed by republicans and middle-class bureaucrats instead of missionaries or empire-minded monarchists.[24]

The government's approach to dredging new canals in the Mekong Delta was a perfect test for a secular *mission civilisatrice*. Not only was canal building "improvement," but in its new form it would now hinge on two key aspects of colonial modernization that made such activity palatable back home: implementing core ideas about labor reform from the French Revolution and introducing new science and technology that would carry out much of the work. Abolishment of corvée (forced labor) had been a central goal of the French Revolution. Le Myre de Vilers, writing for French readers of *La nouvelle revue* in 1913, noted that this practice was formally abolished in Cochinchina by the president of the Colonial Council in 1881.[25] The decision to replace corvée with a requisition system did not change the general nature of unpaid work on canals and roads—peasants still did not receive pay for their work. However, village heads and provincial councils gained some autonomy in choosing who would fulfill government requests. This practice quickly gave way to paying workers, although much of the money likely went to labor contractors and other middlemen. Even paying very low wages, however, the government could not afford to compensate the tens of thousands of people required to dig a primary canal. In 1880 the chief engineer estimated that the cost of building Chợ Gạo Canal with paid laborers would have exceeded the DPW's entire annual budget for all buildings and roads in Sài Gòn and the provinces.[26] Thus, it was crucial that the colony introduce laborsaving machines such as steam-powered dredges to carry out its ambitious plans.

Despite the international reputation for steam-powered dredging that France had gained with the completion of the Suez Canal in 1869, the Minister of the Navy and Colonies did not immediately authorize spending for dredges or waterway projects in Cochinchina but instead focused on roads and railroads. Given the swampy environment, this preference for land-based infrastructure might seem strange, but it stemmed from a number of colonial concerns. First, unlike the Suez Canal, which ran through a desert, waterways in tropical Asia were often already crowded with local commerce. Second, that commerce was generally managed by the networks of Chinese communities operating across Southeast Asia. There was little chance that French merchants or the colony could compete with this network. Working on another hydrographic survey in 1880, Rénaud gives us a glimpse into these frustrations that he and other nation builders encountered on the waterways:

> From a purely economic point of view, in this country of river navigation par excellence, where each center [of the delta] would provide quite sufficient freight to feed a service of large riverboats . . . to move rice freight distances of one hundred miles on assembled longboats with 10 to 15 oarsmen, moored against the bank when the current is opposing, obliged in each *rạch* [arroyo] to wait until high tide to cross the *dos d'âne*, this is nonsense . . . and under this pretext our trade remains in the hands of the Chinese, thus we are conducting our commerce on their terms.[27]

French builders' desires to build a transportation network separate from a Chinese-controlled water world prompted them to build railroads instead of canals to convey their passengers and commodities quickly.

While the colony approved Rénaud's proposals to restore Vĩnh Tế Canal and build a ship canal parallel to Chợ Gạo Canal, it earmarked most of its budget to creating road and rail networks instead. Mimicking the French design of highways at home, the road network was to radiate outward from Sài Gòn with a special link to Mỹ Tho and then a series of steamer routes fanning out to the delta's river towns. The Colonial Council narrowly approved the ten-year public-works package, including a provision that one-third of the 6.4-million-franc annual budget would come from a tax on opium sales.[28] Another third of the budget was to come directly from the Ministry of the Navy and Colonies in Paris, and this perhaps more than the sale of opium drew immediate scrutiny. Alarmed by the ambitious and expensive plan, Minister Jauréguiberry sent one of his senior engineers, Charles Combier, to visit Cochinchina and investigate.

Combier, a civil engineer who had graduated from the École polytechnique, traveled across the colony in 1880–81, studying the proposed projects. The publication of his report to the ministry caused administrative uproar in the colony and publicly in France over financing construction through opium sales. Combier introduced an ethical critique aimed squarely at the *mission civilisatrice* as understood in Sài Gòn. In his report to the ministry he expressed his disgust in quasi-economic terms:

The first wealth of a country is Man. All other wealth proceeds from him and is intended for his use, with the satisfaction of his needs or pleasures. However, it is well known that the abuse of opium, since the first tests, quickly reaches Man's sources of intelligence and life . . . and it promptly makes him useless to the society and himself, before killing him. However, we have created, by the institution of an opium monopoly, a company whose benefit rests only on the disastrous propagation of this addiction.[29]

His report was leaked to French papers, and debates surfaced over the morality of a public-works campaign that was intended to "lift up" indigenous people through new modern constructions but that simultaneously destroyed them through addiction. The new roadways and railroads would allow opium dealers to travel the colony more quickly, thus "accelerating the demise of the Annamite [Vietnamese] people."[30]

It was Combier's detailed cost-benefit analysis, however, and not his ethical outrage, that persuaded the ministry to delay support for much of the colony's proposed public works. While railroads promised a more modern and exclusively French form of movement, Combier opposed building a rail network across the delta on financial grounds. He compared freight costs for shipping rice by river junk and by rail car. Figuring in transshipment costs and required construction of granaries at the terminals, he estimated rail freight costs to be more than triple those of water. He thus favored using the delta's "natural" advantage, extending the waterway network, over building an entirely new one by rail.[31]

Although he supported building more waterways, Combier nevertheless rejected Rénaud's proposals for the Vĩnh Tế Canal and the new ship canal. He criticized Rénaud's hydrographic measurements, noting that the flooding, tides, and terrain would make it very difficult to control water moving between coastal and river zones. On economic grounds, he also criticized redevelopment of Vĩnh Tế because it would only aid Siamese competitors in bringing their merchandise into the delta. The current batch of canal projects, he maintained, would in effect become "works of Penelope," never-ending projects, unless the colony's engineers came up with a new way to stabilize water flow and prevent the waterways from silting up.[32]

With this allusion to the Greek legend of Penelope spinning and unspinning her robe, Combier touched on one of the fundamental barriers to colonial ambitions in the hydraulic landscape. The web of waterways in Cochinchina, constantly shifting with each flood and tide, threatened with each movement of the waters to undo the expensive work carried out before. After Combier's report, Le Myre de Vilers shelved Rénaud's reports and delayed new dredging projects, citing technical and financial difficulties posed by *dos d'âne*. Rénaud nevertheless continued his investigations of water movements in the delta, determined to solve the problem of *dos d'âne* and ultimately build a new kind of waterway to supplement the existing network.[33]

The ministry did, finally, support construction of a seventy-one-kilometer rail link from Sài Gòn to the river port at Mỹ Tho (fig. 6). Work crews began construction in 1882 and completed it on July 18, 1885. Two steel spans crossed the relatively wide channels of the East and West Vàm Cỏ Rivers; Tân An Bridge, one of many spans designed by Gustave Eiffel's enterprise and prefabricated at Levallois-Perret, was 342 meters long and can still be seen today running parallel to two more recently built highway bridges.[34] Once completed, the new railway finally succeeded in moving French troops and passengers quickly from Sài Gòn to Mỹ Tho. It realized the goal of separating and accelerating the colonial flow of people and

FIG. 6. *Tân An Rail Bridge Construction, 1882. Source: R. Gentilini,* Les voies de communication en Cochinchine *(Paris: Imprimerie Chaix, 1886).*

goods by ultimately removing them from the delta's rivers and canals altogether.

With the rail link and a parallel road completed soon after, by 1890 Mỹ Tho had emerged as Sài Gòn's and Chợ Lớn's gateway to the Mekong Delta. A book about the services provided by the Compagnie messageries fluviales (River Transport Company, RTC) described Mỹ Tho as follows:

> From this point radiate many lines of steamers, penetrating the heart of the richest provinces of Cochinchina and heading upward to Cambodia and the upper river. On the famous Chợ Gạo Canal, thousands of junks and long-boats relay all of the riches of the delta and the Mekong Valley to Sài Gòn and Cholon . . . the canal ends three kilometers from Mỹ Tho. The European town is built along the Arroyo de la Poste [see fig. 2], another canal that links the Mekong with the capital; but modern river traffic [to Sài Gòn] has been abandoned because of narrow confines.[35]

Passengers on the train sped past crowded scenes of junks and longboats on the canal running parallel to the tracks. These slow-moving vessels carried the bulk of Cochinchina's commerce while wealthy colonists and a trickle of tourists sped across Eiffel's steel spans to passenger boats waiting at the quay.

Colonial movement into the delta, like colonial residences located in heavily policed centers of colonial towns, required sufficient clearance from the obstructions of everyday indigenous life. These new inventions, the rail line and the steamboat service, were among the first to elevate colonial observers above the water landscape. Thus, these routes enabled a sort of view-from-above with similar effects as airplanes and maps later on. RTC's fleet of 120-ton and 400-ton steamers also introduced a new temporal framework governed by the Western calendar and by the clock. Mail and passenger boats operated according to a printed timetable, delivering mail and goods to newly established provincial towns. Meanwhile, farmers and those still traveling on the water surface continued to follow the seasons of the lunar calendar and the day as divided by the tides.

Besides the locomotives and steamboats—familiar icons in colonial stories at the time—the colonial introduction of prefabricated iron and steel also played an important supporting role in constructing the colonial network. Chinese merchants had controlled most commerce in forged iron tools and weapons for several centuries, and the precious material was rarely if ever encountered in the built environment. In the 1880s, the iron latticework arches most noticeable in span bridges and later in Gustave Eiffel's imposing tower found their way into colonial environments. Not only used in prefabricated bridges and spans, the arches were used for the roofs of many open-air markets—among the most important places in any Vietnamese community. Thus, the iron rails and bridges linking Sài Gòn to the delta also linked the colony more intimately with Paris, as some of France's most famous builders filled huge contracts to supply the prefabricated infrastructure of Cochinchina.

In the 1880s, ironwork construction not only reinforced France's hold on colonial territory but also transformed features of the French landscape. Before Eiffel made millions of francs operating the Eiffel Tower, he had already made a fortune exporting hundreds of ironwork segments for colonial bridges and public buildings, including Sài Gòn's General Post Office and market halls still standing today. The estimated cost for his spans in 1881 was eight million francs, approximately eight times the cost of building the Eiffel Tower in 1887.[36] Downtown Paris in the 1880s, especially the streets around the tower and the grounds of the Universal Exposition, was an intimate quarter populated with headquarter offices for many colonial companies. RTC's headquarters, located at no. 9 rue Bergère, was just a short walk from the tower, and the fabrication yards for its steamships were located on the banks of the Seine not far from Eiffel's yards.[37] Approximately five thousand meters of these interchangeable bridge segments allowed Le Myre de Viler's government to quickly extend a skeleton-like network of roads and rail across the canals and creeks to meet strategic needs for security and surveillance while providing impressive evidence of a *mission civilisatrice* at work.[38] Like the telegraph wires strung up on poles in the 1860s, the new network of rails and bridges lifted colonial traffic out of the existing landscape.

Despite the ministry's rejection of canal projects in 1881, Rénaud and the DPW's chief engineer, Jean Marie Thévenet-Le Boul, nevertheless continued to study *dos d'âne* to find a permanent fix to problems associated with the tides. They examined the dynamics of water flow and sedimentation to determine where flushing basins (*bassins de chasse*) might eliminate tidal "dead points" and provide constant movement of water despite the ebb and flow of tides. Using the "language of exact science par excellence," as another French engineer later observed, the two developed formulas for building such basins as "a fundamental theorem for the establishment of [permanent] canals in Cochinchina."[39] They would have to wait ten more years, however, before the colonial government was willing to fund such constructions, when a new chief engineer of the DPW sent a recently purchased steam dredge to make modifications to the Chợ Gạo Canal. Labor crews dug a short basin connecting Ông Vân Creek to Chợ Gạo and the dredge excavated new flushing basins on either side of the waterway. Results were good, and the flushing basin prevented *dos d'âne*. The chief engineer sent another crew to build a similar basin on the Saintard Canal, which carried river boats into Sóc Trăng.

Despite the successful trials, the breakthrough on *dos d'âne* did not result in a new dredging program. A year after completion of the flushing basin on the Saintard Canal, local people cut through the dam blocking a tidal creek, and within a few weeks, the *dos d'âne* had returned.[40] The apparent "sabotage" of the canal received only passing mention, but evidence from similar incidents a few decades later suggests that such conflicts stemmed not so much from organized political resistance aimed at damaging colonial works as from particular villagers' attempts to restore water circulation that was vital to their survival. By damming tidal creeks to eliminate "dead points," the engineers caused major disruptions to the existing hydraulic landscape. Facing potential bankruptcy or outbreaks of disease, farmers risked arrest or worse to bring back the tides. In 1907 Gilbert Trần Chánh Chiếu, a wealthy Vietnamese landowner from Rạch Giá who advocated Japanese-style modernization strategies in his newspaper *Nông-Cổ Mín-Đàm* [Agricultural Forum], described "une bataille intéressante" on a dam across Cái Bè Creek that ran into the new Thốt Nốt Canal:

> On the banks of Cái Bè a scene most typical has happened. Immense rice paddy is crossed by a canal and a dam, [a paddy that] was in active cultivation. Crack! The floods arrived, and all the part north of the canal was flooded by masses of water stopped by the dam. As the water went up, the owners of the southern part raised the dam to protect against more water to come. Owners of the northern part destroyed this work of their friends to save their crops. Some built, rebuilt, the others destroyed until coming to blows over it. The affair is now in the hands of the administrator and the procurer of the Republic.[41]

Such conflicts over dams and canals highlighted both the fragility of the new colonial transportation network and its unintended destructiveness.

Rather than resolve such conflicts, the colony's engineers instead opted to bring in more-powerful dredging machines to push new canals farther

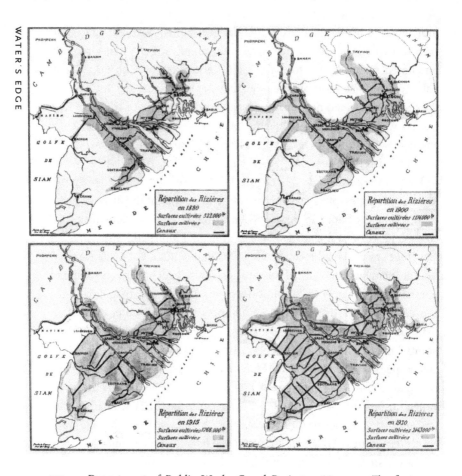

FIG. 7. *Department of Public Works Canal Projects, 1880–1930. The first new project after Chợ Gạo Canal in 1878 was Xà No Canal (1900–1904). By 1920, the DPW had dredged a dozen other waterways, including the Quản Lộ-Phụng Hiệp Canal, which ran to the Cà Mau Peninsula. The 1930 map (bottom right) includes these Hậu Giang region canals and more in the Long Xuyên Quadrangle, with the last major project, the Rạch Giá-Hà Tiên Canal, skirting the gulf coast. Only one major east-west canal crossed Đồng Tháp in 1930, and new projects into its interior were delayed until the 1950s.* Source: *Inspection des travaux publics, Gouvernement générale de l'Indochine,* Dragages de Cochinchine: Canal Rachgia-Hatien *(Saigon: n.p., 1930), 87–90.*

into less-populated regions, the same areas where colonial troops had chased the last rebel leaders a few decades earlier. From 1890 to 1930, a fleet of steam-powered dredges moved more than 165 million cubic meters of earth, a feat comparable to more-famous projects such as Suez (260) and

Panama (210).[42] A time series chart showing canals completed in this period reveals a gradually expanding web of lines that reached slowly outward from Sài Gòn into the forests and swamps of the lower delta (fig. 7).

The colony's return to building waterways depended less on good science or negotiation than on politics and the sheer power of new dredges moving a chain-driven circuit of huge iron scoops. Such machines consumed approximately 150 meters of earth each day and replaced the armies of laborers required to cut a channel with fewer than a hundred men. Machines also rendered the work of digging canals, like the work of building railroads and roads, legible — work could be calculated as a ratio of volume (cubic meters) dredged in a day to various capital and labor costs (fig. 8). Borrowing a term from anthropologist James Ferguson, they were "anti-politics machines" in the sense that such a colonial "apparatus" of men and machines altered the terms in which people interacted with the water landscape to such an extent they could not be easily opposed.[43]

The clanking movement of these machines through the delta signaled the beginning of profound social and environmental transformations in the region. Dredges chewed up fields, forests, and huts in their paths. More than gunboats, locomotives, or machine guns, the arrival of the dredge meant immediate ecological and social change. Following in the wake of the dredges, a steady stream of squatters, private landholders, and, especially, tenants came to work in new plantations that soon lined these waterways. Sơn Nam recalls popular stories told about the dredges in which crowds of people staked claims on lands adjacent to the new canals as soon as they were dug. Even without papers, they nevertheless took a chance on gaining title after having turned the land into fields.[44]

Dredging waterways was very lucrative not because it solved existing hydrologic problems such as *dos d'âne* but because it promoted a contracting model that especially benefited French manufacturers. Dredges became critical instruments for expanding French control over the delta interior. They carved paths for steamboats to penetrate the swampy interior, and in cutting new paths through existing landscapes, they also disrupted existing hydraulic works. In the environmental and social ruptures that followed, new colonial constructions such as public buildings, roads, and plantations were made possible. In this sort of creative destruction, Heidegger's thinking on the relationship of space to place and the importance of such clearing activity is instructive: "A space is something that has been made room for, something that has been freed, namely within a boundary. . . . A boundary is not that at which something stops but, as the Greeks recognized, the

FIG. 8. *Dredge II. Standing atop the dredge at a height of some twenty meters are the three Europeans in charge of the project: the DPW attendant, the dredge operator, and the chief mechanic.* Source: *Inspection des travaux publics, Gouvernement générale de l'Indochine,* Dragages de Cochinchine: Canal Rachgia-Hatien *(Saigon: n.p., 1930), 29.*

boundary is that from which something *begins its essential unfolding.*"[45] Canals in the delta functioned like the bridges Heidegger used in his lecture to explain how clearing space could relate previously unrelated areas such as riverbanks and the interior. In the Mekong Delta the new waterways were effectively water bridges that connected colonial commercial centers on the banks of deeper waters with shallow, swampy interior regions. The new waterways also functioned as important colonial boundaries, destroying and cutting through existing farms and other cultural anchors such as the tombs caught in the dredge's path.

Whereas older canal projects involved negotiations with local officials who gathered thousands of laborers to dig the channels, the machine-dredged projects required a smaller, traveling coterie of about a hundred men. More akin to colonial militias than corvée laborers, they traveled for long distances with the dredge as salaried employees of the French contractor. A list of one dredge's crew in 1908 included a project chief (European), a dredge captain (European), a mechanic (European), eight guards, thirty-nine laborers to clear land ahead of the dredge, twenty-seven laborers to work around the dredge, ten laborers to level tailings in the rear, and five public-works laborers to level a towpath along one of the canal's banks.[46] In the muddy, deforested pathways trailing the dredges, these motley crews of men were the first, temporary inhabitants of the leveled spaces along the new waterway. While the surrounding landscape varied from villages and fields to swamp forests and endless marshes, the scene along the border of a new canal varied little from one place to another. The dredge distributed its tailings on either side in large slices of clay. Lodged in the sulfurous clay were all manner of broken artifacts—bones, bricks, tree stumps, and so on. Given the frequent heavy rains, these surfaces were treacherously slippery. The work crews did not sleep aboard the dredge but atop these muddy banks in lean-tos. Each day, work lasted for a grueling nineteen hours, except on Sundays and during frequent stops for repairs. The giant clanking machinery, with its long arm of scoops and steam boilers, frequently broke down and required all manner of repairs. When spare parts were not available, the crew often had to hire local blacksmiths to fabricate temporary fixes. When work was delayed, crew members spent their free time playing cards, drinking rice whisky, and hunting deer and wild pigs in the cajeput forests or fishing in the rivers. They rarely ventured far from the banks, however, since the forests were still home to tigers, elephants, and venomous snakes such as cobras. Where the dredge broke through existing villages in the alluvial zones, crews gained a reputation for womanizing, excessive gambling, and other corrupt activities. Crew bosses reportedly accepted bribes from landowners in return for redirecting the mountains of dredged clay away from homes and orchards.[47]

While the image of three men standing atop the dredge superstructure in figure 8 suggests that Europeans rode high above the muddy, rough world of laborers and squatters below, they were inextricably involved in surface affairs. Europeans followed their laborers into the surrounding territory. They frequently picked up girlfriends, some of whom traveled with them on the dredges. While readers may imagine such liaisons as temporary affairs, the historical record is far from clear. In French Cochinchina, there were no laws preventing interracial marriage; and legally wed spouses of French citizens received protection under French law. As colonial courts heard various disputes over custody or property, they improvised policies to regulate these engagements among government personnel. Where evidence of these relationships occurs in the records, usually related to legal disputes, it suggests how complex European-native relationships were at the time. On the dredge crew described above, the European mechanic picked up a local girlfriend named Khen who became friends with a Vietnamese foreman's wife—the two Vietnamese women traveled along with the crew. After a fight between them, Khen's teenage son (from a different father, traveling with his mother) challenged the foreman to a fight while his mother hid on the dredge with the mechanic. The mechanic then got involved, and the foreman responded by drawing a knife on the mechanic. Village leaders intervened, and the matter was eventually reported to the chief engineer in Sài Gòn. The chief engineer issued a new rule threatening immediate dismissal and punishment for all crew members (French or Vietnamese) who became involved with *con gái*, a Vietnamese word meaning "young girl" that when spoken as a French word (*congai, encongayer*) was slang for a mistress or for taking a mistress.[48]

Another important feature of colonial dredging was that beginning in 1893 all of this work was carried out by private, monopoly contractors working on extended contracts with the colonial state and without much government oversight. Their only obligation to the state was to meet monthly quotas for volumes of earth dredged and gradually reduce costs. Payment on a ten-year agreement was based on successful completion of canals to specified depths and widths.[49] Montvenoux, a dredging firm in the Loire Valley, was the only firm to respond to the first call. In 1894 company members set up an office in Sài Gòn, and a year later they assembled three steam-powered dredges, named *I*, *II*, and *III*, that had arrived, like Eiffel's bridges, in pieces. Each dredge powered a continuously circulating chain of steel scoops (*chaine à godets*). Once full, the scoops rose along a diagonal arm until they emptied mud and water via booms away from the channel. Montvenoux's two 300-horsepower machines were capable of dredging 90,000 cubic meters per month; their 250-horsepower machine could dredge 50,000 cubic meters per month.[50]

During the first years, work went slowly, with half the funds paying human crews to finish the digging while the machines were stuck waiting for parts. For all of 1894, one crew excavated just 18,000 cubic meters per month, instead of the required 60,000 minimum. Nevertheless, they spent the entire annual budget, most of it on excess workers, overseers, and guards. Repairs cost 20,000 francs, including 2,000 spent on fuel for the boilers.[51] In the first years of their operation, the dredges appeared to be repeating the failures of past projects, creating new "works of Penelope."

The government's handling of the dredging program changed significantly under the administration of Governor-General Paul Doumer (1898–1902), who assumed tighter control over projects in Cochinchina from a new colonial center in Hà Nội. Doumer gave provincial administrators and councils a greater say in paying for and directing what he considered to be essentially local projects. In November 1900, Doumer also reorganized the DPW and renegotiated the remaining portion of the dredging contract.[52] Through his reorganization of provincial councils and provincial planning, Doumer thus brought dredging more within the oversight of provincial councils, whose members were eager to develop more territory and expand revenues. This fiscal and administrative reorganization of the dredging process in 1900 thus created a powerful new alliance of provincial administrators, influential landowners, public-works engineers, and the dredging enterprise that for the next thirty years accelerated the opening of new lands and then profited from subsequent land concessions. The plantation landscape that developed from the boundaries of these new canals is the focus of the next chapter.

In 1904 the government signed a new ten-year contract with a French firm that bought the old dredges from Montvenoux and added two new machines, the *Nantes* and the *Loire*. Members from this company then formed the *Société française d'entreprises de dragages et de travaux publics* (SFEDTP) in 1913, which continued work on canals until 1951.[53] With this new alliance of men and machines, the DPW was able to maintain existing waterways such as Chợ Gạo and rapidly extend the waterway network into formerly inaccessible areas.

One might wonder, with all of the powerful new machines, what happened to attempts to apply a "language of science" to stabilize the canal network. The new machines and the alliance of people directing them simply moved too quickly through the delta to allow any such stabilization to occur. One of the most avid students of the delta's hydrology, Albert Pouyanne, attempted to build a new flushing basin on the Chợ Gạo Canal in 1905, but *dos d'âne* soon appeared at a different location.[54] With a bevy of new projects and wealthy landowners calling on the DPW and the contractor to carry out new projects, Pouyanne abandoned further research into the problem; nevertheless, he still defended Thévenet-Le

Boul's and Rénaud's invention, stating: "The results obtained with the Duperré Canal are absolutely satisfactory . . . we can regard it as having currently its final form."[55] The delta's "final form," however, continued to elude engineers, as changing currents caused by the river and tides as well as by human actions continued to undo the dredges' work.

The Floating State

From 1886 to 1896, Dr. J. C. Baurac of the Navy Medical Service traveled Cochinchina's rivers and canals to every district administering treatments against infectious diseases, especially cholera, which had killed over a hundred thousand persons in the delta region since the early 1800s. The bacterium *Vibrio cholerae* occurs naturally in the zooplankton of fresh, brackish, and salt water, and it is widely believed to have first spread to human populations in coastal regions where people ingested shellfish infected by it. Cholera infections did not become a global pandemic, however, until the nineteenth century, when an 1816 outbreak in the Ganges Delta of India spread along British trade routes to China and west to the Caspian Sea.

In Cochinchina before 1900, cholera spread along the same water network that had fostered the creation of the colonial state: it traveled with colonial troops; it flourished in the polluted water of unfinished canal projects; it passed into new regions upstream through the sewage discharge from steamers departing from Mỹ Tho. Once infected with the bacteria, a person quickly became dehydrated from diarrhea and vomiting, returning bacteria to the canals and creeks where others bathed and took their drinking water. One person could release over a trillion such bacteria back into the water.

As a doctor in France's colonial medical service, Baurac spent much of his time in Cochinchina traveling the waterways to administer vaccines in the countryside, where access to medical care of any kind, French or indigenous, was limited (fig. 9). He and a team of assistants, including nurses and translators, set up a vaccination tent where locals came to be inoculated. After a year of administering treatments for cholera, typhoid, and smallpox, Baurac soon encountered a rapid rise in the numbers of adults he treated on return stops to places such as Vĩnh Tế or Đồng Tháp. Where district and village records indicated three hundred children living in an area, Baurac found seven or eight hundred lined up for

FIG. 9. *The* Vaïco. *The colony furnished Dr. J. C. Baurac with this boat for his vaccination work. He traveled on this boat to every provincial and district center every six months to administer vaccinations and treatments for cholera, plague, typhoid, and malaria.* Source: *J. C. Baurac,* La Cochinchine et ses inhabitants: Provinces de l'est *(Saigon: Imprimerie commerciale Rey, 1899), 240.*

shots.[56] His observations of this difference between recorded versus actual population during ten years of such visits led him to address the Société des études indo-chinoises at a regular Friday night gathering in Sài Gòn with the suggestion that Cochinchina's population be revised upward from 1.8 million to over 4 million people. He went on to suggest that the colony could more than double its head-tax revenue by registering these additional people on village tax roles when they came to get their shots.[57]

Baurac's waterborne, civilizing mission adds another important dimension to the water's edge: it functioned as a threshold for colonial-native encounters in the construction of Cochinchina. In this case, there was a kind of double colonization at work, cholera microbes indiscriminately spreading from polluted water to Europeans and Asians alike and a European doctor using an infectious-disease campaign to draw attention to names yet to be entered on colonial tax rolls. Since the naval attacks in 1859, the water's edge in Cochinchina had been the primary site for colonial encounters. Much of what French observers knew of Cochinchina was mediated by their travels and constructions along this edge. However, Baurac's most significant contribution to understanding life on the water's edge was his two-volume study of everyday life, *La Cochinchine et ses habitants*. The young doctor was an avid photographer and snapped hundreds of pictures while making his rounds. His study was carefully organized by province, with basic geographical and administrative statistics followed by a more random gathering of local historical information, medical oddities, and accounts of visits to key landmarks. While much of this information appears elsewhere, the photographs he included of landscapes, people, and especially buildings constitute a valuable record for many historians in Vietnam. Like the information in Baurac's picture book, most of what historians know about early colonial life in the Mekong Delta was recorded within the relatively narrow slivers of land *(miệt vườn)* along the water's edge.

Because the colonial conquest and subsequent colonial economy were largely shaped by the delta's waterways, the early idea of Cochinchina as a colonial state had less to do with enforcing its vague boundaries and establishing a geo-body of visual impression than with grafting the colonial state on to the existing Vietnamese landscape and Chinese-controlled economy. French gunboats depended on canals built in the 1820s, and early colonial residences were often located inside the ruins of older Vietnamese citadels. Because waterways had been the primary basis of communication in the region for centuries, the region's political and economic activities had always been oriented to waterways and waterfronts. French engineers such as Combier quickly realized the futility of trying to reengineer this waterborne economy; instead, the colonial government opted to build a new infrastructure of railroads and roads that could occupy different niches. Since the first years of the conquest, French success in Cochinchina depended on both co-opting local allies such as Chinese entrepreneurs and Vietnamese commanders and introducing new forms such as railroads, telegraph wires, and cholera vaccines to overcome resistance. Books such as Baurac's and reports such as Rénaud's describe such efforts and reveal how native people and nature frequently opposed them.

Although displacements caused by colonial warfare and dredging operations along the water boundary created openings for the creation of what might be considered a modern state beginning in the 1880s, such displacements were not unique to French conquest. Since the 1700s, Vietnamese and ethnic Chinese had been active in opening new settlements in what was once Khmer territory. Projects such as the Vĩnh Tế Canal were clearly understood at the time of construction as attempts by the Vietnamese government to impose more direct political control over its frontier with Cambodia; and on several occasions, Khmer workers engaged in uprisings against this expanding Vietnamese influence. Though historical records of these precolonial episodes of warfare and canal building are limited, especially in Khmer sources, they nevertheless point to a common theme of displacement in the decades preceding French rule. A French history of Sóc Trăng Province describes one such disruption that occurred from 1836 to 1840, when one of the last Khmer military commanders in the region fought the Vietnamese army before retreating to present-day Cambodia. Vietnamese forces established their main fort at Bãi Xâu—later a key colonial port—and then fought their way to Khmer strongholds in the present-day town of Sóc Trăng. Following the defeat of the Khmers, a terrible epidemic, probably bubonic plague, swept through the region and killed three-quarters of the Khmer population. A terrible famine that killed thousands more then ensued from the loss of labor.[58]

If we keep this turbulent, precolonial history in mind, we see that what makes the colonial period distinct from earlier periods is not so much the violence of the French incursion into the existing water landscape but the new inventions—dredges, Eiffel bridges, steamships, cholera vaccines, photographs, telegraphs, machine guns, newspapers, and military service. These new inventions depoliticized the old water landscape and often allowed colonial actors to float above it for a time. Inventions such as the telegraph and the steam engine compressed distances, while dredges replaced thousands of laborers with small, mobile groups. What distinguished the water's edge in the colonial era was a speeding up and intensification of commerce. While such transformations began at the water's edge with the first cannon shots in 1859, the vast interiors of the delta remained relatively unaffected for decades. This tension of resistance—both political and natural—to colonial inventions continued throughout the succeeding decades of colonial rule.

FIG. 10. *Aerial View of the Gressier Estate. This photograph was taken in 1958 as part of a U.S. military mapping effort. The large canal bisecting the estate's grid of smaller canals is the Xà No Canal. The mill and major buildings of the estate were located at Ấp Bảy Ngàn (Seven Thousand Hamlet).* Source: *Frame 18964, Spot G8714, Aerial Photograph Collection, National Archives and Records Administration, Center 2, College Park, MD.*

In Cochinchina, where there are immense areas without a single
solid structure, without masonry, without any rock, it is not possible
to produce benchmarks even close to the network of Europe.—*P. Régnier*[1]

2 WATER GRID

The colonial dredging program expanded rapidly in the early
1900s, resulting in a rapid boom in population and unprecedented
environmental changes from land reclamation in the swamps of the
Mekong Delta. Of all the lands cleared and reclaimed for rice, the Gressier
Estate developed into one of the delta's largest, most technologically
sophisticated commercial farms. In 1903 Rémy Gressier bought 5,600
hectares of land in a concession running fourteen by two kilometers along
both sides of the recently completed Xà No Canal (fig. 10). He hired laborers
to dig a checkerboard grid of canals at one-kilometer intervals and installed
pumping stations along the main canal bisecting the estate. The estate's
pumps and water gates impressed local farmers, who had never seen such
contraptions for moving water; with the flip of a switch, the devices pulled
water from the interior grid's canals while water levels outside the estate's
dikes were higher. During droughts, they brought water into the fields

while levels outside were lower.[2] At one-kilometer intersections on Xà No Canal, Gressier opened company stores that sold food and dry goods for scrip that he paid his tenants in lieu of cash. The villages today still retain their original, industrial names, which correspond to their distance from the old property boundary: One Thousand Hamlet (Ấp Một Ngàn), Two Thousand Hamlet (Ấp Hai Ngàn), and so forth. Between Seven Thousand Hamlet and Eight Thousand Hamlet, Gressier built one of the first modern rice mills in the region, a six-story cement structure that towered over the fields. He also built shipping docks for a fleet of company barges and after 1930 added an airstrip used for commutes back and forth to Sài Gòn (map 6).[3] Other additions included a maternity ward and for a time an agricultural training school to turn children born on the plantation into future estate managers. He closed the school, however, as most pupils tended to leave for better-paying jobs in the city.[4]

On a recent visit to the site of the former estate (now razed to make way for a highway and market), I had a chance to speak with the operator of a smaller, recently built mill in nearby Vị Thanh, a provincial border post that became the region's first agroville in 1960 and is now one of the delta's fastest-growing cities. Ông Diệu guided me through his mill and its forty-foot-high assemblage of clanking machinery and conveyor belts polishing rice. The husking machine, he told me, was an original piece of machinery from Gressier's mill, taken during the Việt Minh's occupation in 1945 and resold after 1975. Diệu shut down the mill for lunch, and we entered his house behind the mill and talked at length about irrigation and agriculture.

Diệu described life on the plantations before 1945, more or less confirming what I had already read about oppressive colonial taxes, high interest rates, and payment schemes that left tenants in perpetual cycles of debt. He surprised me, however, when we spoke about the effects of the plantations and industrialization on the local environment.

> Before 1945, the Mekong Delta had several large plantations such as the French plantation at Cơ Đỏ, the lands of Mr. Huỳnh Kỳ, the Gressier Estate on Xà No Canal, and in Bạc Liêu some other large French plantations. Those plantations relative to others had advanced technology—machinery, motorized water pumps, and tractor-pulled plows. Gradually, all of their fields were let out as farmers rented the land and bought water buffalo to plow (none of the farmers owned any mechanized equipment). From that time, agriculture developed following this rectangular framework, and any plantation within this frame-work could develop.[5]

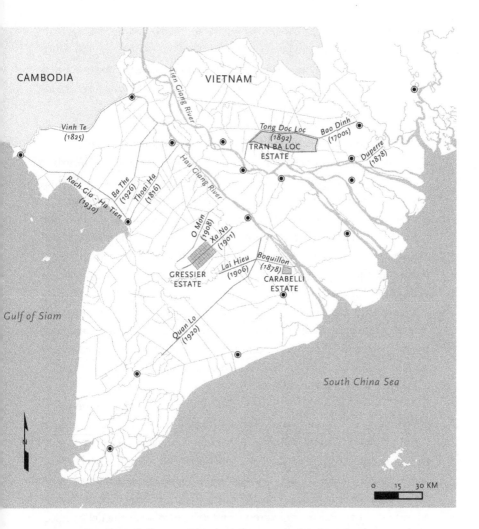

MAP 6. *Canals and Estates. The shaded areas depict three land concessions. Thicker lines show the location of several canals, with their approximate dates of completion.* Source: *Author.*

Rather than drawing ecological parallels to the political and economic disasters of colonial rule, Diêu insisted that such "scientific" farming on the French plantation was far better than other farming techniques in use at the time and perhaps even better than methods used today.[6] In conversations with other people living in neighboring districts, I found a similar attitude toward the industrial irrigation schemes employed by the colonial plantations. Conversely, they held little regard for the few

55

remaining swamps, the dwindling native species, or traditional agricultural practices, which are becoming increasingly rare in the region. With the exception of a few ecologists at Cần Thơ University, everyone I met shared Diệu's enthusiasm for mechanical irrigation and continuing measures to modernize agriculture.

With this widespread adoption of new, industrial technologies in agriculture and the continued spike in the region's population past eighteen million people today, the delta is looking ever more like the urban peripheries of Bangkok, with arrow-straight roads and canals sprawling across flat, borderless plains. Urban growth is limited only by the hydraulic infrastructure that enables commerce, irrigation, drainage, and the removal of waste. In my early ventures to find the last vestiges of wetland wilderness in the delta, I soon came to appreciate that perhaps more significant than any tragic storyline of ecological decline was this other story of how the delta in the twentieth century emerged in this intensely human-manipulated form. In the delta today, almost every plant and parcel of land is touched by human hands. The colonial state certainly influenced this modern transition, but the interrelated processes of urbanization and wetlands reclamation so visible in the delta today were already well under way before the gunboats arrived.

While readers may be inclined to link this trend in urbanization to the introduction of European and colonial models of development, colonial construction was situated within a landscape already subject to earlier trends of urbanism and land reclamation that followed Vietnamese and Chinese models. Since the late 1600s, Chinese settlers had been establishing trading posts along the main rivers; and since the 1750s, the Nguyễn dynasty had struggled to extend its control over the delta region through campaigns to construct forts, granaries, and canals in what had formerly been Khmer territory. A well-defined pattern of early-modern Vietnamese reclamation may help to explain why farmers in the colonial era were so receptive to the new technologies and modes of commerce introduced by the French. Colonial technologies advanced native and French ambitions. The construction of what French engineers described as a hydraulic grid (*réseau hydraulique*) depended foremost on the existing desire of millions of Vietnamese settlers coming from the central and northern reaches of the country to build fields, homes, and villages. The familiar Vietnamese story of southward migration (*nam tiến*), somewhat similar to American narratives of westward expansion, continued under colonial rule, albeit under changed social and political circumstances.

Table 1 compares the populations of three delta provinces and hints at the scale of this migration in the past two hundred years, with a spike following the advent of mechanical dredging and perhaps the abatement of cholera. In the first forty years of colonial rule, population increased five to ten times over precolonial numbers; and from 1900 to the present, it increased another eight to ten times. Despite the multiple wars of the nineteenth and twentieth centuries, the population boom continued unabated, surging after 1975 as millions more migrants moved into the region. Besides the promise of new lands, new medical technologies and a more thorough colonial census may have contributed to the higher figures after 1880.

TABLE 1 Provincial Population Records, 1800-2004.

Province	1802–19	1847–83	1901–11	2004
Tiền Giang	19,800	22,584	234,103	1,681,600
Vĩnh Long	3,700	28,323	132,336	1,044,900
An Giang	26,145	20,858	156,034	2,170,100

Sources: Tiền Giang Province: Đại Nam Nhất Thống Chí, vol. 5 (ĐNNTC, Đại Nam Unification Records) (Huế: Thuận Hoá, 1992), 94; Société des études indo-chinoises; SEI, Monographie de la province de Mỹ-Tho (Saigon: Imprimerie L. Ménard, 1902), 33; General Statistics Office of Vietnam (GSO), http://www.gso.gov.vn/ (accessed December 1, 2006).

Vĩnh Long Province: ĐNNTC, vol. 5, 132; SEI, Monogaphie de la province de Vinhlong (Saigon: Imprimerie commerciale M. Rey, 1911), 33; GSO.

An Giang Province: ĐNNTC, vol. 5, 167, 11; SEI; Monogaphie de la province de Châu-Đốc (Saigon: Imprimerie L. Ménard, 1902), 46; SEI, Monogaphie de la Province d'Hà-Tiên (Saigon: Imprimerie L. Ménard, 1901), 64; GSO.

While colonial projects may have been situated in an already-urbanizing landscape, the ways colonial machines, laws, and business ventures modified the landscape nevertheless brought significant changes to delta society, especially its economy and environment. Contrary to earlier, Vietnamese ideas about land and development, the hydraulic grid envisioned by colonial engineers required the enclosure of water flows into static waterways. The natural ebb and flow of tides and monsoon floods that had animated agricultural cycles and patterns of settlement for centuries thus became problems to be fixed by the colonial state, as they constantly threatened to erode new public works. One powerful colonial agency, the Department of Public Works (DPW), set out to once and for all pacify the unruly waters. The grid (*réseau*) of canals and water control structures they designed extended outward from older water lines and settled areas of the precolonial era to islands, backswamps, sand hills, and marshes. By 1930, even water conditions in the distant, black peat swamps of U Minh in the Cà Mau Peninsula were affected by recently completed canals in the area.

With the extension of waterways came laws and policies to enforce their maintenance. For the first three decades of the twentieth century, French engineers attempted to simplify the delta's complex hydrology by turning the region into a vast, hydroagricultural machine. Mounting ecological, economic, and political problems eventually undermined this enterprise, but over roughly three decades, the DPW effected a powerful transformation in the water landscape. They caused local disputes over water rights and property to move from district and village councils to city courtrooms, provincial planning boards, and legislative meetings where councilors and wealthy speculators angled for new projects to enrich themselves and their friends. In short, water management was taken out of the hands of the farmers and placed instead into the hands of foreign experts and speculators with little or no prior knowledge of the delta's complex hydroecology. Despite the tendency of individuals such as Ông Diểu to idealize the French technocrat's view of the water landscape, the initial expansion of the colonial water grid was highly contentious. While the locals may have marveled at the spectacle of a steam-powered dredge or a diesel-powered water pump, they nevertheless struggled with the terms of land tenure and the subsequent hydrologic problems that such modern wonders brought in their wake. The expansion of a reclamation bureaucracy in conjunction with the waterways alienated not only peasants but also many wealthy French and Vietnamese planters who had lived in the region since the 1880s. A close inspection of court cases, engineering reports, and local memoirs suggests that individual responses to the new water grid were complex, often divided between appreciation of the "scientific" advances of French engineers and resistance to the economic and political workings of the colonial bureaucracy.

As Ông Diểu indicated in his discussion of the Gressier Estate, individuals did not wholly embrace or reject life in the hydraulic grid; instead, they adapted those elements that strengthened their initiatives while opposing or subverting those that did not. The majority of Vietnamese and Khmer farmers who tended the fields and plied the waterways rarely even saw Frenchmen in their daily routines. Interactions with Vietnamese or Chinese foremen on industrial, checkerboard plantations or run-ins with native-born tax collectors or river police were more common occurrences. Whenever possible, locals carried on with their own urbanization schemes in their homes, villages, and associations, much as their ancestors had in the precolonial past.

Precolonial Grids

Colonial efforts to reshape the delta landscape were not so much erasures of natural and historical features as they were expansions and modifications to an existing, skeletal infrastructure of Khmer, Vietnamese, and Chinese constructions, especially the canals, forts, roads, and markets established since the late 1700s. By the early 1800s, Nguyễn military governors and a few hundred thousand Vietnamese and Chinese migrants had significantly expanded and modified older, Khmer river towns. The "Wild West" milieu played a key role in influencing Vietnamese infrastructure projects, which were largely conceived to achieve strategic aims. Nguyễn Ánh (later crowned King Gia Long, r. 1802–20) established several central rice granaries and stone citadels in the 1790s as part of his decade-long military campaign to reclaim the Vietnamese kingdom. His small detachment of French priests and military advisers designed Vaubanesque forts, especially his headquarters at Gia Định (Sài Gòn); and in present-day Chợ Lớn he built a large complex of rice granaries (kho) capable of exporting over a hundred tons daily to the northern front or as payment to other countries for arms and assistance.[7] Former Khmer provinces (srok) such as Gò Công, Sa Đec, and Sóc Trăng also contributed rice and military recruits but remained under locally autonomous Khmer leaders. By 1790 Nguyễn Ánh's strategic network of barracks, forts, and granaries (map 7) made up a powerful political and transportation network reaching to the tip of the Cà Mau Peninsula, where ethnic-Chinese (Hoa Kiều) soldiers and settlers lived with the predominantly Khmer population.[8]

After reunifying the country in 1802, the new royal government established at Huế continued to support expansion of the network of garrisons; beyond this skeletal network they supported settlers building

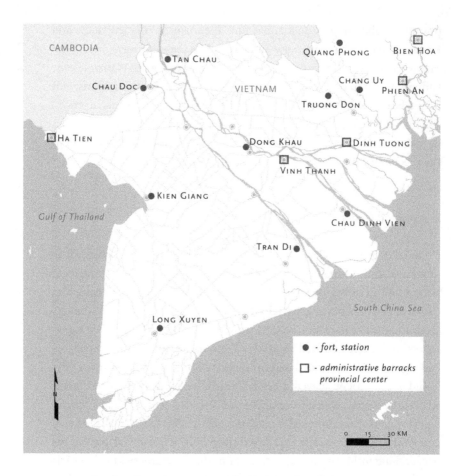

MAP 7. *Nguyễn Administrative Barracks (dinh) and Forts (đạo) in 1790. This map indicates the location of forts (circled dots) and administrative barracks (squares) in the delta. The former barracks at Hà Tiên was still abandoned in 1790 but was later rebuilt.* Source: *Author.*

fortified plantations (*đồn điền*). These settlements were the primary means by which most Vietnamese settled the vast southern frontier in the delta. Early *đồn điền* were organized by military troops who received money, tools, and food from the government for clearing land to build a fort and establish fields. Soldier-farmers split into three units that built the *đồn điền*'s infrastructure (irrigation ditches and communal buildings), performed guard duty, and prepared fields.[9] After defeating the Tây Sơn government in 1802, Gia Long expanded the *đồn điền* policy to others willing to settle the frontier, notably prisoners and debtors. In 1802 he ordered officials at the old barracks (*dinh*) to cede uncultivated land (*đất bỏ hoang*) to poor settlers unable to buy existing farmland. Those who accepted the government's grant and failed to clear the land were then fined three *hộc* of rice (one *hộc* = sixty liters) and required to join the military to repay their debt with service. Those who successfully cleared land then registered it and paid taxes.[10] In 1807 the king also resumed the practice of sending prisoners to the frontier. They arrived in fetters and chains to a *đồn điền* managed by soldiers and were allotted a portion of land, seed, and basic tools. For each month of work, a prisoner received one *phương* (about twenty-five kilograms) of rice. After a year, if he cleared the land and successfully planted rice, then the managing soldier had the fetters released. After three years, if he successfully converted the entire area of land to rice fields, he was free and his chains were broken. His period of chained labor could be shortened if his wife and family joined him and they cleared the land together.[11]

Despite these attempts at expanding Vietnamese influence in the region, the delta's population does not appear to have grown much in the first half of the nineteenth century. Vietnamese official records and early colonial observers remarked that soldiers and settlers often abandoned the *đồn điền* if soils became too acidic and less productive.[12] With abundant land and comparatively few available hands, flight was a common response to adversity. Outbreaks of cholera and other epidemics also limited population increases in some areas.

Instead of converting wilderness into towns simulating the "civilized" streets of Hà Nội or Huế, Vietnamese migrants expanded their kingdom's influence by readily adopting many practices and technologies already in use by Khmers and Chinese. Settlers adapted their agricultural techniques to local conditions and ultimately produced a distinctive riverine culture (*văn minh sông nước*) that often was at odds with royal edicts coming from Huế. The "southward march" (*nam tiến*), a recurring theme in Vietnamese historiography, often comes across as an overly deterministic notion in Vietnamese historiography when considered as a continuous process that has governed Vietnamese migrants over centuries. At specific places and times, however, such settlement was an important factor in the formation of hybrid economic and social identities that emerged as a result of mixing northern Vietnamese ideas with those in place on the frontier. In her study on Vietnamese migration to central Vietnam in the seventeenth and eighteenth centuries, Li Tana suggests that the emergence of the Nguyễn state in the 1600s adapted elements of the earlier Cham culture, including the region's unique mercantile and maritime economy, and incorporated Cham sacred sites into the local Vietnamese cosmography. The Nguyễn Lords went so far as to establish new official titles, modes of dress, state rituals, currencies, and official salary systems that differentiated their southern state from the Trịnh-controlled area around Hà Nội.[13] Such localizations produced distinctive dialects over time and no shortage of rebellions and civil wars. The Nguyễn Lords fought a series of wars with the Trịnh in the seventeenth century. In turn, they were deposed by a rebel army from the central highlands that pursued them to the Mekong Delta, from which the surviving royal heir fled to Siam in 1783.

Like generations of settlers before them, the Vietnamese who arrived in Mekong Delta villages in the nineteenth and twentieth centuries did not faithfully reproduce the bamboo hedgerows and village landscapes of their native lands but instead incorporated local Chinese and Khmer elements into the homes and fields they constructed. In cosmographic terms, many settlers adopted the worship of Bà Chúa Xứ (Lady of the Land), a local protective deity popular with Khmers and Chinese. In a corner of the home or garden, they built a small shrine in her honor. Women especially made offerings of honey and prayed to her for prosperity and good health. Bà Chúa Xứ, associated with the queen bee (*ong chúa*), represented the nexus of fertility, health, and prosperity.[14] Besides Bà Chúa Xứ, local farmers also erected shrines to the Khmer male god Neak Ta (Ông Tà) in the corner of a field or garden. This tutelary spirit protected a household or field from evil. Shrines for this spirit were typically constructed out of brick or stone and can still be seen in many delta gardens and fields today.[15] Perhaps as a public gesture intended to ease ethnic tensions between settlers and existing communities, government officials also paid their respects to such deities, dedicating large state temples to them and including them in royal decrees, which meant that they were recognized as belonging in the official pantheon of gods.[16]

Vietnamese settlers also borrowed local agricultural technologies. They used Khmer tools and work animals to deal with the marshy soils and unfamiliar grasses and adopted the local practice of cutting grass (*phát cỏ*) instead of plowing. If the grass was cut just before the onset of the annual floods, the pooling of water effectively suffocated the roots. Typical species of wild grasses here included *lác* (*Cyperus digitatus*, brown sedge) and *năn* (*Eleocharis*, needle grass), and a Khmer tool called *cây phãng* was especially adapted to these native grasses. Grass cutters swung it in one hand, often using it in conjunction with a sickle held in the other.[17] Working with the *cây phãng* was labor intensive, as the tool weighed over three kilograms. Typically, local strongmen rented out their service, swinging the *cây phãng* in one hand and the sickle in the other. During Tự Đức's reign (late 1850s), one legendary grass cutter, Cai Thoại, traveled from settlement to settlement and was reputed to work as fast as seven men.[18] Once the grass was cleared, Vietnamese farmers used more familiar tools, such as field rakes, to till the soft mud and prepare the fields for transplanted, short-stem rice (fig. 11). Because of this waterlogged land's extreme fertility, it soon merited a new category in Nguyễn tax records: it was called "marsh field" (*trạch điền*), supplementing the older categories of "upland" (*sơn điền*) and "lowland" (*thảo điền*). Marsh fields outproduced lowland fields three to one, producing three hundred *hộc* of grain for every *hộc* of seed. Thus, provincial mandarins were quick to impose the new tax rate.[19]

Rice species also changed in the region as settlers crossed short-stem strains introduced from northern Vietnam and China with long-stem strains favored by Khmer farmers.[20] The two families of rice plants grown in the delta were short-stem rice (*Oryza sativa*) and a floating rice (*Oryza rufipogon*) closely related to a wild, perennial species of rice common in the marshes. Floating rice did not actually float, but because its stem grew rapidly up to four meters, it appeared to float as it responded to the delta's high flooding by growing fast and keeping the rice above the water. Khmer

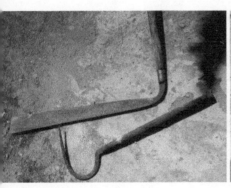

FIG. 11. *Field Tools.* (Left) *Grass-cutting tool* (cây phãng) *and a variety of sickle.* (Right) *Field rake* (cây bùa) *used after cutting to smooth the layer of silt in the field and allow even water coverage during flooding to kill grass stubble and prevent oxidation of the soil. Source: Author photos. The tools in both pictures date to the mid-nineteenth century and are part of the private collection of Trường Ngọc Tường, Cai Lậy, Mỹ Tho Province.*

farmers favored this flood-tolerant, long-stem rice, while Vietnamese farmers preferred higher-yielding, short-stem varieties, including non-glutinous (*lúa tẻ*) and glutinous (*lúa nếp*) types. Over time, villages developed hundreds of local strains differentiated by adaptability, length of growing season, taste, color, and size.[21] In 1900 a French researcher counted over five hundred varieties, including sixteen varieties of floating rice. Names varied with local language, customs, and so on and reflected poetic, religious, or practical themes (e.g., "White Phoenix," "Bird Claw," and "Sweet Girl").[22]

Tools also changed to accommodate the rice. For short-stem rice, farmers used a short-handled sickle. Longer-stem varieties such as floating rice required use of a small blade attached to a longer and curved wooden handle. Handles were typically fashioned from the resinous tree *cây mù u* (*Callophyllum inophyllum*) (fig. 12). Chinese trade also played an important role in settlement, as ethnic-Chinese merchants sold imported iron implements and bought rice with currency imported from the north.

FIG. 12. *Tools Used in the Mekong Delta.* (Left) *This long sickle was used for harvesting the long-stem, or "floating," rice more commonly consumed in Khmer communities. A Vietnamese sickle used for cutting short-stem rice would typically have a handle that extended just above the curved blade in the photo.* (Right) *This tool was used for cutting into clay to create ditches and canals. The iron tip was most likely imported from China, and the Chinese inscription on the wooden handle notes the year of manufacture as Canh Thìn (1880).* Source: *Author photos.* (Left) *Collection of Hoà An Research Station, Cần Thơ University.* (Right) *Private collection of Trương Ngọc Tường, Cai Lậy, Mỹ Tho Province.*

Vietnamese settlers also included wild native plants in their diets and bought Khmer oxen and water buffalo, which could better tolerate the boggy soils.

Juxtaposed against these local adaptations, however, was the continuing pressure from Huế and its regional government in Gia Định after 1802 to consolidate its military and economic control over the region. The Vĩnh Tế Canal and other projects required thousands of conscripted laborers, and these conscriptions often triggered rebellions. Like French colonial projects in the 1900s, these early-modern public-works projects often exacerbated tensions between Vietnamese settlers and Khmer natives and between delta society and Huế. The first of three canal projects, Bảo Định Canal, involved widening an existing waterway dug by Vietnamese troops in 1705 to transport troops to the Chinese-run port at Mỹ Tho. The Nguyễn lord in 1757 ordered troops to deepen and widen the canal to allow larger ships to pass. Beside it, work crews also cleared a mandarin road (*quan đường*) for official communication and patrols. Wars with the Tây Sơn and Siam in the 1780s, however, severely damaged the canal until the reunified kingdom renovated it in 1819. The governor of Định Tường Province (*trấn*) recruited 9,679 laborers, who each received one *quan* (a wooden rack of zinc coins) and one *phương* (twenty-five kilograms) of rice for four months of service. The project lasted the duration of the dry season (January to April) of 1819.[23] After its completion, King Gia Long ordered a stone stele to be constructed alongside the canal to commemorate the work (fig. 13).

Two other canal projects from this era, Thoại Hà and Vĩnh Tế, were much riskier efforts designed to move Vietnamese settlers into the borderlands with Cambodia and protect the delta from future Siamese incursions. Since 1806, King Gia Long's generals had engaged in a series of contests with Siam over Cambodian territory in the Mekong Valley. Although Gia Long had enjoyed good relations with Bangkok in 1787, relations soured over a Cambodian succession crisis in 1806.[24] Gia Long sent one of his most trusted military advisers, Nguyễn Văn Thoại, to Phnom Penh, where he established the La Bích Barracks (*dinh*) and stationed five hundred troops at a garrison outside the Cambodian palace. Finally, Gia Long declared the region around Phnom Penh a new military province called Trấn Tây.[25]

Nguyễn Văn Thoại then was ordered to leave La Bích and return to the central barracks at Vĩnh Long, where he was to start building two large canals and found a series of settlements along them.[26] In 1817 he led approximately 1,500 soldiers to the head of Tam Khê Creek near Long Xuyên, where they began digging a canal that would be over forty

FIG. 13. *1819 Bảo Định Canal Commemorative Stele. This stele is today housed within a small memorial alongside the canal at Phú Kiệt Hamlet, Chợ Gạo District, Tiền Giang Province.* Source: *Author photos, December 2001.*

kilometers long and connect to the Vietnamese garrison at Rạch Giá (map 6). They excavated up the Hậu Giang (Bassac) branch of the Mekong to Long Xuyên and then southward toward Núi Sập, a single granite hill rising some eight hundred meters from the floodplain below. Given their relatively rapid completion of the canal (three months) and the importance of such mountains to the ancient Funan kingdom, they were likely excavating an existing canal trace from either pre-Angkor or Angkor times. That it became immediately viable for large shipping traffic without requiring the usual host of hydrologic fixes suggests this as well.[27] Gia Long's successor, King Minh Mạng, commended the work and ordered a stele be carved and installed at the mountain. He ordered the waterway to be renamed Thoại River (Thoại Hà) and the nearby mountain where the stele was erected Thoại Mountain (Núi Thoại). Nguyễn Văn Thoại was

promoted two degrees in the mandarinate and given the official title Thoại
Ngọc Hầu (Jade Marquis Thoại).

Such ceremonies and historic monuments suggest a precolonial form
of nation-building not so different from the French version several
decades later. The commemorative stone tablet, placed at the foot of the
mountain, highlights how the early-modern Vietnamese state engaged in
appropriation and ordering of this foreign territory:

> The mountain has existed since the days of division between Heaven and
> Earth. It has now received its true name with this royal order. Since that
> moment, the vegetation has flourished and the clouds and mist appear in
> bright colors. The summit, compared with ordinary mountains or hills, is not
> far from the celestial vault. Since antiquity, this territory to which it belongs
> has been under the domination of barbarians [Cambodians] who called it Núi
> Sập. Since the time of the [Vietnamese] conquest of the South by the armies of
> the [Nguyễn] lord, this mountain has been described on the maps as a garden
> paradise. The woods were thick and the fields covered in grass, used for rest-
> ing by leaping herds of deer and stags.[28]

The third project, the Vĩnh Tế Canal, was by far the most ambitious
and contested of these canals, causing several Khmer-led rebellions and
triggering outbreaks of cholera that resulted in thousands of deaths.
Hailed by Vietnamese histories as a key strategic work, the project that
essentially fixed part of the international border is generally viewed
in Khmer literature as an abuse of Khmer workers that severed part of
the ancient Khmer kingdom and subsequently prevented Khmers from
settling eastward in the delta region.[29] In the dry seasons of 1819 and
1820, cholera and dysentery swept through the project site, causing high
casualties. Severe droughts in 1822 brought the project to a halt with severe
shortages of drinkable water.[30] The *Prey Kuk Monastery Chronicle* notes that
abusive working conditions on the canal sparked a rebellion at Ba Phnom,
a nearby Khmer town. Another Khmer source, *Robar Khsat Srok Khmer,*
also describes the rebellion, identifying a Buddhist monk named Kai who
led several thousand Khmer workers. They ambushed an ethnically mixed
Vietnamese military regiment in which Khmer soldiers in the unit refused
to fire on the workers. The Nguyễn viceroy in Sài Gòn sent reinforcements
from Gia Định Citadel and eventually crushed the rebellion.[31] After the
canal's completion, Minh Mạng commissioned another set of stone

monuments and conferred the name Vĩnh Tế on the canal to honor the governor's wife, Châu thị Vĩnh Tế, who had arranged aid for and consoled loved ones of workers killed by disease and fighting.[32]

Mounting tensions between the delta's multiethnic frontier society and Huế finally erupted in a more violent, three-year war of secession following the death of the popular, Sài Gòn–based viceroy Lê Văn Duyệt in 1832. Minh Mạng refused to recognize Duyệt's adopted son Khôi as a successor and instead used the opportunity to convert the old administration of military provinces (*ngũ trấn*) into six regular provinces (*lục tỉnh*) that would form the southern section of the kingdom. He appointed new governors and dismissed most of the veteran officials. Khôi and these ousted officials organized a rebellion against the court, allying with the Siamese king Rama III (r. 1824–51). Khôi's forces quickly seized the citadels and gained control of the region. In the three years of warfare that ensued, most of the granaries, citadels, roads, and canals were ruined. Rama III used the opportunity to launch an offensive against the Nguyễn to gain control over territory in Cambodia, Laos, and the Mekong Delta. He sent a fleet of ships to Hà Tiên and, via Laos, five battalions of troops and elephants to attack at Nghệ An.[33] The Siamese fleet invaded the delta's new waterways and together with Khôi's followers took the citadel at Châu Đốc, holding it for two years. Khôi's followers raided the central granary and treasury at Vĩnh Thành (Vĩnh Long), and many surrounding villages were destroyed by both sides in the fighting.[34] After a prolonged siege that left Gia Định in ruins, the Nguyễn forces finally recaptured the city.[35] Khôi died from illness, and in 1836 the Nguyễn troops finally reclaimed their citadels and granaries in the delta.

The vulnerability of these new canals to invasion by sea may explain why Minh Mạng and his successors abandoned them after 1836. He turned instead to a different process of nation-building involving the consolidation of civil government in all Vietnamese territory. The southern rebellion had cut rice shipments to famine-stricken areas in the north and many had died on the roads; Minh Mạng thus focused on restoring internal links from north to south, pushing for more intensive cultivation of existing fields in the Mekong Delta and urging farmers to use "every morsel of earth."[36] Rather than build new fortresses and canals on his frontiers, he initiated strict reforms across the country on such issues as tax collection, education, and land management. He also reorganized the kingdom's provincial administration by converting the military cantons (*trấn*) into civilian provinces (*tỉnh*) that would be administered by scholarly exam graduates rather than military men.[37]

The 1836 reforms had lasting political and environmental consequences in the delta as the royal government increased its surveillance over land use and encouraged the participation of Khmers and Chinese in Vietnamese forms of governance and education. Huế's ministers of war and finance departed for Gia Định in 1836 to commence the first major property survey (*địa bộ*) in the region. A surveyor (*đạc điền quan*) classified property in the presence of the landowner, village leaders, and a district mandarin (also a representative of the king). The royal surveyors noted major discrepancies between claimed and actual property use; many parcels were illegally subdivided while others stretched several kilometers beyond documented boundaries. Land was also misclassified to avoid higher taxes; for example, houses and orchards often occupied land recorded on provincial rolls as rice paddy. The total area of parcels surveyed amounted to just over 300,000 hectares (less than 10 percent of the region's total area).[38] Most documented holdings were located on the banks of major rivers and creeks. The surveys redefined land spatially and qualitatively with a host of new classifications: mandarin field (*quan điền*), communal field (*công điền*), private field (*tự điền*), garrison plantation (*đồn điền*), monastic land (*phật tự thổ*), pepper land (*tiêu viên thổ*), cemetery (*thổ mô*), and fallow land (*hoang nhàn thổ*).[39] In addition to the land surveys, Minh Mạng's efforts to Vietnamize the delta population produced deep ethnic hostilities that may explain why the French found many supporters in their initial conquest. In a recent survey of Minh Mạng's policies, Choi Byung Wook shows that during the 1830s and for two decades before the conquest, education and assimilation policies increasingly divided Vietnamese communities from Khmer and Chinese enclaves, pushing minorities either to assimilate or to migrate to unsettled areas. This, he argues, may explain why most Chinese and Khmer fought with the French instead of the Nguyễn during the conquest; Vietnamese anticolonial leaders by contrast were mostly literati educated and promoted under these same assimilationist policies.[40]

Regarding local attitudes toward cultivation—both agricultural cultivation (*cày cấy*) and cultural assimilation (*giáo hoá*)—and the still vast, "uncultivated" wilderness (*đất bỏ hoang*) beyond, there were relatively clear definitions in Vietnamese sources of what these terms meant. Since the 1790s, cultivation spread outward from growing administrative centers with central granaries and from smaller fortified plantations (*đồn điền*) that, when successful, evolved into regular villages. From 1836, cultivation was more strictly applied to all people in specific Vietnamese cultural terms. Nonliterate inhabitants, especially Khmer groups, either adopted Vietnamese legal and cultural practices or lost their rights to land and property, causing frequent protests and sometimes violent exchanges. While the royal government had yet to extend its authority to some three-quarters of the delta's land area, in the *miệt vườn* (garden strips) it established the physical and ideological foundations for governance upon which French officials later expanded.

Extending the Colonial Grid

The colonial construction of Cochinchina depended on existing waterways and commercial networks; and early attempts to push beyond them, into *uncultivated* spaces, were often frustrated by natural or political resistance. Moving into the region's cajeput forests and remote enclaves was not simply a matter of clearing or holding terrain; it required coercing or harnessing existing Vietnamese modes of pioneering. The various forms of colonial oppression—military, economic, and political—that people experienced in the port towns and along the main waterways pushed thousands to head out beyond the reach of French boats and guns; but perhaps the greatest incentive to move was the apparent availability of new, uncultivated land for many who had never before owned land. The colonial government since its inception had dispossessed many by seizing land owned by rebels; but to quell rebellion and produce collaborators, it also recognized those who had owned land before the conquest. Ngô Vĩnh Long draws attention to Admiral Pierre de la Grandière (1863–68), who offered even those who had opposed the French the right to retain their property under the colonial government if they returned to their villages by September 1863.[41] While this policy may have quelled fighting, in the longer term colonial land policies generally impoverished the delta's peasantry. The dissolution of traditional usufruct rights, relaxation of restrictions on the size of land holdings for French landlords, and conversion of village communal lands (*công điền*) into private property displaced thousands and established an important basis for peasant resistance against the French decades later. Martin Murray's study on capital formation in Indochina explains how colonial policies not only removed the village's authority over land tenure but also replaced older patterns of land appropriation and distribution, with the market, not village custom, now the sole requirement for land transfers. Decrees in 1871 and 1891 ordered villages to replace the địa bộ (property survey) with new government-directed land lists; and after 1891, villages simply received copies of these lists as drawn up by the government survey office in Sài Gòn.[42]

Colonial land policies were thus instrumental in redefining the economic and legal terms of land cultivation just as the French navy and commercial vessels began transforming the region's commerce in the waterways and towns. Extending colonial rule beyond existing fields and waterways into *uncultivated* regions, however, required the mobilization of new technologies and approaches to reclamation that, in turn, produced a new Vietnamese southward migration (*nam tiến*) in the late nineteenth and early twentieth centuries. From 1881 to 1921, an average of seventy-three thousand people a year settled along new canals, moving outward from the well-patrolled banks to cut or burn forests and drain swamps.[43] This combined effort by pioneers and machines brought the total area under cultivation from 349,000 hectares in 1879 to over 2,400,000 hectares by 1929.[44] Dredging produced over 1,500 kilometers of navigable waterways and 2,500 kilometers of secondary canals—a dramatically expanded grid of waterways—that produced one last frontier boom for migrants, who eventually found themselves displaced again by heavy taxes and a severely disturbed water environment.[45]

What Pierre Brocheux describes as a colonial frontier society differed from precolonial society more in land tenure practices than in actual reclamation techniques. Individuals followed the steam dredges, unloading sampans (*ghe tam bản*) with tools, supplies, and basic building materials. They built huts, burned down sections of the forest beyond, and began the backbreaking work of clearing stumps and forming fields. Once land was cleared and agriculturally productive, however, they often found that landlords had already claimed rights to the land, and they either left for new lands elsewhere or worked out some arrangement.[46] This situation continued into the 1930s, when the last major waterways reached the last forested regions of the Cà Mau Peninsula and the marshes between Long Xuyên, Rạch Giá, and the Vĩnh Tế Canal.

While colonial statistics and maps (such as fig. 7) suggest a continuous and rapid process of expansion, extending the water grid into new areas was frequently accompanied by scandal, lawsuits, and unexpected natural disasters. Canals silted up, soils turned out to be too acidic or salty, and floods sometimes swept through destroying everything. Pitted against the progressive vision of the *mission civilisatrice* was a volatile social and water environment.

There were also more mundane reasons for land abandonment under colonial rule. Many early colonial landowners either went bankrupt or died. Letters concerning the sale of an abandoned plantation near Phụng Hiệp, for example, highlight the economic and ecological problems caused by the failure of many French ventures. The Carabelli Estate belonged to Roccu Francescu Carabelli, who was one of many Corsicans in the colony and served as Sài Gòn's mayor in 1888 and as editor of the city's newspaper, *Courrier de Saïgon*. He applied for a large, undeveloped tract in 1885 and hired laborers to dredge a canal from the existing Boquillon Canal (Kế Sách Canal) to establish a rice plantation on both sides of the waterway (map 6). He died in 1893, at age forty-six, and we have no evidence as to the cause of death. He had failed to deliver a profitable rice crop from the poorly drained, acidic soil and had had to declare bankruptcy.[47] Tenants relocated to nearby villages, while in the abandoned fields rats and birds feasted on the unharvested crops. Three years later, as swarms of birds and rats spread to devour crops in neighboring villages, a group of Khmer village officials from Kế Sách petitioned the government to purchase the Carabelli tract and kill off the pests. Because villagers were not permitted to trespass onto the abandoned plantation, it had become a breeding ground for the pests. The government awarded them the land, and they settled a new village and planted pineapple, which was more suited to the severely acidic soil and had the added benefit of eliminating their rat problem.[48]

Many of the largest land development failures occurred in Đồng Tháp. Since the first years of the conquest, development of this region had been a top strategic priority, given past conflicts and its proximity to Sài Gòn. Ironically, the first landowner to develop new waterways here was a Vietnamese man. Trần Bá Lộc (1829–99), one of Vietnam's most infamous colonial collaborators, had been raised in a Catholic family. In 1885 he retired from colonial military campaigns against Nguyễn forces and became district chief (*tổng đốc*), the highest office a Vietnamese could hold under the French, at the river port Cái Bè, near his childhood home. As a naturalized French citizen, he purchased land from the government and then obtained rights to adjacent, undeveloped tracts. Within a decade he owned over two thousand hectares. With no assistance from the DPW, he hired laborers to dig drainage ditches and canals north from Cái Bè. The DPW later widened them, and today they still bear their original numerical names, designating their order of construction from one to twenty-eight. In 1896, again without government assistance, Lộc hired laborers to dig a canal ten meters wide that stretched forty-seven kilometers across Đồng Tháp from the heavily trafficked Arroyo de la Poste (Bảo Định Canal) in the east to his estate at Cái Bè. The labor crews completed the work in less than a year—a feat for men or machines—and he named the canal Tổng Đốc Lộc Canal (map 6).[49] While Vietnamese historians typically disparage Trần Bá Lộc as one of the worst traitors of the colonial conquest for his role in tracking down many Vietnamese resistance leaders, his role in expanding settlements in Đồng Tháp nevertheless merits attention.[50] Nguyễn Hiến Lê, one of the first Vietnamese to write about the region in a modern, literary form, published a detailed travelogue based on his visits there in the mid-1930s while working as a surveyor for the DPW. Lê attributes Lộc's collaboration with the French to experiences in his youth when local officials in the 1840s detained his father, who taught at one of the larger Nguyễn schools, for several days. Although they eventually released him and allowed him to return to teaching, Lộc nevertheless harbored resentment against the Nguyễn and thus joined the French military. After more than twenty years in the colonial militia, however, he was repeatedly frustrated by the colonial government's racist policies, which prevented him from advancing into the higher ranks of the administration; so after 1885 he commenced on a new path to establish a *đồn điền*, as famous Nguyễn officials had done when he was a boy.[51]

Ironically, the catastrophic floods that wiped out most of the new settlements in Đồng Tháp from 1904 to 1907 harmed Lộc's estate less than French plantations built north of the canals in the heart of the floodplain. Seeing Lộc's early successes, DPW engineers and provincial administrators extended more canals from Lộc's grid through the center of the basin. Two new transport canals, Lagrange and Tháp Mười, attracted thousands of new settlers migrating southward from Sài Gòn and westward from Mỹ Tho. A severe flood in 1904 combined with a major typhoon put the entire region underwater, drowning thousands and washing away their homes. Many people attempted to rebuild, but a major flood swept through again in 1905 and then in 1907. These repeat events caused DPW to abandon its efforts there. A civil engineer traveling along the old canals five years later described the scene as an "absolute desert" with no trace of habitation and not a single encounter with other boats or people for hours at a time.[52]

The eventual center for the largest colonial plantations was the densely forested Hậu Giang region (Transbassac) south of the Mekong River's two main branches. Early colonial and nineteenth-century Vietnamese records describe the forests as being composed of the flood-tolerant species of cajeput (*Malaleuca cajuputi*), which was itself an invasive species that may have colonized more diverse forests that existed before the 1850s. Delta forests since 1700 had been commercially important for honey and beeswax, and the fires used to smoke out the bees may have cleared parts of the old-growth forest. Chinese entrepreneurs paid predominantly Khmer inhabitants to collect honey and beeswax, favoring honey produced by cajeput flowers and a true mangrove species called *cây giá* (*Excoecaria agallocha*). Hives on both species produced so much wax that it could be found floating on the water; Khmers called the region "wax land." The Nguyễn government registered these entrepreneurs in a Wax Taxpayers Association and thus encouraged the cultivation of these forest areas.[53]

With the colonial conquest and the invasion of steam-powered ships, the same cajeput forests became an important source of charcoal, a substitute for coal, which was generally reserved for naval ships in Sài Gòn and stored at island coaling stations such as Paulo Condore (Con Đảo). In the delta, French gunboats, steamers, and dredges burned massive quantities of cajeput charcoal instead. The colonial government issued cutting permits in 1875 that soon accelerated the cutting of trees. By 1905 the Friends of the Forest Service noted that years of unmitigated cutting and annual forest fires threatened to destroy what little remained of the delta forests.[54] Rather than restrict cutting, however, Forest Service officials responded to these concerns by moving the lone forester out of the delta and into the central office in Sài Gòn. They saw little need to conserve the twisted, waterlogged trunks of the "charcoal forests."[55] Annual reported volumes of cut wood approached 2.5 million cubic meters from 1880 to 1910, with approximately five thousand hectares of forest disappearing each year. Actual areas cleared were probably much larger since cajeput (also a source of tea tree oil) was prone to burn and settlers often burned it when establishing rice plantations.[56]

The Hậu Giang region was infamous not only for its vast, flooded marshes but also for river pirates. In 1871 a French naval lieutenant surveyed routes across the interior from the Gulf of Siam to the Hậu Giang branch of the Mekong River. He started from a Khmer village called Vị Thủy on the Cái Lớn River and headed north. The following account reflects a common association of such "wild" interiors with continuing political resistance:

[October 1871] More than 60 miles from the Rach-gia estuary, we arrived on the 26th at eight o'clock in the evening. At midnight we returned to the Khmer village of Vi-thuy, where I prepared 15 xuồng [wooden longboats] . . . the dugout becomes thus a species of broad shoe, slipping with speed on cut or curved grasses. Enough broad packages of rebel grasses form often, causing interruptions where it is necessary to carry the dugout by hand, through what can be called a trập [pit]. Leaving the rice plantations of Vi-thuy, we traveled north until around ten in the morning, the moment when we emerged at the ngon [creek] Cai-Cao, a vast plain from where branches out the Nước-đôc: It is the meeting place of many wild buffaloes, so we took precautions not to surprise them.[57]

The group traveled for four hours through a flooded, bowl-like basin covered in "phantom" rice (lúa ma, Oryza rufipogon) growing a few meters above the surface of the water. Remarking on recently quelled Vietnamese uprisings and acts of banditry, the lieutenant noted that these ghost crops might "sustain the existence of some Robin Hood," but they were insufficient to feed any sizable force. The group reached its destination and then followed a well-worn path created in the dry season by herds of elephants.[58]

When I asked residents living in the area today about elephants and colonial engineers, one explained that the present-day road parallel to a French-dredged canal (Lái Hiểu Canal) was one such "elephant road" (đường tượng) and that it guided colonial surveyors planning the route for the canal. Speaking on the importance of these roads, he said:

There was cajeput forest everywhere here; this road outside here was made by elephants. Because of that, our ancestors came here to clear land and founded the village . . . by having a road, they could attract settlers. When they [the French] dug the canal [Lái Hiểu], people came from every direction; they could then go anywhere and settle . . . so that instantly [after work on the canal was finished] there were settlers, steadily getting more crowded, establishing villages and hamlets.[59]

Even in such remote interiors, then, colonial engineers relied on existing infrastructure—even that created by animals—and expanded it to allow greater numbers of migrants to accelerate the clearing of the forests beyond.

Engineers and Delta Technocrats

As the dredges set to work carving up new paths through the Hậu Giang region and as thousands of settlers turned the forests into fields, colonial engineers emerged as the most powerful arbiters in many disputes between native villages and plantation owners, between neighboring provinces, and even between the colonial government in Cochinchina and more central levels of administration in Hà Nội and Paris. The most powerful engineers were the DPW engineers, young men trained in hydrology, mathematics, and economics at elite French institutions such as the *École nationale des ponts et chausées*. Throughout the years of expansion, they carefully guarded their monopoly on scientific expertise and routinely criticized provincial administrators, village leaders, and others for too often following what they wrote off as self-interest, ignorance, or superstition in proposing their "fixes" to the hydraulic grid. The engineers in charge of canal projects helped create what Theodore Porter calls a "culture of objectivity" that provided the incontrovertible numbers necessary to push their own claims to be the grid's managers.[60] Colonial dossiers associated with these projects are thick with documents detailing past struggles, including court records, letters from Vietnamese village leaders, and correspondence between colonial agencies.

One of the first new canal projects in the Hậu Giang region, the Xà No Canal (completed in 1904), generated extensive controversy, and disputes over damage caused to existing, densely populated Vietnamese villages eventually reached the governor-general's desk in Hà Nội. The new project was one of several "transverse canals" intended to cross the Hậu Giang region and drain into the Gulf of Siam (fig. 14). When dredges cut through these very densely populated areas on the large creeks, they produced walls of clay three meters high that blocked the natural flow of water so that land on one side was submerged in floods while land on the other suffered from drought. Local complaints were especially difficult to resist here since many had property listed on the 1836 *địa bộ* records, and one of these villages, Nhơn Ái, had a total population that was several thousand more than that of the provincial town at Cần Thơ (which had a population of just under eight thousand).[61]

The paper trail of letters, reports, and interagency correspondence reveals the complex interactions between native and colonial worlds as well as the often-competing interests of French officials. The initial move for the project reflects the often-selfish and speculative interests of the

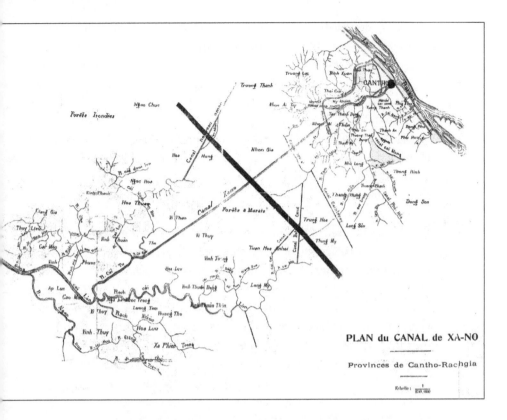

FIG. 14. *Xà No Canal Map. Xà No was one of the first "transverse" canals in the lower delta and was completed in 1904. Source: Plan du canal du Xano (Saigon: Imprimerie commerciale, 1904), file IA 13/232(1), Fonds Goucoch, Trung Tâm Lưu Trữ Quốc Gia II, Hồ Chí Minh City.*

young men assigned to work as provincial administrators in Cochinchina. Administrator Guéry of Rạch Giá Province proposed the project and, once it was accepted, retired from colonial service and applied for a concession of six thousand hectares on either side of the waterway.[62] When the dredge disrupted the irrigation networks of Guéry's neighbors in the densely populated village, he intervened and persuaded a DPW clerk to allow the villagers to make cuts in the embankment to bring water back to their fields. Leaders of Nhơn Nghĩa Village had already written to the Cần Thơ Province administrator complaining of the effects of dredging on their fields:

> Since this part has been dug, there has been no drinkable water; we have had
> to drink water from the swamps, for three months already. Now the dredge   77

has left, completed one section already, so now my village petitions the administrator . . . please allow me to gather 50 men, to make an opening where the dredge had filled, just five days' work . . . if we do not open this back up, our rice fields will be flooded, killing everything, and afterward we will have to find water at a different place.[63]

With the provincial administrator's permission, the clerk permitted them to make the modifications.

The debate quickly reached the governor of Cochinchina and the chief engineer when the same village leader requested that the province compensate him for the expensive work that had been necessary to correct the "damage" caused by the engineers. Somewhat surprisingly, the governor sided with the villagers and awarded them the requested payment of some four thousand piasters.[64] Citing the precedent that such a damage award might set, the chief engineer appealed to the governor-general in Hà Nội to intervene. The ensuing flurry of correspondence between the province, Sài Gòn, and Hà Nội reflects one of the early struggles of engineers to prevail over the interests of provincial authorities, natives, and even governors. The chief engineer argued that the welfare of a village must not jeopardize the viability of such a regional project and put an investment of several million francs at risk. As similar disputes reached Sài Gòn and Hà Nội, the governor-general later issued a decree that was a slight compromise, reimbursing farmers for lost fruit trees while citing that lost income from damaged fields would be counterbalanced by the commercial value of having canal-front property.[65]

Such correspondence suggests that the engineers often gained the political advantage; but it also suggests that many native landholders in older, densely populated villages actively engaged the colonial government in sophisticated ways. The map in figure 15, submitted by Nhơn Nghĩa Village leaders in a bid to regain compensation for land lost to the right-of-way for a canal, demonstrates their facility in producing maps and responding to the precise rules and requirements of colonial decrees. We see that, counter to prevalent historical notions that Vietnamese peasants were largely ignorant of modern instruments such as cadastral maps, those living in such villages as Nhơn Nghĩa demonstrated the ability to challenge the new government on its own legal terms.

Records from other disputes also show that those fighting the engineers, especially in court, did not easily fit into such social categories

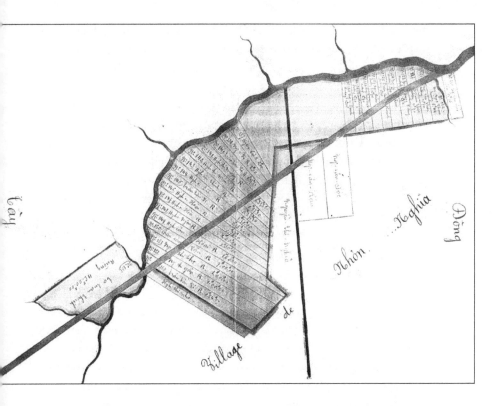

FIG. 15. *Local Land Parcels on Xà No Creek. This plan accompanied letters from the village leaders of Nhơn Nghĩa (adjacent to Nhơn Ái Village at the northern terminus of the Xà No Canal), who complained that the new canal split their parcels and disrupted a key irrigation channel (pictured here as a thick black line running from top to bottom of the figure).* Source: *Nhơn Ái Village, September 27, 1901, file IA 13/232(1), Fonds Goucoch, Trung Tâm Lưu Trữ Quốc Gia II, Hồ Chí Minh City.*

as landowner, collaborator, or peasant. In response to an early project, Lái Hiếu Canal (1902–4), Madame de Lachevrotière brought a 400,000-piaster claim against the government for damages and lost revenues over several years. She was not European but the Vietnamese wife of a French colonist who had died in the colony and left her his concession. They had a son, Henri, who was born in the colony in 1883 and after his father's death in 1894 lived in Bordeaux with his father's family and attended school. He returned to the colony in 1903 and together with his mother managed the plantation.[66] After enduring several years of persistent flooding, the family hired a Paris lawyer, who brought the case to the high court in Hà Nội.[67] The case attracted widespread attention in the colony, and young Henri was very likely the focus of much attention. In a later affair, newspapers described him as a playboy and an opportunist, suggesting that the mixed-race man harbored various conspiratorial ambitions.[68] In the 1912 court case, however, the primary court transcripts reveal a very sophisticated argument that challenged the DPW on technical grounds, offering up calculations of water flow and attempting to demonstrate that the engineers had erred in their supposedly expert calculations.[69]

State engineers responded to these new challenges by French citizens and their lawyers by redirecting the blame for such modifications to provincial administrators who did not carry out all of the secondary works envisioned in various projects. In his response to the Lachevrotières, the chief engineer wrote:

> As MR. POUYANNE indicated on page 64 [of *Les voies d'eau*], certain errors were made repeatedly with regard to elementary truths about the hydrology. . . . I believe it is useful to supplement these by describing aspects where the public and many administrators have used this information wrongly to accept the complaints of taxpayers and give them council. The expression of these errors from the mouths of people having a certain authority, if not from the technical point of view at least from the administrative point of view, can induce public citizens to have misleading illusions and proceed with claims against the colony.[70]

After discussing more details about observed tides, measured mean sea level, and the slope of the terrain, the chief engineer blamed the failed projects on the failure of the provincial councils to complete several provincial projects that were to be part of the overall hydrologic plan. He suggested that lack of technical training at the provincial level was also a cause for widespread problems in the waterway network. The chief engineer confirmed claims that crop yields had diminished by a third or more; but he disputed the causes of the reduction, suggesting that rat infestations and disease outbreaks also reduced crop productivity.[71]

DPW engineers not only responded to individual claims but also frequently intervened in provincial politics, often singling out projects that reflected political, rather than hydrological, concerns. One such project, Bình Hoa Canal, followed the administrative border between Cần Thơ and

Rạch Giá Provinces; its construction was the result of conflicts over one village's flood control structures built along the provincial border. Villagers in Tân Bình Village (Định Hoà Canton, today Tân Bình Commune) petitioned their council in Cần Thơ to resolve flooding resulting from the local canal and embankments built by Bình Hoa Village in Rạch Giá Province. With an extension of the DPW-constructed Lái Hiếu Canal in 1906, water from the river rushed into the area and caused high flooding in Tân Bình. The village head of Tân Bình skillfully argued that it would be impossible to pay provincial taxes if nothing more was done and the rice land perpetually flooded.[72]

Ultimately, DPW engineers could not keep abreast of so many conflicts, and by the 1930s their attempts to maintain the network of waterways began to fail. Nevertheless, they were instrumental in the development of legal institutions such as regional planning commissions and, perhaps more importantly, visual representations—maps and plans—that presented the delta as a single water grid. During this intensive period of public-works construction from 1900 to 1930, the colony sent out successive waves of surveyors to map the territory both above and below the water. Engineers were also key members in colonial planning meetings where provincial administrators, colonial councilors, and the governor decided upon top-priority projects of general interest. Such real and discursive creations—from geodetic survey markers and water gauges to regional development plans and regional commissions—had lasting impacts on the ways that governments and people have interacted in the delta region. Also, because of differing colonial arrangements in Cochinchina (a colony) and Cambodia (a protectorate), work on the hydraulic grid extended, not to the delta's ecological boundaries, but only to its political ones. This confinement of the dense maze of waterways and the *réseau hydraulique* to the boundaries of the political map has continued to play a role in international water disputes, as the governments of Vietnam and Cambodia still negotiate transboundary issues of irrigation, pollution, and flood control.

This colonial-era production of scientific reports, maps, and other artifacts of governance was by no means the first attempt at what Foucault and others might describe as governmentality in the region. Older Vietnamese gazetteers, canal-side stone tablets, and land registers from 1836 accomplished much the same purpose. By 1900, colonial-era products had simply become more extensive in scope and exacting in detail. While scholars such as Benedict Anderson have shown how colonial states used such creations as the census, the survey map, and the museum to organize and frame subject people, environments, and pasts, few have yet to consider how such "totalizing grids" continued to change along with the populations and environments depicted in them. They were works in progress inserted into preexisting works in progress, subject to revision prompted by changes in cartographic techniques as well as modifications such as canals to the existing environment. Early surveys and expeditions such as Rénaud's on the Vĩnh Tế Canal demonstrate what Anderson explains as the necessary business of creating property histories that located the colony geographically and historically, but such acts of nonerasure also advanced and preserved existing framings.[73] French hydrographers and military topographers paid particularly close attention to historic features, often noting place-names in Chinese characters and offering transcriptions into the romanized alphabet developed by missionaries and adapted by French officials. An 1881 *Avertissement géographique et orthographique sur la carte de l'Indo-chine orientale* listed place-names alphabetically within the geographic quadrants (degrees of latitude and longitude) of a map, giving the names in both the missionary script (*quốc ngữ*) and a *transcription pratique* and also supplying corrections to *mots erronés* on the map.[74] Place-names were frequently revised, lines had to be redrawn on maps, and administrative categories had to be reconfigured. As the Lachevrotières' court case above illustrates, errors in canal siting and calculations of water flow opened up colonial spaces to frequent contestation and brought more revisions. Thus, mapmaking, perhaps the signature act of defining territory, was not simply a hegemonic inscription of state power but an enterprise that also revealed the shortcomings and vulnerabilities of an expanding, modern state. Failures to accurately measure canal elevations to the nearest centimeter could not only cost the state huge sums but also bring widespread ecological damage and political fallout. As engineer Combier noted, failures to accurately measure the economic and environmental factors involved in construction ran the risk of creating "works of Penelope," projects without end.

In mapping the hydraulic grid, engineers and surveyors engaged in the difficult process of connecting points on a map to sites on the ground and then connecting each of these sites hydrologically with each other by digging waterways. In dealing with water in one of the world's flattest deltas, the problem that concerned them most—especially after the early court cases and failed projects—was determining elevation as accurately as possible to detect differences of a meter or less so that water would flow in the intended directions. In 1908 the head of the Service géographique de l'Indochine, a lieutenant colonel in the infantry, proposed that a system of geodetic markers be constructed by infantry surveyors in the growing network of new bridges, railroads, and canals so that the colony's elevations could be established more accurately. The resulting network of markers was set up along major "lines" of travel and attested to both the importance that the government attached to this effort—altitudes were recorded down to the millimeter—and the difficulty surveyors faced in calibrating their measurements against anything lodged on solid ground. The chief surveyor noted: "In Cochinchina, where there are immense areas

Matricule	Distances entre les Repères	Cumulées	Définition Graphique	Altitude	Description de l'emplacement des Repères
0ab1	"	6.687		3.111	Borne type du N.G. situé sur le côté droit de la route Bentre-Batri, à 20m devant la maison commune de Luong-My.
0ab1'	"	"		4.019	Extrémité supérieure de la traverse médiane du pont en fer (Côté N.) situé sur le Rach Bavong au Km 12 de la route Bentre-Batri.
0ab1''	"	"		2.923	Rondin scellé dans le pilier S.E. du mur d'enceinte de la maison commune de Binh-Chanh.
	11.925				
0ab2	"	18,612		2.747	Borne type du N.G. situé à 15m devant la maison commune de Cho Giong-Trom.
0ab2'	"	"		3.485	Repère pris sur la plate-forme marquée par trois traits de ciseaux du tombeau en granit situé à 185m au N.E. de la maison commune de Binh-Thanh et à 20m à l'E. de la route Bentre-Batri.
0ab2''	"	"		2.755	Partie supérieure d'un tombeau en granit situé à 55m à l'O. de la maison commune de Tan-Thanh-Dong vers le Km 21.500 de la route Bentre-Batri.
	5.699				
0ab3	"	24,311		3.073	Borne type du N.G. situé à la jonction des routes Bentre-Batri et Bentre-Sandoc au Km 24.

FIG. 16. *Survey Markers along the Road from Bến Tre to Bà Tri.* Source: *Service géographique de l'Indochine*, Répertoire des repères du réseau de nivellement de la Cochinchine *(n.p., 1911), 149–50; file IA 19/232(1), Fonds Goucoch, Trung Tâm Lưu Trữ Quốc Gia II, Hồ Chí Minh City.*

without a single solid structure, without masonry, without any rock, it is not possible to produce benchmarks even close to the network of Europe."[75] The benchmarks thus clung tightly to the few solid points available in this landscape: trusses on the Eiffel bridges or the bridgeheads, the cement bases of roads and canal markers, and cornerstones of key government buildings. The tops of granite tombstones and the base steps of village meeting halls (đình) (fig. 16) were used as a secondary, less-precise array of markers.[76]

Even after such trigonometric surveys were completed, colonial knowledge of the water landscape in three dimensions was still severely limited to existing lines of movement—canals and a few roads—where surveyors were guaranteed clear lines of sight and relatively solid ground. Knowledge of the vast cajeput forests in the Cà Mau Peninsula or the winding arroyos crowded with homes remained quite limited until the advent of aerial photography in the 1920s. The chief surveyor's recognition of different levels of exactness (or solidness) in his measurements should suggest that not all areas were mapped equally; the hegemony of colonial rule diminished the further one traveled from the main lines of the hydraulic grid into the interiors.

Far more complex than measuring solid ground, however, was measuring the flow of water through this environment. By 1911, colonial water records, especially rainfall records, varied widely from station to station. An irrigation engineer inspecting the construction of irrigation and drainage systems in Cochinchina pointed out extreme errors in these records. For example, rainfall in September 1910 for two neighboring provinces, Mỹ Tho and Gò Công, was recorded as 567 and 939 mm, respectively. He thought this error could in all likelihood be attributed to "the native in charge of the readings neglecting to regularly empty the apparatus after each daily reading."[77] However, he also pointed to French engineers and surveyors who failed to apply appropriate mathematical models to calculate intensely variable hydrodynamic conditions on canals such as Lái Hiếu Canal (at the heart of the Lachevrotière court case) or in coastal regions affected by strong tides. Instead, many engineers and the private company that dredged the canals proceeded by "trial and error," considering water flow in general, rather than locally specific terms and thus disregarding the annual autumn floods, the daily influence of two tidal regimes (Gulf of Siam and South China Sea), and the influence of newly dredged waterways on water flow in existing waterways.[78]

If we return to the notion of maps and scientific practices framing colonial landscapes and people, we see that such errors in calculation produced openings through which people could challenge the engineers and ultimately colonial authority. Whether attributed to "ignorant" native employees unfamiliar with data collection techniques or European firms pushing ahead without sufficient preliminary studies, such errors brought direct and often-devastating consequences: lost crops, bankruptcies, abandoned lands, and disease. This more detailed glimpse of the production of maps and data on the delta suggests that such paper representations of the delta as a single hydraulic region, while voluminous, were nevertheless more imagined than one might think when confronted with the hundreds of pages of rainfall tables, flood gauge readings, and tide charts. The scientific authority of the DPW engineer was still in part a spectacle.

Besides mapping efforts, two other institutions created in the colonial era played powerful roles in reinforcing the idea of a single hydraulic grid: colony-wide *procès verbal* proceedings on public-works campaigns and the French company that carried out all of the dredging projects in a multiyear, monopoly contract. Administrators from every province, the governor, colonial councilors, and representatives from every department of government met annually to prioritize major projects and to appropriate funding for three-year campaigns. Beginning in 1903 and meeting less frequently after 1930, such meetings were important for determining which areas the colony would concentrate its efforts on and which areas it would ignore. For example, at the 1908 meeting (held in Sài Gòn from July 21 to July 24) the chief engineer explained to disgruntled administrators from the Đồng Tháp region that no money from the general budget would be forthcoming to dig new canals or fix old ones, as some 55,000 settlers had abandoned the region in the past five years.[79] While the chief engineer and the governor frequently prevented funds from reaching what they considered peripheral regions, they also frequently prevented administrators from these provinces from taking actions locally. An administrator from Châu Đốc, for example, collected over 56,000 piasters from voluntary subscriptions in each district to purchase a small dredge from France to handle his province's needs independently from the DPW in Sài Gòn. After a year of correspondence with the governor and a dredge manufacturer in France, his request for the acquisition was refused by the chief engineer, who cited the potential damage to the regional grid that such local initiatives might cause.[80] Thus, through such meetings and extensive correspondence preceding them, central officials and public-works engineers reinforced the hegemony of the center over the periphery.

Finally, dredging contracts not only pressed contractors to rapidly dig new waterways so they could be paid but also resulted in the most politically important measure of progress: monthly and annual statistics showing the total volume dredged. Dredging campaigns and their associated contractors were organized in multiyear contracts. Notable gaps occurred in 1926–28 and 1939–41 due to prolonged court battles between the government and the contracting company. Contract records also show that in 1913 one company, the Société française d'entreprises de dragages et de travaux publics (SFEDTP), reached a quasi-institutional status when it became the only contractor to carry out state projects (table 2). With just one firm operating the colony's dredges from 1913 on, possibilities for corruption were obviously high. The SFEDTP evolved into a formidable institution. Except for two prolonged legal disputes over payment, public criticism of its close relationship to the DPW did not emerge until after the Great Depression, when colonial officials moved to break up its monopoly and recast development policy in the delta.

TABLE 2 Dredging Contracts

1893–1903	Montvenoux Company (sole bidder)
1904–1912	Société française industrielle d'Extrême-Orient
1913–1926	Société française d'enterprises de dragages et de travaux public
1929–1936	Société française d'enterprises de dragages et de travaux public
1937–1939	Société française d'enterprises de dragages et de travaux public
1941–1951	Société française d'enterprises de dragages et de travaux publics

Sources: For all contracts from 1893 to 1939, see file VIA 8/186 (31), Fonds Goucoch, TTLTQG2. For 1941–51, see file 14094, H61-38, TDBCPNV, TTLTQG2. The final contract was interrupted by the outbreak of the First Indochina War, and records indicate that the contractor never completed the final program of projects.

The often poorly conceived, rapidly deployed projects suggest a massive construction effort in which engineers and scientists often struggled after the fact to understand the complex hydraulic (and legal) processes that their works unleashed. Once a canal was finished, undoing it was not as simple as Penelope's undoing of her night's weaving. Waterways brought thousands of settler "pioneers" into new territory, cemented powerful political alliances in Sài Gòn, increased the need for more accurate mapping, and reconfigured the flow of water through many delta areas. Meanwhile, failures in the hydraulic grid often brought severe economic and political disruptions. Thousands of tenants soon abandoned the depleted soils of Đồng Tháp after the waterways succumbed to several years of bad floods. Over a million hectares of "charcoal" forests were eliminated in this period, replacing once-common wetland forests and estuaries with treeless horizons of plantations built in checkerboard plots of land framed by canals and dikes. The dredging program never achieved a "final form" for the water landscape, nor did it ever completely "pacify" the region. Instead, it merely redirected for a time its powerful machines and several million settlers into relatively uninhabited terrain, away from past problems.

As engineers ran out of "empty" land to cultivate, environmental and economic conflicts escalated, eventually threatening the future economic and political stability of the region. The onset of the global depression in Indochina in 1931 bankrupted hundreds of thousands of farmers; and the combined economic and environmental problems finally caught up with the DPW. New disputes emerged in the 1930s that ultimately allowed nascent nationalist movements to comment on the *crisis agricole*. The origins of these conflicts, however, were present from the early days of colonial expansion. Combier's social, moral, and technical criticism of projects funded by opium sales in 1880, for example, and other critiques of insufficient project preplanning in 1913 foreshadowed the political and technical criticisms of the 1930s. Poorly conceived projects such as the Lái Hiếu Canal justified Combier's fears that engineers would engage in projects that would have no end.

In 1930, however, while anticolonial uprisings spread and new nationalist voices emerged in the press, colonial officials clung tightly to their story that the machines and infrastructure they had introduced proved the benevolence and sophistication of colonial rule. On September 15, 1930, just three days after French troops and aircraft opened fire on thousands of protesters in the northern city of Vinh, a steamer carried the governor-general of Indochina, the lieutenant-governor of Cochinchina, and the chief engineer of the DPW to the docks at Rạch Giá for the inauguration of the last major colonial canal project, the Rạch Giá–Hà Tiên Canal. The new canal ran sixty kilometers through swampy, deforested terrain along the gulf coast, a thirty-meter-wide path carved through peat bogs, salt marshes, and mangroves. The colonial officials met a welcoming party divided into two lines: one of about a dozen Vietnamese district officials dressed in the traditional mandarin tunic (*áo dài*) and the other of about twenty colonial troops wearing conical hats and white uniforms. The Frenchmen, mustachioed and dressed in the suits and pith helmets of the civil service, shook hands with their Vietnamese counterparts and spoke to a small crowd gathered around a dais (fig. 17).

Governor-General Pierre Pasquier delivered a carefully crafted speech that lauded the French "hydraulic management" in the delta. He defended this aspect of the French colonial project against his Vietnamese enemies

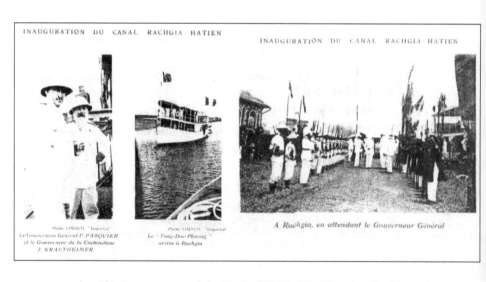

FIG. 17. *The Inauguration of the Rạch Giá–Hà Tiên Canal, 1930. (Center) A common steamer used in the Mekong Delta for mail and passenger travel. (Right) The two "faces" of a colonial reception: militia on the left and provincial leaders in* áo dài *on the right.* Source: *Inspection des travaux publics, Gouvernement générale de l'Indochine,* Dragages de Cochinchine: Canal Rachgia-Hatien *(Saigon: n.p., 1930), 69–70.*

protesting outside factories and violently seizing rural districts in the north. In an allusion to Rudyard Kipling's controversial 1899 poem "The White Man's Burden," he began his speech by criticizing the "cruel deception of the English poet," since the burden had been carried not only by the French but also by "indigenous brothers."

> It would be necessary to doubt the intelligence and heart of the Asian people if they were thought to be blind and insensitive to the unfolding of the French miracle.
>
> ...What brighter proof of the fertility and continuity of our politics than this hydraulic management of Cochinchina, methodically led for over 60 years without fail, since the first days of the conquest . . . a canal network tended by our engineers over the deltas of the Mekong and Dong Nai . . . developing it for the profit of the Vietnamese populations in these alluvial lands . . . heavy with silt, heavy with their future crops.[81]

Pasquier noted the dramatic increase in cultivated land, rice exports, and population to make the case for colonial rule. For him, these statistics and the machines that supported them were proof enough of the benefit of *"l'oeuvre française"*:

> these dredges, instruments of Progress moving untiringly through the forests of tram [cajeput] and mangroves—swamps inhabited until recently by herds of wild elephants . . . are opening up these waterways to the sun, great life-giving furrows traversing an uninhabited, uncultivated plain. I would like to show this to all denigrators of *l'oeuvre française,* these immense expanses . . . yesterday they were dismal, vast solitudes. Today they are rich patchworks, sumptuous cloisonné in which are set as far as the eye can see the gold and emerald of the peaceful fields.[82]

The governor-general's speech gave an impression of colonial dredging gradually transforming the delta landscape. This idea of colonial machines moving steadily and "tirelessly" forward through an empty terrain, however, was an idea born of maps rather than any actual experiences on the boggy ground. Those who traveled across its creeks and swamps knew that converting forests to rice fields was not such a straightforward business. The dredges and their DPW engineer-pilots did not expand the hydraulic grid in any logical fashion, and they expanded into uncultivated areas where their knowledge of vegetation, soil, and water was minimal. The idea of water management achieved via these "instruments of Progress" was the colonial engineer-politician's idea: controlling the movement of rivers and people in a steady state of mechanical hydraulics, industrial agriculture, and carefully structured institutions. The failure of colonial engineers and administrators to achieve the steady hydraulic state thus implied a possible failure to control the flow of politics as well.

Back at the inauguration festivities, a Vietnamese district chief (*tổng đốc*) followed the governor-general on the podium and took a very different tone when speaking in Vietnamese about the project. He duly noted the technical prowess of the French, but then he delved into the efforts of the many Vietnamese people who had cleared the lands beyond the canal— thus engaging in the work that really settled the region. The current project was for him one of a long line of projects over several centuries where Vietnamese in conjunction with Khmers and Chinese had "cleared wastelands" (*khẩn hoang đất*) and thus extended civilization. He described in very different physical and narrative terms what he considered to be the Vietnamese oeuvre.[83] This minor emphasis on indigenous, human work rather than the French, mechanical work recalls the ambivalence of Ông Diều toward the design of the Gressier Estate. Foreign technical interventions were acknowledged and even lauded, but they ultimately were just steps in a longer settlement history that extended both temporally and geographically beyond the visions of colonial engineers and surveyors.

The colonial-era expansion of the hydraulic grid represented one phase of a longer history of civilizing missions still in progress. Even within elite circles of colonial society, landowners, politicians, engineers, and entrepreneurs envisioned the hydraulic grid of the 1920s and 1930s in different ways: as a source of irrigation, a network for surveillance and patrols, or a poorly functioning pathway that could nevertheless be expanded and would allow the damage caused by the initial construction to be repaired. Colonial canal projects thus advanced different visions of the hydraulic grid, visions that after 1930 threatened to bring their constituencies into conflict with one another.

I have spoken about slavery: it is worse. The owner of slaves had interest to spare his livestock, which represented a value; on the other hand, he who buys a Tonkinese for five years sees every year the value of his purchase decreasing by a fifth. He thus may find it beneficial to draw from this purchase in five years all that he can give. . . . What matters that the man is spent by this time, good for nothing? The master will not lose a penny there.[1]

3 HYDROAGRICULTURAL CRISIS

When the Great Depression reached Indochina in late 1930, landowners and tenants alike suffered from a severe drop in rice prices. The price of Saigon No. 1 polished grain slid from a peak of $13.10 (piasters per 100 kilograms) in 1930 to $3.20 in 1934. Relative to other commodities—rubber, tin, corn, and cotton—rice lost 51 percent more value in this period.[2] While farmers attempted to expand their production to meet financial debts, total exports fell from 1.8 million tons in 1928 to 1.2 million in 1933, and the total area of land in cultivation decreased for the first time in seventy years, from 2.2 million hectares under cultivation in 1929 to 1.85 million in 1933. Two very severe floods in 1929 and 1937 amplified the effects of this crisis by wiping out crops and settlements along the most recently completed canals in the Long Xuyên Quadrangle and Đồng Tháp.[3]

The general malaise that ensued from these social and environmental

FIG. 18. *The Inauguration of the Tổng Đốc Lộc Canal, 1898.* Source: *J. C. Baurac,* La Cochinchine et ses habitants: Provinces de l'est *(Saigon: Imprimerie commerciale Rey, 1899), 32.*

events in the early 1930s provided openings for emerging Vietnamese-language political commentary and political action in the countryside aimed at exposing flaws in past policies, especially the severe abuse of farm labor, and the urgent need for land reform. Both nationalists and colonial reformists used the agroecological crisis of the 1930s to focus urbanites' attention on the countryside, especially distant plantations and recently settled areas, where few urbanites, much less Europeans, ever traveled. In these vast areas, European and especially native landlords increased their holdings while thousands of small landholders who had taken out loans to buy small tracts went bankrupt. Land values slid with rice from 1,000 piasters per hectare in 1930 to less than 200 piasters per hectare in 1934. The colonial government forgave debt for many large plantations and enterprises, but owners of smaller plots received little relief and pre-1930 debts compounded to cause widespread foreclosures. Tenants also had to work much harder, selling off two or three times the pre-1930 amount of rice to cover taxes that were calculated in piasters (then tied to a gold standard) rather than a percentage of the harvest. Where fifteen days of agricultural labor once sufficed to pay a poll tax, after 1930 a farmer had to work two or three times as long.[4]

At the same time as this economic disaster, underground political parties established in Sài Gòn, Hà Nội, and northern Vietnam turned their attention to the countryside, demanding reduced taxes, lower rents and interest rates, a "land to the tiller" policy, and wage-labor reforms.[5] While the Great Depression raised public awareness of the dire conditions in the countryside, Vietnamese political parties had already been working to build their influence in the countryside for several years. Native political movements had been growing fast since the mid-1920s, after the Ba Son Shipyard strike in Sài Gòn in 1925 and especially after the funeral of the famous nationalist Phan Châu Trinh in 1926. Indochinese Communist Party members established their first secret cells in delta towns (Mỹ Tho, Vĩnh Long) several months before the Great Depression hit Indochina; they coordinated mostly peaceful mass demonstrations on May 1, 1930, and then fled as colonial security police rounded up many key organizers. Other Vietnamese nationalist movements, such as the Nationalist Party and the Constitutionalist Party, had alternative visions for an independent Vietnam in the future. Political activity coincided with economic catastrophe, and throughout the rest of the decade various groups used the economic and political problems to promote various political solutions.[6]

The delta in this period, with its huge plantations, hastily constructed infrastructure, and increasing numbers of landless peasants, became a kind of social laboratory where political activists, colonial officials, and new groups of scientists and engineers experimented with new approaches to worsening environmental, economic, and political situations. France was also in political crisis after 1930; and the election of the Popular Front in 1936 brought a brief barrage of inquiries into colonial problems. The Department of Public Works (DPW) and the dredging enterprise became targets of these inquiries, and new actors emerged to fill political vacuums left after the DPW's reorganization in 1936. Colonial politicians and Vietnamese researchers led programs to form farmer cooperatives while social scientists published many new studies on farming and rural life. In response to new political trends, engineers began drawing up new plans to rehabilitate and settle abandoned areas such as Đồng Tháp. In the 1930s these new actors redefined the terms of development in the water landscape and rejected older notions of a water grid managed by a centralized engineering agency in favor of large, self-enclosed settlements called *casiers* (similar to polders).

During this period a growing cadre of French and Vietnamese social scientists laid the theoretical and ideological foundations for local public discourse on development, land reform, and the environment. This discourse shaped successive government policies in the delta through the end of colonial rule in 1954 and into the Green Revolution and throughout the Indochina Wars. This growing network of researchers and sympathetic officials sought to understand such "troubled" landscapes in economic, political, and ecological terms. New technologies such as aerial photography and popular theories in such fields as human geography gave them new tools for understanding peasants and the delta landscape. Major works such as Pierre Gourou's *Les paysans du delta Tonkinois* (1936) guided social scientists, who after 1930 entered into consultative relationships with the colonial government and were tasked with describing traditional rural cultures and the physical environment to better aid concerned officials.[7] New technologies available in this period, especially aerial photography, became key to this shifting colonial discourse on development and the rural landscape. Aerial photos shifted the colonial gaze from horizontal views, where interior spaces of villages and homes were hidden to surveyors behind orchards and hedgerows, to vertical views "peering over the village hedge" to show vibrant mosaics of fields, dikes, and villages. DPW engineers soon also recognized the importance of such intricately parceled interior spaces, and they began planning to artificially reproduce such landscapes in resettlement *casiers* intended for thousands of migrants. Given increasing threats of anticolonial political activity across the region, such settlements were appealing as a containment strategy, and this helps to explain why *casiers* were attractive to not only Socialists in the 1930s but Fascists in the 1940s and the southern Vietnamese government after 1954.

The water landscape became a social and ecological laboratory where a broader cast of characters attempted to create new agricultural and social conditions through settlements aimed at solving the region's growing environmental and political problems. Such experiments did not break up old alliances (landowners, entrepreneurs, engineers, and officials), but they often reconfigured them with the addition of new groups. In such a social and environmental laboratory, ideological and scientific foundations were laid by different groups with often-conflicting solutions to the "rural problem" and different appeals to the "hearts and minds" of farmers.

This crisis period was thus an intensely experimental era when popular, scientific, and political debates emerged over rural development, aided by new surveying technologies and increased attention paid by cosmopolitan Vietnamese to the troubles of the countryside. It was beginning in this period that some of the most troubled interior regions of the delta became southern "cradles" of revolutionary activity (*nôi cách mạng*). Such early, underground activity produced the ideological and geographical foundations for guerrilla bases and communication networks later during the Indochina Wars. These clandestine activities accompanied a relative explosion in new outlets for vernacular media, including hundreds of short stories and novels in the genre of documentary fiction (*văn chương phóng sự*); these works of fiction filled a niche in political writing because Vietnamese writers were generally prohibited from publishing nonfiction on the same topics.[8]

Abandoned Lands and the Ecological Crisis

The treeless horizons of abandoned lands (*terres abandonnées, đất bỏ hoang*) in the delta's most inaccessible interiors were physical reminders of the failures of past projects. With each new canal into such regions, forests and wetlands disappeared, giving way to wide vistas of grayish clay, polluted, stagnant water, and the skeletal remains of abandoned shacks (fig. 18). After just a few years of cultivation, tenants often abandoned plantations in these areas because of poor soils and terrible working conditions. Other areas that had once been relatively productive were abandoned as new canals penetrated the region and altered water conditions. The Quản Lộ–Phụng Hiệp Canal (1918), for example, remedied earlier flooding as described in the previous chapter on the Lachevrotière Estate, but it brought new flooding problems to the Cà Mau Peninsula, drowning fields there and producing what one provincial administrator described as a "vast pool good only for hatching moths and other insects."[9]

One important ecological factor in the growth in abandoned land was the buildup of alum (aluminum sulfate) from canal drainage in these areas.[10] New canals often reduced the tidal fluctuation of water levels to just a few centimeters, thus preventing farmers from draining acidic water out of their fields. In the Long Xuyên Quadrangle, canals also lowered the water table during the dry season so that recently cleared soils were exposed to the air, and through oxidation much greater amounts of acidic sulfate were produced. Lower water levels also allowed saltwater to intrude deeper inland, exposing many fields to the added danger of salinity.[11]

Forest destruction, mentioned in the previous chapter, also played an important role in the creation of abandoned land by eliminating natural buffers to water acidity. Before 1906, the Long Xuyên Quadrangle was still mostly covered in freshwater and brackish mangroves that prevented rapid evaporation of water from the soil and slowed the exit of freshwater to the sea. Such waterlogged soils rarely oxidized and thus kept alum levels low.[12] Rapid extension of new canals into these regions in the 1920s eliminated this buffering effect and lowered the water table, exposing the peat layer to fires. In 1931 one administrator in Rạch Giá complained of worsening forest fires each year for three dry seasons as new immigrants burned off more trees and vegetation to clear soil for rice. On the Ba Thê Canal, a debris fire ignited the peat layer and burned out of control over fifteen thousand hectares in one season. Such fires occurred annually until peat areas were completely destroyed, leaving only marine clays and surface layers of organic deposits.[13] Typically, a brief period of high productivity followed these burnings: farmers reported harvests double the average productivity of one ton per hectare. Within a few years, however, the parched soils became depleted of carbon, produced toxic levels of alum, and killed off crops.[14] Canals that did not drain properly often concentrated these toxins, making irrigation of crops in prolonged dry seasons extremely risky because outside water might be more toxic than water in the fields.

With the elimination of forests and the creation of new water pathways into these areas, catastrophic floods on the Mekong destroyed crops and forced thousands to abandon fields for higher land. In an average year, the river rose two to three meters above mean sea level in September and October, emptying across the Long Xuyên Quadrangle and Đồng Tháp (these ecoregions are described in the introduction). The flood moved in directions produced by new canals, dikes, and other features on the terrain. Water levels gradually dissipated eastward into the delta's winding creeks and branches, effectively defining boundaries between historically productive land and endangered new plantations as well as different agricultural regimes. More permanent farms were most dense in the eastern regions of the delta where annual flooding was least pronounced. In Long Xuyên and Đồng Tháp, farmers had planted "floating rice" (*Oryza rufipogon*), a fast-growing long-stem variety that could survive the floods, but colonial directives to plant the exportable, short-stem rice further exacerbated local losses.

New infrastructure and plantations situated in the western delta were extremely vulnerable to floods. In September 1923, the river flooded a few weeks earlier than normal, rising 5.8 meters above sea level at Châu Đốc and rushing over riverbanks and dikes to cover 80 percent of the province. After the flood receded, the administrator of the province requested 25,000 tons of rice in immediate aid. The province's average harvest of 125,000 tons of rice was lost. Downstream on the Phụng Hiệp plantations, flooding was less severe but prolonged. The waters crested on three separate occasions—September 28, October 15, and November 12—with floodwaters further downstream reaching 2.8 meters above sea level. Wealthier landlords used dikes and diesel pumps to protect their fields, while less-prosperous farmers and tenants were forced to harvest quickly and wait out the floods. As the 1923 flood reached Mỹ Tho Province (east of Đồng Tháp), the administrator there noted how farmers became fishermen and spent their days casting nets from boats.[15] With several weeks' warning of the coming waters, they had had enough time to harvest rice and prepare. Canal embankments and highways constructed on them also affected the severity of floods. The Rạch Giá–Hà Tiên Canal (1930) and the highway running parallel to it atop one of its banks produced in effect a thirty-kilometer earthen dam that prevented water from draining quickly into the sea. It prolonged flooding in the region by several weeks. Engineers responded by constructing mobile barriers and drainage gates, but expansions of new waterways and roads inside the plain continued to restrict flood drainage.[16] Flood events were thus both social and natural phenomena, exacerbated by past policies and alterations to terrain. Meanwhile, colonial scientists continually lagged behind such constructions; with so much new construction going on each year, they were unable to predict how a flood would affect a given area.[17]

The most important flood year with respect to the development of political and economic crises was 1929. The flood that year, approximately one year before prices began to slide, left thousands homeless and without their harvests; most tenants and many landowners took on new debt in 1929 to recover. In Tân An, on the eastern edge of Đồng Tháp, four hundred people—mostly women and children—took refuge from the flood at the provincial Société indigènes de crédit agricole et mutuel (SICAM) office. SICAM was the principal government lender for delta farmers. The crop losses of those who had borrowed money from SICAM and private moneylenders led to hundreds of foreclosures as rice prices fell during the next harvest.[18] The colonial government refused to forgive these individual loans, but it provided emergency loans, such as a million-piaster fund, to rubber plantations and large enterprises, a move that they justified by declaring that these enterprises produced essential commodities. Colonial economist Paul Bernard noted that the slide in prices and the failure to alleviate agricultural debts caused widespread social and political crises. In interior regions, far from towns and markets, rice had always been used as currency—and now it lost most of its value relative to the piaster, which was pegged to a gold standard. Debts and exchanges were calculated in piasters but paid in *giạ* of unpolished rice (one *giạ* was about twenty kilograms). Debts incurred after flood losses in 1929 would have been payable at a rate of one *giạ* equal to 1.2 piasters. Four years later, however, the value of a *giạ* had decreased to 0.3 piasters, requiring farmers to supply four times the rice to meet outstanding debts.[19]

With proportionally more rice going to government and private granaries after this devaluation of rice, tensions with tenant farmers increased. The next major flood, in the fall of 1937, especially damaged harvests in Cà Mau Peninsula and caused food shortages as rice was collected in a few granaries. For the remainder of 1937 and again during the floods of 1938, bands of farmers raided these granaries and seized money from landlords. A government investigation concluded that these organized raids reflected an increasingly well-organized leadership, as groups had carefully coordinated their attacks and manipulated provincial boundaries to thwart local police. The report also suggested that the root of the problem was insufficient regulation of landlord-tenant contracts and favored replacing complicated arrangements of "pseudocontracts" with a standardized wage for seasonal work. By creating a *prolétariat agricole,* the investigator argued that farmers might not be reduced to the desperate situations of the tenants who suffered from usury and other abuses.[20]

Labor Conditions and the Social Crisis

The above report responded to labor conditions that had grown progressively worse since the 1920s, as the last unclaimed land disappeared in corrupt sales to large estates. The colonial apartheid system of land rules produced extreme conditions, especially in the newly settled areas of the Hậu Giang region. Older, historic villages in the delta's densely populated alluvial regions were largely protected from the consequences of environmental catastrophes in this era because the farmers there had greater access to merchant networks and education, whereas those living in the western plains lived more nomadic, frontier-style lives. Conceived as legal "empty zones," however, the western regions of the delta and Đồng Tháp gave way to large estates eventually owned almost wholly by French and naturalized citizens.

The devaluation of land after 1930 and the bankruptcy of many planters—both French and local—led to a sudden shift in the old distribution of French versus indigenous landholdings, often with severe implications for tenants. When I asked about landlords in the Cần Thơ area, for example, farmers repeatedly told me about the rapid sale of lands from bankrupted Europeans to naturalized Vietnamese, Chinese, and Khmer landlords. The new owners also included many native wives of Frenchmen and their métis descendants.

Contrary to what most might assume, the older farmers I spoke with repeatedly emphasized how conditions worsened when European estates passed to local landlords. Mr. Mười, who was a young man working along the Saintenoy Canal in the 1930s, noted that French-born planters were more lenient about tenant debts, often forgiving old debts at the start of the new year. Tenants were also free to gather fish and glean rice from most French plantations after the crop was gathered. The new, local-born landlords, however, enforced debt terms more strictly and compounded unpaid loans from year to year—especially after losses in 1930.[21] Another former tenant, Mr. Rì, noted that French plantations had more tenants than locally owned plantations because French owners typically granted farmers free fishing rights and allowed tenants to eventually own the water buffalo they rented, paying in rice or piasters.[22] After the onset of the Great Depression and many land sales to indigenous owners, conditions became harsher, with little check from French officials. During harvests, landlords often locked the gates on dikes and guarded fields to prevent tenants from gleaning grain or fishing. Mr. Hai related how the new landowners not only abused their tenants in these ways but also forced them to do much unnecessary work:

> Before the wet season arrived and the grass was still young, they asked us to clear it—we had to! After that, the grass was still young, and without water [covering it] it grew fast. Then they forced us to clear it again! Just like that, we worked a lot—"giang lưng lớn" [our backs facing the sky]. Just working for some rice to eat. Then the harvest came, the canals were dry around here, and they came around to take the rice. If we wanted to eat, we had to beg for some

rice. But it was not easy. . . . They cut it, and when it was harvested, they gave us one or two *giạ*. Then we beat the rice and exposed it to the sun to dry it and eat. When the harvest came, they brought their canoes we called "striped tigers," and people went to our houses to steal our rice! They did not even leave a cup of rice for the children's food. The rice straw that we used while threshing was also checked. They thought we hid rice in the straw, so they took everything, there was nothing left.[23]

Consolidation of newly titled lands in the Cà Mau Peninsula led to several outbreaks of violence before the Great Depression that caused a stir in Sài Gòn when a serial account of the conflict blamed the violence on the worsening disparities in conditions between ethnic Khmer farmers and powerful local officials. Lê Quang Liêm, a wealthy landowner from Rạch Giá who served on the Colonial Council, reported the events of a "scuffle" in the remote village of Ninh Thạnh Lợi, where several colonial troops, a few district officials, and scores of villagers died over several days of fighting in 1927 (map 8). Ninh Thạnh Lợi, a Khmer village in the southern reaches of Rạch Giá Province near Bạc Liêu, was home to mostly Khmer people who settled here as Vietnamese and French colonists continued to claim lands closer to the main rivers. After completion of several canals into the region, the district chief, Cai Tổng Ngô, obtained title to all of Ninh Thạnh Lợi's lands.

Under several aliases, Ngô amassed over 11,000 hectares of land in the region—much of it already farmed and inhabited. After gaining title, he demanded that villagers pay him agricultural taxes. Hương Chủ Chot, a village leader from Ninh Thạnh Lợi, organized a protest along with a local healer named Thầy Cả, who prepared spells and amulets to make villagers immune to harm. Beginning in late April 1927, the village organized loud parties, during which they proclaimed their independence from taxation and declared the Celestial Emperor as their only overlord. They designated Chot as king, carrying him on a makeshift palanquin. On May 4, the group traveled to neighboring Vĩnh Phong Village, and the following night they visited the Vietnamese village of Vĩnh Thuận.[24]

The district's vice-chief visited the village with an armed escort several days later but was rebuffed by a crowd of angry villagers holding torches and knives, who dismissed his requests to discuss matters. A band of eight villagers then followed him back to the district town and broke into the district chief's home. Finding nobody there, they visited one of his business associates, an ethnic-Chinese merchant whose son is listed in

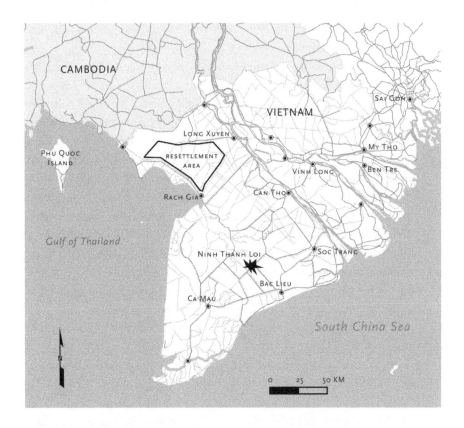

MAP 8. *Ninh Thạnh Lợi Uprising and Post–1930 Resettlement Zone.* Source: *Author.*

provincial records as the government's village chief of Ninh Thạnh Lợi. At the time, this son was away serving in the Foreign Legion, so the band of villagers decided to kill the father in the son's place, decapitating him and bringing his head back to the village communal house.[25]

As news spread from Bạc Liêu of this violence, the provincial administrator sent one French policeman with eight Vietnamese officers armed with rifles on a DPW steamer to apprehend the party at Ninh Thạnh Lợi the following evening. When they reached the village, the group split up, and the soldiers who left the village center were ambushed by a large group waiting for them in the forest. Realizing he might be overpowered, the French commander raced back to the boat and prepared his escape. He abandoned three Vietnamese officers on the canal embankment. Only one of them knew how to swim, and he survived by jumping into the canal and swimming to the boat. The other two were killed, leaving their guns and bullets to the villagers.[26]

After hearing about the worsening situation in the village, merchants and wealthy landowners abandoned mills and houses for the nearest town, Long Mỹ. They feared that a more general insurrection might be under way. At 6 a.m. the following morning, a French lieutenant accompanied by thirty well-armed Vietnamese soldiers arrived at Ninh Thạnh Lợi. After a brief battle, they torched the communal house with Chot and his band inside.[27] A political inquest committee interviewed Khmer monks some days later to determine if the uprising was part of a larger conspiracy. When the committee arrived at the village, they found thirty corpses in the charred remains of the house, the bodies burned too badly to determine if Chot was among them. Liêm argued repeatedly that the cause of the tragedy was not nationalism but economics. Under the French land system, canton chiefs gained legal title to form small fiefdoms, dispossessing farmers from lands they had claimed by virtue of clearing them years before.

Such episodes of violence also highlighted the role that ethnic tensions played in land tenure disputes. Lacking the ability to read or write in either French or Vietnamese, many Khmer farmers were left without standing in either the French or Vietnamese legal systems. The Colonial Council attempted to respond to this issue not by incorporating Khmer land rights but instead by relocating dispossessed Khmer farmers into abandoned areas closer to Cambodia in the western floodplain. They became the colony's first populations targeted for resettlement. An Office of Colonization offered five-hectare plots for each applicant family and located these plots adjacent to the newly completed Rạch Giá-Hà Tiên Canal, Tri Tôn Canal, and Ba Thê Canal (see map 8). The new settlers, eager to gain legal title, quickly set up their houses and fields along the main canals. Each household was required to put the land into production and pay taxes with rice. The result was a flood of applications, including many from Vietnamese farmers. Colonial officials worried that they could not adequately control the "type of person" who staked a claim. Noting that these tenants had worked for landlords in a state of "semislavery," provincial administrators also worried that they did not possess a suitable "love of the land whose demonstration is the care taken in cultivation."[28] Settlement was uneven, and the clearing of forests in these areas coincided with forest fires that spread and depleted soils in the region.

Social unrest in the years before the Great Depression was also due to increasing problems associated with migration, especially migration of farmers from the densely overcrowded Red River Delta (on the Gulf of Tonkin). These workers, especially contract workers called *engagés,* were almost all young men who left their homelands with hopes of earning enough to eventually own land in the new agricultural regions of the south. The contract labor program began in 1907 as the newly formed Office of Colonization in Cần Thơ brought 84 *engagés* to plantations near Phụng Hiệp. Facing unfamiliar agricultural practices, harsh working conditions, and so much open land beyond the plantation, this initial group quickly fled and hid in the swamps. Police later found them and returned the survivors to their home province of Thái Bình in 1908.[29] Only landlords could initiate this emigration, requesting the number of persons and paying for their transport.[30] Once *engagés* arrived at a plantation in the Mekong Delta, they had to work off the debt from their passage and their provisions at interest rates set by the landowner. In smaller concessions, native landowners often modified or abandoned their obligation to pay salaries as stipulated in the contracts. Conditions on larger, industrial plantations were slightly better; owners were more likely to offer all laborers a basic standard in housing and supplies.[31]

By the late 1920s, growing concern for the welfare of these Tonkinese laborers led both nationalists and colonial reformists to describe the contract labor program as a form of slavery. Plantation owners paid 2,500–3,000 francs for each contracted laborer, who could not choose where he would be settled in the Mekong Delta. Laborers were frequently "bought and sold" by the owners of their contracts during the five-year period of their contracts. The quotation at the beginning of this chapter highlights a popular sentiment among reformists—that such contracts amounted to slavery. In his studies on the Red River Delta, Pierre Gourou estimated that about ninety thousand persons emigrated in these work programs over several years before 1930. After the Great Depression hit, about fifty-five thousand of them returned to the Red River Delta.[32]

Tonkinese migrants in the Mekong Delta developed a reputation for being "unruly," especially in the mid-1920s. One French writer explained the "psychological factor" behind this: "A Tonkinese coolie *obeys badly* in spite of coming to Cochinchina, where one is unaware of the general Tonkinese mentality. According to us, therefore, the use of the Tonkinese laborer in the rice plantations is not to be advised, except that it can be likened to *tá canh* [wage laborers] and then it would be preferable to bring entire families."[33] Another factor was that members of the Revolutionary Youth League (founded in 1924) decided in 1928 to proletarianize themselves and work undercover through such programs on plantations and in factories. Although he claims he was not a member of the Revolutionary Youth before embarking as a contract laborer, Trần Tử Bình's memoir *The Red Earth* offers an in-depth account of how a highly educated, disaffected youth from the Red River Delta soon met such agents at the Michelin Company's rubber plantation at Phú Riềng and then organized one of the first mass labor protests there in February 1930 just as delegates of Vietnam's three Communist Party organizations met in Hong Kong to form the Indochinese Communist Party.[34] Although highly educated, undercover members of the party targeted factory workers and wage laborers, their greatest support in the first organized protests for May 1, International Labor Day, in 1930 came from farmers.[35]

Colonial Experiments

The protests of 1930 and the violence that followed, especially in northern Vietnam, combined with the economic and ecological crises to cause a widespread reexamination of colonial development policies in the Mekong Delta. Colonial social scientists and others responded to the agricultural crisis of the early 1930s by comparing water management in the Mekong Delta with other agricultural regions, especially the Red River Delta. They sought to explain how Tonkinese peasants had managed for hundreds of years to protect their fields from floods and achieve steady crop yields while plantations in the Mekong Delta routinely suffered from flooding and other disasters.

This new strain of colonial research in the 1930s was heavily influenced by new ideas in human geography coming from French and German geographers and Orientalist theories that sought to define "modes of production" specific to Asian places. Paul Vidal de la Blache, who taught at the University of Paris from 1898 to 1918, opposed then-prevalent ideas of environmental determinism in geography and instead considered the importance of region and locality in his analyses of landscape change and economic development. He proposed a theory called "possibilism" that asserted that environments set certain constraints or limitations on a culture but that human use of landscapes — especially intensely constructed environments such as river deltas — depended on unique cultural and historic factors.[36] This strain of thought in geography was readily taken up by both Socialists and Fascists, whose settlement programs assumed that the right people (Tonkinese farmers) would be able to overcome the environmental challenges in the Mekong Delta.

Related to these ideas of possibilism in geography was Karl Wittfogel's influential work in Germany. In several important papers and two books, notably his 1926 book *Das erwachende China,* he emphasized the natural rather than the social context of production and built upon Marx's concept of the Asiatic mode of production. He argued that Chinese society progressed through different stages of social organization and economy from Europe because its extensive use of irrigated agriculture enabled powerful hydraulic bureaucracies to emerge.[37] Though scholars in Europe and the Soviet Union contested such ideas, Wittfogel's assertion that something different was going on in China (and Asia) because of the orientation of classical societies to intensely managed hydraulic environments soon pervaded colonial scholarship in the 1930s. Agricultural researchers and geographers focused on traditional agricultural landscapes—especially in Mandalay, Java, Bali, and Tonkin—to identify locally appropriate modes of traditional agricultural production. Precisely because of the growing social and economic problems in places such as the Mekong Delta, colonial researchers sought to combine the traditional with the natural in the hope of stabilizing such places economically and politically. Still, this view of traditional agriculture was a wholly colonial, Orientalist creation—one produced and reproduced by European and European-educated observers peering over village hedges to describe what they believed were fundamental features of Vietnamese life.

In Indochina, the French School of the Far East (École française d'Extrême-Orient; EFEO) in Hà Nội became the most important center for such research, and one of its researchers, Pierre Gourou, became one of its most famous with regard to agriculture. Published in 1936, Gourou's *Les paysans du delta Tonkinois* quickly drew widespread attention both inside and outside Indochina.[38] Born in Tunisia, educated in Paris, and then assigned to teach at the Lycée Albert Sarrault in Hà Nội in 1927, Gourou readily adapted Vidal de la Blache's ideas to the water landscapes that he visited in his travels around the Red River Delta on weekends and vacations.[39] Gourou was one of the first geographers to make a systematic use of aerial photographs to identify different patterns or types of settlement in the Red River Delta and later in the Mekong Delta. Gourou's book, thick with photographs and detailed drawings, circulated widely and profoundly influenced the thinking of many other researchers and officials on rural problems.[40]

From Gourou's work and these broader theoretical trends emerged an important idea for colonial planners in the 1930s: the polder, or *casier*, came to represent the ideal landscape unit merging the wetland environment in the river delta with the traditional culture of Tonkinese peasants. To Gourou and others, northern farmers possessed a more ancient, local environmental and cultural knowledge necessary to maintain the elaborate system of dikes and canals built over hundreds of years. The sight of thousands of farmers *voluntarily* maintaining a *casier*'s enclosing dikes to protect fields and villages from severe floods invited comparisons from visiting French writers to the construction of the pyramids in Egypt or the stone temples in Angkor Wat. Each dike was built from millions of blocks of clay; women carried smaller blocks in baskets while men carried larger blocks on their backs. Six or seven thousand people might engage in one construction project for a week or more at a time.[41] This effort was a communal duty, required to preserve the community as a whole. *Casiers* combined physical, environmental, and social aspects and presumably had their origins in the eleventh century, when the Lý dynasty first expanded settlements in the region by building a network of flood dikes. Gourou noted, however, that while dikes protected settlements from floods, they also complicated problems of drainage—in effect causing floodwaters to rise higher. At Hà Nội, the Red River rose some ten meters during floods. Thus, over decades and centuries, preserving this built, cultural landscape became ever more difficult as the walls of the dikes had to rise ever higher. As the *casiers* were extended farther outward into the delta, flood damage was contained within individual cell-like structures rather than spreading across the entire region.[42]

Gourou and other colonial observers helped create a notion of Tonkinese peasants as almost superhuman in their ability to overcome extreme environmental conditions. André Touzet, on a fact-finding mission from Paris in 1934, described one such scene: "One must see these instances of great danger that leave one speechless at the sudden buildup of the flood . . . to judge the fearsome mass of water rushing six or eight meters above the plain, villages, and cities . . . it is necessary to witness the defense against this invading water, to have participated with these armies of courageous peasants who fight from *casier* to *casier*, desperately, to save life and possessions." He praised the "genius" and solidarity of the peasants, suggesting that there were even hints of Goethe in this mass oeuvre but without the assistance of "diabolical sorcerers."[43]

While praising Tonkinese peasants, many colonial observers used the same logic to condemn farmers in the Mekong Delta as lazy and unfocused. One observer blamed the thousands of tenants for lacking patience in clearing new lands. They appeared to move ceaselessly—especially in the Hậu Giang region. They cleared fields, planted a crop or two, and then abandoned the area to try again elsewhere: "Rather than make an effort, tiny as it may be, they prefer to move in the province or to another, according to the climatic conditions, to cultivate lands and possibly abandon them because they are too high or too low. The risks and the expenses that the *indigène* incurs because of these displacements are as large, if not larger, than if he had remained on the plantation working just a little more."[44] This increasingly common tendency to compare water landscapes in these two river deltas fostered a new preoccupation in Cochinchina with creating a water landscape more like that in the Red River Delta, built around the *casier* as a unitary landform.[45]

The move from building an *extensive* water grid to a system of self-contained *casiers* was further bolstered by new visual evidence coming from above. Aerial photography, first used for land surveys in the 1920s, allowed researchers to finally look inside the formerly inaccessible, unreadable interiors of Vietnamese villages as well as the impenetrable swamps and forests (fig. 19). Most colonial officials spent little, if any, time in such places, which were far from urban downtowns and major roads. Gourou and others used the new spatial perspective, armed with Vidal de la Blache's ideas, to place villages into new categories based upon patterns detected in the photos. The following quotation from *Les paysans* indicates the sense of power that this new surveillance technology imparted to Gourou: "In this petri-dish-like land of humanity, where man created everywhere the landscape such as we see it, the unity of the peasant population is powerful; the natural uniformity of the deltaic country has also played no small part in creating a human unity. Natural uniformity and human unity, by aiding one another, have created a remarkably homogeneous land and a nation perfectly coherent."[46] Relating the surface of the Tonkinese landscape to the microscopic surface of a petri dish, Gourou suggests that such peasants were *petit colons*, tiny colonizers. The aerial photo, in which individuals were reduced to microscopic dimension, offered visual support to such assertions of "unity."

Another EFEO fellow, archaeologist J. Y. Claeys, contributed similar

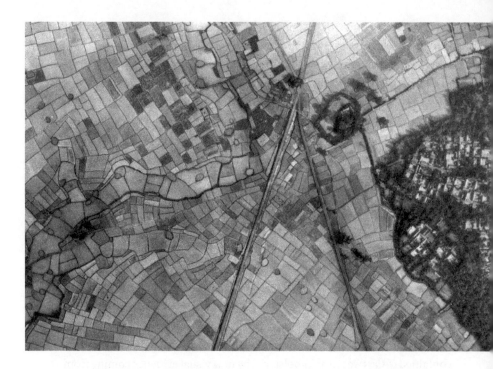

FIG. 19. *The* Casier *Landscape. This aerial photograph of the Red River Delta shows the "cloisonnée" of rice paddies enclosed by field dikes and villages enclosed by tree-lined dikes (indicated by the thicker black lines). The village is surrounded by trees and hedges and is located on higher ground above the floodplain. Gourou studied hundreds of aerial photos and then grouped villages into different types depending on their topographic and spatial configurations.* Source: Pierre Gourou, Les paysans du delta Tonkinois: Étude de geographie humaine *(Paris: Éditions d'art et d'histoire, 1936), pl. 36.*

musings on the surveillance power of aerial photography, referring in particular to northern villages that had been involved in the Communist-led insurrections of 1930 and more protests in 1932:

> On the ground, even traveling at low speed on the roads, one does not see into the villages; one sees of it the small woods and hedges of high bamboos. The aerial view transforms these screens into plumes of palms densely planted in clusters around the houses. The plan of the village is extremely variable. . . . Materially, the village is enclosed in its hedge of bamboos as hermetically as in its social rules . . . the greatest punishment that district prefects could inflict on the villages, as a collective punishment, was to make them raze this edge of

bamboo. They still inflicted this sanction in the villages active at the time of the unrest in 1932 in the area of Vinh. . . .

The Tonkinese will always remain stubborn movers of earth. They were the ones who raised these dams and dikes that compartmentalize the delta into an infinity of *casiers*. In these *casiers*—Vidal de la Blache too quickly calls them "natural," forgetting the human side in human geography—the bird's-eye view shows that the Vietnamese agricultural landscape is born of the masses, a characteristic fact.[47]

The bird's-eye view, however, by flattening the landscape into a two-dimensional plane, may have overemphasized the fractal-like repetition of human life in this "infinity of *casiers*," leading officials in Cochinchina to believe that such designs should be propagated across the Mekong region's landscapes, where canals stretched for "hundreds of kilometers, absolutely fixed and lost to view."[48]

Struggling to make sense of land abandonment problems in the western Mekong Delta, administrators and researchers readily absorbed such ideas from the north and believed that more stable yields would result from development of smaller land parcels and denser populations. In Long Xuyên, a provincial administrator noted that small landowners in downstream Mỹ Tho and Vĩnh Long Provinces doubled and sometimes tripled the average yield of one ton per hectare.[49] Such densely occupied places contrasted sharply with the situation on the barren estates in Long Xuyên. Another administrator praised the "typical picture of Vietnamese fields, where houses stand in the rice fields surrounded by bamboo and fruit trees." This was to him "an extremely verdant landscape, very fragmented, where the view is broken at each instant by lines of trees." As he traveled to the center of newly opened lands in Long Xuyên, the view changed dramatically to a treeless horizon with mats of floating rice growing in flooded fields. Houses here were built against the banks of the canal and roadway, and workers came in small boats to build temporary dwellings. If contracts were not renewed, they demolished their houses and carried the wooden house piers to another destination. Plantation owners failed to encourage their tenants to settle permanently. Contrasting this view with the ideal, the administrator remarked, "They never settle definitively, and consequently, what good is it to build a garden and to plant fruit trees or bamboos from which others would profit?"[50] While he identified key economic and legal differences in land use between these regions, he nevertheless ignored the ecological and hydrological differences between such garden strips (*miệt vườn*) and the "barren" regions that were large sinks.[51] Gourou's colonial followers may have taken Vidal de la Blache's idea of possibilism too far in thinking that by simply adding more people and dividing up the flood basins they might reproduce the agricultural results of other areas without concern for variations in water and soil.

The Popular Front, Casiers, and Petits Colons

Besides the Great Depression, the pro-Left Popular Front in France (1936–38) played a formative role in reshaping debates over land and water, just as Roosevelt's New Deal had done for farming in the United States. Settlement *casiers*, first attempted in the Mekong Delta in 1930, soon attracted Socialists and Vietnamese nationalists interested in rationalizing agriculture, turning peasants into proletarian wage earners, and settling several hundred thousand people into the colony's "empty" areas.

With the election of the Popular Front government in France in May 1936, many Vietnamese and French expected sweeping changes in the colonies, perhaps even moves to recognize their independence; however, when the new minister of colonies, Maurius Moutet, convened France's governors-general in November 1936, he made it clear that the coalition of French Radicals, Socialists, and Communists would not support independence from the empire. Rather, he called for the governors to replace selfish colonization (*colonization égoïste*) with what he called altruistic colonization (*colonization altruiste*). Of course, the term "altruistic colonization" is an oxymoron. Moutet's program called for only minor humanitarian and social reforms, as it was still tightly constrained by the economic terms of French political and economic domination.[52] Although a certain percentage of the Popular Front's base was anticolonial, its leading officials achieved only limited reforms in French colonies.

This more limited view of the achievements of the French Left in the colony helps to explain the somewhat independent development of settlement *casiers* and labor reforms before and after the Popular Front's brief reign. The first government-planned settlements were begun in 1930 in Rạch Giá Province along the new canals dug in the relatively barren Long Xuyên Quadrangle. This program granted five-hectare and ten-hectare plots of land to Khmer farmers who had lost their lands to foreclosure and corrupt practices (see the "scuffle" in Ninh Thạnh Lợi, discussed earlier in the chapter) in former Khmer centers such as Cà Mau, Cần Thơ, Sóc

Trang, and Bạc Liêu. The DPW dredged a primary grid of irrigation canals before the *petit colons* arrived. Hundreds of families rushed to gain title to these lands on Tri Tôn, Rạch Giá–Hà Tiên, and Ba Thê Canals.

Despite attempts to control the settlement process, authorities soon found themselves overwhelmed by squatters and wildfires that reached beyond the boundaries of the settlements into nearby forest reserves. Demand for plots far exceeded the available number, requiring a lottery system to distribute parcels. The government later prohibited settlements within a kilometer of major canal intersections, reserving this space for police, navigation, and commercial property. In just three years, the new settlers cleared over one hundred thousand hectares, although much of the work was done by fires. In the spring months of the dry season, they burned out of control, incinerating the peat soil as well as the trees. In 1933 the government stopped the program due to a reduced availability of dredges to open new parcels and concerns over forest loss.[53] The dredging contractor had reduced operations by 75 percent because of severe shortages in colonial revenues.[54]

DPW engineers nevertheless continued planning new settlements, and in 1935 a special commission considered the possibility of developing new settlements for Vietnamese migrants coming directly from the Red River Delta. The project reflected contemporary views of northern agricultural landscapes, of the "genius" of northern peasants, and of the persistent fear in Cochinchina of threats from organized bands of settlers in the remote, western lands. The project sought to extend settlements farther west from the Khmer zone between the Tri Tôn Canal and Canal No. 1, an area over one hundred thousand hectares in size (fig. 20). The project sought to stabilize the region economically and politically by building new northern Vietnamese enclaves and more generally infiltrating northern migrants into the existing southern population, a new version of the Nguyễn Lords' southward march: "It's estimated that the establishment of Tonkinese colonists in the open lands of Cochinchina could be achieved by two different processes: the first envisages the establishment of immense groups, constituted in autonomous communities, and the second supposes a progressive influx of immigrants filtering into the Cochinchinese agricultural masses."[55] The Popular Front government under Governor-General Jules Brévié continued support for these preliminary studies of what came to be known as *casiers tonkinois;* there is no evidence, however, that such an immigration program began until several years later.

The Popular Front was perhaps most influential in widening debates

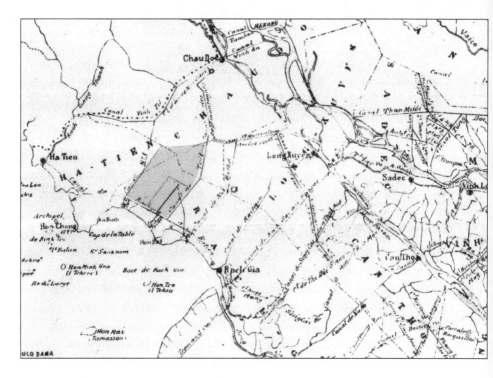

FIG. 20. *Proposed Tonkinese Settlement, 1935–37 (shaded area).* Source: *File N21/15, Toà Đại Biểu Chính Phủ Nam Việt, Trung Tâm Lưu Trữ Quốc Gia II, Hồ Chí Minh City.*

over land reform and tolerating an increasing number of protests. French officials affiliated with the Socialist and Communist Parties encouraged the transformation of tenant contracts into wage-labor contracts, under which tenants were paid cash as agricultural workers. Popular Front politicians sought to turn the tenants into a working class and into consumers who could then purchase French manufactures. Shortly after arriving in the colony in November 1936, Governor-General Jules Brévié established by decree an inspector general of labor responsible for ensuring worker safety and hygiene and for enforcing contractual obligations with employers. The same decree also encouraged the free migration of colonists from crowded regions such as the Red River Delta to more open areas such as the Long Xuyên Quadrangle and the central highlands in an effort to redistribute population more evenly across Indochina.[56]

One reason the Popular Front may not have begun any major settlement projects in the delta was the severe floods that inundated the region in

1937, causing widespread crop losses followed by new outbreaks of disease, bankruptcies, and famine. Floods hit the Cà Mau Peninsula especially hard, a region where Indochinese Communist Party (ICP) cells had been active since the early 1930s. As landowners scrambled to seize from tenants what rice remained, food shortages spread. For the remainder of 1937 and again after floods in 1938, ICP-organized bands of farmers raided granaries and held up landlords for cash. A government investigation concluded that these raids showed an increasingly sophisticated level of tactical planning, as the groups had carefully planned the attacks and escape routes across district and provincial boundaries to slow down local police.[57]

Peasants in the Public Sphere

These internal dialogues on peasants and *casiers* among colonial officials were just a smaller part of a much broader public discourse on the fate of the peasantry, especially in the Mekong Delta, under way in Cochinchina's newspapers in the 1930s. While a flourishing vernacular print culture in the cities permitted the expression of various identities—Communist, non-Communist, Buddhist, and Confucian—it was nevertheless confined to the relatively small population of Vietnamese living in towns and cities at the time.[58] The vast majority of Vietnamese living in the countryside, with the exception of wealthy landowners and district officials, did not participate in this public sphere, though they were frequently a topic of interest. In such newspapers as the pro-Communist *La lutte* and the reformist *Tribune indochinoise*, a new generation of Vietnamese writers engaged in contests to define the peasantry. At the heart of these debates was the question as to whether the peasantry was an "agricultural proletariat" made up of millions of workers or a rural society with unique moral and cultural values.

La lutte, a newspaper produced by prominent Vietnamese Trotskyites such as Tạ Thu Thâu, featured numerous articles about conditions in the countryside but focused attention on the struggles of village teachers (often involved in the Trotskyite underground) and agricultural workers involved in various industrial occupations such as dredging. A regular series in the newspaper, "The Life of Workers," featured news snippets about protests and strikes in the rural provinces. In April and May 1938 the series featured accounts of a strike led by over two hundred laborers employed by the Société française d'enterprises de dragages et de travaux publics in Mỹ

Tho Province. The strike involved the enterprise's refusal to raise wages and lasted for fifty-five days before the local director left the colony and returned to France.[59]

While the *La lutte* group focused on building support from such industrial classes, the pro-Stalinist ICP continued its efforts to organize tenant farmers and mobilize the vast population of landless peasants, especially in the flood-stricken Hậu Giang region. After severe floods destroyed crops in late 1937, ICP cadres organized peasants both in protests at district markets and in raids on area granaries. They especially promoted use of the term *tá điền* (tenant farmer) and strove to differentiate them as a separate class from peasant smallholders or the bourgeoisie. Such characterizations, however, did not go uncontested in this period, as the centrist *Tribune indochinoise*, a newspaper of the Partí constitutionaliste indochinoise, regularly attacked such protests as carried out by ignorant peasants being "duped by agitators."[60] Referring to the protests organized by the ICP in response to flood-induced famines, one article sharply criticized the "Stalinists and Trotskyites," who threatened to induce fratricide among Vietnamese over ideological differences. The article suggested that the peasantry—largely illiterate and susceptible— would only suffer.[61]

Although none of these groups succeeded in fully mobilizing or defining the peasantry as a political entity in this era, the debates waged among Vietnamese bourgeoisie, Trotskyites, and Stalinists led to a more thorough consideration of the peasantry as a target population by nationalists and colonial officials alike. The 1938 government investigation into the strikes and raids in the Cà Mau Peninsula, besides identifying ICP cadres as instigators, suggested that solving problems for the *tá điền* required strong regulation of wage-labor contracts and replacement of existing "pseudocontracts" with a government-standardized salary for seasonal work across the region. By creating a *prolétariat agricole,* it argued that farmers in the future could avoid usury and severe privation.[62]

Finally, the language of social scientists such as Pierre Gourou and demographer Yves Henry, describing peasants through aerial photographs and statistics, entered the popular press at the same time as the reading public in France and Indochina was for the first time made aware of the problem of overpopulation in the Red River Delta. The *Tribune indochinoise*'s account of a session of the Popular Front's Commission of Inquiry attended by M. E. Outrey, Pierre Gourou, M. A. Varenne, and other colonial figures related Gourou's and others' basic findings that population densities in the Red River Delta were simply too high to support even subsistence agriculture, while large areas of Cochinchina, especially in the Mekong Delta, were uncultivated and could be settled by northerners to both alleviate population pressures in the north and perhaps improve the rural economy in Cochinchina.[63]

Such news, while factually accurate, nevertheless conveyed a new, rationalized view of the peasantry that further reduced them from victims of landlords or "agitators" to mere statistics. Rural people and rural settlements became increasingly subject to new methods of surveillance and representation. However, where the colonial state in Indochina had until this time favored the creation of large plantations to increase the efficiencies of taxation and surveillance, by the mid-1930s key colonial leaders appear to have begun reversing their interest in plantations since it had become increasingly difficult for the authorities to influence corrupt district officials or large plantation owners.

Through recently published research and public commissions, colonial officials drew upon new ideas to propose smallholder settlements in the *terres abandonnées* as a solution to the continuing troubles. Reformist groups such as the Partí constitutionaliste indochinoise and the lesser-known Partí démocrate indochinoise latched on to such colonization schemes, attempting to position themselves in the center between Communist "agitators" and corrupt rural officials. Nguyễn Văn Thinh, president of the Partí démocrate indochinoise, wrote the governor to strongly urge the rapid development of settlement *casiers*:

> This work, the utility and urgency of which are shown by the havoc of the flood, is likely to bring work and an immediate help to the populations of the disaster victims. . . . Regarding social aspects, we know too well how misery is often a bad adviser. He [the peasant] risks being exploited by adversaries of the current regime, partisans of the class struggle, and enemies more or less declared against French influence in Indochina. They will be too happy to appeal to the worst instincts, on a ground already prepared by disappointments and deprivations, to destroy the social order.[64]

Thus, while peasants had yet to establish their own perspectives in the public sphere, they were nevertheless subjects of debates central to colonial and anticolonial projects.

Vichy in the Water Landscape

The fall of the French Third Republic to the Nazis on June 17, 1940, and the subsequent establishment of a Vichy-led, Fascist government in Cochinchina under Japanese military authority resulted in the violent suppression of nationalists and the closure of many newspapers. However, it also resulted in more intense support for *casiers* and other initiatives developed by the Popular Front. The Fascist government's violent suppression of Communists after the aborted Nam Kỳ Uprising of November 23, 1940, caused a major shift in tactics among nationalists as the number of political prisoners at Poulo Condor nearly doubled, from 2,119 in May 1940 to 4,203 in June 1941.[65] While Vichy rule and Japanese military occupation brought extreme privation to most, the period was also one of intense experimentation as Governor-General Jean Decoux started work on a *casier tonkinois* and proceeded to develop plans for northern migration that would have long-reaching implications for nation-building efforts after 1954.

The reason the Vichy government strove to implement *casiers* instead of protecting the old system of plantations was most likely the extreme privations encountered under Japanese occupation and wartime interruptions of commerce from France. The colony was forced to rely upon its own means for basic goods and machinery that had previously been imported. Wartime interruptions of kerosene, medicine, textiles, and other basic goods and Japanese fixed-price quotas on rice hit the peasantry especially hard, causing the countryside figuratively and literally to fall into darkness. One farmer explained how his family coped during this time:

> In the South, especially in forty-three and forty-four, when the Japanese kicked the French out of Vietnam, there was no kerosene, no fuel, so we used *mù u* [*Callophyllum inophyllum*] nuts for a lamp. We cut the nut into small pieces, dried it, and then burned it. Sometimes we used pig fat or mouse fat to burn. We just used it awhile for dinner only.
>
> . . . at that time we didn't even have clothes, so we saved our mosquito nets for clothes, because at that time we didn't sleep in the mosquito nets anymore. No one could buy new clothes, and our old clothes were worn out and torn after two or three years. Mosquito nets were used to make outfits for women while men just wore shorts. We also washed sacks to wear as a shirt without sleeves . . . there was no cloth, no kerosene, people died of diseases (in forty-three, forty-four, forty-five, forty-six) like malaria and cholera. They died because they did not have food and medicine.[66]

In such extreme circumstances of poverty and repression, the Vichy government pressed its engineers and planners to respond with new social-engineering efforts.

To improve crop yields, in 1942 the government established a rural engineering corps (Service du génie rural) to focus on agricultural improvement, especially in the proposed *casiers*. After eighty years of colonization, a system of agricultural field stations was finally established. Génie rural offices were organized into distinct agroecological sectors with research stations to be located in the centers of planned *casiers*. Unlike the hydraulic engineers and the dredging operators in Sài Gòn, agricultural engineers supported decentralized water management and improved conditions for smallholders. A 1944 map of the génie rural's operations in Cochinchina describes each research center, sites that after 1954 continued operation for research on irrigation and settlement (fig. 21). Long Xuyên and Phước Long, in particular, received a lot of government attention into the early 1960s.

While his secret police continued to pursue Communist agents in the U Minh Forest and Đồng Tháp, Governor-General Decoux encouraged a relatively active debate among colonial officials over land and engineering practices. From the génie rural's inception in 1942 to 1945, a heated debate was waged between the génie rural and the DPW over past causes of the agricultural crisis. Agricultural engineers criticized the DPW for failing to build waterways that improved both navigation and irrigation in any logical fashion: "There is always the risk of seeing, one day, one's efforts destroyed by a modification of water resources in an entire region, or even more by the execution of one significant work, not envisaged at the appropriate time and whose repercussions had obviously not been considered at the time of secondary installations."[67]

Another report accused DPW engineers of following political interests rather than good scientific evidence: "In the course of fiery meetings at the Colonial Council a certain number of Vietnamese councilors asked the administration to dig channels crossing their grounds, and the administration for political reasons agreed to their request. It is obvious that they created the system of channels haphazardly for sentimental and political reasons."[68] DPW engineers responded to these critiques by adopting the cause of *casiers* as a new approach to irrigation in the delta. They fired back at agricultural engineers for writing "pessimistic reports" that "all of Cochinchina is in danger."[69] They in turn blamed the region's irrigation problems and abandoned lands on uncontrolled local

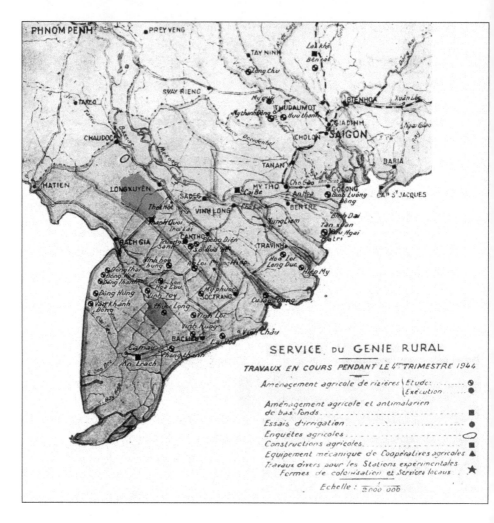

FIG. 21. *1944 Agricultural Research Projects and Proposed* Casiers. *This excerpt from a colonial map shows the locations for planned and active rice research projects in the Mekong Delta. The shaded areas (added by author) show projected agricultural* casiers *at Long Xuyên and Phước Long. Source: File H62/14, Toà Đại Biểu Chính Phủ Nam Việt, Trung Tâm Lưu Trữ Quốc Gia II, Hồ Chí Minh City.*

practices in newly opened regions. Unlike farmers in the Tonkin region, their reports argued, farmers in the Mekong Delta refused to build ample irrigation or flood control works, and there was little to no cooperation among neighbors.[70]

In this unusual period of Japanese military occupation and increasingly dire conditions in the countryside, Governor-General Decoux essentially co-opted earlier schemes and proposed a new plan to resettle 750,000 northern Vietnamese in the *terres abandonnées* of the Mekong Delta. Under a new budget item (Paragraph U, "Aid to Rice Farmers"), he requested five million piasters to send entire villages of peasants down the recently completed Trans-Indochina Railway to populate new *casiers*. The same budget category also was to fund not only the development of the génie rural's research stations but also a series of new feasibility studies on development of sea dikes, movable dams, and water-pumping stations to complete the establishment of fields in Đồng Tháp, the Long Xuyên Quadrangle, and the Cà Mau Peninsula. Despite the governor-general's ambition, however, the project was scaled back to a budget of just 540,000 piasters to be paid out over four years.[71] Nevertheless, DPW engineers commenced building the first *casier tonkinois,* which was intended for approximately 750 families who arrived in mid-1943.

DPW engineers drafted the plans for the *casier tonkinois* and sent dredges to prepare the main canal grid as well as other nearby canals for future waves of settlers (map 9).[72] This was to serve as a model settlement, and the engineers expected both future immigrants and even the locals to copy it once its success had been demonstrated. In keeping with what Eric Jennings describes as the "neotraditional" tendencies of Vichy, the *casier tonkinois* not only was a continuation of older settlement plans but also embodied Vichy aesthetics, which mixed extreme nationalism with an idealized notion of the pastoral modeled on the landscapes of the Red River Delta. The settlement included the modern machinery of the state — schools, a clinic, pumping equipment, and at its center a sports stadium to coordinate youth athletics and group activities.[73]

Workers completed the main canals of the *casier tonkinois* in August 1943 and approximately 750 families voluntarily moved there from Thái Bình and Nam Định Provinces in early 1944. The immigrants received new clothes, mosquito netting, raincoats and hats, blankets, and matting upon arrival. They also received a five-hectare lot upon completing required manual labor on canals, one month's supply of food, cooking supplies, farming tools, and a small boat. Besides these personal amenities, the government built a primary school, a government field post, a market, and a meeting hall (*đình*). A sports stadium was to be completed later in the year.[74]

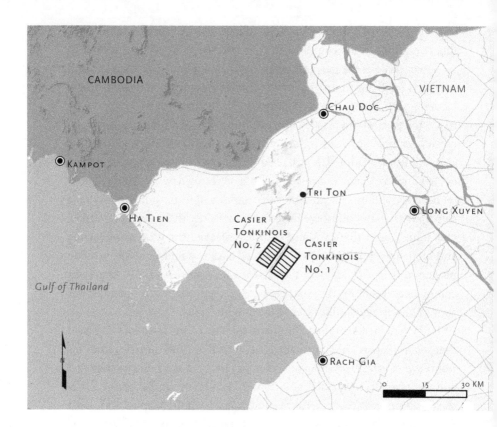

MAP 9. Casier Tonkinois. *Beginning in 1943, the Vichy government resettled over seven thousand Tonkinese within a constructed grid of canals adjacent to the Tri Tôn Canal. Construction of the first casier commenced in 1943, and in late 1944 crews began construction of a second grid on the opposite bank of the Tri Tôn Canal across from the first settlement.* Source: *Author.*

Before the year's end, however, the farmers had cleared only one-third of the land and were suffering from severe water shortages. Unfamiliar with the local influence of tides and the annual floods, they dug deep canals that drained floodwater outside the protective dikes, but once the rains ended they were unable to keep enough freshwater running in the canals. The government continued to spend another 175,000 piasters into 1945 to provide sufficient food for the families.[75] Still, work continued in 1945 on a second *casier tonkinois* (Casier Tonkinois II) and the next wave of immigrants arrived just as the Vichy government collapsed in March and a few months before the Việt Minh led the August Revolution.[76]

While such projects were extremely limited compared with the initial proposals, they were nonetheless important as experiments given the attention that the Republic of Vietnam and U.S. aid workers directed to settlements after 1954. Decoux's vision of resettling a million northern Vietnamese into the delta materialized in 1955, when approximately one million refugees, especially from the Red River Delta, arrived in temporary camps built in the same "empty" lands. Even upon completion in 1945, however, the *casier tonkinois* attracted American attention. While U.S. military planners in 1945 were primarily occupied with targeting Indochina's oil depots, coal mines, bridges, and railroads in preparation for an invasion, a few experts in the Roosevelt administration were aware of the *casier* project (but were unaware about plans to use atomic bombs on Japanese cities). Henry Field, an anthropologist and grandson of Marshall Field (benefactor of the Field Museum in Chicago), directed a top-secret wartime study group for President Roosevelt on problems of migration and food shortages called the M Project. He joined Roosevelt's administration in 1941 as a member of the Special Intelligence Unit and proceeded to document resettlement in other countries. Field's staff focused on problems worldwide, anticipating a future contest with the Soviets for the loyalties of millions of people plagued by starvation, abandoned fields, and wartime dislocations. Field's group continued to operate even after the Japanese surrender, and they translated a French report on the *casier tonkinois* in October 1945. The project continued to 1946; later, President Truman transferred its reports to his Point IV Program, which was in turn folded into successor aid programs.[77] Thus, while such experiments in the water landscape may have had very limited social or environmental effect, they were nonetheless important as models that traveled, guiding not only colonial but also postcolonial ideas about developing the water landscape.

Decoux's *casier* program had another long-term effect: the creation of massive project studies for the other major "empty" or "troubled" areas of the delta. Wartime scarcities essentially cloistered the colony's engineers in their offices, which led those charged with improving irrigation and expanding settlements to produce extensive desk studies for *casiers* with no real concern for working within budgets, which did not exist. P. C. Jammé, chief engineer of irrigation in Sài Gòn, authored reports complete with maps and appendices that he believed would finally permit the colony to "fix the type of water management for the region" and stabilize agricultural production in the future. His report narratives are especially valuable as condensed histories of development in each area, with clear opinions expressed about past research and surveys. A 1943 Đồng Tháp proposal, for example, discussed past proposals debating the relative virtues of canals and dikes and arrived at a kind of compromise plan involving the construction of a network of drainage canals in the western region most prone to flooding and construction of a sixty-kilometer flood barrier across the middle of the basin to protect a proposed network of *casiers* to the east (fig. 22). Jammé's reports embraced both the idea of *petit colons,* native colonizers, and new, large-scale technologies such as pumping stations, moving floodgates on the dikes, and interlaced grids of irrigation and wastewater ditches.[78]

Schizophrenic Spaces

Such projects, both implemented and imagined, attempted to realize a modern development philosophy: engineered environments intended to deliver technical and social changes at every level of human activity in formerly nonstate, nonterritorialized spaces. Yet the colony's engineers and its officials had never been more removed from actual conditions. While they articulated ever-heightening desires for greater productivity, stability, and order in such plans, the canal network was falling into disrepair, and various political and religious groups continued organizing their own bases of political power in the region, some with support from Japanese authorities. In the economically and ecologically "troubled" areas, peasants were suffering from untreated diseases and severe shortages in basic goods while revolutionary youth, educated in the city, hid out from secret police and organized cells associated with the ICP.[79] Rather than make the delta landscape more legible to colonial authorities, projects such as the *casier tonkinois* initiated a new splitting of the landscape and flows of people and water through it with proposed settlements bounded by encircling dikes and populated by groups as ethnically and ideologically homogeneous as possible. Drawing on new technologies of visualization such as aerial photography and ideas current in the social sciences, colonial planners altered earlier notions of expanding the water grid—dredges and colonial laws alternately

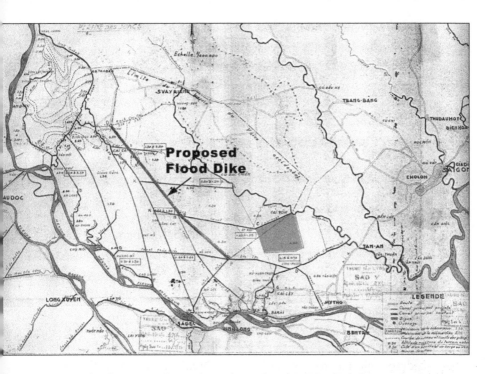

FIG. 22. *Plan for Major Dikes and Canals in Đồng Tháp. The shaded area indicates a zone under consideration for possible settlement. Note that the village located just west of this area is Ấp Bắc, where a key battle took place in 1963.* Source: File 312, Bộ Giao Thông Công Chánh, Trung Tâm Lưu Trữ Quốc Gia II, Hồ Chí Minh City.

destroying and opening up new plantation landscapes—and replaced this goal with a program to reshape "troubled" regions by encouraging northern migrants to colonize these regions in what social scientists such as Gourou identified as traditional family and village structures.

The economic, ecological, and social crises of the 1930s and 1940s produced what Deleuze and Guattari might call schizophrenic flows in the water landscape: the breaking down of traditional relationships in rural families, the growing trend with every new tenant bankruptcy to drift into an informal system of slavery, and increasing instances of protest and revolt among the peasantry. Capitalism and capitalist civilization, they argue, is "defined by the decoding and the deterritorialization of flows."[80] Regarding colonial developments in the Mekong Delta, instances of decoding and deterritorialization included the often-violent reworking of water flow through new canals; also, frequent acts of dispossession and reprivatization of land thoroughly reworked almost every facet of village life.

An emergent genre of Vietnamese documentary fiction from the 1940s, including such works as Bạc Liêu–born author Phi Vân's quartet of novels published from 1943 to 1949, pointed to many ways that such decoding upset even the most intimate of social relations in rural families. Such stories detail frequent accounts of parents selling children as servants to pay taxes and instances of rape and widespread government corruption.[81] Citing Franz Fanon's work psychoanalyzing patients in Algeria, Deleuze and Guattari argue that especially in colonial settings, the family unit of mother-father-child is a "poorly closed triangle, a porous or seeping triangle," given that the parents and children are often forcibly coupled to corrupt officials, dirty cops, soldiers, plantation bosses, and others who routinely "break all triangulations" in what might be called a traditional family structure.[82]

Since the first gunboats launched their assault on Sài Gòn in 1859, the expansion of colonial rule and the development of the colonial economy produced all manner of such schizophrenic flows; after the Great Depression, however, such disruptions outpaced colonial attempts to contain them. Abandoned land, ICP-led protests, riots, and catastrophic floods—all of these events signified the unraveling of colonial structures intended to maximize production and revenues; and yet such "crises" were often set into motion by colonial expansion in the first place.

Casiers represented the most recent colonial attempt to respond to schizophrenic flows that had only expanded with Japanese military intervention and growing anticolonial movements. Past hydraulic failures, a worsening political and economic situation, and new ideas supported with visual props from aerial photography prompted engineers and governors to attempt a re-creation of traditional village landscapes by digging channels, erecting some communal buildings, and transporting thousands of Tonkinese peasants to live inside spaces surrounded by flood dikes. However, such artificial landscapes failed to halt the delta's ecological and social unravelings and to approximate what Gourou saw in the Red River Delta as a "Petri dish of humanity."

Critics in the colonial government and in sanctioned indigenous political parties remind us, however, that the metropole—whether Sài Gòn, Hà Nội, or Paris—was similarly schizophrenic in this era, subject to radical shifts in political currents and alliances. The colonial bureaucracy was further complicated by a major political shift from the Left to the Right: the tenure of the Popular Front (1936–38) was followed by Vichy Fascists and the Japanese Imperial Army (1940–45). Another recent trend in colonial cities was the growing number of indigenous scholars, engineers, and social scientists. These new forces in colonial and world politics divided government officials as well as Vietnamese nationalists; with the 1945 August Revolution and the First Indochina War, they spilled out onto the canals and creeks of the delta.

FIG. 23. *Detail of Bas-relief Commemorating a Việt Minh Ambush at Láng Hầm on Highway 40 in 1948. The bas-relief is part of a state historic site commemorating the ambush of a French military convoy near Cần Thơ. The artillery gun was loaded onto several attached sampans and floated off to a nearby base area. The flags indicate that the soldiers were a unit of Military Region IX, which had its headquarters at U Minh.* Source: *Author photo.*

It is a terribly human war, constant harassment, not allowing for rest; where a smile, understanding, occurs as much as the furious cracking of the machine gun. Indochina: an immense mountain of rice . . . but to master it, it is necessary to conquer each grain one after the other.
—*Jean Leroy*[1]

In 1945 we had French soldiers again, and we had the uprising, the August Revolution. From then we called this canal intersection Burned Mill Junction. The French had built a big mill here, six milling units, very big; but in 1945, we rebelled and burned down the factory, even digging up the floorboards below it so that now this place is known as Burned Mill Junction.—*Ông Rõ*[2]

4 BALKANIZATION

The first indication of the problems that the French were to face in their bid to regain control of Cochinchina from the Việt Minh was that they returned prepared to fight on land instead of water. On October 22, 1945, a thousand men of the French Expeditionary Corps Second Armored Division under the command of General Jacques Philippe Leclerc disembarked at Vũng Tầu (Cap St. Jacques) with tanks and armored vehicles but no floating equipment, no gunboats, and no engineering troops capable of rebuilding the many bridges that had been blown up by the Allies before the end of the war.[3] In their first operation, to recapture the delta gateway city of Mỹ Tho, the French experienced logistical problems that would plague them throughout the war. The armored division, traveling on the main colonial highway running alongside the Sài Gòn–Mỹ Tho railway, was repeatedly delayed by destroyed bridges and sections of road. To convey the level of popular support for the resistance, a French correspondent noted that long sections of iron-latticed Eiffel bridges and reinforced-concrete highway bridges had been dismantled using only hand tools and mass labor.[4]

While the tanks and armored cars proceeded slowly alongside the railway (also damaged by Allied bombings), a separate group of commandos borrowed British landing craft and traveled from Sài Gòn on the canals. The boat convoy, departing at the same time as the tanks, broke through a single barricade of boats left by Bình Xuyên supporters on the Cây Khô Canal and by evening reached the primary water route to Mỹ Tho, the Chợ Gạo Canal. Colonel Jean Leroy, a half-French, half-Vietnamese commando born in Bến Tre Province, recounted the Japanese troops, still posted in watchtowers along the canal, looking on silently as they moved down the historic canal.[5] The first major French military operation of the First Indochina War, the seizure of Mỹ Tho, began at three o'clock in the morning with commandos seizing main government posts while some top leaders of the Vietnamese resistance retreated under fire, setting up temporary battle lines along the Xáng Canal ten kilometers west of town to stop French troops in pursuit.[6]

In this brief, opening exchange of fighting over a year before the generally acknowledged start of the Indochina war, the French army and the Vietnamese resistance quickly reoccupied historical territorial positions as French commanders gained control of key river ports on the water's edge while the Việt Minh retreated to more isolated interior areas such as Đồng Tháp with bases not far from where Võ Duy Dương's royalists operated from 1862 to 1866. What differed, however, was the French command's insistence on reoccupying a relatively fragile, land-based network of roads and commercial outposts beyond the ports. Colonial commerce and travel had moved to the roads and railroads from the waterways.

The nine years of war that followed the French assault on Mỹ Tho in 1945 may be read not only as a political or ideological struggle but also as a struggle to come to terms with incompatibility between colonial and indigenous spaces of the delta. As early as 1881, colonial nation builders such as Charles Combier (see chapter 1) had readily identified the economic and political dangers inherent in the government's attempts to bypass the native water landscape with railroads. In Combier's estimation, the French could never outcompete local merchants in the rice economy or in native commercial traffic. Since the establishment of rice, alcohol, and opium monopolies in Cochinchina, the government instead maintained its political and economic dominance through complex power-sharing arrangements with mostly Chinese-owned monopolies and through the levying of taxes. Native commerce continued largely at the same slow pace on the canals while Europeans and wealthier natives whizzed by in speedboats, private cars, trains, and, for the wealthiest, airplanes. Colonial space was built upon this relatively fragile, "floating" infrastructure — roads, railroads, steamers, and telegraphs — while native space continued to occupy the older, largely natural landscape of creeks and footpaths. Most people in 1945 still traveled by sail, oar, ox cart, foot, or the ubiquitous *ghe tam bản*. Each *ghe* was a narrow, long boat that, depending on size, could carry anywhere from two to ten people. These canoes, along with the larger junks, were still made locally; sawmills along the riverbanks produced planks from giant, hardwood logs typically floated downstream from Cambodia. The colonial transport network was, in the words of French historian Jean Chesneaux, "stuck onto the Vietnamese organism; it did not really bring life to the regions it traversed." The same peasants who were primarily responsible for its upkeep through taxes and required labor were often denied the opportunity to travel on it.[7] Thus, when peasant groups dismantled long sections of bridges and tracks in preparation for the Second Armored Division's advance in 1945, it is unlikely that they were concerned that such a "scorched-earth" tactic might inconvenience them.

The ecological and social crises of the 1930s and the Japanese military occupation of the early 1940s resulted in degradation of the canal network; and the diminished ability of the French to patrol the countryside allowed several emergent groups to vie for control of areas cut off from the main rivers. These politico-religious groups competed with the Communist-led Việt Minh and the French government and had established virtual fiefdoms by 1954. From controlling key plantation zones to regulating the transport of rice and revenues, this new cast of actors included revolutionaries, charismatic religious groups, and pro-French collaborators who stepped in to replace the colonial administrators and redefine economic and political order in the water landscape. Such changes ultimately required the French high command in 1947 to compromise with all Vietnamese groups except the Việt Minh simply to allow French troops to resecure major transportation routes through the delta. The Hòa Hảo and Cao Đài religious sects expanded control over large areas while the Bình Xuyên mafia network operated checkpoints on major transportation throughways into and out of Sài Gòn. By 1954, the sects and the Việt Minh controlled their respective zones with their own militaries; the Việt Minh even issued their own currency and banned use of Indochinese piasters.

Bernard Fall, in a 1955 essay, included a map showing each of these zones except for the Việt Minh areas. Each was located either around a historically significant anchor point (such as the Seven Mountains area, which was controlled by Lâm Thành Nguyên, a commander in the Hòa Hảo Buddhist sect), or along a strategic corridor such as the national highway and canal linking Mỹ Tho to Sài Gòn (controlled by the Bình Xuyên) or the routes between rivers (also controlled by the Hòa Hảo). While Fall's assessment of the fiefdoms expressed common French prejudices toward sects as fanatical, tribal, or mafia-like, he nevertheless conveys how thoroughly balkanized the region had become in less than ten years (see map 10). Fall's map (map 10) likewise exhibits a French tendency to assign borders to zones under competing authorities even though the territories controlled by the sects overlapped extensively. Each group collected taxes, maintained armies, and operated moneymaking ventures separately from one another. Much like contemporary reports on sectarian strife in such regions as the Balkans or the Middle East, reports to 1954 described instances of intersectarian violence as often as they did violence directed at foreign troops or the Việt Minh.[8]

The First Indochina War (1945–54) thus not only contributed to the erosion of the colonial grid but also fostered construction of new, heavily fortified enclaves claimed by competing groups. While many colonial-era waterways deteriorated from war-induced neglect, war also reconfigured the colonial water grid in less-obvious ways. Frequent instances of political and ethnic "cleansing" compelled refugees to move from one zone to another, thus changing the ethnic character of certain districts. The sporadic expansion of zones liberated by the Việt Minh from French control facilitated a return to more natural movements of rivers and tides, which played into war strategies as old canals became filled with silt, stranding convoys of deep-hulled ships. Perhaps most important for the several million human inhabitants, the war—especially in the liberated zones but also in zones controlled by other groups—permitted the reorganization of the water grid as farmers and political leaders renegotiated the terms of land tenure, taxation, and the individual's relationship to the state. The nascent discourse on the plight of the tenant farmer that began in the 1930s continued to develop during the First Indochina War as all sides struggled to enlist their support and cooperation.

The water landscape and its several million inhabitants presented a challenge that thwarted the attempts of any single group to control

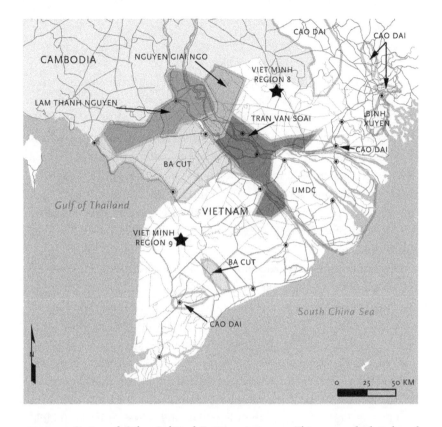

MAP 10. *Sects and Other Political Entities circa 1954. This map, which is based in part on a map from Bernard Fall in 1955, shows approximate areas controlled by various political and religious groups affiliated with the Franco-Vietnamese regime as well as approximate locations for the Việt Minh military headquarters in Đồng Tháp and the Cà Mau Peninsula. The Hòa Hảo zones were divided among four different leaders and are the shaded areas. Note that these zones were not uniformly controlled, and boundaries shifted from one month to another.* Source: Bernard Fall, "The Political-Religious Sects of Viet-Nam," Pacific Affairs 28, no. 3 (September 1955): 235.

the whole area. Once the French had incorporated most of the sect-controlled areas into a pro-French military alliance after 1947, two primary governments were left in the delta, each with its own political, strategic, and environmental characteristics: the liberation zones (*đất giải phong*) of the Việt Minh and the controlled landscapes (*terres controllées*) under a Franco-Vietnamese authority stretched along the riverbanks and highways.

Dividing the Water Grid

While American readers may be quick to associate images of warfare in Vietnam with aircraft—Huey Cobras and F10 Phantoms swooping over rice paddies and jungles—the First Indochina War, especially in the Mekong Delta, did not involve significant numbers of aircraft. It was a war still largely confined to the surface. The navigability of roads and waterways was vital to French military circulation; and it meant that if major routes of communication were interrupted long enough, then isolated areas would become subject to competing groups. Narratives of French or Việt Minh "progress" during the war typically emphasized opening or closing flows of traffic on the roads, of rice convoys on the river, and of police and troops.

One account by a French sailor of an operation to rescue a stranded rice convoy in Đồng Tháp on the Tổng Đốc Lộc Canal in 1947 illustrates the intensity of efforts by both sides to wrest control over the flow of water and waterborne commerce and the potent historic significance of such struggles. Tổng Đốc Lộc, a key collaborator in the French conquest, had developed plantations along the southern fringe of Đồng Tháp. He managed the digging of the long canal that until 1975 bore his name. North of the canal was territory largely controlled by the Việt Minh, who maintained mobile bases on the islandlike sand hills (*gò*) in the middle of the floodplain. To protect armored convoys of rice junks attempting to transport rice to mills, the French established small forts protecting markets along the canal. Việt Minh units used shallower creeks draining into the canal to ambush passing traffic, often seizing rice for the bases. By 1947, they had effectively stopped commercial traffic on this canal, and in April they attacked a garrison at Market 17 on the canal, leaving the soldiers inside stranded for several days.

The French command at Mỹ Tho ordered the armored barge *Devastation,* an old rice barge covered in steel panels and equipped with high-caliber machine guns, to reinforce the beleaguered troops. On its mission along the Tổng Đốc Lộc Canal, the barge encountered a barrier consisting of a row of parallel stakes driven into the mud and spanning the channel bed. The stakes were approximately half a meter in diameter and twelve meters in length, and they were held together by a steel cable. They were reinforced by a second row of stakes leaning against them. The crew crossed this first barrier by waiting for high tide, but they then encountered a similar barrier the next day. This one took six infantry platoons and a demolitions team six hours to destroy. The barge encountered two more such barriers on the thirty-kilometer route and did not reach the garrison and return with the wounded for two more days.[9]

The details of this small rescue operation are interesting for a couple of reasons. First, the guerrilla tactic employed—submerged pilings—was an important symbol of resistance for Vietnamese nationalists: the same tactic had been used against invading Mongol forces at the Battle of Bạch Đằng Estuary in 1288 and against invading Chinese forces in 938. Second, the construction of such barriers meant that, over several years, the canals would naturally fill with silt, thus increasing shallow flooding in the region and preventing French forces from easily crossing the area along the few roads, which would be submerged in the flood season.

At the Việt Minh bases in U Minh, resisting a militarily superior enemy meant that guerrillas not only fought to control waterways but became allies with the swamp as it encroached over roads and plantations. They first retreated to the depths of the freshwater, mangrove forest when about two thousand French, Algerian, and Vietnamese troops landed at Rạch Giá in March 1946 and reclaimed key markets and posts on area canals. After several months of French gains, the guerrillas began to use submerged barriers and to ambush French vessels, waiting until the French had exhausted their ammunition and supplies before seizing the vessels. French forces tried using flamethrowers and incendiary bombs to burn away the forest, and aircraft repeatedly bombed the earthen dams that Việt Minh militias had built to maintain high water levels. After each such attack, however, local crews worked quickly to rebuild the dams. Such barriers played a key role in protecting the Việt Minh bases. The larger dams required hundreds of laborers working in dangerous conditions to repair, and given their new permanence, they soon earned names.[10]

Although the French war in the Mekong Delta began with the assault on Mỹ Tho in 1945, the nationwide declaration of war on December 19, 1946, resulted in escalated conflicts, especially as the Việt Minh, organized into formal military units, expanded beyond base areas to attack surrounding areas. French publications denounced their destruction of bridges, roads, and canals as a "scorched-earth" tactic, but given the French advantage on navigable roads and waterways, destruction of these features was inevitable. By allying themselves with the forces of tides, siltation, and plant succession, rebels by necessity embedded themselves in the landscape.

During visits to one contested agricultural region between Cần Thơ and U Minh, I asked several Việt Minh veterans whether farmers at the time, facing greater flooding and interrupted irrigation systems, supported the revolution even though it meant suffering from more floods. Though deterioration of the canal infrastructure led to hardships, these farmers said that most former tenants in the area supported the Việt Minh because they stood to gain clear title to land and low tax rates if the revolution succeeded. By shifting cultivation techniques and crops, they adapted to the tactically inspired regeneration of wetland. Mr. Rỡ explained both why he supported the Việt Minh and how he adapted to survive the higher flooding:

> In about 1953, the revolutionary government got together and they granted land rights to the people first thing. They granted land from here to a buffer zone one kilometer wide from the bank of the river. With extra land, they granted that to us too. . . . Generally speaking, the [post-1945] Vietnamese landlords were awful; they were traitors . . . when the French left, they followed, so the Việt Minh claimed the right to manage and grant the land to the people. Because we wanted to keep the land, we later offered our children to the revolution against the Americans and to our victory.
>
> . . . In that time agriculture was not successful, because the elevation was only 0.2 meters above sea level, very low, so we could use this land only for growing tobacco, but for paddy we couldn't—we planted sugar too . . . we made raised beds, plenty of grass, it was this high [two to three meters] . . . we had to cut the grass in order to make the raised beds to grow tobacco. Then it was just us farmers, living with the Việt Minh . . . we'd sell the tobacco for rice at Long Mỹ and bring it back here. Long Mỹ was higher in elevation, so you could have paddy . . . here, the elevation was too close to water level, you couldn't dry out the fields; you couldn't burn the straw because it was too wet.[11]

The Việt Minh's campaign to destroy roads and bridges in the delta eventually crippled provincial administrations, especially those established under the Bảo Đại–led State of Vietnam formed on June 14, 1949. At Tầm Vu, site of a major Việt Minh ambush of a French armored convoy on April 19, 1948, guerrillas again in 1949 and 1950 destroyed nearby sections of the same highway (fig. 23). The Vietnamese military officer assigned as administrator in the newly formed government submitted a request for additional funds to the director of finance for South Vietnam seeking funds from an extraordinary budget to pay for repairs to the road. The provincial government was already in severe deficit, but the French high command was demanding that the road be restored quickly.[12] Thus, the continuing disruption of road and waterway networks not only prevented state forces from easily patrolling the liberated zones but also put continual pressure after 1949 on relationships between the all-Vietnamese provincial administrations, their Vietnamese superiors in Sài Gòn, and the mostly French high command that oversaw military and security operations.

Besides coordinating attacks on infrastructure, the Việt Minh also made clever use of natural processes such as floods and the rapid sedimentation of canals to their advantage. The problem of *dos d'âne* that had vexed Public Works engineers such as Rénaud in the 1880s returned again as colonial dredges were increasingly prevented from keeping channels clear. Without any systematic cleaning of waterways, *dos d'âne* soon blocked many major canals. These natural barriers quickly became a cause for concern when they stranded a number of military escorts and rice convoys. Near the river port Bãi Xâu (Sóc Trăng), one convoy became stranded for three days. Because the heavy barges full of rice invited a Việt Minh raid, about two hundred troops were required to guard them day and night before a full-moon high tide lifted the vessels off the bottom.[13]

The Việt Minh (and to some extent the politico-religious sects) profited economically and strategically from the regeneration of the precolonial water landscape. Once again, the *dos d'âne* turned into important meeting spots (*giáp nước*) for the exchange of goods and information. In French military literature, such places formed important bottlenecks that permitted the Việt Minh to control the flow of sampans and larger water traffic through tight channels protected by heavily fortified positions along either bank. The Việt Minh forces exacted taxes in money or kind to allow local boats passage.[14] While the Việt Minh were not alone in employing such strategies of surveillance and tax collecting by controlling the flow of water traffic through a few major points, because their base of power was centered in well-hidden forests and wetlands they depended on naturally produced bottlenecks more than did the Hòa Hảo, state military, or Cao Đài forces, which established checkpoints along the old highways or at entry points through blockades.

Despite having established bases for their gunboats and landing craft in the major delta ports, the French forces had difficulty controlling even the largest waterways that traversed the delta's vast interiors until they entered into tense alliances with former anti-French, non-Communist groups. During the first year of undeclared war in Cochinchina, other militant, anti-French groups, such as the Hòa Hảo sects, the Cao Đài, and the Bình Xuyên, cooperated with the Communist elements of the Việt Minh in Đồng Tháp and U Minh to prevent the French from passing through areas they controlled. After the formal declaration of war against the Việt Minh on December 19, 1946, the French high command moved quickly to reallocate its small fleet of river craft into northern and southern flotillas and, recognizing the severe shortage of equipment and troops, to form alliances with some of the non-Communist nationalist groups that French authorities had previously suppressed. In August 1946, the high pontiff of the Cao Đài Church, Phạm Công Tắc, returned from exile in Madagascar and together with his generals began negotiations to form an alliance with the French in return for quasi-autonomous control of territory. The agreement, signed in January 1947, led to the recognition of 1,470 Cao Đài troops organized into twelve mobile *supplétif* units of sixty men each and sixteen fixed bases in Tây Ninh Province, an important Cambodian border province west of Sài Gòn.[15]

The Hòa Hảo Buddhist sects were the major non-Communist group that controlled territory in the delta, especially in the Hậu Giang region (Transbassac). Numbering about eight hundred thousand adepts living on the large islands between the two branches of the Mekong River and in the Long Xuyên Quadrangle, the Hòa Hảo sects developed first as part of a millenarian Buddhist movement popular with peasants in the western delta region. They followed the teachings of a charismatic leader, Huỳnh Phú Sổ, who claimed to have been born again as the Buddha Master of Western Peace (*maitreya*) during his convalescence in 1939 at the temple dedicated to the Buddha Master of Western Peace (Chùa Phật Thầy Tây An) near Châu Đốc. A home to the Bửu Sơn Kỳ Hương movement that began in the 1850s, the Seven Mountains region became a key base for Hòa Hảo partisans, who drew direct geographic and historic connections between their sect and the anticolonial resistance in 1873 and the resistance led by Nguyễn Trung Trực from 1862 to 1868 (chapter 1).

The move from being a primarily religious movement to a military one was caused by the political crises during the Japanese occupation before 1945. Huê Tâm Hồ Tai describes how Sổ cooperated with the Japanese in exchange for protection against French secret service agents. In return, he mobilized his followers, many of whom worked on the old French estates, to produce rice that was desperately needed for the war effort in 1945. In spring 1945, after the Japanese coup, Sổ met with key Communist leaders in Cần Thơ to arrange an alliance of forces to oppose the French. One of Sổ's military commanders at the time, Trần Văn Soái (Năm Lửa), rose to prominence because he and his lieutenants had developed a lucrative business extracting protection fees from boat drivers crossing the two main river branches close to the major ferry routes. Soái, nicknamed "fire" (*lửa*) for his old job stoking the fires on the ferry that crossed north of Cần Thơ, made use of his extensive contacts developed on the river before he converted to Hòa Hảo Buddhism.[16] After the August Revolution, Sổ's commanders continued to build their forces in tense agreement with the Việt Minh despite occasional outbreaks of violence between the groups. Soái organized the Nguyễn Trung Trực Division to control much of the alluvial region between the two major river branches and the fertile area around Cần Thơ. As clashes between the Hòa Hảo and Việt Minh increased in 1946, however, Sổ finally moved to form his own political party in January 1947. In late April, Sổ was abducted during a trip to meet with Việt Minh leaders, and a month later the Việt Minh Executive Committee of the South claimed responsibility for his murder.[17]

After Sổ's death, sources take various views on the May 18, 1947, agreement signed by Trần Văn Soái and Colonel Cluset of the French high command, but the ensuing French armament of approximately two thousand Hòa Hảo troops allowed the French military to regain movement on several major colonial waterways in the region, including the Xà No, Ô Môn, and Thốt Nốt Canals, which were then under General Soái's control.[18] Soái, with his headquarters at Cái Vồn, an arroyo on the Hậu Giang branch of the Mekong River downstream from Cần Thơ, organized village self-defense militias and mobile forces that also controlled the major highway running alongside the Hậu Giang branch. Soái and his lieutenant Ba Cụt also reopened rice mills on several major colonial estates, including those on Émery, Gressier, and Red Flag (Cờ Đỏ) lands. Hòa Hảo mobile units also set up camps along the precolonial Long Xuyên–Rạch Giá Canal and the colonial-era Ô Môn and Thốt Nốt Canals. The large mill on the Red Flag Estate again began shipping rice to Chợ Lớn.[19]

These uneasy military alliances with former adversaries allowed the French military a measure of control over major waterways and highways in the delta but at a price: ceding control of the old water grid to Vietnamese nationalists who were for the most part anti-French as well as anti–Việt Minh. Besides Soái, other Hòa Hảo commanders (see map 10) formed personal fiefdoms in the western delta region. What followed for the next several years were episodes of fighting even between sect commanders. Some occasionally switched sides between the French and the Việt Minh. However, the majority of the commanders were violently opposed to the Việt Minh. Bernard Fall conveys one French observer's report of Hòa Hảo treatment of captured militants: "The Hoa-Hao had the habit of tying Viet-Minh sympathizers together with ropes and throwing them into the rivers to drown in bundles. . . . One could see those bundles of bodies floating down the rivers like so many trains of junks, at the mercy of the currents and tides."[20] Over the next several years, from 1947 to 1950, all three Vietnamese groups moved to expand control over portions of the delta. A popular phrase at the time associated the three groups with their three centers of power: "Cao Đài Tây Ninh, Hòa Hảo Làng Linh, Việt Minh Cán Gáo."[21]

In the midst of fighting, all three groups also worked within their violently defended zones to build new physical and social grids. By 1949, Việt Minh successes around the U Minh Forest and the liquidation of the old estates brought them significant support from former tenants. They reestablished political offices at An Biên and Vĩnh Thuận Villages and regularly ambushed French patrols on nearby waterways. They stockpiled captured weapons in the forest and grew increasingly bold, even staging conventional military attacks on French forts and towns. They even initiated work on new canals in the area, notably the People's Army Canal (Kinh Quân Dân), to allow quicker travel from U Minh eastward to coastal bases on the South China Sea.[22] General Soái prevailed upon the provincial administration in Cần Thơ to pave new roads to his private homes and businesses, while the Hòa Hảo commander in Châu Đốc, Lâm Thành Nguyên, reinvested some of the profits from rice-milling operations in the construction of roads and schools.[23]

Rehabilitation of some segments of the old water network in controlled zones was further enhanced by the operations of French riverine forces known as *dinnassaus* (Divisions navales d'assaut), a modern incarnation of the French gunboat navy of the 1860s and a predecessor to the American brown-water navy of the 1960s. Organized in early 1947 after the formal declaration of war, the units' primary purpose was to protect convoys of equipment and rice moving through the Red and Mekong River Deltas. Unit 8, headquartered along the river quay in Cần Thơ, was primarily responsible for patrolling the Hậu Giang and alluvial regions. A memoir published by the first commander of this unit highlights the difficulties in navigating not only the embattled waterways but also the regions held by Hòa Hảo commanders. The units devoted much of their efforts to restoring traffic on major transportation corridors. In spring 1947, they protected a dredging operation on Nicolai–Mang Thít Canal and established guard towers every few kilometers along its banks. The canal permitted rice convoys to pass quickly toward Vĩnh Long from the Hậu Giang region.[24] In another major operation in May 1950, the group participated in a joint offensive against Ba Cụt's Hòa Hảo forces, who had switched sides against the French. The boats, amphibious tracked vehicles, and several thousand infantry troops reclaimed Thốt Nốt Canal and destroyed a number of earthen barriers built across it. They then pressured this most notorious of Hòa Hảo commanders to realign his troops with the French.[25]

If we step back from the shifting political and military events of the First Indochina War to the broader perspective of changes in the water landscape, we can see that this period of French intervention and resistance from 1945 to 1949 produced several key changes in the older, colonial landscape, which had been undergoing various ecological and social crises since the early 1930s. Through destruction of the floating infrastructure of roads and bridges, the Việt Minh restricted the French largely to patrolling vulnerable highways and a handful of major canals. By constructing barriers and becoming "friends" with the natural forces of sedimentation and flooding, the Việt Minh also played an important role in regenerating wetland conditions that had existed before regions such as Cà Mau were reclaimed as plantation land.

As the Việt Minh and the sects established their bases of power in 1946–47, the water landscape gradually split apart (socially and hydrologically) into separate water enclaves. General Soái and other Hòa Hảo commanders managed several of the largest colonial-era plantations in collaboration with the French and with the original owners, while areas closer to the frontiers of Việt Minh–controlled territory suffered increased flooding and deprivation of supplies as the French attempted to block the traffic of basic commodities into the liberated zones. Yet in the liberated zones, cadres worked to build up an alternative infrastructure of schools, underground bunkers, and clandestine routes of communication. From these early struggles there emerged two very different water landscapes, that of the French and that of the Việt Minh.

Perhaps the single most important political factor encouraging this enforced separation of the water landscape was the French blockade of the Hậu Giang region that coincided with the formation of the Associated State of Vietnam (ASV) in July 1949. While the Việt Minh capitalized on French difficulties in responding to natural problems such as flooding and sedimentation, the French military command together with a new Vietnamese state authority attempted to limit the flow of commodities—especially oil and industrial goods—outside controlled corridors. Oil and lubricants, all imported to Vietnam at the time, were essential to the operation of machinery in old rice mills. Polished rice could be distributed to troops or sold to raise money. The borders of the blockaded area were the Vĩnh Tế Canal on the west, the Hậu Giang branch on the north, and the ocean along the east and south. The French military command and the ASV, headed by Bảo Đại, announced that the following items headed into or out of this area were to be seized: salt, fruit, green vegetables, construction materials, snakeskin, and salted fish. Rice and fresh meats exiting the Hậu Giang region were subject to seizure if they were being transported by vessels carrying large quantities and not traveling in scheduled military convoys. The French wanted to restrict most traffic of rice and meats to the road network, where it was permitted only in approved vehicles carrying valid papers issued by military and provincial authorities.[26]

The French emphasis on restricting traffic in the Hậu Giang region to the roads had major social and economic consequences in the region. Along this fragile network, the military command attempted to relocate populations of supporters, refugees, and newer settlers, who, because of the tariffs and restricted travel, soon became dependent on government aid for survival. The blockade likewise strained provincial budgets just when Việt Minh assaults on roads and other infrastructure were increasing. The administrator of Rạch Giá Province reported that in the first year of the blockade total tax revenues dropped from 1.6 to 1.1 million piasters while rice excise revenues dropped to 50 percent of preblockade levels.[27] The blockade and continuing militarization along major traffic routes also resulted in stark visual changes in the landscape as watchtowers and pillboxes appeared every few kilometers along the major routes. One reporter traveling the road to Mỹ Tho in 1949 noted guard towers whose silhouettes "were eerily evocative of France in the Middle Ages."[28]

Considering Foucault's notion of the watchtower as panopticon, we can interpret the rapid appearance of watchtowers on controlled waterways and roads as a desperate effort by the state to monitor all movement of people and things. The presence of so many towers and bunkers, hiding soldiers within, must have altered the behavior of those moving under their surveillance.[29] Unlike Foucault's prison model, however, the spaces under the watchtowers were bounded, not by the fortress walls of a prison, but by barbed wire yielding to the endless horizons of swamp and fields beyond. In opposition to the watchtowers, the Việt Minh established their own *invisible* observation networks; and on the periphery of the liberated zones, camouflaged bunkers permitted a different sort of surveillance effect on traffic moving through liberated zones. The juxtaposition of the exposed watchtower and the camouflaged bunker symbolizes an important opposition between visible and invisible governmentalities located within two different terrains in the water landscape. For many farmers and others in the region, their daily challenge was not only to move along these deteriorated waterways or bombed-out roads but to navigate from checkpoint to checkpoint between these different zones.

Tá Điền and Land Reform

During the First Indochina War, the "peasant question"—what to do about several million tenant farmers living in poverty on the large plantations in the Mekong Delta—continued as a major issue, especially after the catastrophic famine in 1945 and each year thereafter as the Việt Minh redistributed land owned by French and Vietnamese elites to the workers (*tá điền*) on these plantations. State officials worried that a large majority of *tá điền* would respond to Việt Minh calls for "land to the tiller" and support liquidation of the large, colonial estates. Vietnamese writers had begun describing the plight of *tá điền* in documentary fiction in the 1930s and continued to do so during the years of the Popular Front and even Vichy rule. Land reform evolved into perhaps the single most important political issue of the revolution, especially in the rice-producing regions of Cochinchina. Beginning with the establishment of a provisional Cochinchinese republic in 1947 and especially after the creation of the ASV in 1949, both the Việt Minh and ASV governments (and to a lesser extent those of the Hòa Hảo and other sects) strove to develop alternative land reform strategies based on their respective Communist and liberal economic ideologies. All groups struggled with the basic issue of rebuilding the agricultural economy to provide much-needed revenues, and they utilized either socialist or colonial legal precedents as well as existing, colonial-era maps and property records to govern parts of the water landscape.

In this evolving discourse, farmers repeatedly found themselves negotiating labor contracts, paddy taxes, basic economic transactions, and even disaster relief—in some instances with multiple authorities. They were often "caught in the middle," left to maneuver between military checkpoints, economic blockades, and different currencies and administrations; however, there is evidence to suggest that, as the main producers in this agricultural economy, they nonetheless exacted compromises from both governments as they resisted measures to increase taxes or "contributions" to either cause. The fact that the Việt Minh had to make repeated appeals to peasants to pay their taxes and make patriotic contributions (đóng góp) suggests a general resistance among peasants to excessive taxation even within the liberated zones.[30] Drawing primarily upon interviews with prisoners of war conducted from 1965 to 1971 by the Rand Corporation, David Elliott likewise emphasizes inconsistencies with stated policy and frequent modifications in Việt Minh tax and land redistribution practices. Elliott suggests that peasant support for revolutionary schemes appears to have correlated roughly with how much they stood to gain from land redistribution and with how well local resistance committees operated. Resistance or cooperation also may have depended upon whether peasants before 1945 already owned some small piece of land and thus had been classified as "middle class" landowners by Việt Minh cadres. After 1949, with more direct Chinese Communist support of the Việt Minh, cadres even in the south appear to have begun quietly removing many such "middle-class" farmers from key political positions in the liberated zones.[31]

Although a detailed picture of farmers' relations with Việt Minh cadres from year to year after 1945 is difficult to ascertain given the lack of local Việt Minh records, regional and provincial statistics suggest a widespread redistribution of land from large plantations formerly owned by French and Vietnamese owners, who fled the fighting for the cities. Lâm Quang Huyền's *Cách mạng ruộng đất ở Miền Nam Việt Nam* (Land Revolution in Southern Vietnam) states that 567,547 hectares of land belonging to French planters and Vietnamese "traitors" (*Việt gian*) was redistributed to 527,163 people, an average of 1.1 hectares per person.[32] A series of provincial monographs produced by the ASV in 1953 gives updated information on both "noncontrolled" and "controlled" areas, with additional information about some areas under sect rule. While the monographs lack the depth and completeness of the colonial-era geographies published from 1902 to 1911, they nonetheless follow the pattern of previous provincial monographs by including basic statistical information on the economy, population, and land area of the province as well as more anecdotal accounts of recent local events.[33] The 1953 series offers a glimpse of broad changes in population and land use during the Indochina War.[34]

In most provinces, the area of land under cultivation fell while populations increased significantly. This increase in population may have had much to do with the catastrophic 1944–45 famine in Tonkin and northern areas, when over one million farmers died from starvation. During those years and after, many more may have migrated southward. Other causes for the population increase were high birth rates and lower infant mortality. It was common in the Vietnamese countryside to encounter families with ten or more children who had survived infancy. Meanwhile, the fall in the total area of cultivable land was directly linked to the Việt Minh's scorched-earth policy, rendering rice fields back into swamps as a means of protecting the liberated zones. In July 1949, soon after the formation of the ASV, the president of a provisory assembly addressed the newly appointed governor of South Vietnam: "The area of cultivable lands has diminished in catastrophic proportions: many hundreds of thousands of hectares are returning to fallow or to forests to become, if no action is taken to stop this disastrous trend, 'dead lands.'"[35]

The Việt Minh effectively controlled less densely populated provinces such as Bạc Liêu and Rạch Giá Provinces, more than half of which were undeveloped or classified as forests and swamps. Anecdotal evidence from individual reports suggests correlations between specific landscapes and political conditions in these areas. For example, in Châu Đốc and Long Xuyên Provinces, where there were large populations of Hòa Hảo followers, 477,000 hectares were listed in 1936 as under cultivation, and 87 percent of this land was classified as planted in floating rice, not the more common, short-stem rice planted in other parts of Vietnam. These two provinces were located in a flood-prone landscape surrounding the islandlike Seven Mountains region, where the Hoà Hảo religion started.[36] In Cần Thơ Province, important for its large-scale, colonial estates and rice mills, 60 percent of this area was listed as "noncontrolled," but more important was the decrease in total land listed under cultivation, from 206,000 hectares in 1928 to just under 150,000 hectares in 1953. Of the 56,000 hectares that had been abandoned, just 10,000 hectares were located within "controlled" territory, meaning that the Việt Minh campaigns to render land unproductive through construction of barriers and attacks on dredging had eliminated 25 percent of productive lands and the taxes they generated from the province's budget.[37]

Contrary to the catastrophic reports issued by the government leaders, however, farmers in Việt Minh–controlled areas may have actually begun to improve rice yields before the end of the First Indochina War. This not only brought more food and revenue to the Việt Minh but also resulted in the first major shifts in *tá điền* fortunes since the beginning of the agricultural crisis in the 1930s. Abolition of the head and land taxes and decreased land rents may have spurred many farmers who previously grew only one rice crop per year to grow two. Mr. Diều, a Việt Minh veteran living near the former Gressier Estate, compared life during colonial times and the changes experienced after the Việt Minh controlled the territory in 1950:

> Before, farmers rented land from the French landlords. If you rented one hundred *công* [1 *công* = 0.1 hectare] of fields, Gressier could lend you one or two hundred *giạ* [two to four metric tons] of rice. Even if people didn't borrow a lot, they still borrowed a little to cover household goods and tools to work this one hundred *công* of land. They could exchange this rice to buy fish sauce, diesel fuel, cloth, or tools sold on credit only to *tá điền*, to be repaid at harvest season again in rice. Paying in rice! At the same time, we also had to pay the agricultural tax to Gressier. Thus, on the surface, the farmer's life looked stable, but in truth it worked out that he didn't have a thing; first, the goods [Gressier] sold us took up a large portion of our harvest, and then on top of this he took out the agricultural tax. When their work was done, farmers were left with just the tip of the rice pile.
>
> From that time, when the Việt Minh distributed land for farmers on the Gressier Estate, farmers only had to pay a reduced agricultural tax; besides that, there were no other taxes, so farmers could get ahead. Today, using new agricultural technologies to increase the harvest, the Gressier region can produce three crops per year.[38]

Memoirs and government documents suggest that by 1952, at least inside Việt Minh and sect enclaves, local authorities had begun building new infrastructure and expanding agricultural production and services such as schools and hospitals. Around the U Minh Forest, the Việt Minh established major caches for storing weapons as well as facilities to accommodate new arrivals of matériel and people, especially the families of high-ranking party members. The population in the area is reported to have tripled from 1947 to 1953 as refugees and middle- and high-ranking cadres moved into the region for protection. Leading figures of the Việt Minh such as Lê Duẩn, head of the party's Southern Regional Committee (Xứ Ủy Nam Bộ) and future general secretary, moved to the base area in 1948 and continued to conduct major meetings in the area to 1954.[39] After the arrival of Lê Duẩn and other party leaders, work accelerated on expanding the base area's ability to handle the traffic of key political figures as well as supplies and more troops. In the winter dry season of

1949, workers began dredging the eleven-kilometer People's Army Canal (Kinh Quân Dân) to facilitate the movement of people and matériel into and out of the base area on the South China Sea side of the delta near Bạc Liêu.[40] Formerly sparsely populated cajeput forests and marshes in the liberated zones thus became bustling, hidden towns through which some of the most illustrious members of the revolutionary movement passed.

The increased Việt Minh presence in the swamps and liberated zones resulted not in the reversion of certain landscapes to their natural state, but instead in a kind of managed nature that hid the growing revolutionary infrastructure. Beginning with a series of decrees issued by Hồ Chí Minh in 1949, the Southern Regional Committee began issuing legal contracts to *tá điền* that regulated their obligations to Việt Minh authorities and, more interestingly, built a new landowning class using colonial-era property maps. For example, one 1951 contract issued to a farmer in Mỹ Tra Village (Cao Lãnh District, Sa Đéc Province) records that the local Resistance Committee in Ba Sao consented to rent 1.9 hectares of land confiscated from Mr. Tomasi, a French planter, noting a specific lot number from the colonial cadastral survey. The Việt Minh did not remap the landscape in this initial phase of occupation; rather, they improvised from existing documents. Besides offering a substantially lower rent (twenty-eight *giạ*, or roughly half a metric ton in rice), the contract also promised many of the basic measures—disaster relief, fixed interest, labor guarantees—that colonial reformers had pushed for since the days of the Popular Front.[41]

Besides creating a legal infrastructure, the Việt Minh also worked to build a new social infrastructure through mass literacy campaigns, nationalist music, and nationalist theater. Literacy was a powerful tool for recruiting local farmers to join political and military organizations. Basic primers, teaching farmers to read and write the romanized script *quốc ngữ*, were supplemented by simple moral plays produced along the same lines as the documentary fiction of the 1930s. Local cadres in musical or theatrical troupes used familiar forms such as *cải lương*, a regional opera similar to popular forms of Chinese opera that were performed across Southeast Asia. They also adapted patriotic and revolutionary songs from Russian and French sources. Impassioned by local performances, thousands of children of *tá điền*—male and female—joined voluntary aid groups or militias at the outbreak of fighting in 1946. Once literate themselves, they then often spearheaded efforts to teach reading and writing and simultaneously moved on to more difficult political writing in the Marxist-Leninist tradition. In the 1960s, American interrogations of prisoners of war and "ralliers" (those who surrendered to the government) offer an unusual, rich window into the lives of people growing up in these areas. One man, interrogated in 1971, was born near Ninh Thạnh Lợi just two years before the 1927 massacre. He joined a Việt Minh militia at age twenty and learned to read at twenty-one in the first year of fighting. After fighting with the local militia until 1954, he was imprisoned from 1956 to 1959 and then joined the National Liberation Front (NLF). As a cadre in the NLF, he managed an all-women performing troupe from 1960 to 1970. The interview revealed that some of the women in the theater group also operated a primary school in Ninh Thạnh Lợi from 1946 until 1969, when intensive bombing forced it to close.[42]

Such stories highlight the violent yet socially unique conditions for young, poor Vietnamese in the countryside living in the base areas. Future party secretary Lê Duẩn met Nguyễn Thụy Nga, a party member and performer in an all-women singing troupe from Cần Thơ Province, and they married in the U Minh Forest in 1950. The marriage was something of a celebrity marriage given Lê Duẩn's stature and Nga's reputation as a skillful fighter and beautiful young woman who as a teenager had participated in many daring escapades against the French. They reportedly had several children, who lived with their parents in the base area before moving north to Hà Nội.[43]

Sơn Nam, one of the best-known writers from the Mekong Delta, lived in the base area from 1943 to 1954 and became one of its more famous historians, directing his intense interest as a novelist and journalist to the stories of revolutionaries and common people living together in the region. His memoir Ở Chiến Khu 9 (In Military Region 9) gives detailed accounts of his activities in the base area as a writer, teacher, and political adviser who frequently traveled with Việt Minh troops on operations and the theater troupes performing in the forests.[44]

During the First Indochina War, areas controlled by sectarian groups such as the Cao Đài, Hòa Hảo, and Colonel Jean Leroy's Unités mobiles de défense des chrétiens (UMDC) likewise developed local education programs and political networks, albeit in close connection with the ASV and the French military. In Jean Leroy's memoir, he describes forming ten brigades under his command, comprised primarily of fellow Catholics but also Moroccan legionnaires and Hòa Hảo and Cao Đài followers. By 1947 and for the remainder of the First Indochina War, Leroy controlled the islands of Bến Tre Province with almost no disruptions from the Việt Minh.[45] Leroy, writing in 1955, made a strong case for his model of rule over the province, citing the following figures as evidence of his successful reoccupation and development of the province:[46]

	1945	1950	1952
Population	353,000	129,000	385,000
Area cultivated	116,000	59,000	187,000
Schools	39	39	153
Hospitals/clinics	5	5	120

In describing the Hòa Hảo–controlled areas in Long Xuyên, Châu Đốc, Cần Thơ, and Sa Đéc Provinces, journalist Bernard Fall harshly criticized Trần Văn Soái and his lieutenants for repressive taxes against farmers as well as heavy transportation taxes for merchants passing through Hòa Hảo–controlled territory. Lâm Thành Nguyên, with his base area near Châu Đốc in the Seven Mountains area, fared better in Fall's account, as he had ordered some one hundred new schools to be built and had lowered taxes.[47] A Hòa Hảo account of this period does not do much to refute these criticisms, but it explains that Hòa Hảo commanders were forced by the French to be self-sufficient—they had to purchase their own weapons from the French military, for example—and thus had to resort to sometimes-desperate measures to raise funds for self-defense.[48] There are few Hòa Hảo memoirs to place French or Việt Minh critiques in context. In one of the most thoroughly researched accounts of Hòa Hảo economic and social life drawn mainly from French military records, Pascal Bordeaux shows how individual Hòa Hảo leaders responded differently to economic and social conditions in areas under their command and how within each fiefdom there were often still more internal divisions among lieutenants. Lâm Thành Nguyên appointed his father, a man partly descended from local Chinese families, to manage the collection and exportation of rice. This action drew strong criticism from unit commanders, who refused to aid such a "clique of Chinese merchants" and accused Lâm Thành Nguyên of supporting these "infidels" over followers of the religion.[49]

Finally, although the ASV (1949–54) and its predecessor governments, the Republic of Cochinchina (1946–47) and the Republic of South Vietnam

(1947–49), exercised very limited authority in the Mekong Delta outside the major towns, they nevertheless played an important role in continuing state discourse on questions of land reform and *tá điền* into post-1954 nation-building efforts. Centered in Sài Gòn, these provisional governments were led by southern Vietnamese elites, most of whom were owners of large estates who had attended elite schools in the colony and France before entering politics in the 1930s. Many of these elites, born in the 1880s and 1890s, had become French citizens and, after retiring from government or professional service, entered politics. Dr. Nguyễn Văn Thinh, first president of the Republic of Cochinchina, had completed a doctorate at the Pasteur Institute in Paris before returning to Cochinchina in 1926 and entering politics. In 1937 he founded the Partí démocrate indochinoise and began to urge the colonial government to develop *casiers* and improve working conditions on the large estates.[50] Along with Dr. Thinh, a group of other wealthy landowners made up the initial provisional government, holding primarily consultative roles with the French High Commission until 1949. Among them were District Chief (*đốc phủ sứ*) Nguyễn Văn Tâm, known as the "Tiger of Cai Lậy" for his brutal suppression of protesters in Đồng Tháp since the 1930s; Henri de Lachevrotière, a landowner from the Cần Thơ area and the son of a Vietnamese woman and a French soldier (he brought a major lawsuit against the Department of Public Works in 1912); and Nguyễn Tấn Cương, a relation of de Lachevrotière's with strong ties to the security service (Sûreté).[51] Tâm, a naturalized French citizen since 1927, later served as prime minister of the ASV in 1952–53, and his son, Nguyễn Văn Hinh, served at the same time as chief of the Vietnamese armed forces.[52]

This network of wealthy, French-educated Cochinchinese elites, often dismissed in Vietnamese histories as "lackeys," nonetheless played a pivotal role in land reform as they continued advancing such concepts as *casiers* and labor contracts while they fought vigorously to protect the rights of landowners. When asked by French authorities about how to solve the "*tá điền* problem" in 1947, Dr. Lê Văn Hoạch, president of the republic and a Cao Đài follower, responded that the primary problem occurred in the Hậu Giang region, where over a million laborers made up a "floating population." The first task, according to Dr. Hoạch, was to bring French civil authority to this mass of people, giving them identification cards and enforcing contracts that, he argued, would protect worker rights as well as those of landowners.[53] The Provisional Government issued a decree establishing such *tá điền* contracts on May 21, 1947; however, there is little evidence to suggest that provincial administrators in government-controlled areas actually implemented its major stipulations, including the establishment of local tribunals to mediate claims brought by workers against landowners.[54]After the ASV's inception in July 1949, there is no significant evidence that it managed to carry out any significant land reforms either.

As in the 1930s with peasant protests, Việt Minh actions were largely responsible for moving the ASV's recalcitrant leaders to adopt stronger measures for land reform. Following a radio address by Hồ Chí Minh, broadcast on transmitters in the liberated zones, Tâm urged his minister of information to counter immediately with government broadcasts highlighting a campaign to repartition large estates and establish credit unions for farmers. Tâm, addressing his three regional governors, acknowledged a preliminary stage of "voluntary dismemberment" of some of the large colonial estates by landowners. Tâm, whose large holdings in Đồng Tháp had already been confiscated and redistributed by the Việt Minh, urged his peers to voluntarily sell large portions of their land at fixed rates. He also called for the establishment of provincial agricultural banks to help farmers come up with the necessary means to purchase such lands and stated that already over 12,000 hectares had been resold.[55] Tâm and his cohort eventually responded in the newspapers, too, describing Việt Minh seizures of land as only a first phase of redistribution that would ultimately lead to collectivization. In contrast, they promised to protect farmers' rights to individual property and to counter the Marxist threat of state domination.[56]

Not only did the First Indochina War disrupt the colonial water grid, its canals slowly filling with silt and annual floods breaking its dikes, but through the actions of all sides in the war, it resulted also in some creative responses to basic problems of security and survival. Farmers, especially former *tá điền*, participated in a variety of efforts, most notably the Việt Minh campaigns but also those undertaken by the Hòa Hảo and other sects, to build societies that differed from the colonial one they had endured through the financial crisis of the early 1930s and the famine years under Japanese rule. Joining either the Việt Minh or the sects offered farmers some measure of upward mobility, but it also required, as Mr. Rõ explained above, that they give up their children to the revolutionary authority offering these opportunities. The First Indochina War also brought more and more children of the middle and upper classes, often speaking fluent French and coming into direct contact with the hundreds of thousands of peasants living in the Hậu Giang region. As Sơn Nam has written in his memoirs and in historical fiction such as *Hai Cõi U Minh* (Two Worlds of U Minh: Stories), the "jungle" was not just a place for hiding weapons and troops but a platform from which to build a society and an alternative history, one centered on stories, songs, and poems of national resistance.[57]

With regard to the water environment, the war was also a period of alternative constructions such as underwater barriers lined with mines to counter French efforts to patrol the region. Abandoned land (*đất bỏ hoang*) reverted to swamp and, in some cases, young cajeput forest. What French and ASV officials called *terres mortes* and criticized as part of the Việt Minh's scorched-earth tactics was for the resistance a terrain that suited the terms of survival in this war. This period of strategically planned degradation of agricultural landscapes opened up the possibility, unique in the mid-twentieth century, for the restoration of large areas to precolonial ecological conditions. While certainly not friends of such re-wilded landscapes, Vietnamese farmers who supported the revolution adapted to them, often switching crops and trading patterns to survive higher floods.

The First Indochina War, especially as it wore on in the early 1950s, was also historically important for creating the physical landscape that American advisers encountered after 1954. The continuing ideas of *casiers* and *tá điền* contracts also shaped the policy environment that Americans encountered after 1954. The war provided the ASV with an important means for continuing older land reform ideas first posed by elite Cochinchinese in the Popular Front era and during World War II. Although recent historical studies of Ngô Đình Diệm's rural development schemes tend to attribute their "model" to British counterinsurgency tactics in Malaysia or to other counterinsurgency measures adopted after World War II, this chapter's study of Việt Minh and ASV programs and measures suggests that Vietnamese attitudes toward the economic and strategic situation in the countryside had much deeper roots in late-colonial Indochina, where individuals such as Dr. Nguyễn Văn Thinh drew from ideas developed in Cochinchina in the 1930s.[58] The basis of colonial authority over land—land tenure agreements, cadastral surveys, and property maps—likewise continued to influence not only ASV-related programs for land tenure but to some extent even Việt Minh programs. Contrary to government propaganda suggesting that Việt Minh forces intended to eliminate private landholding and any vestiges of a landowner class, in reality the development of a redistribution program and the creation of an alternate form of government often depended on occupying the conceptual territories left behind in colonial land documents.

The particular strategic and environmental circumstances of the First Indochina War saw the emergence of various enclaves from the schizophrenic landscapes of the 1930s and 1940s and also led to the creation of new physical and conceptual spaces, although parts of the older, colonial landscape and the colonial discourse over land reform persisted. The war initiated two powerful discursive contests, one over who should govern the Mekong Delta and the othr about the forms of landscape necessary to support this governance. American advisers entered both contests as early as 1950 through their military support of the French and through several nation-building programs begun in 1953. After the 1954 Geneva Accords, they arrived in the area en masse, largely unaware of the historical reasons that helped to explain the division of the region into separate enclaves and the various attitudes to land reform.

FIG. 24. *Cái Sơn Agroville Inauguration Pamphlet, 1961. This pamphlet in Vietnamese celebrates the creation of a new "agroville" at Cái Sơn Village near Vĩnh Long. The hospital, maternity ward, high school, church, and market pictured were all common features of agrovilles and earlier settlements. Source: File 6361, Phủ Tổng Thống Đệ Nhất Công Hoa, Trung Tâm Lưu Trữ Quốc Gia II, Hồ Chí Minh City.*

The simple, unadorned truth is that in Vietnam the peasant

is the center of the piece. If we are to help him to become a useful,

self-reliant citizen, making the most of his land, and giving his

allegiance to the national government, then we must make an effort

equal to this goal.—*Wolf Ladejinsky*[1]

5 MODERNIZATION

The negotiated end to the First Indochina War at Geneva in July 1954 brought in its aftermath a rapid expansion of American activities south of the seventeenth parallel through both military and civilian channels. The broad array of military and civilian efforts sponsored by foreign governments to create a client state (an endeavor that diplomatic historians typically refer to as modernization) affected not only political culture in Vietnam but also the environment, especially in areas targeted for bases, agricultural mechanization, and especially refugee settlements. After the signing of the Geneva Accords in July 1954, the growing numbers of American advisers, the mass shipments of heavy equipment, and several hundred thousand northern Vietnamese refugees reconfigured social and physical landscapes in the Mekong Delta. The vast network of canals and the villages and war-torn plantations were subject not only to the new policies of a government led by Ngô Đình Diệm but also to the modernizing influences of the Green Revolution and American-sponsored mechanization programs. American equipment and funds flooded the Sài Gòn government; in just three years, the annual operating budget for its Ministry of Public Works and Communication (Bộ Công Chánh và Giao Thông) increased fortyfold from four million dollars in 1953 to one hundred sixty million dollars in 1957.[2]

Despite the windfall, or perhaps because of it, the relationships that developed between the United States and the Republic of Vietnam (RVN) over the next several years were contentious. Amid this weighty presence of American experts, Vietnamese leaders such as Diệm struggled to realize their own visions of development, visions often influenced by past experiences in the Bảo Đại government, in the First Indochina War, and with the colonial administration before 1945. Department chiefs repeatedly complained to their ministers and the president of severe staff shortages, unrealistic American contracting deadlines, and the hopelessly bureaucratic reporting procedures involved in using American aid funds. Meanwhile, they were forced to compete with colonial-era French companies and recently arrived American companies, which quickly moved in to fulfill some aid contracts. The private contractors were formidable competitors with Vietnamese public agencies, which struggled throughout the 1950s and the Second Indochina War to retain personnel. Changing environmental and political conditions in the field also undermined their efforts, as floods, guerrilla attacks (on people and machines), corruption, and increasing militarization frequently caused people to abandon projects. Failed canals, broken machines, and crop losses undermined not only the perceived legitimacy of American nation-building programs but ultimately the Sài Gòn government's authority over people and places that for a decade prior to 1954 had existed semi-autonomously under the domains of Việt Minh, Hòa Hảo, and Cao Đài groups.

Because the early stages of American intervention occurred in such a politically and ecologically complex environment, nation-building in this era was less an ideological campaign drafted in Washington and Sài Gòn and more a series of concrete events involving transfers of technology, bodies, and new commodities into heavily contested regions beyond the major roads, canals, cities, and airports. By following this latest procession of advisers, allied authorities, heavy equipment, troops, and refugees into the water landscape, it is possible to trace how such projects were ultimately transformed and reinterpreted by local leaders. A small but growing literature in Cold War diplomatic history draws on Vietnamese and other archival sources to question common stereotypes of the RVN as a "puppet regime." Philip Catton suggests that Diệm and other officials exercised a high degree of agency in implementing American modernization programs; on many occasions they also subverted American designs and resisted American calls for reform.[3] By traveling beyond the high-flying world of Sài Gòn politics to the water landscapes of the delta, it is possible to see how local people—refugees, tenant farmers, and provincial authorities—and local nature also sometimes subverted or resisted American programs. By following the course of land reform programs, refugee resettlement, and attempts to rehabilitate the damaged colonial-era canal system, it is perhaps easier to detect how colonial ways of seeing nature and people persisted and shaped American experiences in Vietnam.

In the United States and Europe in the late 1950s, critiques of modernization were commonplace, but they rarely went so far as to suggest that peasants or rural officials might know best how to handle such problems as land reform. Vietnam in the 1950s was the setting for one of the best-known critiques of American technical and military aid in the developing world: Graham Greene's best-seller *The Quiet American*. First published in 1955, the story captured the imagination of Americans and, by many accounts, accurately captured the mood in Sài Gòn in the mid-1950s. The fictionalized portrayal of a love triangle between a British journalist covering the First Indochina War, a Vietnamese beauty named Phương who stokes his opium pipe at the Continental Hotel, and a freshly arrived American who holds a vague position at the U.S. Embassy as a cover for his real work as a spy amounted to a controversial critique of American naiveté and arrogance.[4] Viking Press first published the book in the United States in 1956, and it became an immediate best-seller, prompting a Hollywood film adaptation with Audie Murphy in 1958. Keyes Beech, a journalist with the *Chicago Daily News* working in Saigon in 1956, recalled that "nobody was talking—nobody in the American colony there, the American community, excuse me—was talking about anything else, and it was an under-the-counter item. I don't know whether it was officially banned or not."[5] Beech's reference to the American community as a colony is a telling slip; like the *Quiet American*, it alludes to the intimate, colonial downtown landscapes run by French and cosmopolitan Vietnamese in which Americans started working in greater numbers after 1954. The slip might also suggest the relative chasm that separated the Americans, like the French before them, from most Vietnamese people. Americans stayed at the same hotels, ate at the same restaurants, and worked with many of the same Vietnamese officials as French predecessors. Likewise, their ideas about Vietnamese people and places were frequently interpreted to them by Francophone writers such as A. M. Savani, who published such texts on southern Vietnam as *Visage et images du sud Viet-Nam* in Sài Gòn in 1955.

Another popular stereotype was the American technical adviser as a tragic hero pitted against high-ranking American bureaucrats, the local elite, and a shadowy, Communist insurgency backed by the Soviet Union. *The Ugly American,* published in 1958, was also an instant best-seller at home in the United States. It portrayed the struggles of American development officers working in Southeast Asia; its heroes were the "ugly" Americans who did real, nitty-gritty work such as building dams, setting up irrigation pumps, and working closely with rural populations. Besides the external threats from the shadowy insurgency, the book suggested repeatedly that such noble nation builders were more often thwarted by senior American officials and local elites, who worried more about their image and petty rivalries than actual results.[6] The book sold over a million copies and in 1963 was adapted into a film starring Marlon Brando. This book, like *The Quiet American,* produced a pervasive narrative image of technical advisers as tragic, neutral heroes that, while a critique of American policies, nevertheless misrepresented the nuances and complexities of nation-building at the work site. Even the "ugliest" of Americans, from tractor technicians to livestock experts, moved as frequently through the downtown streets of Sài Gòn and embassy cocktail parties as they did through villages in the Mekong Delta; and often even high-level American and Vietnamese officials expressed strong critiques about nation-building's failures.

To avoid both of these popular interpretations on American intervention, one might view American nation-building programs, like nation-building in previous eras, as a real and imagined possibility space that, regardless of intention, allowed new flows of people, technology, and ideas back and forth from centers of American and Vietnamese power to rural peripheries and politically contested, liberated zones. American journeys from the comforts of French hotels, swimming pools, and lavish dinner parties attended by such personalities as Madame Ngô Đình Nhu (wife of Diệm's brother and a de facto first lady) to villages, canals, and former "killing fields" of the First Indochina War brought new flows of ideas and technology into a water environment already deeply divided by past military and ideological struggles. Project sites such as new canals and refugee settlements became important contact zones where such flows were subject to modification or even attack, as debates continued over the physical and ideological terms of development into the 1960s. This more-dispersed, situated view of nation-building not only shifts the historical gaze from the designers of specific policies to the implementers working at specific sites; but it also opens up new possibilities for local histories, the landscape, and individuals living in these areas to play into the broader narrative of modernization.

Into the Political Vacuum

After the signing of the Geneva Accords in July 1954, travel into many areas of the Mekong Delta remained severely limited for another year, as the Hòa Hảo and Cao Đài paramilitary sects remained in control of large areas and the Việt Minh evacuated thousands of troops from their strongholds in Đồng Tháp and the U Minh Forest. Through the winter of 1955, Ngô Đình Diệm's government appeared likely to fall as a coalition of paramilitary sects in the countryside and the Bình Xuyên with their extensive ties to mafia, police, and French agents in the city challenged his authority. Bernard Fall, an American journalist embedded with French and Vietnamese troops in 1954 and 1955, noted that not until June 29, 1955, when a colonel in the Vietnamese army planted the national flag on the summit of the Seven Mountains, did the nationalist government establish its presence in all of the former enclaves of these rival groups.[7] For the American press corps living in the downtown French quarter of Sài Gòn, several days of urban warfare beginning on April 28 and end-ing on May 3 served as a violent climax to what had been a months-long diplomatic and political struggle between Diệm and the sects. Just a few kilometers from rue Catinat, renamed Liberty Street, nationalist troops battled the Bình Xuyên with tanks, howitzers, and mortar fire in some of the poorest neighborhoods of Chợ Lớn. Caught in the crossfire in a square mile of densely constructed shacks and tents were thousands of northern Vietnamese refugees, who frantically fled the bullets and a rag-ing fire that soon burned some neighborhoods to the ground.[8] Not until late May, with Diệm finally in firm control of the military and with sect leaders either retreating or dead, did American discussions about nation-building in Vietnam really begin.

In the aftermath of the fighting in Sài Gòn, American advisers began working on a slate of programs organized around one issue in particular: the settlement of refugees. Because of the terms of the Geneva Accords, as well as over a decade of fighting, Vietnamese cities and towns were crowded with small tent cities housing mostly displaced rural families. Complementing the refugee problem was the near-total absence of communication networks between the Sài Gòn government and distant rural areas. Unlike in postwar Japan or Taiwan, land reform and mechanization programs could not have been easily implemented by a strong, central bureaucracy in Vietnam because its control over the grass roots existed only on paper. The early influx of American agricultural experts and American aid out into the delta countryside thus tended to concentrate on solving the refugee problem and building acceptable provincial and district administrations. While Diệm's commanders finished off the remaining pockets of sectarian resistance in May 1955, U.S. Operations Mission (USOM) advisers began traveling to inspect rural conditions for themselves. Speaking directly with tenants and landowners at various meetings, they learned just how tenuous was the Sài Gòn government's hold on power in provinces and districts that for the past several years had been under Việt Minh or sect control.

From these first few trips, some of the most insightful reports came from Wolf Ladejinsky, one of the most recognized American names in agricultural reform in Asia. Ladejinsky, born in 1899 to a Russian Jewish family that operated a flour mill in the Ukraine, fled the Soviet Union in 1921 after his family was dispossessed of all their property. He landed as an immigrant in New York City, and by 1926 he had learned enough English to attend Columbia University. He pursued a doctorate in economics before dropping out with a master's degree during the Depression. He then took a job with the Department of Agriculture and, after writing about the failures in Soviet collectivization, started writing about agricultural reform in Asia. By the end of World War II, Ladejinsky was one of the few Americans who had written and published anything on agricultural reform in Asia; thus, he played an increasingly powerful role in shaping land reform in postwar Japan and Taiwan after 1949. In his papers and memos, he became known as an ardent opponent of collectivization while at the same time arguing that governments should support smallholdings and provide reliable credit to individual farmers rather than favoring wealthy landlords and private companies.[9]

Ladejinsky had, for a brief time in late 1954, been at the center of ideological struggles in the U.S. Congress when the secretary of agriculture dismissed him after twenty years of government service on suspicion of being a member of the Communist Party. Following new security protocols that resulted from the McCarthy hearings on suspected Communists inside the government, the secretary fired Ladejinsky for having briefly worked as a Russian interpreter in New York for the Soviet trading company Amtorg in 1931.[10] After being cleared of any wrongdoing by Congress, in January 1955 Ladejinsky accepted President Eisenhower's offer of a new job to oversee land reform in Vietnam. In contrast to the relatively straightforward challenges to development work presented in *The Ugly American*, Ladejinsky's experiences in steering land reform in Vietnam point to the complexities involved. His reports, issued in a series of memos from March to June 1955, provide clear examples of the unique circumstances in Vietnam. Just a few weeks after settling in with his family in Sài Gòn, Ladejinsky ignored warnings from the Vietnamese Ministry of Agriculture against traveling in the countryside and immediately set out with an interpreter and a Vietnamese staffer from the USOM office to assess rural conditions. His first report, an account of travels to central Vietnam, was highly critical of existing State of Vietnam rent reduction programs and the behavior of Vietnamese provincial authorities, noting that the Việt Minh rent ceilings in liberated zones were significantly lower and that former Việt Minh troops showed more discipline and restraint in dealings with farmers.[11] In his first trip to the Mekong Delta, Ladejinsky traveled the main highways and visited four provinces over several days. Noting the widespread availability of land in the delta compared with central Vietnam and the precipitous drop in lands under cultivation, Ladejinsky was most surprised by the "political and administrative vacuum in the countryside," where provincial and district officials had almost no communication with villagers more than a few kilometers distant from their offices. He noted a "woeful lack of a reasonably authoritative administrative machine and a political stagnation that leaves the countryside wide open to the enemies of the national government."[12] This report reached Washington over a month later just as the street fighting erupted in Sài Gòn.

After Diệm's defeat of the sects, Ladejinsky returned to the delta to assess the potential for initiating land reform programs. His trip to Cà Mau, the Geneva-designated disembarkation point for thousands of Việt Minh soldiers based at U Minh, was perhaps the first by any American civilian since the signing of the Geneva Accords. There he found former Việt Minh officials running the provincial government and levying taxes at old Việt Minh rates rather than Diệm's decreed 15–25 percent. In the middle of this trip, Ladejinsky's small group was required to join a five-car procession led by the minister of agrarian reform to several delta provincial towns. This much larger procession was greeted by brass bands and lavish luncheons, the streets lined with gold and red-striped flags. Ladejinsky noted that the arranged meetings that followed the luncheons were with the government officials and wealthy landlords, who were dressed in "impeccable white sharkskin" and contrasted sharply with the mass of peasants at the same gatherings.[13] Despite the intimidating spectacle of the "white sharkskin," tenants emboldened by years of fighting with the Việt Minh and the absence of landlords spoke in frank terms without hesitation or deference to the wealthy visitors. Ladejinsky observed that both tenants and landowners spoke of the inevitability of massive land sales and the dissolution of the old estates. They differed mainly on the terms; and in one case a province chief "got carried away" and said that one of the ultimate goals of the national government was land redistribution. He then tried to recover, chiding the tenants: "Don't you go home beating your breasts and telling the other tenants that the land is theirs."[14] Ladejinsky called for USOM and its parent agency, the Foreign Operations Administration, to initiate an emergency loan program of thirty million dollars to finance loans to tenants, and he suggested immediate commitments in material aid such as flying in ten thousand water buffaloes from Thailand to replace the tens of thousands of work animals lost during the fighting. As with the previous report, this one was not transmitted to Washington for two more months. Ladejinsky waited while little was done by the United States or the Vietnamese government to remedy what he saw as an emergency in the countryside.

The Vietnamese government's position on land reform in the delta, especially that of Diệm, is difficult to ascertain based solely on the documents. Diệm was limited by violent challenges to his authority before May 1955 and his need to form political alliances with Vietnamese elites, many of whom were the wealthiest landowners in Cochinchina. Many Vietnamese with more administrative experience than Diệm, such as former State of Vietnam prime minister Nguyễn Văn Tâm, had just regained massive tracts of land in the delta region and repeatedly refused to accommodate tenant demands. In one of his early proclamations, Diệm actually relaxed a 1953 policy fixing land rent at 15 percent and allowed it to fluctuate between 15 and 25 percent. The proclamation also reaffirmed earlier policies to create written, regulated tenant contracts.[15] According to Ladejinsky, this decision incensed farmers, who at the very least expected that the new prime minister would continue the 1953 rent ceiling and perhaps match or exceed Việt Minh rates to gain support in the former liberated zones. Ladejinsky

not only criticized these measures in his reports to the Foreign Operations
Administration but also had the privilege of speaking directly with Diệm
on multiple occasions about land reform and the refugee situation in the
countryside. On one such meeting on June 1, 1955, Ladejinsky attempted
to persuade Diệm to convene a national conference on land reform and to
abandon his failing contract program in favor of land redistribution and
sales, but the prime minister refused. Diệm appeared to show only slight
interest in Ladejinsky's comment that to date nothing real had been done
to permanently settle several hundred thousand refugees still living in
temporary camps.[16]

Refugee Settlers

While Ladejinsky's campaign for land reforms continued to linger on
the margins of discussions with other Americans and Diệm, refugee
resettlement emerged as the one issue on which Americans and Vietnamese began working together on specific nation-building schemes.[17] The
first and largest settlement, soon referred to as Cái Sắn (for a creek that
drained one side of the area), is especially instructive because it reveals
the complexities of nation-building as applied to a specific landscape with
its own unique history and ecology. The relatively abundant records in
both Vietnamese and American archives suggest that it was taken seriously by both sides as a potential model for nation-building. On the
surface, Cái Sắn's rectilinear grid of canals and its schools, clinics, and
infrastructure upgrades might appear as a fitting example of what political anthropologist James Scott calls high modernism, a project born out
of a "self-confidence about scientific and technical progress, the expansion of production, the growing satisfaction of human needs, the mastery
of nature (including human nature), and, above all, the rational design of
social order commensurate with the scientific understanding of natural
laws."[18] However, upon closer inspection, there were highly unmodern,
nonrational features built into such projects. From its creation in 1956,
Cái Sắn undermines assumptions about the central role that Americans
played in nation-building and the extent to which American ideas of
modernization, the kind of high modernism Scott is referring to, traveled from the downtown offices of aid agencies in Washington and Sài
Gòn to the refugee field offices, settler villages, and tractor depots in the
hinterlands.[19]

While Americans can be credited with delivering an unprecedented quantity of new equipment, weapons, and money into the region—actions that had substantial environmental and social repercussions—their role in the design of projects such as Cái Sắn and later programs such as agrovilles (*khu trù mật*) and strategic hamlets (*ấp chiến lược*) was limited. And the many instances of corruption, factionalism in the provincial administrations, and frequent episodes of criminal activity on lonely delta highways limited even the Sài Gòn government's role. American advisers such as Ladejinsky played more of a supporting role as enablers rather than as architects of such programs. What was planned at Cái Sắn thus grew out of many different, some not-so-modern ideas and circumstances. In particular, past designs from the colonial era and earlier Vietnamese ideas about settlement on the frontier, ideas such as the southward march (*nam tiến*) or agricultural garrisons (*đồn điền*), figured heavily in the design of Cái Sắn.

Though the first evidence of plans for a refugee settlement at Cái Sắn appears in a Vietnamese memo released on November 24, 1955, the location in the Long Xuyên Quadrangle and its design strongly resembled the *casier* settlements attempted in the same region beginning in the early 1930s and culminating in the *casier tonkinois* (see chapter 3). Like Cái Sắn, these earlier projects involved construction of a grid of canals surrounded by an encircling flood dike. The 1944–45 *casier tonkinois* settlements were just thirty kilometers from the southern end of the Cái Sắn settlement. From the economic and political reasons for the earlier projects—alleviating severe poverty and preventing peasants from siding with the Communists—to even the notion of moving in northern Vietnamese migrants, Cái Sắn had a precedent in the *casier tonkinois*. The area of *terres abandonnées* chosen for Cái Sắn had already been legally designated for refugee settlements by the Vichy-era Decoux regime. In 1942 the governor-general had outlined a plan to resettle some 750,000 northern farmers into the *terres abandonnées,* and the colonial government had already begun the work of pressuring absentee landlords to accept government-imposed terms for rental and possible sale of their land.[20]

Another set of influences on project designs was the colonial-era experiences of Vietnamese leaders such as Diệm. From the political and economic crises of the 1930s, especially during the politically liberal years of the Popular Front, they staked out various positions on "the agricultural crisis" that continued to shape their attitudes in the 1950s. American adviser and CIA agent Edward Lansdale recalled that almost every time he visited Diệm in his office, he was "deep in the study of some new program, often of vast dimensions." The Vietnamese president was known to be personally interested in the settlement schemes, his desk often covered in maps. Since his days as a province chief in the 1920s, Diệm encouraged peasant settlement on empty lands and supported calls for reforms in the 1930s.[21]

Finally, with no real field studies begun in the first few years after 1954, nation-building in Vietnam depended on the stacks of technical reports and field data that had accumulated in colonial offices such as the Department of Public Works since the 1880s. As Benedict Anderson shows in *Imagined Communities,* colonial maps, museums, and census projects aided the reordering of colonial subjects at the beginning of colonial rule; colonial-era reports and studies likewise influenced postcolonial schemes. Faced with continuing resistance in former Việt Minh areas and a political vacuum in the countryside, the Diệm government constructed several key feasibility studies from existing colonial engineering data and old property maps.[22] Diệm even relied on several French colonial experts who stayed on after 1954 as consultants with a French technical aid mission.

Even American support for Vietnamese nation-building projects had precedents before 1954. Americans working in Hà Nội supported a resettlement and pacification effort in the Red River Delta from 1953 to 1954. Following Eisenhower's election and the end of the Korean War, USOM's agricultural and land reform advisers in Hà Nội pushed the Associated State of Vietnam (ASV) to engage in a demonstration project in the heavily contested Red River Delta. The Đồng Quan "new life" (*đời mới*) hamlet was located off the Nam Định Highway (Highway 1 in present-day Hà Tây Province). In a matter of months beginning in early 1953, work crews with newly contributed American bulldozers and heavy equipment razed an existing village center and constructed a grid of paved streets lined with concrete buildings and an open-air market. They installed a water-pumping station for irrigation of surrounding fields, and they added a perimeter road and a small airstrip just inside a perimeter fence dotted with watchtowers—in design, the settlement resembled a military base. USOM advisers even planned for visits to the site by Vietnamese and American dignitaries, including Vice President Nixon.[23] A Vietnamese official visiting the project in 1953 later disclosed in a memoir that the shiny new buildings and well-supplied market disguised what remained a dire situation for farmers at Đồng Quan. The project did little to redistribute property, and the Việt Minh moved freely through the town by day or night. They did not attack it because they needed the market to sell black-market goods and to find reliable guides into Hà Nội. Meanwhile,

Franco-Vietnamese troops refused to attack the town because they feared jeopardizing American military support.[24] Beginning with Đồng Quan, American advisers likely figured out that a well-functioning settlement might in fact have little to do with the logic or modernizing technologies involved in such plans.

Local, Vietnamese, and American institutional histories reveal that the actions of Vietnamese leaders such as Ngô Đình Diệm were especially significant for the circumstances of nation-building, as these individuals translated and interpreted between past and present as well as among American, Vietnamese, and French communities. With a lengthy report issued by the secretary of state for land reform on November 24, 1955, Diệm unofficially presented Americans with a plan at Cái Sắn to open up some seventy-seven thousand hectares of land in the Long Xuyên Quadrangle to roughly one hundred thousand refugees. The plan's primary purpose, not unlike the earlier *casier tonkinois,* was the "permanent implantation" of northern Vietnamese refugees into rural areas that had long been abandoned (*đất bỏ hoang*).[25]

Another aspect of the project that contradicts some basic assumptions about the failures of modernization, especially if one looks at later projects in Vietnam such as the "agroville," is that Cái Sắn was economically and politically a success. In several stages, refugees moved into the area and established permanent, viable settlements. The success of the model, at least in the unique area in which it was situated, continued to attract interest even after 1975. In 1979 the Socialist Republic of Vietnam's Ministry of Water Resources drafted plans to build new flood control structures there and further expand the network of canals.[26]

The problem with Cái Sắn in the context of nation-building was not its eco-logic within an already highly altered, plantation landscape but the political and economic terms of land tenure linking settlers with the central government. A map produced by the Vietnamese Land Reform Commission and subsequently transmitted to American advisers in January 1956 suggests the government's intense push to render former terra incognita legible through a highly rationalized canal infrastructure. New canals were labeled in ascending numerical order in one province and ascending alphabetical order in another (fig. 25). Along this new grid, land lots were measured in 20 × 1000 meter lots perpendicular to the canal bank.

Of the thirty thousand settlers who moved to Cái Sắn in 1956, all except six hundred were Catholic; and rather than subdivide Cái Sắn into

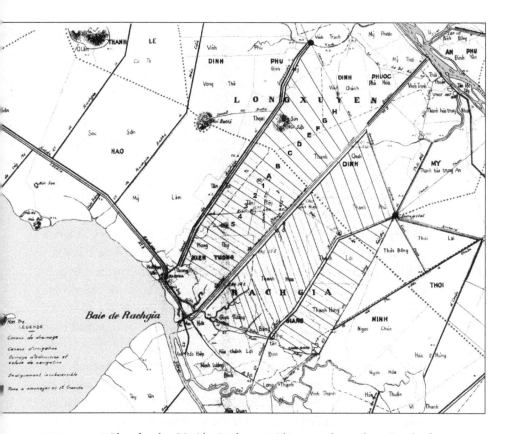

FIG. 25. *1956 Plan for the Cái Sắn Settlement. This map shows the network of canals planned for over roughly 77,000 hectares in the Long Xuyên Quadrangle. The northeast-southwest line running through the center of this area was the Bassac–Rạch Sỏi Canal and the main highway connecting Rạch Giá with Long Xuyên and the rest of the delta. The numbers 1–5 and the letters A–F (added by author) indicate the first series of canals dug in 1956. The other lines running parallel indicate planned canals, many of which were dug in the successive stages of this settlement after 1957. Source: "27 Jan 1956. L. Cardinaux, Chief, Resettlement Division. Cai-San (Long Xuyen-Rach Gia Project)," box 13, U.S. Operation Mission, Vietnam, Security Classified Files, RG 469, National Archives and Records Administration, Center 2, College Park, MD.*

secularly administered villages, the Commissariat General for Refugees divided it into parishes, each parish under the authority of a priest who was to administer aid payments and the sharing of equipment from a central church to be constructed on each canal. On Canal 1, a few kilometers south of the project headquarters and district town Tân Hiệp, Father Nguyễn

Ba Lộc presided over a parish of 2,500 persons. He was the government's main liaison, and his parish managed distribution of food and tool rations, registered settler families on individual plots, and managed their labor contributions to building the canals. There was only one non-Catholic settlement, which was under secular authority.[27]

Instead of guiding nation-building at Cái Sắn, Americans spent much of their time interpreting it to themselves and American taxpayers. USOM advisers sent regular updates to senior officials in Washington, and American journalists occasionally wrote stories on nation-building exercises. Robert Alden, writing in the *New York Times* on February 9, 1956, announced the arrival of the first wave of refugees at Cái Sắn. His headline presented the project as a frontier tale: "535 Refugees in South Vietnam Turn the Earth in Vital Project; They Dig Canal That Not Only Will Give Them a New Life, but Also Will Enable Settlement of Foes to Red Penetration." Even in such favorable stories, however, there were continuing indications of trouble. Alden reported that Wolf Ladejinsky, the best-known American involved in Vietnamese land reform, had been fired from USOM for violating a relatively obscure conflict-of-interest rule. Alden credited the American (with no attributed source) for working with Diệm on the "nucleus of the idea" for Cái Sắn and added that Ladejinsky would stay on as a personal adviser to Diệm. Locating Americans at the center of nation-building, even inside the Vietnamese government, Alden concluded the article with the news that the United States would provide one million dollars' worth of tractors, plows, and harrows to the project.[28]

Despite such stories and Ladejinsky's sudden move to the Diệm administration, American involvement in Cái Sắn remained strong though mostly peripheral through 1956. Advisers regularly visited Cái Sắn and conveyed an optimistic appraisal of development efforts. Leland Barrows, chief of USOM-Vietnam, reported in a field trip on July 16–17, 1956, that the refugees had made great strides in bringing former abandoned areas back under cultivation. The rows of newly transplanted fields contrasted sharply with the surrounding, empty plains. An estimated 40,000 refugees were expected to arrive by the end of the year, and already some 12,000 hectares had been planted. The former village of Tân Hiệp, once a small roadside village, had grown in several months into a boomtown with over ten thousand people and a new project headquarters for Vietnamese officials and equipment hangars for the hundred new tractors that arrived in March and April. In his report to Washington, Barrows noted the extensive activities planned by Vietnamese ministries and suggested

only a few areas for American aid: new schools and clinics; Paris green
(lead arsenate) and other chemical pesticides; renovation of two nearby
airstrips; and widening of the main highway connecting the project office
to Rạch Giá.[29]

By October 1956, however, Americans expressed mounting concerns
about increasing tensions between the settlers and the government. Since
January 1956 the government had provided refugees with a monthly
allowance of food and funds as well as tools and other necessities; this
led farmers to believe that they would receive title to the land they had
rendered into fields along the edges of canals dug by hand. On August
29, 1956, however, Diệm issued an order that caught American advisers
and the settlers by surprise: in two days all authority over each village
would shift from the parish to a provisional village council; priests were to
cease all administrative functions and assume only spiritual guidance over
their parishes. The order also stipulated that refugees would no longer be
considered to have a special status and would instead be considered regular
citizens, thus eliminating all special privileges to monthly aid. Finally, the
order reversed earlier intimations that refugees would become owners of
the land outright and reiterated that the refugees would be required to
sign tenant contracts with the owners of the land where their plots were
located.[30]

The order triggered protests in the villages as farmers reacted
angrily to the news that their months of hard labor had only resulted in
their becoming tenants subject to land rents and other terms fixed by
landlords. Government authorities, traveling from Tân Hiệp to villages
nearby on Canal 1 and Canal A, met so many angry villagers that they
called in military troops to impose martial law and prevent villagers
from circulating beyond checkpoints at each canal intersection. In
searching for the reasons why Diệm acted so suddenly, the American
field representative suggested Communist infiltration and sympathies
among the entirely Catholic villages, noting that the refugees had come
from Communist-controlled areas of the Red River Delta and that they
had organized a protest denouncing Madame Nhu (who they alleged had
recently smuggled a fortune into secret accounts in France) on the eve of
"an important Communist holiday."[31] As tensions mounted between the
priests and secular authorities, the rumors flew. American advisers had
been troubled since the first few months of the tractors arriving at Cái
Sắn by rumors that the new machines were being sent first to plow lands
owned by the minister of agrarian reform and "resident minister" for Cái

Sẵn, Nguyễn Văn Thời.[32] Even as American advisers planned for a potential visit to Cái Sẵn by Vice President Richard Nixon during his July 6–9 visit to Sài Gòn, they expressed concern about rumors of protests and about the detention of twenty known "agitators" at Cái Sẵn, who were to be released a few weeks after all festivities commemorating the "double seven" (July 7, 1954) creation of the southern Vietnamese government had ended.[33]

All shipments of money and rice to the approximately thirty thousand refugees stopped in September and October, and government authorities backed by national security forces threatened to force every family to sign the new contracts. During a meeting in Father Lộc's parish on Canal 1 to voice concerns, the priest claimed that Diệm, in an April 1956 visit, had promised to give the land to the refugees provided that after one or two years of work turning it into viable fields and canals they started to pay taxes on it. This had been a traditional incentive for frontier settlement in the Mekong Delta since King Gia Long's rule (1802–20). State authorities, particularly provincial representatives and project staff, however, expected to implement tenant contracts modeled on earlier ASV edicts. Father Lộc angrily demanded to know why such arrangements were being forced on his parishioners. The villagers refused to let the officials leave the village until a company of soldiers arrived to escort them back to their headquarters in Tân Hiệp.[34]

Although the standoff was eventually resolved when the settlers agreed to sign tenant contracts in return for continuing government financial support and promises to arrange land sales at fixed rates, the conflict illustrates a critical problem that remained largely unresolved in the early years of Diệm's rule. Even with relatively massive amounts of American foreign aid and persons such as Ladejinsky urging immediate land transfers to small farmers, Diệm and other officials in his cabinet continued to push colonial-era schemes that reworked the water landscape but preserved the rights of landowners, especially the wealthiest, over lands brought into cultivation with canals and other infrastructure provided by others. Even though Cái Sẵn continued after the protests to be an economic and political success story in an otherwise-dismal history of such projects, fundamental differences between individual farmers and the state over the specifics of building fields, canals, and villages continued. What is perhaps most surprising, in light of contemporary historical characterizations of the northern, Catholic refugees as pawns of a staunchly Catholic president, is that even in the relatively peaceful days of 1956, deep divisions existed between the mostly Catholic refugees and their priests, on the one hand,

and politically connected landowners and government authorities, on the other.

Just a few weeks after the protests at Cái Sắn, while government police followed up on their own accusations of fraud and corruption among priests such as Father Lộc, Diệm finally acceded to a program to limit the size of landholdings and to sell land at fixed prices to tenants.[35] On October 22, 1956, he issued Ordinance 57, which in essence addressed the following three issues: it effectively limited the size of landholdings in the delta region to one hundred hectares; it guaranteed tenants already working such lands the first rights to buy it at fixed interest rates and in installments over multiple years; and it established the government's role in purchasing surplus lands from landowners and then managing the resale to tenants. Wolf Ladejinsky, Diệm's personal adviser on land reform, likely played a key role in the drafting of the ordinance, as the above stipulations corresponded closely with previous reform programs he had developed in Taiwan and Japan.[36] In keeping with Ladejinsky's claim that the biggest deterrents to the program's success were the Communists, David Elliott's history of revolutionary activity in Mỹ Tho Province confirms that the measures presented the first significant challenge to older, land-to-the-tiller campaigns in the liberated zones. He cites one village cadre who recalled many tenants cheering Ngô Đình Diệm upon hearing about the reforms.[37] These reforms appear to have been most successful in locations such as Cái Sắn where Communist groups had little sway and government officials worked under close supervision after the protests and investigations.

Venturing into Rebel Terrain

After some measure of success at Cái Sắn, which confirmed his government's authority over new villages of mostly Catholic refugees, Diệm embarked on a far more ambitious plan to extend government authority into two of the most bitterly contested and environmentally challenging regions in the delta, Đồng Tháp and U Minh. After many meetings with USOM staff and Vietnamese officials in various departments, Diệm announced the formation of a Land Settlement General Commission (Tổng-Ủy Phủ Dinh Điền) on April 23, 1957, to carry out a series of reclamation and settlement projects, including four "special projects" at Cái Sắn, U Minh, Đồng Tháp, and the central highlands. He named the director of the refugee commission, Bùi Văn Lương, as head of the new program and explained that Cái Sắn and the other three sites would also serve as Agricultural Development Centers (Công Trường Khuếch Trương Nông Nghiệp), centers for disseminating new agricultural technologies and offering agricultural extension programs. The settlements came to be referred to as Dinh Điền, an indirect reference to the Nguyễn-dynasty term *đồn điền*. This new wave in refugee settlements featured an Agricultural Mechanization Campaign (Quốc-Gia Nông-Cụ Cơ-Giới-Cuộc) supported by several hundred tractors and tillers as well as thousands of newly arrived diesel engines used as outboard motors and water pumps.[38] Whereas Cái Sắn was organized in parishes of Catholic refugees, the new projects were built for veterans of the national army and the security police. Not only were the projects targeted at eliminating Communist influence in the former liberated zones, but they were also intended as bold measures to increase technological development in a countryside that Diệm noted had been "retarded and dominated by foreigners" for so many years. On the third "double seven" anniversary, in July 1957, he explained Dinh Điền in the following terms:

> Parallel with the establishment of the General Commission and the Agricultural Development Centers, the president has ordered the Army of the Republic of Vietnam [ARVN] and the Civil Guard to maneuver troops close to the end of their service to the Settlement Centers . . . to create Agricultural Centers and find land that is agreeable, to organize their own defense, to clear the land by means they already possess, and to erect houses so that gradually their families may join them.[39]

In reality, the projects borrowed heavily from older, colonial plans for *casiers* in the same troubled areas. Diệm drew upon familiar, Vietnamese ideas to explain such projects, but his land development commissioner, Bùi Văn Lương, worked closely with USOM staff and other foreign advisers. Plans for the settlements at U Minh and Đồng Tháp were largely drafted from advance project reports produced in the early 1940s. The former chief engineer of irrigation, P. C. Jammé, even returned to Vietnam as a consultant in 1957 to assist Vietnamese engineers and planners in interpreting his office's pre-1945 research.

The return of a former colonial, the chief engineer of irrigation, to work in Vietnam after independence was part of a broader trend in the late 1950s in which former employees of government and colonial services joined private consulting firms to undertake projects in postcolonial countries. As Dutch hydraulic engineers returned to Sukarno's Indonesia and British engineers returned to Nehru's India, a growing cohort of French, Japanese, Israeli, Taiwanese, Dutch, and other nationals joined Americans and Vietnamese in Sài Gòn to consult on individual contracts, most funded by the United States through the USOM and some funded through the United Nations and foreign embassies. Jammé joined a French firm founded in 1954 that specialized in irrigation and water engineering. As a consultant with the Société grenobloise d'études et d'applications hydrauliques (SOGREAH), he returned to Vietnam in 1957 on a contract paid for by the French Technical and Economic Cooperation Mission in Sài Gòn to investigate the Dinh Điền project at U Minh.[40] Two other French engineers accepted a similar contract to make recommendations for development of Đồng Tháp.

Before investigating these two projects more closely, it is important to recognize their embeddedness not only in a local political discourse on nation-building in Vietnam but also in a broader, international discourse on modernization shaped in part by the actions and policies of the United States. Three major changes occurred in this era that had long-term consequences for nation-building and the water landscape in the Mekong Delta: the promotion of public-private partnerships for design and construction of dams and other hydro projects, the collapse of the Chinese Nationalists on the mainland in 1949, and the creation of international agencies to oversee regional and river basin development schemes. In the hydraulic-engineering community, the completion of Hoover Dam in 1936 brought international recognition to the United States Bureau of Reclamation (BoR) dam designers and to the six private companies that carried out most of the work. As Indian and Nationalist Chinese engineers traveled to visit the new facilities, the BoR sent engineers to consult on projected dams in such places as the Damodar Valley in India and the Yangtze Valley in China. In an interview looking back on the bureau's foreign training programs, former commissioner Floyd Dominy described them as "breaking ground for U.S. companies."[41] With the People's Army victory over the Chinese Nationalists in 1949, President Truman quickly redirected U.S. interests in the Pacific from the "great market" of China to its peripheries, Northeast and Southeast Asia. Under his Point IV Program, a plan to encourage modernization in developing nations, Truman ordered the BoR to commence dam surveys and other technical assistance projects overseas. As part of a World Reconnaissance Survey, by late 1950 the BoR's investigational teams in Thailand, the

Philippines, and Indonesia had identified several dozen sites for irrigation and hydroelectric projects.[42] The third important change that occurred in the 1950s was the creation of new, international agencies charged with supporting infrastructure development in international river basins and in individual countries. The U.N. Economic Commission for Asia and the Far East (ECAFE) was the primary conduit for channeling funds from donor nations (and many ex-colonial engineers from these countries) to specific projects. Set up in 1947 with headquarters in Shanghai, the agency moved to Bangkok in 1949, where it began coordinating studies for projects especially in Southeast Asia.[43]

These events converged to produce new, transnational flows of engineers, project ideas, and investment capital into areas such as the Mekong Delta and the Mekong Valley. One of the more noteworthy spectacles in 1957 was the establishment of the Mekong Committee. Created by ECAFE and supported by several years of BoR surveys, the new agency was headquartered in Bangkok and charged with coordinating the development of a cascade of hydroelectric dams and irrigation schemes in the valley from the Chinese border southward to the Mekong Delta. In December 1957, an all-star cast of international engineers led by General Raymond A. Wheeler, former chief engineer of the U.S. Army Corps of Engineers, set out on a river tour of projected dam sites. Accompanying the American engineer-general were some of the most powerful figures in hydropolitics: Kanwar Sain, chairman of India's Central Water and Power Commission; John W. McCammon, former general manager of Quebec Hydro; G. Duval, director, SOGREAH, France; and Yutaka Kubota, president of the Nippon Koei Company, Japan. At a press conference following the tours, General Wheeler described their trip down the river as a modern-day version of the first French surveys of the Mississippi in the seventeenth century: "There were no maps of the country, we had to make them. Nobody had any data on river flow, or even any idea how to keep data. What I saw was a truly virgin river. Such sights disappeared in our country long before I was born."[44] Besides the fact that the river had been surveyed and explored extensively, notably by French adventurers in the 1860s, the spectacle signaled a very different kind of beginning in 1957: the "opening" of the river and a violently contested region as a place for private foreign companies to make money. Both SOGREAH and Nippon Koei thrived and expanded because of contracts funded by the Mekong Committee, USOM, and other sources.

This turn of events, the invitation of private international (and transnational) firms to undertake the work of nation-building and the signaling by the United States and its allies of a willingness to protect such projects militarily if necessary, produced a new gold rush for private companies, especially newly formed companies in Japan, Taiwan, and Korea, that were willing to accept the security risks. The establishment of the Mekong Committee in 1957 and the further commitment of the United States economically and militarily in the region produced a second construction boom in Indochina not unlike the colonial boom that resulted in creation of the delta's major canal and roadway infrastructure built by private companies from 1879 to 1930 (see chapter 1). Comparing these two very different boom periods, what was similar in both was an alignment of powerful commercial interests in their home countries with a more liberal political belief in the civilizing mission.

Organizations such as the Mekong Committee communicated the idea not only that modernization was a morally defensible position but that it opened up areas formerly dominated by enterprises from a single nation— France, Japan, the United States—ideally, at least, to the lowest bidder. Although U.S. corporations received a predictably large share of such contracts, a closer inspection of the bidding process shows that even U.S. firms were becoming increasingly multi- or transnational in their response to such projects located in Asia. A USOM document drafted in Sài Gòn titled "Japanese Technicians for Resettlement Project 030–82–075" shows that even contracts opened to American companies for bidding often involved specific requirements for minimal numbers of Japanese and other foreign staff. All three companies that bid for the contract included twenty-two Japanese personnel, to be paid approximately six thousand dollars each, and four to seven American personnel, to be paid approximately twenty thousand dollars each. The winning company, U.S. Consultants, Inc. of Los Angeles, beat two competing companies by charging significantly less overhead, as its American personnel came from the Tokyo branch office instead of the United States. Subsequent exchanges between the firm and USOM over security clearance for U.S. staff reveals another important aspect of the contract. The Americans employed by U.S. Consultants in Tokyo were mostly Japanese Americans. The American selected to manage the 1957 project at Cái Sắn was thirty-seven-year-old Saburo Sugitani, born in 1920 in Huntington Park, California, and educated at Los Angeles City College before the internment of Japanese Americans ended his studies in 1942. After additional study at Berkeley, he joined the Tokyo office of U.S. Consultants in 1951, where he worked as an inspector-engineer and administrator on construction contracts in Japan.[45]

Given the increasing flows of foreign experts, the relative successes at Cái Sắn, and the growing budget for new projects supplied largely by the United States, Diệm responded by sending an advance team of engineers and equipment to two of the troubled regions in the delta. Vietnamese memos on the special projects reflect the same language being used by the Mekong Committee at the time, that of massive new water control structures "stabilizing" or "harmonizing" a local environment that had been devastated and upset by past struggles.[46] A 1960 booklet highlighting the government's achievements in irrigation with pictures of recently finished dikes, pumping stations, and canals likewise contrasted the government's "concretization" of the local landscape with the Việt Minh's scorched-earth tactics.[47] However, as reports on the projects at Đồng Tháp and U Minh show, the introduction of dredges, canals, and other works into the relatively fragile, flood-prone wetlands was far more disruptive than harmonizing or stabilizing. The environmental failures that followed many efforts in both locations may have increased rather than decreased the appeal of the Việt Minh.

At U Minh, both Diệm and American advisers realized the strategic importance of "winning the peace" in this former stronghold of the Việt Minh's Military Region 9; but from the early planning stages for this settlement both groups failed to overcome the intertwined political and ecological challenges to state authority here. According to Commissioner Lương, development and irrigation here needed to be "immediately viable and also future oriented"; however, from the beginning the project was repeatedly hamstrung by poor knowledge of local conditions and controversial responses to a local population that had for over a decade largely supported the Việt Minh in a liberated zone.[48] Diệm's most controversial intervention was to populate the settlement with ethnic-Khmer veterans of the national army. The move upset not only the locals living in U Minh but also the Khmer veterans. As small attacks and Việt Minh traffic increased in the western border region of Đồng Tháp, Diệm was concerned that native-born Khmer veterans might either desert to the Việt Minh or return to Cambodia.[49]

The Sài Gòn government's approach to the peat forest at U Minh was no less controversial. Military commanders of the province, one a former Việt Minh officer, persuaded the Land Development Commission to dredge two canals through the center of the forest, cutting it into quadrants, and to post decrees for all inhabitants of the forest to settle along its edge on border canals. Anyone remaining would be considered a rebel.[50] Thus, from the beginning at U Minh, the planned settlement resembled the rectilinear grid of Cái Sắn and past *casier* projects, but in practice it amounted to a coordinated military assault on the wetland forest, piercing it with canals.

As the first groups of Khmer soldiers and their families arrived in the summer of 1957, problems surfaced almost immediately. A small American dredge named "U Minh" and several bulldozers on loan from Cái Sắn created part of the canal grid for 660 families (2,696 persons) to settle north of one of the forest's border canals, Ranh Hạt Canal (fig. 26). With seventeen additional canals planned, the settlement was scheduled to receive 3,000 more families (15,000 persons) within three years.[51] By October, however, it was clear that water conditions in the canals would not support good rice harvests. In his capacity as a consultant with SOGREAH, Jammé visited the area in October 1957 with the Vietnamese director of irrigation to inspect work on the settlement. In his report, he described settlers digging the branching canals by hand and using newly donated water buffalo—part of the aid project—to stir up the layer of peat along the banks and wash it downstream. Also, because the area to the north of the settlement was still forest, many farmers preferred hunting and collecting wood there to growing rice. Instead of living within the bulldozed plots between the canals, many chose to roam the forest, harvesting the cajeput trees and selling them off as charcoal. Witnessing this rapid decimation of the forest, Jammé advised the government to immediately relocate the families. Also, the American dredge U Minh was stalled and waiting for spare parts, having been damaged by the dense roots and ancient trees submerged in the peat.[52]

The relatively prolonged demise of the U Minh settlement over the next year and a half speaks to the multiple failures of the Sài Gòn government to understand and respond to the interconnected political, economic, and ecological challenges at the edge of its authority in the water landscape. Far from the gaze of Sài Gòn officials and far from any sizable military bases, boundaries between government and rebel spheres became as muddied as the waters. One American visiting the site before work began on the settlements noted with alarm that members of the Civil Guard and the army, including many former Việt Minh officers, had regularly engaged in private business with rebel groups in the forest to manufacture and sell charcoal from the cut wood.[53] As individual members of the provincial

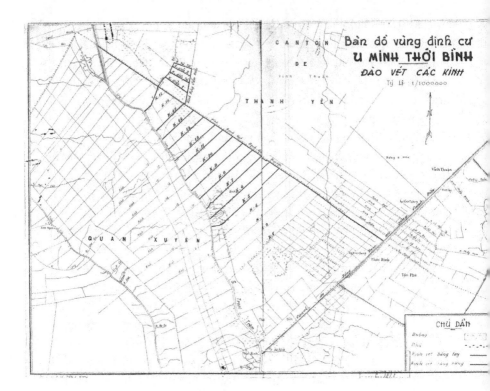

FIG. 26. *U Minh Settlement. This plan shows several sections of settlements in the U Minh region. A major east-west canal, Ranh Hạt Canal, bisects a portion of the forested area of U Minh Thượng. The Ranh Hạt Canal formed both drainage canal and dike on the southern border of the forest. The new grids of canals and settlements also covered the important intersection of creeks and canals at Thới Bình, indicated in the bottom center. Source: Khu Thủy Nông, "Đào Vét Các Kinh Nhỏ và Kinh Ranh Hạt Thuộc Vùng U Minh Thới Bình," 1957, file C18/1, Bộ Giáo Thông Công Chánh, Trung Tâm Lưu Trữ Quốc Gia II, Hồ Chí Minh City.*

government and military continued to forge ties to targeted rebel groups, conditions for Americans and government engineers grew more and more unsafe. The chief engineer of public works declared the U Minh region completely off-limits for dredging in 1958 after newly organized guerrilla groups ambushed the dredge "Cần Thơ" on the Sông Trẹm Canal, killing the captain and critically wounding the chief surveyor. At Canal 5 on Ranh Hạt, a battle erupted between the army troops and guerrillas, who retreated into the forest. The chief engineer rejected requests for equipment and engineers, stating that he "would not send his staff off to die."[54] Meanwhile, flooding in the half-finished grid threatened to ruin the several thousand people who had moved there in 1957.[55]

In February 1959, political and environmental conditions had deteriorated so much that Commissioner Lương convened a meeting with President Diệm, a USOM representative, and several of the foreign consulting engineers who had been involved with the project.[56] The winter harvest in Cà Mau was largely ruined by flooding, and to keep settlers from moving, Diệm's cabinet minister authorized immediate payments in cash equivalent to several months' salary in the army to those who stayed at the settlement. The agricultural centers had flooded in October, ruining the rice harvest; and in January, as the dry season progressed, saltwater began to intrude into the canals from the sea.[57] Salty and brackish water seeped through parched, peat soil and caused some embankments to dissolve. Foreign advisers cited other examples of irrigation projects in peat soils in Holland, the United States, and Israel; but in none of these places did farmers have to contend with a six-month dry season and a dramatic reversal in water flow. Unlike the dense, marine clay common in the delta, peat acted as a sponge and soaked up saltwater. Only a peat layer kept wet by freshwater, not drained by canals, could prevent salt intrusion.[58]

The Americans, other foreign consultants, and Vietnamese engineers agreed to terminate the project at U Minh. It is instructive to look at their solution to the growing political instability in the region: forest preserves. Following Jammé's advice from his 1957 visit, Vietnamese engineers drew up plans to fence off areas that Jammé had noted might be more valuable as inundated peat, as a "vast freshwater reservoir," rather than as drained farmland.[59] Rice agriculture was to be encouraged along the major streams and transport canals, with the rest of U Minh protected as a forest preserve. The map in figure 27 indicates three preserves intended to protect the freshwater mangroves of cajeput, as well as several coastal reserves to protect saltwater mangroves.[60] This particular response, drawing up forest enclosures and separating spaces for settlement along deeper-flowing waterways, can be read as a retreat from rebel-controlled portions of old Việt Minh enclaves. In the wake of rising guerrilla aggression, government officials retreated to the water's edge while attempting to prevent others from traveling through the porous borders beyond market towns and forts into terra incognita.

It was precisely the porosity of borders that focused Vietnamese and American attention on the flooded basin of Đồng Tháp. In March 1957, a Vietnamese military commander overseeing a small settlement project in

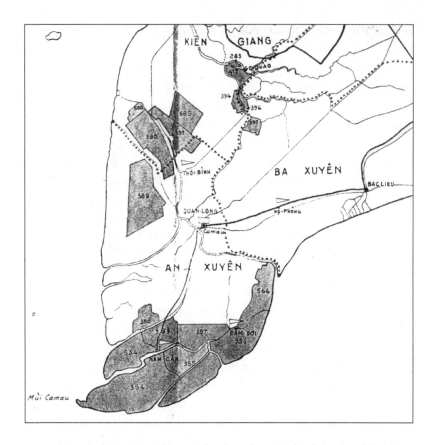

FIG. 27. *U Minh Forest Preserves. The plan shows three areas slated for forest preserves at U Minh Thượng and U Minh Hạ as proposed first in 1943 and again in 1957. Each conservation area was also designed to include surrounding dikes to prevent water drainage from within these important freshwater reservoirs. Source: File 2584, Bộ Giáo Thông Công Chánh, Trung Tâm Lưu Trữ Quốc Gia II, Hồ Chí Minh City.*

Mỹ An, not far from the Cambodian border, discovered a "secret canal" running just a few kilometers beyond one of the military outposts. Called Resistance Canal (Kinh Kháng Chiến) by the locals, the canal ran some twenty kilometers and connected two major creeks in the western end of Đồng Tháp to a river that formed part of the border with Cambodia. Alarmed that the Việt Minh not only moved freely among the local population but also had organized their own public-works project, the Vietnamese commander suggested building a road running just inside the Cambodian border to cut off such clandestine traffic across the border.[61]

Such reports from the frontier helped reinforce President Diệm's obsession with security and his desire to fortify his new state's boundaries through the creation of the settlements as human walls or "security cordons."[62] Diệm's concerns and the real threats that regrouping Communist political and military cadres posed produced increasingly desperate measures such as hastily constructed flood dikes and airlifted emergency supplies to counter the problems caused by annual floods that swamped many of the new works. It also resulted in frequent "ethnic-cleansing" operations, either to remove suspect people such as Cambodian-born veterans from the border to isolated settlements in U Minh or to insert "loyal" settlers such as northern Vietnamese Catholics into areas such as Cái Sắn. This practice, historically influenced by the French military's approach to sectarian fighting and the recognition of allied Hòa Hảo and Cao Đài enclaves before 1955, continued well into the 1960s as the government targeted people by ethnicity or religious affiliation for settlement into specific locations. This intentional balkanization of the delta's population coincided with the fragmentation of its physical topography as American dredges and bulldozers carved out new canals and encircled the grids of refugee settlements with dikes topped by roads and watchtowers with machine gun mounts.

Of any place in Vietnam, Đồng Tháp was the epitome of a real and figurative quagmire for nation builders in the 1950s and 1960s. With its eastern edge less than an hour's drive from Sài Gòn and over eight hundred thousand hectares of swamps, marshes, sand hills, and cajeput, this region had frustrated all the colonial government's efforts to drain and settle it. Đồng Tháp likewise had long since earned a reputation as a harbor for rebels and fugitives (chapter 1). Việt Minh propagandists exploited this history repeatedly in their efforts to gain support from local villages during the First Indochina War. The long list of projects included Lagrange Canal, Tháp Mười Canal, Canals 1–10, and Canals 25–29—all dredged in the first contract with the dredge operator before 1904. Disastrous floods then almost completely wiped out new plantations along the canals from 1904 to 1908.[63] During the peak of French power in the region, Đồng Tháp lay mostly deserted until the weak economy and anticolonial uprisings in 1930 brought French engineers back. Over the course of the next fifteen years or so, various French and Vietnamese hydraulic engineers wrote extensive studies on it, and these generally presented one of two approaches to the region. Benabencq (1916) and Svigliani (1942) suggested a plan that "allowed the flood to pass" by building a network of massive drainage channels that would direct floodwaters into temporarily raging torrents that would empty close to the sea. Engineers Nguyễn Ngọc Bích (1938), Lefebvre (1942), and Jammé (1943) favored a plan to build a cellular-like series of dike-enclosed *casiers* that would prevent the floods from entering cultivated areas, reclaiming land more in the manner of the Dutch coastal flats.

Given Đồng Tháp's proximity to Sài Gòn and its history as a rebel landscape on a porous international border, Diệm and American advisers immediately identified it as a target not only for land reform but also for more military-led "pacification" operations. As at Mỹ An and other small centers in Đồng Tháp regularly visited by USOM field staff, the sheds housing American tractors and the cement buildings housing foreign visitors were never far from the military garrison. In the 1950s, such centers were not heavily fortified, often constructed of cement and bricks and surrounded by a few circles of metal fencing and barbed wire. While there were increasing instances of Việt Minh attacks on local government officials, mid-1957 attacks on equipment sheds or adviser quarters were rare. At Mỹ An and Cái Sắn, Việt Minh agents told people to cooperate with the Sài Gòn government and American programs to improve the land before the Việt Minh returned to claim the area.[64]

In this tense political environment, Diệm targeted the region for a "special project" in the Land Development Commission, and he assigned two French consultants to draft up a feasibility study that he could then forward to USOM and start channeling funds to the area. The French consultants, working closely with Vietnamese engineers in the Ministry of Public Works, decided upon a mixed solution given past approaches to reclamation and suggested a variety of projects: several new canals to drain the floods in the western reaches near the Cambodian border and dike-enclosed settlements for refugees in the eastern region.[65] They intentionally located the first settlement in one of the most hotly contested sites in the area between Lagrange and Tổng Đốc Lộc Canals (fig. 28). Local people called the site the Indigo Forest (Rừng Chàm), and it was just several kilometers from Hưng Thạnh Mỹ Village. This forest of indigo enclosed five square kilometers of rice fields and it had been a Việt Minh forward base and administrative retreat on the eastern edge of Đồng Tháp during the First Indochina War. The good terrain and productive fields attracted Communist Party committees from surrounding villages to relocate here during the worst of the Franco-Vietnamese military campaigns from 1951 to 1953. By 1953, the site had become notorious as a killing field where hundreds of soldiers had died.[66] Rather than attempt a settlement in Đồng Tháp, however, the government planned something more strategic, a new canal that would penetrate the heart of the area and quickly speed government troops to the Cambodian border near former Việt Minh bases. Republic Canal, indicated in figure 28 by a line of soil coring sites pointing to the northwest, was a bold move to extend the circulation of government military craft, mainly inherited French and American river vessels used by the *dinnassau* units in the First Indochina War.

New Lines in Old Networks

The old symbol of colonial technological prowess in the Mekong Delta— the towering, clanking apparatus of the dredge—returned after 1954 in the form of smaller (but no less expensive) American dredges. Although the new machines still signified the power of the state and the promise of this advanced technology to quickly render wasteland into fields, reha- bilitating and extending the colonial water network was no longer a cen- tralized task. The authority of the colonial Department of Public Works to draw new water lines in unknown terrain had been fragmented by differ- ent interests and approaches to irrigation since the 1930s; and aside from the strong resistance mounted against efforts to deepen waterways in the Việt Minh's liberated zones, efforts to rehabilitate waterways were further hampered by complications in Sài Gòn with American-funded contracts to operate the newly donated fleet.

One of the first American aid contracts in fiscal year 1955–56 was awarded to the colonial-era dredging enterprise Société française d'enterprises de dragages et de travaux publics (SFEDTP) to organize and train operators for the new Vietnamese fleet. It included some of the French machines (refurbished with diesel engines) and two American eight-inch cutter- suction dredges manufactured by the Johnson Corporation.[67] Like many colonial-era firms, SFEDTP continued to operate as a private company after 1954 on various contracts with USOM and the RVN until its dissolution in 1960. Such competition between older, French enterprises and Vietnamese ministries created logistical and personnel conflicts as the Vietnamese state struggled to build its corps of skilled technicians. SFEDTP charged triple the government rate for its services in carrying out American dredging contracts, but its total operating capacity by 1957 was still triple that of the government.[68] The French firm discouraged its

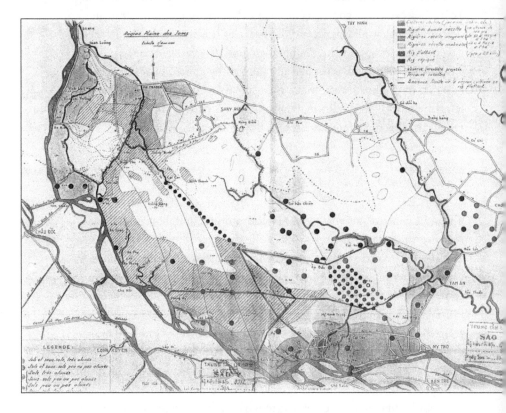

FIG. 28. Đồng Tháp. *This map shows major canals and different areas of cultivation circa 1943, with the dots representing soil surveys conducted after 1955 in preparation for settlements and one large canal project. Gò Bắc Chiên, the center for the Việt Minh Military Region 8 before 1954, is labeled in the center of the plain. The area of the large block of soil samples in the southeast corresponds to the limits of a planned casier that became a special project in 1957. The line of dots in the northwest corresponds to the path for what in 1958 became the Republic Canal (Kinh Cộng Hòa). The map shows the approximate location of the Indigo Forest, a Việt Minh base area, with a grid of dots representing soil cores taken by the French consultants during their short visit to the site in 1957. It is likely that Diệm and the Land Development Commission had abandoned their plans for a large-scale settlement by 1958. Source: "Aménagement de la Plaine des Joncs: Carte des cultures, Annexe no. II jointe au rapport de l'ingenieur des P. C. Jammé," file 312, Bộ Giáo Thông Công Chánh, Trung Tâm Lưu Trữ Quốc Gia II, Hồ Chí Minh City.*

newly trained Vietnamese crews from serving the government, enticing
them instead to stay on in the private sector with higher salaries.[69] After
the Ministry of Public Works took control of the French- and American-
donated machines in 1960, American construction firms entered Vietnam
and continued this competition in the construction sector.[70]

Thus, by continuing to insist on using such expensive machinery,
American advisers perpetuated an old colonial problem: associating
nation-building with preferential treatment for home-based manufacturers
and parts suppliers. Since the 1880s, the expensive work of building
Indochina's canals, roads, and railroads, part of the "civilizing mission,"
was made politically feasible by granting French manufacturers exclusive
contracts to deliver the materials and equipment involved in this work.
Most of Indochina's steel bridges and heavy equipment such as dredges
were preassembled in Paris yards and then shipped to Sài Gòn for final
assembly.[71] Although American leaders often encouraged international
approaches to nation-building, American contracting agencies such as
USOM typically limited bids to American-based firms and manufacturers.
The tendency to favor plans to import expensive, high-end machinery
(such as the cutter-suction dredges, which cost about one million dollars
each) instead of funding more feasible, low-tech alternatives (such as hiring
local labor contractors to dig canals by hand) reproduced the old colonial
dilemma: a high proportion of currency flowing back to home-based
companies rather than into the local economy, increased vulnerability of
projects due to equipment failures or insurgent attacks, and, in the case
of SFEDTP, a perpetuation of colonial-era enterprises that competed
directly with new Vietnamese agencies for skilled labor.

American machines were slowed down not only by soft mud and
insurgent attacks but also by the Vietnamese state. Because of the size and
expense of machines such as bulldozers and dredges, there were routine
delays at customs. Transporting the equipment from the Sài Gòn docks to
remote work sites typically required large military escorts, moving slowly in
military convoys, which raised costs further. Finally, the ultimate Achilles'
heel associated with the machines was the globally extended pipeline of
spare parts needed to keep them operating, often in extreme conditions
that hastened breakdowns. Repairmen and parts traveled across the globe
from dredge manufacturers in Baltimore and Amsterdam to shipyards in
Japan (that fitted equipment with armor plating) and finally to sites in the
Vietnamese countryside. A broken fuel injector or other minor part might
stop operations for days or weeks.[72] In a report to President Diệm about

progress in digging the canals at Cái Sắn in 1956, the administrator general of financial affairs reported that, in the first days of dredging canals, five USOM-contracted dredges sank into the soft mud, their hulls too heavy for the shallow water. The machines were excavated and removed, and for the remainder of the project, the Ministry of Public Works made regular payments to eleven labor contractors who each mobilized a team of five hundred laborers who earned approximately 35 piasters per day and could dig a two-kilometer stretch of canal in about eleven days. Judging from the tone of such correspondence, with Vietnamese engineers frequently complaining about the inappropriate American machinery, it appears that Diệm and others were happy to opt for more low-tech, locally enriching methods of work.[73]

One nation-building project born out of Diệm's obsession with blocking the movement of people across the Cambodian border and the delivery of American high-tech equipment was the one new canal project attempted in the 1950s, the Republic Canal (Kinh Cộng Hòa). The idea for the Republic Canal in Đồng Tháp was born out of colonial-era discussion on draining the floodplain in the 1930s and 1940s. After delivery of two American dredges in 1956 and the French consultants' survey in 1957, the Ministry of Public Works commenced dredging for the new canal with support from the SFEDTP, which operated the dredges under a USOM contract. However, hard clay below the surface caused frequent delays and cost overruns; by late 1957, American advisers and the French contractor recommended abandoning the project. The dredges were sent to other sites. Determined to complete the project at all costs, however, Diệm ordered the Ministry of Public Works to continue digging the channel using labor contractors.[74]

A lengthy government pamphlet highlighting recent achievements described the inauguration ceremony for the new canal, which was completed in June 1958. Diệm gave a short speech, followed by speeches from the minister of public works and several area officials. Such ceremonies were commonplace in colonial times (see chapter 2) and served to remind the local population of the government's paternal benevolence, building infrastructure that would bring "prosperity and peace." The 1958 ceremony, however, was not so spectacularly staged as its colonial precedents. Instead of a parade of military and civilian boats or a welcoming party composed of well-heeled mandarins dressed in traditional *aó dài*, Diệm and the party of officials, all dressed in white suits, traveled on a small motor launch to the designated inauguration site. Their audience appeared to consist mostly of laborers and settlers, standing along the banks of the canal and dressed in ragged clothes. A snapshot of the ceremony shows Diệm cutting a thin ribbon stretched across what looks more like an irrigation ditch than a major new canal, set in a treeless, muddy plain. Rather than transmitting a message of state power and grandeur, the photos instead suggest a struggling state, its leader staking a temporary flag on a far-flung frontier.[75] As if the photos were not telling enough, within a few months the river's annual floods rose higher than normal and swamped the new canal and the Dinh Điền settlement constructed along its banks. By October, most of the canal banks were completely submerged; and by December, after the floods receded and the dry season caused water to stagnate, Diệm began authorizing airlifts of food and supplies to keep the soldier-settlers and their families from abandoning the area.[76]

Remilitarizing the Water Landscape

Looking back on the South Vietnamese president in the summer of 1958, cutting a ribbon aboard a small motorboat while floating on a canal carved precariously into the muddy basin of Đồng Tháp, it is tempting, given the events that followed, to read this relatively minor episode as a sort of zenith for Diệm's career and his government's coercive hold on people and the water landscape. Several months later, Communist guerrilla groups began attacking tractors, dredges, and isolated outposts; and by 1960, government officials in many districts traveled only with armed escort and rarely stayed overnight in villages. However, the resumption of warfare in the water landscape was more geographically and historically complicated; there was no general ebb and flow of insurgent or government control over large areas of territory but instead a more gradually intermeshed presence of government-controlled points and lines—bases, centers, towns, major roads, and deep waterways—and less discernible, insurgent-held areas situated beyond the edges of new settlements, typically in vast interior regions accessible only by small boats, by foot, or by the few helicopters then available. This intermeshing produced, in all but the most firmly held revolutionary base areas or government centers, a perpetual, low-level traffic of people and things between government and revolutionary zones.

Whereas both nationalist and military historiographies tend to portray revolutionary cadres, government soldiers, peasants, American advisers, and so on as faceless individuals cut into heroic or villainous molds, local memoirs and accounts of the period inevitably complicate these histories by showing how individuals affiliated with different sides traveled between government-held and revolutionary spaces, navigating a human and historical landscape deep in symbolic meaning. In many cases, individuals acted independently of distant government authorities, implementing their own version of punitive laws and revolutionary retributions on the population. Recently published memoirs of local revolutionary actions suggest that some ex–Việt Minh leaders engaged in military actions before having received approval from Hà Nội. David Elliott's study of cadre memoirs and military history in Mỹ Tho notes that local party cadres, responding to several years of violent suppression, organized military and political actions in advance of directives that came from Hà Nội. He relates how Trần Văn Trà, a southerner and a general of the People's Army living in Hà Nội, first learned of a platoon-sized engagement in Đồng Tháp while tuning into the BBC. Party leaders in Hà Nội may have in fact first issued orders to send military advisers to the south only after learning that such engagements were already happening in the revolution's name.[77] A USOM field adviser, when asking a Vietnamese provincial commander about traveling up the Vàm Cỏ Đông River to see refugee settlements near Đức Hoa, was told that the area was not secure. The Vietnamese commander informed the American that recent government assaults on dissident Việt Minh bases had reduced their numbers by 80 percent, but he claimed that they still posed a dangerous threat.[78]

Diệm responded to the increasing number of attacks on remote outposts and officials in 1958 with his own set of proclamations and schemes to strengthen the government's hold over particularly resistant areas. On May 6, 1959, Diệm decreed Law 10/59, which authorized military tribunals to hear cases against people accused of terrorist acts against individuals, sabotage of any public works or buildings, and belonging to any organizations believed by the government to be involved in such actions. This law, widely acknowledged by Vietnamese and foreign observers as one of Diệm's most repressive laws, authorized military leaders and secret police to dispense with civil courts, try suspected individuals directly in military tribunals without the possibility of appeal, and enact sentences, including death.[79] Memoirs of party cadres such as Nguyễn Thị Định's *No Other Road to Take* describe in graphic terms what this expansion of military judicial authority meant in delta villages in her native province of Bến Tre. An effective female leader who joined the revolutionary cause, she recounts numerous stories of women who were detained, beaten, raped, and tortured by military and police investigators at this time. Often, these officials were searching for their husbands, who were known to have been active in the Việt Minh or who had relocated north as stipulated in the Geneva Accords.[80]

At the Fifteenth Central Committee Conference in January 1959, party leaders had privately expressed their support *in principle* for party leaders in the south to resist government attacks on their organization. A week after Diệm issued Law 10/59, the Politburo in Hà Nội issued a communiqué affirming its support for armed struggle in the south. The timing of the communiqué and a spate of newspaper accounts published in the Hà Nội papers the next day suggest that party leaders were taken by surprise by the harshness of Diệm's repressive policies and finally agreed to take a decisive role in aiding and supplying southern revolutionary groups.[81]

While the exact timing and original responsibility for increased violence in 1959 may never be fully resolved, such orders opened the way for insurgents as well as government soldiers to take action. Among the first targets for revolutionary action, besides particularly notorious district chiefs and police, were the symbols of American nation-building: the scores of tractors and other heavy equipment that since 1956 had served as symbols of American assistance. Reports from various Dinh Điền sites in 1959 describe well-organized, platoon-sized assaults on the equipment. For example, on April 24, 1959, forty men armed with a variety of machine guns attacked four International-McCormick 650-D tractors. After the operators and farmers scrambled for cover, the group riddled the tractors with bullets and then set fire to them, destroying their engines.[82] Earlier, on March 24, ten "Việt Cộng" dressed all in black had launched an assault on two John Deere 80 tractors in Đồng Tháp. Local officials had been using the tractors to plow an area about ten kilometers from the Cambodian border at Rạch Sa Rài (near Binh Thành Thơi; map 11). After scattering the crew operating the tractors with several warning shots, two men placed improvised explosive devices inside each tractor and detonated them. Other reports of attacks on tractors, equipment depots, and a rice mill in Bạc Liêu raised a general alarm among those involved in such projects, especially Americans. In retaliation for these actions, district officials associated with the Dinh Điền projects held large community gatherings

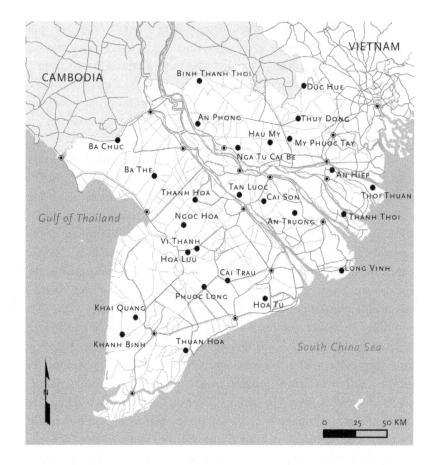

MAP 11. *Agrovilles Proposed and Completed, 1959–61. Dots show sites for twenty-six proposed agrovilles, of which twenty were constructed in 1960 before the government abandoned the program in 1961. Determining which of the twenty-six were not constructed is difficult because all were listed in a 1960 document as "under construction," and some, such as the three around U Minh, were later developed on a similar model as strategic hamlets. Older Dinh Điền sites and projects are indicated with shading. Source: List of supplies received for agrovilles, February 8, 1960, file 13419, Phủ Tổng Thống Đệ Nhất Công Hoa, Trung Tâm Lưu Trữ Quốc Gia II, Hồ Chí Minh City.*

where apprehended suspects were charged in connection with the attacks and subjected to verbal and physical abuse before being sent off in police custody.[83]

While party leaders in Hà Nội developed a new political and military program in the south, the Diệm government responded to such episodes of increasing violence with a new measure to reassert its authority: what English-language sources call the agroville. In February 1959, Diệm's Ministry of the Interior began investigating new methods to increase its control over rural communities and to increase agricultural production. The president had reportedly visited a lieutenant stationed in Vị Thanh, a market town on Xà No Canal, who had relocated villagers from isolated areas to the outskirts of the market town. The military commander had not only relocated them but also divided them into settlements based on whether they had any past connection to Việt Minh troops.[84] Working from this example, the Ministry of the Interior developed a larger plan to move peasants into such "agglomeration" zones divided into zones for "Việt Cộng families" (*khu trù mật*) and zones for families known to be patriotic to the southern government (*ấp trù mật*).[85] Each agroville was to have four to six hundred households, and each household was to have a home, a garden plot, and approximately one hundred square meters for domestic livestock and a vegetable garden. Families would live separately from their fields (and ancestral tombs) but closer to government services and surveillance. One argument behind the plan was that concentrating people into one densely occupied area supported more efficient delivery of modern services such as schools, maternity care, agricultural extension, and agricultural modernization.[86]

Whereas all earlier settlement schemes, even the highly utopian *casiers*, involved reclamation of relatively uninhabited land (*đất bỏ hoang*), the agroville marked an abrupt, violent transition to forced evacuation of *inhabited* lands as several hundred families in an area were forced, sometimes at gunpoint, to clear away productive orchards and fields before moving into bulldozed, treeless grids. Unlike the Dinh Điền or *casier* programs administered by local civil or religious leaders, agrovilles were for the most part managed by district military authorities, who exercised far greater control over subject populations than civil officials had in prior schemes. The relative absence of central-government checks on management of the agrovilles coupled with recent decisions such as Law 10/59 that sanctioned military courts to imprison and even execute suspected Communists produced widespread popular protest and political resistance. In her memoir, Nguyễn Thị Đình describes how soldiers in Bến Tre forced some five thousand farmers to destroy fields and cut down fruit orchards to make way for an agroville settlement at Thành Thới (map 11). The site and the families had been selected because many had relatives who had relocated to the north with the Việt Minh after 1954. The purpose of this agroville was to concentrate and put under surveillance families suspected of having continuing sympathies for the party. After farmers ignored government orders to clear an area approximately ten kilometers long for the new settlement, two battalions from the ARVN Seventh Division moved into the area in December and forced approximately five thousand villagers to clear the surface of the area to make way for a new grid of housing plots. Đình reports repeated incidents of physical beatings, rapes, and shootings as farmers, especially women, tried to resist.[87]

More interesting than her graphic stories of military violence, however, is an account of a staged protest led mostly by women at an inauguration ceremony attended by Diệm for the agroville's opening just after the Tết (New Year) holiday in February 1960. About one thousand villagers staged a public spectacle designed to capture the attention of the journalists and the lower officials in the entourage. When Diệm's convoy arrived, they threw off their outer garments to reveal ragged, filthy clothes underneath. They wrapped mourning cloths around their foreheads and rushed the president's car, moaning and weeping as reporters and photographers arrived to document the scene. Village notables pushed past the security detail and handed petitions to Diệm while women handed out similar petitions to soldiers and reporters. Đình writes, "Seizing this opportunity, many women and children clung to Diem and the officers by hanging onto their jackets, weeping pitifully and demanding the release of their husbands and parents."[88] The protest so embarrassed the president that he cut the ceremonies short and canceled all but a few other inaugurations. It also convinced many high-ranking Vietnamese officials that Diệm was unable to reduce rural tensions and suspicion of the central government.

Although American advisers from USOM had been involved in earlier settlement schemes such as Cái Sắn, they did not involve themselves in the development of agrovilles until relatively late in the process, after the protests in Bến Tre and after more serious opposition to Diệm was expressed in Sài Gòn by a growing number of high-ranking officials in the spring of 1960. The first official American visit to an agroville was made by Ambassador Elbridge Dubrow and several USOM advisers to the "model" agroville at Vị Thanh on April 30, 1960. During this field trip, they noted that, while Vietnam's prize-winning architect Ngô Việt Thu had been involved in the design of a central administrative and shopping area with tile-roof, cement buildings and a landscaped park with large, stylish ponds, there was no indication that the farmers, now moved several kilometers from their fields, would manage to make ends meet. One adviser, upon seeing the as-yet-unfinished tract plans for the settlement, suggested that it resembled a modern American suburban development with a shopping center located in the middle. Besides a new dispensary and maternity clinic, one of the first buildings to be completed in the agroville was a large, open-air market, which was later surrounded by streets lined with cement buildings with shops below and apartments above (for a similar graphic of Cái Sơn, see fig. 24).[89]

Photographs taken during Diệm's inaugural visit on March 12, 1960, and later published in his official newspaper, *Cách Mạng Quốc Già* (National Revolution), indicate the stark contrast between the relatively barren stretches of land designated for rural settlements and the movie set–like downtown center, with a medical center, shopping outlets, and even a two-story hotel, all draped in national flags in anticipation of the president's visit. They reveal what Americans and Vietnamese alike observed over the next several months as Diệm announced seventeen such settlements in construction by August 1960: the relocation of established rural communities en masse to such distant and strange centers not only reiterated the stark divide between the urban and the rural worlds of Vietnam but also the increasingly violent attitude of the urban-based government toward rural populations living in the interior regions that had for decades been beyond the reach of colonial and post-colonial authority or surveillance.

The agroville was in essence a heavy-handed attempt to respond to the growing disenchantment in the former enclaves and vast, inaccessible interiors of the water landscape by forcibly moving the population to the edge of the major canals and roadways on which government troops, foreign advisers, and commercial traffic circulated. Joseph Zasloff, participating in a study with a Vietnamese colleague on rural resettlement for the Michigan State University Group in Vietnam, reported President Diệm's vision for the program as conveyed in a July 7, 1959, speech: "The agroville, the President said, might well be the happy compromise between hustling, teeming city life and placid rural existence. In the ensuing discussion of the program a French term was coined for the centers — *ville charnière* or 'hinge city.'"[90] The presence of this French term in Diệm's radio broadcast points to an essential spatial conflict that characterized the enclave landscapes of the First Indochina War as well as seven decades of conflict since the French conquest in 1858: the struggle to develop a state within the narrow confines of deep-water canals, paved roads, and buffer zones that hugged the edges of rivers, canals, and highways.

Agrovilles thus became the subject not only of a renewed revolutionary struggle from the old liberated zones of the First Indochina War but also of a brief flash of internal criticism led on the streets of Sài Gòn by student groups and elite politicians. On the same day that the American ambassador and his advisers visited Vị Thanh, a group of eighteen Vietnamese politicians and former government ministers published a manifesto at the Caravelle Hotel in downtown Sài Gòn that called upon Diệm to begin immediate reforms to allow the formation of political opposition groups to respond to growing political and economic crises in the countryside and in the cities.[91] Dr. Phan Quang Đan, a political adviser to the group who had repeatedly opposed Diệm through the formation of opposition parties and an opposition newspaper *Thời Luận* (The Times; 1957–58), added his voice to calls for reform with an open letter to Diệm published on October 6, 1960: "On the Subject of Agrovilles." In this lengthy letter, Đan, who had recently won an election in a landslide against his Diemist opponent but then had his candidacy rejected on a technicality, pointed out that the agroville program required several hundred thousand peasants to participate in corvée labor, which had been outlawed by the French colony in 1879. Himself an émigré from the north after 1954, Đan concluded his open letter with a reference to earlier, failed attempts to resettle peasants from the more densely populated Red River Delta before 1954: "It is finally useful to recall that the delta of North Viet-Nam, including the densest rural and urban concentrations, was nonetheless lost to the Communists because colonialist policy alienated the hearts and spirits of the people, which proves that regrouping South Vietnamese peasants in agrovilles by itself would not be enough to combat and defeat Communism."[92]

Đan capitalized on the growing tide of dissent in Sài Gòn until November 13, 1960, when a coup attempt he had supported in an advisory capacity failed. He spent the next three years in jail until Diệm's assassination in November 1963. The long summer of internal dissent in Sài Gòn in 1960, the increasing frequency and intensity of "Việt Cộng" military actions, and finally an attempted coup in November signified several major transitions from civil to more military government authority in the Mekong Delta as well as a rapidly diminishing American role in programs. Since 1958 Americans had distanced themselves from supervising or financing such programs as the agrovilles. On October 14, Ambassador Dubrow recited in person to Diệm a carefully crafted, fourteen-page memorandum in

French expressing official American concerns for the rising "Việt Cộng" threat in rural areas and the severely diminished popular support for his administration nationwide. The memo was a list of American suggestions that amounted to a call for Diệm to democratize his government, stop the violence carried out by district officials in the countryside, and, finally, sack his brother Ngô Đình Nhu and Madame Nhu by reassigning them to an overseas post. As the architect behind many of the republic's more coercive policies, Ngô Đình Nhu's involvement with secret police and counterinsurgency operations had repeatedly made him a target in the foreign press as well as in southern opposition pamphlets and North Vietnamese papers. According to Dubrow, Diệm assumed a "slightly grim" manner after hearing his statement in its entirety and calmly responded that such accusations about his brother were nothing more than rumors spread by the Communists.[93] Thus ended not only the conversation but also, over the next several months, chances for a return to the sort of land reform and modernization programs that American civilian advisers had envisioned since 1954.

Abandoning Modernization

These failures to resolve older crises in the swampy floodplains of the delta—abandoned plantations and liberated zones—by the early 1960s began to affect the foreign community inhabiting the French-styled hotels, villas, and cafés of downtown Sài Gòn through a number of high-profile departures and new arrivals. One of the notable departures was Wolf Ladejinsky, who in mid-1961 accepted a post with the Ford Foundation to work on land reform issues in Nepal. He made his first trip to Nepal in 1960 over several weeks that coincided with a protest of the founding of Diệm's republic (October 26) and an attempted coup against him on November 12. By the time Ladejinsky returned to Sài Gòn, his patron's future as president was in serious question. One of Ladejinsky's last published papers on Vietnam highlights the success of Diệm's earlier ordinances, which he argued continued to stabilize land rents and move an increasing share of land from large, French-owned estates into small-holdings. After December 1959, when government soldiers began moving into delta villages to force villagers, often at gunpoint, to work on agrovilles, Ladejinsky continued to trumpet Diệm's earlier "successes," likely unaware of the changes occurring in 1960 with the agroville program. He presented a paper "Agrarian Reform in the Republic of Vietnam" at a Conference on Social Development and Welfare in Vietnam held in New York City, and the paper mentioned nothing of the agroville policy of relocating farmers into concentrated settlements. Either he had no knowledge of the program or else he chose not to criticize it before securing new employment. Even two years later in 1962, a published version of the paper highlighted the older agrarian reforms and made no mention of agrovilles or the strategic-hamlet program that replaced it; it merely updated figures on land ownership and productivity. Such an omission suggests that this American architect of land reform in Asia, a target of Senator Joseph McCarthy's anti-Communist witchhunt in 1954, self-servingly chose to avoid mentioning the worsening political situation in Vietnam. He left Sài Gòn for good in early 1961 and stayed at the Ford Foundation in New York until January 1962, when he moved to Kathmandu as an adviser to King Mahendra of Nepal.[94]

Ladejinsky's departure was followed in June 1962 by that of another well-known figure in Sài Gòn, Professor Wesley Fishel, who had led a Michigan State University Study Group that since 1955 had advised Diệm on the drafting of the 1956 constitution, the development of the secret police, and more mundane matters such as public-policy training courses, standardization of bookkeeping procedures, and training traffic police. The short, mild-mannered assistant professor from East Lansing who had befriended Diệm during his two-year stay in the United States from 1952 to 1954 occupied a bigger-than-life position as Diệm's American confidant, enjoying more regular meetings with the president in the 1950s than the American head of USOM, Leland Barrows, or even the American ambassador. Together with Ladejinsky, Fishel often ate breakfast with Diệm at the Presidential Palace and enjoyed a close relationship few others possessed.[95] Despite the rising criticism against Diệm coming from Vietnamese and American channels, Fishel and Ladejinsky were Diệm loyalists. Only when two other MSU professors wrote a scathing critique of Diệm in the *New Republic* in 1962 did Diệm, enraged by the article, expel the MSU Study Group and Fishel with it.[96]

Thus, as military commanders replaced civilian officials in rural provinces such as Bến Tre, foreign military advisers, counterinsurgency experts, and proponents of such euphemistic "pacification" or "villagization" schemes replaced such individuals as Fishel or Ladejinsky and, finding themselves in opposition to leaders such as Diệm, sought alliances with Vietnamese military leaders and the anti-Communist opposition. Nation-building as a more general exercise of foreign assistance in material and military aid did not end in 1962—as most people familiar with American involvement in Vietnam know, such aid was just the tip of the iceberg. However, nation-building as a civilian campaign engaged in by Americans, Vietnamese, and others to solve such issues as land reform did essentially end as the new wave of arrivals in Sài Gòn in the Kennedy administration stressed security and counterinsurgency above all else.

Finally, getting back to the water landscape in the Mekong Delta, we must ask who were the real agents of modernization and its political and economic failure to solve the "agrarian problem" during the "six years of peace"? Evidence from Vietnamese and foreign sources suggests very clearly that Americans, even Ladejinsky, held at best a peripheral role in designing such projects as Cái Sắn, the Dinh Điền settlements, or the agrovilles. Diệm and many of his ministers were instead strongly influenced by their involvement and familiarity with past solutions to the *crisis agricole* as proposed and developed by French and Vietnamese engineers since the 1930s. Besides the often-mentioned intransigence of ex-colonial Vietnamese engineers and wealthy Vietnamese landlords to support land reform, a less obvious cause for nation-building's failures in the water landscape concerned the persistent political, economic, technological, and ecological relationships implicit in the ways in which the *work* of clearing new fields, digging new canals, and building new settlements was undertaken. As with the colonial enterprise in the 1890s, the hundreds of John Deere tractors and the growing fleet of diesel-powered, armored dredges were a temporary fix that solved the needs of nation builders to justify their project to taxpayers at home while simultaneously disarming local inhabitants with the spectacle of rapid, mechanical production. "Việt Cộng" units, striking out against the tractors and dredges rather than their human operators in early 1959, understood the strategic and political value of such machines. Ultimately, as the women and children's protest at Thành Thới in 1960 and the Catholic protests at Cái Sắn in 1956 illustrate, nation-building failed politically and ecologically because it did not allow those living closest to the water landscape to determine the direction of reclamation and agricultural modernization in a manner that would have solved some of the underlying causes of the agricultural crisis that had persisted since the 1930s.

FIG. 29. "CH-21 *Shawnee helicopters of the 57th Transportation Co. prior to returning to Cà Mau airstrip after airlifting Vietnamese troops into a combat zone. Cà Mau is approximately 55 miles from Sóc Trăng.*" Source: *Ricardo A. Hinojosa, May 10, 1963. Army Signal Corps Still Photographs, SC 604626, National Archives and Records Administration, Center 2, College Park, MD.*

The bombs in this area were uncountable because this was the central village in the district, a liberation base area. The Americans bombed everywhere, and if they had any bombs left in the day, they dropped them here. At night, the fighters from Trà Nóc Air Base came shooting through the night. We couldn't sleep . . . many people died then . . . just a few survived. Just imagine you step everywhere and see all the bomb craters and bullet casings. Cluster bombs were used the most here; chemical poisons were also dropped many times, but we couldn't dredge the canals to drain them. We could only clear a little bit of silt and debris in the main waterways to make passage for the movement of our soldiers. It would take four or five people with big branches to push the water hyacinth out of the way so that they could pass.—*Ông Rở*[1]

6 AMERICAN WAR

The arrival of American troops in Vietnam in 1965 inaugurated one of the bloodiest engagements of the Cold War; it also triggered a surge of writing on the conflict that has yet to abate. As a literary genre represented in many languages, the events of the war form the backdrop in many memoirs, novels, and films in which authors and protagonists strive to work out the ethical dilemmas associated with American intervention. As Colonel Kurtz explains in the final scenes of the movie *Apocalypse Now,* many attempt to reconcile the personal and collective horrors of this brutal engagement in which more than four million Vietnamese, Laotians, Khmers, Americans, Koreans, Australians, and others died in just eight years. Besides the literary realm, historiography of the war has likewise grown steadily, from military and diplomatic works to social and cultural histories. Yet despite all of this artistic and scholarly work, few works have yet to consider the role of environments—historic, built, or natural—

in shaping the events of the conflict. Nor do very many postwar studies consider lasting effects of the conflict on Vietnamese places except for some studies on bombing, unexploded ordnance, and sites damaged by chemical defoliants.[2] The figurative quagmires identified in much of the war literature are the sticky moral, political, and diplomatic situations that enveloped people at all levels, while little attention is paid to how places such as the Mekong Delta also shaped policy and played into the successes and failures of war campaigns.

The rapid growth of an American military and civilian infrastructure in the 1960s altered Vietnam's urban and rural landscapes in different ways that reflected evolving concerns over movement, visibility, and each place's perceived importance to the war. As a densely occupied, agricultural region far from the demilitarized zone, the delta environment largely constrained American military operations to the deep waters of the main rivers and the wide streets and airport tarmacs of larger towns. Until the Tết Offensive in January 1968, most Americans and other foreigners working in the Mekong Delta lived in relatively small numbers with a relatively small presence of troops living for the most part on floating base ships. Americans served as advisers to Vietnamese units and provincial governments, as pilots of helicopters and jets providing air support and surveillance, and as volunteers and consultants working in towns (fig. 29). By 1965, the National Liberation Front (NLF), or "Việt Cộng" (VC), had reoccupied most of the pre-1954 liberated zones (đất giải phong) and expanded into some new areas, while American advisers set up quarters inside South Vietnamese bases and offices. The war in the delta was a counterinsurgency war, defined less by major combat operations than by a host of programs aimed to "pacify" the population through refugee settlement, psychological operations, agricultural mechanization, police surveillance, and small-unit patrols into contested areas. The 1968 Tết Offensive caused a shift in American military planning with a series of highly destructive campaigns launched against the NLF base areas, but the boundaries between government and NLF territories did not move much until American ground forces left in 1973.

What Vietnamese typically call the American War—short for the War of Resistance against America to Save the Nation (Kháng Chiến Chống Mỹ Cứu Nước)—differed the most from past conflicts in the delta with respect to the new technologies it introduced. Americans brought a spectacular array of jet aircraft, helicopters, jeeps, patrol boats, radar, microwave communications equipment, television cameras, munitions, and chemicals to places where before 1965 only the wealthy owned televisions and only large towns had electricity. For Americans, the delta was both a counterinsurgency and a nation-building laboratory. A generation of social scientists from American think tanks and universities worked alongside military advisers, private contractors, and CIA agents to study the effects of this mass deployment of new machines.

While delta residents had grown accustomed to seeing Americans and their equipment since the late 1950s, there was no precedent for the massive buildup that followed President Johnson's decision to send ground forces to Vietnam. Gargantuan bulldozers, the latest military hardware, and warehouses filled with dry goods, liquor, fertilizer, and cigarettes were part of one of the largest military infrastructure campaigns in modern history. Beginning in 1965, American agencies and contractors began coordinating base construction at sites all over Vietnam, including airports and ports in the delta. Though most of the large base complexes such as Biên Hòa, Đà Nẵng, and Pleiku were located north of Sài Gòn and in central Vietnam, there was a detectable shift in the scale and intensity of the American presence in the delta. Forty-two military construction battalions (approximately 30,000 persons) were deployed, while American companies supplied an even greater construction capability with specialized machinery and technicians to specific projects. Fulfilling both military and civilian contracts, conglomerates such as RMK-BRJ and DMJM brought thirty-inch pipeline dredges, thirty-ton dump trucks, and four-hundred-ton-per-hour rock crushers to speed up work on big jobs such as airport runways and all-weather highways.[3]

This unprecedented investment in military technology and construction soon facilitated a new era of military destruction, but it also prompted a revolution in everyday technologies such as small engines attached to boats and pumps for irrigation. These small-scale, everyday technologies became essential to survival, compressing times and distances required to travel across dangerous terrain. While this radical change in individual experiences of time and space can be associated with the expansion of a more global, capitalist economy to delta farmers, it was farmers who drove this revolution in everyday technology.[4] More than the violence or spectacular displays of military hardware, the proliferation of boat engines, radios, and motor pumps played a central role in the delta's environmental history. One older farmer, when asked about his first outboard motor purchase in 1963, explained the importance of the new motor in this way: "In the time fighting the Americans there wasn't a house that didn't have the motors. When the kids ran away from the enemy [American/Republic of Vietnam] soldiers, they took the boats with the motors, lifting the propeller up when they saw water hyacinth and letting it down again after to keep going. If they got stuck and the water hyacinth prevented them from moving, then the [American] jets would swoop down and shoot them dead."[5] Such machines were a matter of life and death for many in the countryside.

Vietnamese museums around the delta have picked up on this theme in revolutionary perspectives of the war, too. At the Cần Thơ Province History Museum, a six-horsepower motor manufactured by Kohler Corporation in Wisconsin is mounted on a *ghe tam bản,* the ubiquitous wooden canoe (fig. 30). Next to this display are various photographs of revolutionaries in checkered scarves and black outfits transporting supplies in the motorized canoes. The name for the motors in Vietnamese, *máy kô-le,* is a lasting tribute to the American company and town (Kohler, Wisconsin) where the engines were made.

Another technological object at the museum, a mimeograph machine hidden inside a camouflage of branches and leaves, points to another important struggle during the war: visibility and invisibility. The American War meant increased capabilities for the state to penetrate the delta's swampy interiors and observe from the air. Through remote sensing and aerial reconnaissance, American units were able to convey detailed images of the ground to distant observers in minutes. Perhaps no country at the time was as extensively mapped and photographed as Vietnam. During nighttime firefights, too, the Americans turned night into day with flares and other devices. Harvey Meyerson, a *Chicago Daily News* correspondent, described the AC-47 flare and gunship aircraft nicknamed "Spooky." From dusk to dawn, at least one circled above the airfield in Cần Thơ, awaiting orders to provide two-million-candlepower flares and streams of bullets from its three howitzers mounted along the left side of the fuselage to selected positions.[6] Against such invasions of the cover of darkness, NLF units often managed to continue their attacks concealed inside mud embankments.

This spatial and technological opposition between the gunship above and the guerrillas below reflected a widespread difference with regard to individual orientations in the delta landscape. Revolutionaries struggled to stay hidden within it while Americans and their allies strove to remain floating above. American manuals even coined the term "immersion foot" for a medical condition suffered by troops who had spent too much time

FIG. 30. *A Kohler Engine Mounted on a* Ghe Tam Bản *in the Cần Thơ Province History Museum. The same engine could be quickly swapped out and used as a water pump.* Source: *Author photo.*

wading through the bogs. The leather boots worn by infantry soldiers were slow to dry and promoted fungal growth on damp skin. The manual recommended rotating platoons so that a unit could rest once every three days to dry out.[7]

Reclaiming Waterways

As in former colonial and postcolonial struggles, dredging was instrumental to controlling the flows of traffic and people through the delta landscape; however, due to guerrilla attacks and bureaucratic delays in American aid, dredges often became more symbolic of the failures of large-scale machinery to overcome the forces of an intertwined human and natural resistance. The Republic of Vietnam's (RVN) fleet of eight American dredges moved slowly and required extensive military escorts. They were perhaps most valuable politically in Sài Gòn and for the publicity they generated in newspapers; at inauguration ceremonies well-dressed audiences viewed a craft's impressive engines and listened to hopeful visions of economic prosperity delivered by Vietnamese and American officials. At one such inauguration ceremony on the Sài Gòn waterfront in August 1961, Ambassador Frederick Nolting addressed the RVN's minister of public works and, like colonial officials before him, stressed the importance of this new equipment in "extending civilization" and preventing the countryside from falling into the hands of the Communists:

> The Kim Giang [Golden River] here is not just proof of the cooperation between two free peoples; it is also part of a combined struggle to build a better world and a life that is more satisfying for humankind. . . . Esteemed Minister, I, along with Mr. Gardiner and our American colleagues, wish for the government and the people to realize success in the development of the waterway system. I envision one day in the near future when every village in the Mekong Delta will become a center for peace and prosperity.[8]

As a symbol of renewed American support for Diệm under President Kennedy, the dredge's first task was to rehabilitate and extend the Republic Canal, Diệm's 1958 project partially funded by the U.S. Operations Mission (USOM) and eventually completed with conscripts and hand tools. Kennedy advisers Eugene Staley and General Maxwell Taylor included the project in a list of infrastructure and strategic projects to be funded as part of the Staley Plan proposed in July 1961.[9] From its inauguration in August 1961 until March 1962, the dredge and its Vietnamese crew worked at digging a thirty-five-meter-wide channel in the Republic Canal.[10] Costing more than a million dollars, work again halted before the canal's completion. This time, however, it was not hard clay or shallow water but mortar attacks and underwater mines that stopped the work.[11]

As the war escalated, dredges and other expensive equipment became prime targets for attack. The dredge "Bac Lieu" was severely damaged by underwater charges placed on its hull and detonated on May 22, 1959.[12] By May 1962, USOM was arranging to airlift replacement engines and other heavy equipment from the United States to sustain "high morale in this activity important to both economic and military efforts."[13] However, this high point in U.S. support for dredging appears to have quickly diminished with every successive attack delaying more of the routine dredging work in the delta region. By December 1963, the Ministry of Public Works routinely denied provinces access to dredges for reasons of poor security. Instead, the Vietnamese military—later followed by the U.S. military in 1965—commandeered the machines to perform relatively safe work building up fill for runways and base areas near the major cities.[14]

Even without the attacks on the dredges, wartime fragmentation of the landscape into shifting zones of controlled and uncontrolled territory forced many delays. Seen from Sài Gòn, the lack of security in the countryside prevented any realistic, economical scheduling of operation, even in secure areas, as dredges typically had to cross insecure areas en route to work sites. The convoys of dredges and supporting equipment required a military escort with upward of four hundred soldiers placed at intervals along the canal banks. Another problem in moving through the delta was the distance of the central repair shop from remote sites separated by hostile territory. The central repair yard at Phú An near Sài Gòn in Military Region III was more than fifty kilometers from most of the sites located in Military Region IV. Compared with the French dredges, for which many parts could be retooled locally, American equipment also presented problems since spare parts could not be procured. Small components, if they failed, could stop operations for days or weeks while replacement parts started their journey in Baltimore, Holland, or Japan. Once arriving either by ship or by plane, the parts then had to pass through either military or civilian import procedures, be delivered to the central yard, and then travel by highway through various military commands and possible ambushes before reaching a stranded dredge. Facing these delays and the target that such a stalled machine presented to NLF patrols, crews on the American dredges often took matters into their own hands, repairing the machinery with the tools available. One report on dredging operations noted their heroic resolve to keep the dredges working with the following remark: "The only saving feature has been the ability of the Vietnamese artisan to improvise and make do with basic tools. A 24-inch cast iron pipe is attacked with a hand hacksaw. Half inch steel plate can be cut with a hammer and cold chisel."[15] Despite the increase in the size of the fleet from three dredges in 1958 to eleven in 1965, productivity during the war plummeted from 4.5 million cubic feet dredged in 1964 to less than a million from 1965 to 1971 and even less from 1972 to 1975.[16] Thus, for most of the war, dredges and other heavy, slow-moving equipment symbolized the near paralysis of the government and Americans on the water.

The facility with which the NLF's military branch, the People's

Liberation Armed Forces (PLAF), controlled movement on the waterways was the result of decades of hard work with frequent loss of life in many unsuccessful attempts to mine boats, conduct ambushes, and avoid detection. A captured PLAF document from 1964 explains that besides sapper (demolition) units, since the early 1950s engineering units had worked to develop tactics for employing newly imported or captured seventy-millimeter howitzers, recoilless rifles, and rocket launchers as well as improvised underwater explosives developed to handle the unique depths and conditions of the muddy waterway bottoms.[17] From the beginning of American military intervention in 1965, American observers were well aware of the many sophisticated ways that PLAF troops used the waterways in the delta region. Captured soldiers revealed that they moved almost exclusively by water. In Đồng Tháp, the PLAF 502nd Battalion had ordered construction of 350 boats, with gunwales built several boards higher on either side to accommodate movement of troops and heavier weapons. Especially around the two major PLAF base areas, almost all troops and supply movements were coordinated in convoys of sampans with occasional use of larger boats.[18]

Survival for the guerrillas required a detailed, intimate knowledge of water conditions, including the location of key channels and the timing of tides, which, if not accounted for, could leave a convoy stranded in the daytime hours, when it would be most vulnerable to spotter planes and jets. The PLAF also relied on detailed knowledge of local water traffic. Ambushes were typically laid at bends in creeks and canals, on the side of the bend in the river where the channel cut closest to shore. Underwater mines were often laid in such channels with nondescript, buoyant matter such as driftwood tied to them with a line to allow guerrillas hidden on the water's edge to estimate the proper time for firing. Besides such small-unit activities, the PLAF also developed means for rapidly moving heavier guns across the water. In one event in February 1966 when PLAF forces successfully disabled a radar and communications center at Cà Mau, they had moved two seventy-millimeter howitzers mounted on tires onto a muddy bank for firing and then immediately pushed them back onto an array of sampans for water transport into a well-covered creek.[19]

Contrary to the French experience in the gunboat exchanges of the 1860s, the PLAF demonstrated repeatedly throughout the American War that it held the advantage over larger American and RVN vessels on freshwater; nowhere was this demonstrated more clearly than on one of the main French canals, the Nicolai–Mang Thít Canal, that formed a strategic connection between the two main branches of the Mekong (see map 12). In December 1966, the United States together with the Sài Gòn government vowed to regain control over this canal, which had effectively been under the control of the NLF since 1963. On March 26, 1967, units from the American Ninth Infantry Division's floating, amphibious base at Đồng Tâm and other encampments engaged the PLAF 306th Battalion, one of the most famous PLAF units from U Minh. Heavy losses were incurred on both sides: approximately 142 PLAF and 40 Americans and an unknown number of Army of the Republic of Vietnam (ARVN) soldiers died. The Americans declared "victory" and rapidly constructed watchtowers along the waterway's thirty-kilometer course. However, over the next two months, the PLAF steadily eroded government authority by capturing and destroying individual watchtowers each night. For the remainder of the war, the canal was never fully reopened to barge traffic and never redredged. The constant threat of ambush coupled with the continuing deposition of silt (*dos d'âne*) in the canal prevented most barge owners from risking damage to their vessels by venturing into such canals.[20] Meyerson's account of American activities in his book *Vinh Long* (1970) is unparalleled for its analysis of how American military and civilian advisers dealt with specific problems posed by the natural terrain.

Perhaps even more striking than the accounts of their knowledge of the landscape, however, were accounts of the ways that units also adapted imported technologies into their tactics. Old oppositions between indigenous and foreign technologies from past conflicts were turned on their head in the 1960s. Drawing on captured documents and prisoner interviews, Meyerson reports that PLAF forces managed to down three American helicopters and regain control over the canal by communicating with telephones linked by thousands of meters of wire stretching across the district. American soldiers surveying the scene after the battle found some of the PLAF dead entangled in the wires and quickly learned that the enemy units had moved from radio to wired communications to prevent interception. Also, the telephone lines permitted them to communicate while they were jamming the American and RVN radio communications in the area. Meyerson described the battle as a "violent pulsation issuing from a weblike system that blankets the Delta."[21] Compared with French naval units stringing up telegraph lines in the 1860s to outmaneuver Vietnamese rebels, NLF planners in the 1960s demonstrated incredible facility mixing modern technologies with everyday conditions.

Meyerson also hit upon one of the Resistance's strongest weapons against

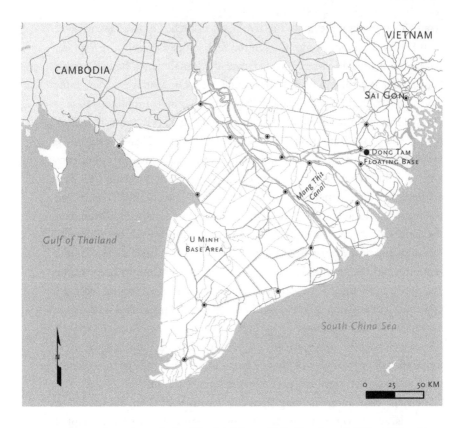

MAP 12. *Location of the Nicolai–Mang Thít Canal and Đồng Tám Base.*
Source: *Author.*

Americans and the Sài Gòn government: time. He noted how in many
delta villages the Resistance had been building its "weblike" infrastructure
politically since the 1930s and militarily since the 1940s. Việt Minh and
later NLF leaders had since the 1940s realized the importance of claiming
the slower-moving, everyday routes of movement—footpaths, canals,
and creeks—not because this was all they knew but because it gave them
advantages over the faster-paced, heavily mechanized forces of the French,
the RVN, and the Americans. In the delta, the NLF typically engaged
U.S. and RVN forces far from roads and airstrips, deep in mangroves and
rice fields. Vulnerability to ambush, slowdowns in dredging, and other
delays can be contrasted with quick PLAF attacks, fast withdrawals, and
intricately coordinated operations.

Islands of Innovation

Beyond the battlefields and base areas, however, many more experiments were under way with new technology—pumps, motors, and generators—that profoundly altered the terms in which millions of inhabitants engaged with the delta's water environments. The sudden flood of new imports into the delta fueled a kind of modern agrarian revolution quite unique from that in neighboring countries, where the Green Revolution meant a state-sponsored push away from traditional, subsistence agriculture and toward chemical fertilizers, pesticides, tractors, and industrial farming. Works on the Green Revolution in Southeast Asia address the interconnected ways that booming rural populations, modernist state policies on land tenure, commercialization of agricultural crops, global commodity markets, and new technologies transformed rural societies across Southeast Asia.[22] Vietnam was somewhat exceptional because many of these agents of change, especially global markets and powerful central states, did not really reach beyond the edges of national highways or downtown quays. Nevertheless, people in the delta were experimenting with similar technologies.

The portable engine (*máy kô-le*) was one of the most powerful agents for environmental change. Assembled by the Kohler Corporation and then sold in government towns, the engines were used as both outboard boat motors and water pumps. In dozens of conversations with farmers about their experiences during the war and with the local environment, no topic came up as often as *máy kô-le*. As boat engines attached to sampans, they quickly traveled beyond government checkpoints into NLF base areas. The standard-issue sampan, so vital to PLAF troop movements, was overnight transformed into a speedboat capable of covering ten times the distance in a single night. When not used for movement, the small motors could be mounted to a frame and used as water pumps. In a period when the canal system was in disrepair and flooding no longer manageable, water pumps allowed farmers to individually manage water levels within the paddy dikes. While Americans sponsored many different programs through the U.S. Agency for International Development (USAID) with little success, sales of the motors skyrocketed far beyond anyone's expectations.

Provincial capitals such as Mỹ Tho and Cần Thơ functioned as islands of diffusion for the lightweight, affordable engines, despite resistance to the unregulated use of the engines by the Sài Gòn government, the NLF, and even USAID. Farmers modified the pumping apparatus attached to the motors and in the process revolutionized age-old routines and technologies for field irrigation. Phạm Văn Thành, a small-engine merchant in Mỹ Tho, was reported by some to have been the first to adapt the engine for use as a water pump. He sold the motors in a shop after having worked twelve years for the French dredging company (SFEDTP) in Sài Gòn. Just twenty-three years old in 1963, he accompanied a friend, an ARVN military engineer, to watch a dredging project in progress nearby. Studying the old German and Japanese diesel engines powering the French dredges and the centrifugal pumps powering the newer, American equipment, Thành began experimenting with German-made impellers (reversed propellers to create suction) attached to the shaft of the lightweight, American-built engines. After developing a successful water pump with sufficient lift, he began selling the new pumps in 1964. He sold on average six hundred motors a month through mid-1967. By that time, at age twenty-eight, he had become one of the richest men in town, owning three cars and a hotel. Robert L. Sansom's research in the area in 1967 suggests that the laborsaving technology was quickly copied and spread across the delta independently of American, RVN, or NLF authorities.[23]

Despite the American media's praise of such instances of ingenuity and modernization, the Sài Gòn government took a generally prohibitive stance against the diffusion of motorized technology to the rural masses. This resistance stemmed from earlier colonial and Japanese wartime prohibitions on the ownership or transfer of motor-powered boats and equipment. Especially under Diệm, the Sài Gòn government conveyed to American advisers their dire need for motorized craft to police the waterways, while internally it expressed severe concern over the rate at which such equipment was falling into the hands of their enemies in the countryside. In 1958 Diệm pressed USOM for 3.6 million dollars worth of motorboats for the delta provinces—an array of ten-horsepower canoes, seventy-five-horsepower fiberglass launches, and larger, seagoing vessels.[24] While officials in Washington moved at their usual, slow pace to process such requests, the Resistance ramped up its own campaign to procure sampans through the levying of new taxes, especially on the periphery of liberated zones such as Đồng Tháp.[25] By 1961, government reports from the provinces included frequent accounts of "Việt Cộng" raids to steal motors or, even more troubling, of people who had purchased equipment under various aid programs hauling it to NLF zones for resale.[26] While Sansom suggests that NLF political cadres may have railed against farmers using the engines that typically bore a stamp with the American flag and the shaking hands insignia of USAID, PLAF forces appear to have adopted the engines as readily as farmers for military craft.[27]

Often it was farmers rather than technical advisers who provided the practical experience necessary to make such equipment useful and profitable; in some cases they even retrained extension agents in techniques of operation. Mr. Rỡ, a farmer who had lived in a heavily contested "free fire zone" during the war, explained how farmers in his district showed a university extension agent how to modify the engines to work in the soft clay:

> At first, the university introduced their machines to us (those of us who worked with irrigation), . . . but their use of them was not as effective as the farmers'. They mounted the engines too high up, causing them to tip over into the water . . . the engine got wet, the spark plug got wet . . . not effective. We would used wooden scoops [sa quạt] for moving water; but soon after that, we gave them up for the pumps. Everything takes some time to understand.[28]

By the war's end, so many of the little engines were rigged as pumps that a team of Dutch hydrologists in 1974 estimated that, with more than a million such pumps in operation, they exerted large-scale influences on the direction and movement of floodwater.[29]

A similar phenomenon occurred when portable rice mills were introduced. The Japanese-manufactured Yanmar rice mill was sold in larger towns such as Mỹ Tho and Bạc Liêu. An American Civil Operations for Rural Development Support (CORDS) study noted the rapid sale of the small mills and focused on the RVN's attempts to restrict sales because local milling upset the owners of the large mills who had controlled rice milling for decades. In Gía Rai District (Bạc Liêu), one American adviser estimated that as many as sixty Yanmars were in service. The introduction of these mills presented a direct economic challenge to the ethnic-Chinese families who had controlled milling in the delta as a virtual monopoly since the colonial era. The RVN charged high fees for mill licenses, in effect preserving this exclusive right. Licensed firms paid province officials an estimated 200,000 piasters ($30,000) per year to keep their permits. A former province chief used his cut from the license receipts to buy semiannual draft deferments.[30] The RVN and licensed mill owners thus attempted to prevent the sale of the mobile mills because they threatened their businesses. Banning the use of small mills, however, merely led to the relocation of mobile milling to NLF-controlled areas. Some mill operators in the liberated zones even sold rice below rates in government markets to further undermine the influence of the monopolies. One American advisor assessing the problem concluded:

> They could gain rice, political support, and seriously damage GVN [Government of Vietnam] tax revenues by such a tactic. If the people are allowed to operate the mills themselves, with a minimum of GVN harassment, the Government stands to gain political support and break the Chinese stranglehold over the economy of the Delta. A responsive government, not economic controls, is the key to successful counterinsurgency.[31]

The provincial CORDS headquarters was a site for an endless array of optimistic experiments, the perspective of the laboratory. However, the real laboratory for testing and operating such equipment was in the field.

While most American archival sources concern the machinations of the military bureaucracy, files of provincial advisory teams offer some glimpses into changing conditions at a more local level in the countryside. The province senior advisor (PSA), typically a colonel in the army or a senior foreign service officer, was the senior scientist in the counterinsurgency laboratory, often improvising new approaches to achieve political and socioeconomic goals. PSA reports were composed in simple, straightforward prose; they offered many insights into the complicated ways that the water environment influenced local economic and political struggles. For example, one report submitted by the PSA of An Xuyên (Cà Mau) Province in 1967 details development of a light drilling rig used to drill new freshwater wells. By developing a drilling rig that could be carried by airlift from one site to another, the adviser was able to undermine a key source of NLF authority and revenue: their provision of potable water by barge to the populace during the dry season. In regions affected by saltwater inundation, the NLF charged water merchants high taxes to deliver freshwater to area villages; in some cases (according to the PSA) they took over the trade altogether.[32] As the advisory effort changed along with the events of the war, however, their experiments and observations became less cheerful and at best guardedly optimistic as the security and political situation rapidly deteriorated after 1968. Despite the worsening political situation, American advisers nevertheless documented environmental and social changes that were rarely mentioned in reports coming out of the press offices in Sài Gòn or Washington. The following end-of-tour report from a provincial adviser in Cà Mau epitomizes changes in the delta countryside in 1971:

> There is a change in Vietnam and the country will never be the same again. Look at the skyline full of TV antennas, and then choke on the Honda fumes. These gadgets are just the beginning. Now that these people have a taste of them, for better or worse they are not going to let them go—to Charlie or anyone else. It is these materialistic gains that the average VN will try to hold on to and sustain himself with over any and all mellifluous philosophical doctrines.[33]

In spite of the fighting and the restrictions of various governing forces, individuals throughout the region adopted new technologies that altered ages-old patterns of work and communication, compressing distances and speeding up daily activities.

Asian/River Regionalism

Besides the widespread, local alterations to the water landscape that the mass importation of motors, radios, televisions, and other equipment accelerated in the 1960s, Americans and their allies also participated in numerous international and river basin development schemes beyond the borders of Vietnam. These schemes and contracts generated hundreds of scientific and policy-oriented studies and third-party survey work, especially in the "counterinsurgency laboratory" of the Mekong Delta. Development of the Mekong became a leitmotif of American nation-building projects in the 1960s, and under President Johnson, a Texas politician who came of age in the New Deal era, the model for that development was the Tennessee Valley Authority (TVA) with its federally initiated programs to build hydropower dams, extend electricity into rural areas, and act as a regional economic development agency. On April 7, 1965, one month after American Marines had begun landing in Danang, Johnson attempted to counter critics of the war by proffering a plan for "peace without conquest" by offering one billion dollars to develop hydroelectric dams, irrigation systems, and other structures that would "provide food and water and power on a scale to dwarf even our own TVA."[34] In

Thailand he pointed to plans to build the largest dam in the world on the Mekong mainstream and a cascade of dams similar to those of the TVA stretching downstream into Cambodia, with additional irrigation and flood control structures built in Vietnam. Glossy pamphlets published by American engineering agencies with offices in Bangkok explained that the dams might generate twenty billion kilowatt-hours of electricity per year, enabling the region to "lift itself out of debt by its own bootstraps through the sale of electric power."[35]

While such proclamations from afar had little impact on the day-to-day lives of farmers and soldiers living in the delta, they nevertheless point to significant historical changes in the growth of international engineering firms, technocratic state agencies, international development banks, and (proposed) monumental projects in the region that continue to capture the imaginations of national leaders. The formation of the Mekong Committee in 1957 combined with increased commitments of American funds to regional development produced a kind of postcolonial "gold rush" in which foreign firms, especially Japanese and Korean firms, made sizable fortunes as their units produced surveys and feasibility studies. The reports generated from such contracts have had a lasting effect on development attitudes in the region. For example, the Mỹ Thuận Bridge, completed in 2000, was the first span bridge to cross the Mekong. The design for the bridge and its site were first outlined in a 1963 study by the Nippon Koei Company.[36]

American journalists often presented such sites for development as fiercely violent landscapes superimposed upon places with tremendous economic potential, "new frontiers" for the forces of liberalism and modernization. Peter White, writing for *National Geographic* and visiting the river several months after the Tết Offensive in 1968, described the delta as a place "of terror and hope," with rockets and tracers splitting the dense greenery while a brown-water navy patrolled the waterways. Upstream in Thailand, the article introduces readers to a cigar-chewing, leather-skinned Wyoming native, Lyle Mabbott, on loan from the Bureau of Reclamation to monitor soil coring at the Pa Mong Dam site near Vientiane, Laos. Under a makeshift tarp, Mabbott managed Thai technicians who were using a Swedish drill powered by a clanging Volkswagen motor to bring up three-inch cores of siltstone. The samples were capped in wax and airmailed to the bureau's Denver Hydraulic Laboratory for analysis. Meanwhile, a visiting Lao economist from the other side of the river explained that Pathet Lao guerrillas, using recoilless rifles and backed by several thousand

Vietnamese troops, had recently started shooting at the engineers and technicians. Mabbott explained to White, "Our fighter bombers are hitting the enemy hard. But he infiltrates more troops, and heavier weapons."[37] This unusual sort of fieldwork, carried out amid the rattle of small-arms fire and nearby air strikes, manifested in concrete terms the visions expressed by American modernization theorists such as Walt Rostow.

With regard to the Mekong Delta and this era of TVA-inspired development, no figure better embodied its principles and shortcomings in the face of the Vietnamese Revolution than David Lilienthal, widely known in the 1960s as the "architect" of the TVA and by the press as "Mr. TVA." As one of the first directors of the New Deal agency, he became famous in the late 1930s for easing popular fears about an impersonal, government agency controlling the Tennessee Valley's water by insisting on grassroots involvement by people living in the region. As recent biographies on Lilienthal attest, however, problems inside the TVA in the 1950s and 1960s followed river basin planning schemes overseas.[38]

Robert Komer, a veteran of the CIA and a special assistant to President Johnson in charge of developing the CORDS approach to "pacification," or what Johnson called "the other war" in Vietnam, contacted Lilienthal in February 1966 with a proposition that his private consulting firm Development and Resources Corporation (D&R) consider a contract to develop a regional development program in the Mekong Delta. Komer's call was followed by one from Walt Rostow, the national security advisor, who outlined the basic idea of the program:

A critical part is giving these people a sense that they not only have a future, but what shape it might have. This means a postwar plan; but it would have to be a particular kind of postwar plan. . . . If we get that kind of postwar plan [i.e., one focused not on gross national product but on tangible development projects] we can begin to find ways to carry out aspects of an aid program while the fighting is still going on.[39]

Lilienthal then submitted and "won" (although he knew it was likely that no other consulting firms wanted the task) the contract to develop a "Mekong Delta Development Program," and on February 13, 1967, he arrived on his first visit to Sài Gòn.[40]

Lilienthal's published journals from these years offer a unique, high-level American perspective on the likelihood of actually developing such a regional development authority as the TVA in a country sliding into an increasingly violent war. On his approach into the Sài Gòn airport, he describes his aerial perspective on two American jets bombing a target just several miles off from the city and later recalls flashes of B52 strikes in the distance, wondering in his writing about the chances for postwar planning. However, as a true believer in the promise of high technology and modernization to empower grassroots participation, Lilienthal is at his most insightful on the changes happening around him in the countryside and the increasingly apparent disconnects between the American pacification mission, the counterinsurgency laboratory, and the military conduct of the war. While traveling by boat around Bangkok and then again on a foray into the delta, he notes the particularly innovative nature of farmers. As a sampan with a long-tailed outboard engine passes, he is told by his American guide that the design was not introduced by Americans but instead developed by a Thai engineer who claimed to have been trained at MIT. Lilienthal then reflects that "even on many technical matters it is *we* who have a lot to learn."[41] As American diplomatic historians have noted, Lilienthal grew increasingly critical of Johnson's conduct of the war in the early months of his fact-finding missions to Vietnam. While attending a conference between the United States and the RVN on peaceful goals on Guam in March 20–21, 1967, he pondered how odd it was for Johnson to select the very base where B52's took off hourly to pound North Vietnam to rubble for a conference to discuss *peaceful* solutions to end the war through modernization.[42]

Although support for such American-funded postwar development largely faded with Johnson's decision not to run for a second term in 1968, development planning did not end. Government support for Lilienthal's firm D&R and for the Mekong Committee (what Lilienthal himself called an "international pork barrel approach" to development) dissolved under Nixon; but postwar planning accelerated into the early 1970s under a new goal of Asian regionalism.[43] Upon taking office in 1969, Nixon moved away from the older bilateral model of United States–led aid projects to a more multilateral form to be partially funded and provided by Vietnam's Asian neighbors. Nixon widely publicized this program at a July 1969 press conference on peaceful development strategies also held on Guam.[44] Project documents submitted by D&R in May 1969 and later studies contributed by American, Taiwanese, Korean, and Japanese contractors reflect this abrupt shift from American-centered programs to less-comprehensive, individual projects managed by Asian firms. Despite this decentralization of modernization and postwar planning in Vietnam, however, most contractors continued to propose large-scale, high-tech solutions, often reusing large chunks of late-colonial research on water management (such as Jammé's 1943–44 studies) with little criticism.

Rather than propose new visions for state-centered regional development, feasibility studies, including D&R's "Appraisal Report" submitted in May 1969, merely carried colonial and earlier American ideas forward with some additional references to newer technologies and assessment methods. Asian contractors continued what Theodore Porter describes as an American "cult of objectivity" in engineering and public works that involved the adoption of a French tradition for mathematical models adapted to such American creations as cost-benefit analyses and risk assessment models.[45] Lilienthal's report exemplified such a synthesis in its approach; for example, it imported French plans from the 1940s, such as engineer Jammé's ideas for post–World War II development of *casiers*. D&R's small staff in Sài Gòn, together with a group of Vietnamese engineers, presented to USAID a thin document essentially cobbled together from older reports and with no new field data.

While political fallout from the Tết Offensive spelled the end of such TVA-style initiatives in Vietnam, curiously it spurred the American military to take up "the other war" as an important strategy in defeating the NLF, especially in the Mekong Delta. After losing control over significant areas of the Mekong Delta in 1968, the U.S. Defense Advanced Research Projects Agency (DARPA) focused new attention on Đồng Tháp with a plan for "accelerated development." The chief of the army's Engineering Agency for Resources Inventories argued that the military, strategic, and social benefits to be derived from a widespread reclamation project that was started here in advance of other areas justified immediate surveying and research so that implementation could "begin as an impact program at the time of phase down for military operations."[46]

Although this project, like Lilienthal's, largely expanded on the ideas of colonial-era engineers, it was unique in two key ways. First, DARPA commissioned ecologists and geologists to travel to secure parts of the region and develop more nuanced maps of the region's subecologies— specific ecological communities defined by plants, water and soil conditions, and land use. Rather than view the floodplain as a vast "empty" space, the ecological surveys presented it more as a mosaic, as was increasingly popular in landscape studies in the late 1960s. Second, the DARPA study avoided any discussion of existing government agencies guiding the work or of proposed construction timetables. All of the recommendations were contingent upon a "post-hostility scenario," and absolutely no mention was made of guiding Vietnamese agencies in carrying out the work. A successive study by the Rand Corporation, a Santa Monica think tank with many retired military and CIA officers on staff, echoed this noncommittal stance, pointing to the troubling situation across the border in Cambodia as one major crisis to be resolved before major reclamation projects might be undertaken.[47] These reports were presented, in Vietnamese translation, to President Nguyễn Văn Thiệu's government, but with no expectations of them being taken up.

As the NLF's hold on the delta countryside strengthened, especially with American troop withdrawals in 1972–73, the cadre of engineers, scientists, and contractors distanced themselves from the Sài Gòn regime while retreating into a perhaps more utopian (but no less contested) faith in what one American systems theorist described as a singular ecological philosophy: "There seems to be no basic conflict in [numerical] values that needs to be worked out. The battles that have been going on in the region are about who shall govern, not about different ecological philosophies. If the facilities are designed properly it is the human population that benefits and all the ideologies are willing to take the credit."[48] Coming from the air-conditioned offices of Sài Gòn and Bangkok, such proclamations failed to reach the millions living in the delta. Drawing upon such evidence as the booming numbers of long-tailed outboard motors and TV antennae, Americans assumed it to be true without any serious solicitation of local opinion.

With regard to Nixon's Asian regionalism plans, one generally overlooked change during the era of American involvement was the return of Japanese construction firms to the region in the 1950s followed in the 1970s by Taiwanese, Korean, and other Asian firms. While Asian firms and consultants typically worked on American-funded contracts, their growing economic and political presence in the region had a significant effect on reframing the Mekong Delta as a new frontier for investment and business in Asia. One firm in particular, Nippon Koei, exemplified the complex transnational dimensions and post–World War II legacies involved in the return of Asian businesses. Formed in 1946 during the American occupation of Tokyo, Nippon Koei took on some of the more dangerous public-works projects in Vietnam, projects that frequently placed survey teams and construction consultants in less-secure areas. Beginning in 1957, the company sent engineers to a series of salt intrusion barriers in Sóc Trăng that had been abandoned since 1946. Intermittently into the 1970s, Nippon Koei fulfilled contracts to redevelop the barriers, and in 1972 actually completed construction of one barrier at Tiếp Nhứt. Funded by the World Bank, the project aimed to protect some fifty thousand hectares of farmland from salt intrusion in the dry season. Nippon Koei's engineers continued visits to the site as late as 1974, when they noted that the new project had stopped saltwater from intruding but had created other problems due to stagnating freshwater behind the dam. Were it not for farmers inside the area using an estimated one thousand water pumps to move wastewater, the dikes would have been of little use in increasing productivity.[49]

Finally, in the violent aftermath of the Tết Offensive and with Nixon's impending withdrawal of American troops and materials, President Nguyễn Văn Thiệu in 1970 launched a Land to the Tiller Campaign that once and for all aimed to solve the rural crisis by awarding tenants what they had sought since the 1930s: ownership of land. Contrary to the 1950s, when landowners formed a powerful block in the Vietnamese government, in 1969 a majority of legislators in the National Assembly (Quốc Hội) backed President Thiệu's plan to transfer land to farmers and simultaneously reimburse former landlords through a combination of direct payments and bonds. In his 1974 study of the program, C. Stuart Callison noted that by 1973 the government had surpassed its goal of redistributing over one million hectares to the farmers. Land to the Tiller, inaugurated on March 26, 1970, even recognized historic Việt Minh and NLF land grants made after 1945, providing those farmers government-issued deeds that recognized the same land plots as had the latest revolutionary papers.[50]

While American advisers and Vietnamese politicians trumpeted the successes of the program in terms of land redistributed, Thiệu's land reform appears to have been issued too late to have swayed farmer loyalties from the NLF to the government. While the reforms may have solved the historic land crisis, they did little to change farmers' minds about which authority was most legitimate in the countryside. Since the 1940s, older farmers had participated in a revolution that was not only economic or military but cultural, offering the means for them to gain literacy, participate in local government, and define their places within a broad-based social and military movement. Furthermore, by 1971 because of the escalated violence there was no shortage of land to farm. Since the Tết Offensive, tens of thousands of families had left their villages for the cities and towns; and landlords had not set foot on former parcels since the mid-1960s.[51] Finally, the period from 1971 to 1973 marked a long period of cease-fires punctuated by resumptions of B52 bombing and large-scale offensives as the United States, the Democratic Republic of Vietnam (DRV), and the Provisional Revolutionary Government of South Vietnam (PRG; an NLF-sponsored government-in-exile since 1969) met for negotiations in Paris. With the signing of the Paris Peace Accords on January 27, 1973, the PRG was officially recognized as the legitimate government in liberated areas that had effectively been under its control since the 1960s.[52] Thus, while the Thiệu government might have offered precisely the land tenure terms farmers had wanted all along, by the early 1970s it became increasingly apparent that NLF authority in the countryside was increasing.

Escalation

After the Tết Offensive commenced on January 31, 1968, the American-RVN military infrastructure in the delta shifted to a ramped-up, offensive strategy that had dire consequences for much of the rural population and the water environment. Liberated zones and many contested areas were designated on maps as free-fire zones, where anyone caught moving under certain conditions or at certain times was subject to be fired upon. In local parlance, however, the same areas were referred to by the more general term wasteland (*đất bỏ hoang*). The term in Vietnamese suggests land put back (*bỏ*) into a virgin or uncultivated (*hoang*) state; more than being left fallow, the term has a negative connotation. After 1945, and especially after 1968, farmers spent more and more of their time traveling through such lands.

Fields often became wasteland when farmers abandoned them or when guerrillas constructed barriers in irrigation works; after 1968, increased bombing led to more and more personal decisions to abandon land. Farmers grew accustomed to unprecedented instances of violence coming from the sky. Mr. Dang, who lived south of the Vị Thanh agroville in Hòa Lựu Village, recalled:

> At the place where I was living at that time, they shot down a jet from Vị Thanh, and in one day they dropped bombs nine times. Then they sent airplanes to scatter poisonous chemicals at the place where they were shot down. Because of that, at the time my land had a lot of bomb holes, like a *khọt* pan. [A *khọt* pan is a clay pan with an array of depressions used for making small cakes.] Other kinds of marks from the fighting have disappeared, but the bomb holes

are still there as evidence. They were always dropping M105's [leaflet bombs] wherever they thought necessary. At night, wherever the B57 [a high-altitude reconnaissance and bomber aircraft] dropped its bombs, there was no one left alive. People called that stealth bombing; they flew around at night and dropped bombs anywhere they wanted to. During the days, they had scout planes that would go out and drop a mortar at the place they wanted to bomb; then they would leave and pin the spot [on the map], and at night they would return and bomb it; they called that stealth bombing. During the day, also in this village, they sent the wing sprayers, the C-130's. They went up high, spraying down like fog. After that they carried it on helicopters and flew closer to kill us. They got my place with a helicopter. If I had been inside it, I would have been soaked, too. After that, when the poison dried, it looked like lime; just three days later, the trees dropped their leaves.[53]

That this man could, thirty-five years later, accurately identify the bombers, the leaflet bombs, and the winged sprayer aircraft using American military acronyms suggests how intimate farmers had become with the American arsenal. Daily life in the delta was increasingly punctuated with the droning engines of small, scout aircraft, the roaring sonic booms of jet fighters, and the sudden, deadly thunder of bombing runs and shelling. On some occasions, cargo planes passed overhead spraying chemicals such as Agent Orange to defoliate selected areas.

Although farmers no longer used these lands for commercial agriculture, they nevertheless continued to depend on wild rice and wild fauna for survival. In what is one of the more ironic twists of the American War, the intensive bombing and dislocations caused by post-1968 strategies encouraged farmers to become allies with the delta's wild environment and species. They shifted cultivation techniques from transplanted, short-stem rice (*Oryza sativa*) to long-stem floating rice (*Oryza rufipogon*), which tolerated higher flood levels and spontaneously regenerated. Once a staple in the floodplains before 1900, phantom rice (*lúa ma*) again flourished in the region. Other farmers stopped farming rice altogether and instead constructed temporary clay mounds for raising tobacco. Rice became so precious that in some outlying areas one kilo of rice traded for three of tobacco. In interviews, farmers also recounted many wild plant and animal species, especially native migratory fish that returned to flooded fields. Contrary to modern conservationist ethics, most did not consider this return to wilderness a good thing. More often than not, they recalled swarming mosquitoes:

Because the canals and creeks were all torn up, the mosquitoes here were ten times worse than before; wherever the bombs were dropped, the water was stagnant, and stagnant water produced a lot of mosquitoes! We had a hut made from scrap rubber here; we used it for sleeping when we traveled through the area during the war ... I'd keep swatting back and forth at them with my head scarf—swat one way and they would come from the other side—and they still bit me.... There were thousands of them; they just bit me freely—I could not kill them all.[54]

The war forced people living beyond the perimeters of government towns and bases to improvise some basic necessities. NLF field hospitals sometimes relied on coconut juice as a substitute for saline solution. Mr. Mười recalled its preparation: "We'd cut away the outer husk, then we'd stick the needle into the middle of the coconut. Other soldiers that were injured, they had penicillin and bromine solution [mercurochrome], and on the inside they used only saline solution. We also used honey to apply to the wound, then we bandaged it."[55] Fuel was also often difficult to obtain for household use in outlying areas; people saved it for their boats and water pumps. During shortages, for lighting around the house, farmers used the oleoresinous nut of the Calophyllum tree (cây mù u) as a lantern wick. They pounded the nut until it formed a fibrous pulp; then they drew it into a long wick and burned one end of it. Other farmers recalled using animal fat from pigs or field mice in their lamps.[56]

Although American bombing and ARVN troop movements often limited guerrillas' movements, the NLF worked to expand its own governmental and physical infrastructure from the base areas. Controlling local traffic on waterways was a crucial source of revenue. For local farmers and merchants traveling the waters, NLF control was achieved not by ambush but by tax collection checkpoints. American advisers as early as 1963 recognized that the NLF controlled most of the delta's waterways except for the widest canals and rivers.[57] During severe floods in 1966, the NLF made additional gains as roads in Đồng Tháp Mười and around Long Xuyên were submerged. NLF tax collectors traveled by motorized boat and intercepted travelers; only women and children were permitted to pass without paying. RVN officials, soldiers, or businessmen caught were subject to having their boats seized or destroyed.[58]

When Sài Gòn forces regained control over some key waterways in 1970–71, however, the practice of informal toll points did not cease. One American report discussing "extortion on the waterways" noted that one merchant traveling from Sài Gòn to the Cambodian border near Châu Đốc had to make thirty-six separate payoffs, ranging from one hundred to several hundred piasters ($5–$20), to persons posing as National Police, Customs, Maritime Police, and Army representatives.[59] Besides navigating the ever-present tax collection points and avoiding the occasional, violent episodes of bombing, farmers for the most part based their survival upon a kind of postmodern, pioneering ethic that required innovation of new technologies such as motorized water pumps and motors as well as a constant readiness to pay off the local tax authorities regardless of affiliation. Earlier creations such as agrovilles and strategic hamlets further hampered farmers' movements between government- and rebel-controlled territory, but for the most part they did not significantly influence the larger, fragmented, and ever-shifting geography of wastelands.

Despite persistent natural and human threats, there was no large exodus of refugees out of the countryside until after the Tết Offensive. As part of the new offensive strategy, the U.S. Navy inaugurated SEALORDS (South East Asia Lake Ocean River Delta Strategy) on November 5, 1968, and continued operations until July 1, 1970. The strategy's operations included campaigns to interdict major lines of NLF communication in the delta and to deny the NLF sanctuary in its historic bases in Đồng Tháp and the U Minh Forest. One of Admiral Zumwalt's "wild ideas" was an operation to encircle the U Minh bases with a network of pontoon bases where Swift Boats, helicopters, and other units could then penetrate and destroy core zones. Operation Sea Float commenced in June 1969 and over the next year was strategically successful in interrupting the PLAF's major supply routes into the lower U Minh Forest north of Năm Căn. A second operation, Breezy Cove, commenced a few months later on the Ông Đốc River near the upper U Minh Forest (map 13). This period of intensive bombing and large-unit fighting was extremely disruptive not only for PLAF movements but especially for the local inhabitants who had survived to this point. During the course of operations, the American-RVN force succeeded in defending the floating bases and in some cases reopening waterways. However, military accounts of the numbers of PLAF troops killed—forty to fifty per month—suggest that perhaps twenty thousand troops and their families either remained dug in or exited along with the refugees.[60]

According to both American and Vietnamese sources, this two-year series of operations was one of the most destructive in the delta. A Vietnamese memoir of the base area in the upper U Minh Forest notes

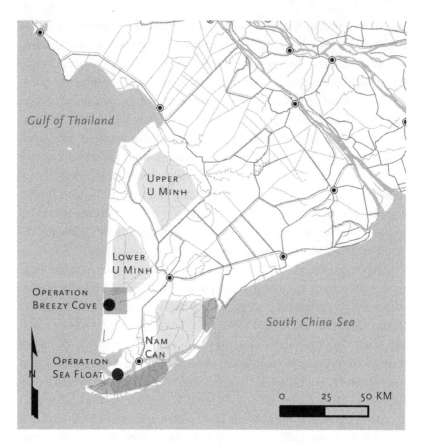

Gulf of Thailand

UPPER
U MINH

LOWER
U MINH

OPERATION
BREEZY COVE

South China Sea

NAM
CAN

OPERATION
SEA FLOAT

N

0   25   50 KM

MAP 13. *American Operations and Spray Areas, 1969–70.* Source: *Author.*

that a single B52 strike in November 1969 killed 27 people and wounded many more. In Vĩnh Thuận District, an area east of the upper U Minh Forest, out of 12,000 young men and women who served in the area during this period, 2,073 were killed and 1,194 were injured. Sixty-two families in the district had lost two or more children in the fighting.[61] An American survey of refugees prepared after American operations were handed over to ARVN units in 1971 estimated that roughly 63,000 people had fled their homes in the base areas to request government assistance and relocation. An American adviser traveling in the Cà Mau Peninsula described the waterways around the provincial seat as "wall to wall boats" where families had brought on their sampans stores of food, house frames, and all personal belongings. The overwhelming majority of these persons were old men and women and children. When asked where the younger men were, people replied that they had disappeared after the Tết Offensive. Perhaps most interesting in the report was that the majority of persons interviewed responded that until 1969 living conditions under NLF control had been good compared with past times. It was only the intensified bombing that forced them to move.[62]

Finally, while the U Minh campaigns caused widespread disruptions primarily through combat and B52 bombing, disruptions caused by defoliation—the aerial spraying of chemicals under the Air Force Operations Trail Dust and Ranch Hand—were limited to areas surrounding the U.S. Navy floating bases (map 13).[63] Contrary to popular conception, defoliation played a relatively minor role in forcing people to flee base areas. Because the sight of planes with spray rigs passing overhead created such an agitated response from farmers, American advisers were reluctant to call for defoliation except to clear areas around downed aircraft. One American observer wrote:

> Presently it is necessary only for an airplane with a spray rig to fly over, or the sight of a vehicle or man-packed apparatus, to generate a rash of claims. Much of this is no doubt opportunism, i.e. an attempt to recover some (any) loss by blaming defoliation. Some of it is no doubt a product of enemy propaganda, but a rather significant amount represents a belief that herbicides are responsible for the loss, whether imagined or real.[64]

While large patches of forest along the Sài Gòn River and in the Central Highlands lay in waste from years of fighting, defoliation, and bombing, the majority of the delta's agricultural areas suffered primarily from neglect while wild plant and animal populations may have rebounded from colonial-era reclamation.

Denouement

In many ways the American War in the delta ended where it began. Areas such as U Minh and Đồng Tháp that had been cradles of the revolutionary cause since the 1930s returned in 1973 to being areas now governed by the NLF. The Provisional Revolutionary Government, founded in 1969 as a government-in-exile for the NLF, organized provincial People's Committees after the signing of the Paris Peace Accords on January 27, 1973; and thousands of military and technical advisers from North Vietnam arrived in PRG areas to rebuild irrigation works, reestablish schools, and fortify PLAF battalions and regiments. The American role in the war effectively ended with the signing of the four-party agreements in Paris and the release of American prisoners of war. On March 29, the last American troops left Vietnam; and from then until April 30, 1975, America's involvement reverted to the advisory role it held from 1950 to 1965. One *New York Times* article in 1974 estimated that the American population in Vietnam amounted to about three thousand military contractors and advisers working at the large air bases and two thousand civilian personnel working at the embassy and corporate offices in Sài Gòn.[65]

The American role in post-1973 Vietnam, by far the least-studied era of American involvement, in many ways resembled the technical and advisory efforts of the Military Assistance and Advisory Group in post-1954 Vietnam. Daily news from Vietnam diminished in the American media, and the news that did reach American audiences tended to confirm an impression of a slow demise for the Sài Gòn government. In January 1974, the month leading up to the Tết holiday, senior General Electric jet engine mechanics worked twelve-hour shifts at double-overtime wages with double-salary benefits to keep the aging fleet of American-donated aircraft operational. Meanwhile, the seventeen- and eighteen-year-old Vietnamese men assigned to learn from these men exhibited little interest, as they earned from ten to thirty-five dollars per month to perform the same maintenance jobs.[66]

While there was a lull in the fighting in some areas, the conflict nevertheless continued to grind on at the boundaries between Sài Gòn- and PRG-controlled areas. In Đồng Tháp, fighting raged as it had in the 1860s at the water's edge where deep canals around Mỹ Tho and the Mekong gave way to shallow, flooded plains. Reinforced by northern Vietnamese troops and Soviet weaponry, NLF forces pushed outward from their bases to extend control to some district capitals such as Vĩnh Kim near Mỹ Tho. District officials were reluctant to travel more than a kilometer outside well-defended compounds, and sniper and grenade attacks on town markets became more frequent as ARVN patrols slackened and American air support disappeared.[67]

Vị Thanh, site of the first agroville, was surrounded by some of the worst fighting in the delta from 1973 to 1975. Joseph Treaster, a *New York Times* reporter visiting in July 1973, noted that approximately twelve thousand government troops were garrisoned in the town while an almost equal number of PLAF and North Vietnamese Army (NVA) troops were

quartered in NLF-controlled parts of the province. Like Đồng Tháp, the
province straddled an important hydraulic border between deep canals
extending southward from the Hậu Giang region and the swampy, cajeput
forest stretching north from U Minh. While most villages between the
major bases had been laid to waste by shelling and were now only ghost
towns inhabited mainly by the elderly, the fighting in the region continued
month to month in what Treaster described as a kind of "ballet" as each
side tended to avoid large-unit encounters and instead waited for the other
side to make a mistake and fall into an ambush. As a sign of the changing
times, when a government adviser interviewed a farmer living just
outside Vị Thanh on agricultural practices, he answered politely and then
asked whether the adviser worked for Sài Gòn or the liberation.[68] Such
ambiguities between pro–Sài Gòn and pro-revolution "nation builders"
continued until the fall of the Sài Gòn regime on April 30, 1975, and the
numbers of Russian-trained, northern Vietnamese technical and military
advisers increased. In the liberated zones, farmers returned from military
service to the abandoned lands and began the long process of repairing
war-damaged homes, fields, and infrastructure.

FIG. 31. *Mercury Outboards with Fiberglass Shells, 2005.* Source: *Author photo.*

EPILOGUE

"**B**uilding the nation" (*xây dựng nhà nước*) has remained a central priority for the Vietnamese government in the delta region since 1975. As with many new projects, however, older environmental and legal problems persist. Today, as in past eras, there is still one fundamental problem in the delta: finding solid ground. Today's nation builders are faced with a more socially and environmentally complex situation as well. Population since 1975 has more than doubled to over eighteen million persons. Engineers and planners must navigate the historic built infrastructure that links old colonial-era towns that have grown into cities. The threat of rising sea levels has only amplified long-held concerns over the long-term viability of maintaining dikes and elevated roadways that may yet again become works of Penelope (never-ending projects). Furthermore, life in the delta in recent decades has been complicated by globalization of the Vietnamese economy. Increasing privatization of property and decentralization of state planning since the 1986 renovation (đổi mới) — market-oriented reforms — have allowed a host of local agencies and private firms to replace the state in some water management decisions. With the delta's booming economy in export agri- and aquaculture, "building the nation" has thus become more deeply intertwined with building private fortunes. After a century of war and intense reclamation, the delta today, including many newly reclaimed areas in eastern Cambodia, is starting to resemble many other densely populated, highly litigated wetlands where powerful agribusiness interests and local powerbrokers lobby government officials and management boards to advance their interests. One need only attend one of the annual provincial trade fairs to see many of the same corporate actors — Mercury Marine, Bayer CropScience, Monsanto, ADM, and Nestlé — that one finds at similar events in Mississippi or the Loire Valley (fig. 31). Although there have been numerous stunning success stories such as the delta's explosive growth as a center for rice and fruit exports in the global market and the much celebrated improvements in infrastructure such as the opening of a highway suspension bridge across the Mekong at Mỹ Thuận, many of the same environmental and social challenges that undermined earlier projects persist.

With every severe typhoon or flood come breaks in river and sea dikes and consequent destruction of hundreds of thousands of hectares of farmland that force more than a million displaced people to scramble to precious strips of elevated land. Since the late-colonial infatuation with casiers (polders), successive governments have continued a "Dutch dike" strategy to enclose floodplains such as Đồng Tháp and the Long Xuyên Quadrangle. Until the advent of shrimp and fish aquaculture in the late 1990s, saltwater and floodwater were anathema to the state's "rice everywhere" strategies, which were begun after 1975 to combat hunger. At first, with little access to foreign capital, the national government embarked on a series of large reclamation projects using mass labor; however, with market reforms in 1986 came access to foreign equipment and hundreds of millions of dollars to build and expand the system of sea and flood dikes. Combined with use of the International Rice Research Institute's high-yield rice, Vietnam went from being a net rice importer in the 1980s to becoming the world's second- or third-largest rice exporter in the 1990s.[1]

As in the past, the national government in Vietnam faces intertwined environmental and economic dilemmas. Recently completed dikes funded by several billion dollars in international loans were designed for freshwater rice irrigation; however, as international rice prices slumped in the late 1990s, more farmers in coastal areas entered into the highly lucrative business of shrimp farming. To flood their plots behind the dikes with saltwater, many made incisions into the dikes to permit seawater to flow in. These largely unregulated acts have severely undermined the structural integrity of large sections of dikes as farmers and state engineers again get litigious over the function and form of the built environment.[2]

Often only a spectacular natural or man-made disaster is sufficient to bring debates over continuing problems of changing environments and public works into the limelight. In the United States, this happened after one-hundred-year-flood levees in New Orleans burst during Hurricane Katrina (2005) and inundated much of the city, killing over 1,800 people and incurring over one hundred billion dollars in damage. Four years later, the U.S. National Academy of Engineering concluded its study of the hurricane by declaring that ever-bigger dikes would not save a city that lies below sea level. The solution to future flooding and storms, it stated, was not to continue expanding the dike system but to relocate key services to higher ground.[3] During severe floods in the Mekong Delta, dikes routinely fail, and a large percentage of the eighteen million inhabitants are accustomed to moving rapidly to higher ground.

Vietnam has had its share of national and international public attention because of forest fires, floods, and in 2007 the collapse of a second suspension bridge under construction over the Hậu Giang branch at Cần Thơ. At over four kilometers long, the new span would have completed an old dream of urban engineers to extend the highway network from Sài Gòn to the farthest reaches of the delta and on to Cambodia. But on September 26, 2007, after several days of torrential rains, a section of an approach ramp collapsed, killing over fifty people and injuring one hundred more.[4] Subsequent investigations pointed to the unexpected sinking of a newly completed, six-thousand-ton supporting structure as the cause. The engineers had again failed to reach solid ground. Within a day, President Nguyễn Minh Triết was on hand to comfort victims' families. He called the disaster the worst in the history of Vietnam's construction industry.[5] As Chief Engineer Combier reflected in 1881 and certainly national agencies have considered since the bridge's collapse, expanding such a floating infrastructure above a soft, dynamic environment runs the risk of producing projects with no financial end.

Vietnamese from Cần Thơ to Hà Nội, however, express a strong desire to see bridge and highway projects completed. Because such bridges do not interfere with water flow and offer faster, easier access to "the city" (Hồ Chí

Minh City), there is little question that the bridge that collapsed in 2007 will eventually be completed. The city of Cần Thơ has in just a few decades grown from a regional town with about three hundred thousand persons to a sprawling city with a population of well over one million. Today rice fields are liable to be taken not only by floods but also by developers. Especially since the late 1990s, waves of new housing and industrial development projects have eclipsed the contested landscapes of the 1960s and erased the downtown facades of colonial storefronts and villas built in the early 1900s. Except where historical preservation authorities and communities have intentionally preserved old villas or war-damaged structures, it is increasingly difficult for tourists today to recognize any traces of the violent wars that once ravaged the landscape.

Given the traumatic events of Vietnam's long twentieth century, the coming of new architecture and the focused preservation of the old is by most accounts a very good thing. French tourists may stroll along the river quay in Cần Thơ or Mỹ Tho and eat a French meal inside a refurbished colonial-era building. American veterans may visit the sites of old bases and recognize such remnants as rusting petroleum tanks and cracked airport tarmacs that to most other eyes appear as generic, industrial decay. If one looks more closely at the cutter-suction dredges cleaning canals on the river or the ferries carrying motor traffic across the river branches, one may recognize beneath dozens of layers of paint the beaten-up shells of craft that have been in operation since the 1960s. However, if one actually boards these vessels and ventures into their engine rooms, he or she will likely find that the original Caterpillar or General Motors engines have been replaced, often in Frankenstein fashion, with parts from Japan, China, Europe, and the United States.

With the lifting of the American trade embargo against Vietnam in 1994 and the signing of a bilateral trade agreement in 2001, some of the original American suppliers involved in the military-sponsored construction of the 1960s have even returned. In 2000 *New York Times* reporter Wayne Arnold interviewed a fisherman who had just outfitted an eighty-nine-foot fishing trawler with a 480-horsepower Caterpillar engine and who expected to now get rich exporting tariff-free seafood to the United States.[6] In 2007 a representative from the Kohler Corporation even contacted me to get an opinion of Kohler's brand recognition. He had Googled the terms "kohler" and "Vietnam" and found a conference paper I had presented.[7]

I do not know what became of Kohler's plans to reenter the Vietnamese market, but I responded by pointing out that Kohler (*Kô-le*) was a household name for many older Vietnamese, especially the patriotic supporters of the Revolution. I am not sure that this response enthused Herb Kohler, Jr. (the president of the company and reportedly interested in this venture), but it does point to the ways that such American objects and historic built environments are being framed and interpreted in Vietnam today. Such objects as a *máy kô-le* mounted on a *ghe tam bản* are familiar fixtures of history museums that have sprouted up across the region. They almost always figure into exhibits describing the political activities of the National Liberation Front in that province. Similarly, some built environments such as the first agroville at Vị Thanh have since become thriving towns, but the memory of the agroville has been preserved in a museum located in the old town center. Visitors to the museum at Vị Thanh walk through a series of dioramas depicting the atrocities associated with forced relocation. Finally, along the highways there are many statues, billboards, and other historic markers to focus the traveler's attention on the region's revolutionary past (fig. 32).

Especially in the current climate of "market-oriented socialism," other elements of the delta's history, especially its economic and environmental history, are largely ignored. A closer look at nation-building in specific places reveals many lingering tensions over water management, land rights, and political access that have been there in some cases since the days of the Nguyễn before colonial rule. In that sense, many of today's problems in the delta are newer versions of much older problems and tensions in the region. Were Jacques Rénaud to return to the Vĩnh Tế Canal today, he might be surprised to find the borderland almost as tranquil and uninhabited today as in 1879. The ethnic-Chinese-supported Temple to the Lady of the Land (Bà Chúa Xứ) has recently become a magnet for national and international pilgrims, attracting well over one million visitors per year; however, a few kilometers down the canal toward the sea, the waterway still probably looks much the same as it did in 1879. The middle portion is annually submerged in autumn floods, and villages in this section use mostly thatch construction. Such scenes contrast sharply to the booming cities of the *miệt vườn* (Cần Thơ, Mỹ Tho, and Long Xuyên). Most of the water traffic is still local: fishing boats returning from the Gulf of Thailand or long, low passenger boats powered by smoky diesel engines bolted on the back. The old road built in 1820 on the eastern side of the canal to the border crossing at Tịnh Biên has been raised, widened, and covered in asphalt; and motor traffic has picked up considerably. One can still find the same stone tablets at the tomb of Thoại Ngọc Hầu and visit the Pagoda of Western Peace.

FIG. 32 *Billboard along Highway 40, Láng Hầm. The caption reads: "Hậu Giang is stepping up its processes of industrialization and national modernization to realize the goal of 'rich people, strong country, just society, civilized people.'"* Source: *Author photo.*

The 1816 citadel that guarded the entrance to the canal in the 1820s is still occupied by the military, and a certain amount of transborder smuggling and other illicit activity continues to attract occasional attention.

Such landmarks, particularly the Bà Chúa Xứ Temple, suggest the persistence of precolonial history and even a partial return to an even older, Chinese-influenced business network on the water frontier. The delta has emerged as a modern Chinese business frontier, as catfish farms and seafood factories do most of their trade with Taiwanese, Hong Kong, and Singaporean firms.[8] If anything, Rénaud today might express amazement that, despite all of the French dredging, the post-1960s urban growth, and the devastating wars, the built and natural landscapes today are still subject to many of the same environmental and social influences as they were before 1860.

Less obvious to visitors in the Vĩnh Tế region and other areas, however, are persistent ethnic and class tensions that have resurfaced with the departure of the Americans in 1975. A newer monument, an ossuary, near the canal in the village of Ba Chúc commemorates a series of violent clashes between Khmer and Vietnamese forces in 1977. In April 1977, Cambodia's genocidal leader Pol Pot ordered his Khmer Rouge forces across the Vĩnh Tế Canal to attack ethnic-Vietnamese villages. After a Vietnamese counterattack on the Khmer Rouge bases, Pol Pot sent his troops to destroy the village of Ba Chúc on Vĩnh Tế Canal, where, according to Vietnamese accounts, only 2 of the village's 3,157 people survived.[9] The ossuary serves a dual purpose, commemorating the atrocity and reminding visitors of the violent intraregional engagement that followed the American withdrawal.

The resurgence of private enterprise in the region in the 1990s has given rise to disputes over access to land and property rights. Tensions between ethnic Khmers in the delta and both the Vietnamese and Cambodian governments have been expressed in protests led by Khmer monks and in court cases where ethnic-Khmer citizens claim that they are being discriminated against in land deals and other big development projects.[10]

While museums continue to reinforce the main historical narratives of the region and various protests attract attention to the views of ethnic minorities and the poor on contemporary issues, very little attention has been paid to the ecological philosophy behind many of the large development projects. One reason for the relative absence of discussion about contemporary environmental values may be that powerful international lenders such as the World Bank and the Asian Development Bank have partnered with the national government to push primarily large-scale projects. One might look at several catastrophic failures such as the broken sea dikes or the Cần Thơ Bridge and conclude rather that the national government favors such schemes for their political impact and the fees they bring to Hà Nội–based consultants. To be sure, one can find instances of corruption and bid-rigging in New York, Paris, and other places too. However, an emphasis on the national government as the primary actor in shaping the water environment and the discourse concerning it neglects the important roles that provincial governments, local governments, private enterprises, international organizations, universities, and individuals have come to play in environmental management and development policies. Different visions for the Mekong Delta play out in different contexts and venues.

Certainly with regard to government texts, the technocratic language of state-centered regional water management plans and basin development schemes of the 1960s continues to serve as a framework for updated plans. Decrees issued since the mid-1990s by the prime minister have emphasized the national government's role in long-range regional management of the delta's waterways and flood control structures in a manner reminiscent of the Army Corps of Engineers, the federal agency responsible for managing most major water control structures in the United States, including the levees in New Orleans. Politically and economically, such large-scale features as hydroelectric dams or shipping canals are of interest to the whole nation and justify a national agency presence. Similar to other basin management schemes as well, these decrees are sweeping documents that envision an array of works to be built in stages over ten or twenty years.[11] Such documents are often intended to respond to concerns voiced by citizens and officials about the hazards associated with living in such unpredictable regions. With enough investment and construction, such plans promise to rein in rivers and tides to achieve some kind of "final form."

Meanwhile, this national vision for the delta is tempered not only by available funds and budgetary fights but also by ongoing developments at both the international and local levels. The very source of the delta's rich sediment and freshwater, the Mekong River, is increasingly becoming subject to modification by over a dozen dams in the upper valley in Yunnan, China; and various groups, including the Vietnam National Power Company, have proposed ventures to build several large mainstream dams in the lower valley. While the Vietnamese government has for several decades now strongly advocated building dams on the Mekong and other rivers to generate electricity, its officials are also beginning to voice concerns that projected dams may have severe environmental and economic consequences for people in the delta. Alterations to the volume of water and sediment traveling into the delta may stop the seaward growth of the delta's coastal areas and require far greater expenditures to protect low-lying areas from floods and salt intrusion, as parts of the delta may sink below sea level.

Other challenges to a state-centered vision of development come locally from the millions of people and local authorities directly responsible for shaping specific features of the delta. A different disaster, a wildfire in one of the last vestiges of the peat forest in U Minh, illustrates the powerful role that local farmers play in triggering larger events. Increasing settlement in the area after 1975 coupled with increasing use of shallow wells and the cutting of new drainage canals gradually lowered the water table several meters. During one particularly severe drought in 2002, this dried the peat soil layer in the forest and it caught fire. The blaze continued for almost two months. Several thousand army troops, police, and forest rangers struggled to extinguish the fire, ultimately pumping in saltwater to douse the flames.[12] The difficulty that state officials have had in controlling the behavior of internal migrants who settle in such areas has generally increased as more people migrate to the delta.

Returning to the question of an ecological philosophy, it may be crucial to the development of a more sustainable economy and environment here to understand how local inhabitants view nature. Political disruption and economic hardship associated with colonialism, postcolonial wars, and the economic depression of the 1980s not only undermined more traditional modes of rural life but also prevented the development of any coherent conservation ethic with regard to natural resources. Most farmers in the delta today are the descendants of former tenant farmers and revolutionary soldiers whose primary goals were to survive. Although they share the view common throughout the world that wetlands and swamps are wasteland, the current generation is really one of the first to be able to contemplate how a conservation ethic might be woven into ongoing plans for economic development, infrastructure, and responses to various environmental challenges.

By looking more carefully at the environmental assumptions implicit in nation-building, we can better appreciate not only why states continue to pursue the kinds of projects that they do but also why individuals may or may not support these schemes. By examining nation-building at specific sites to assess particular social and environmental factors, we may gain a better idea of the ways that institutions work (or fail) to mediate among the natural environment, various constituencies, and local inhabitants. Considering the quagmire as a metaphor for the ways that specific environments and groups of people figure into nation-building, let me conclude by suggesting that the metaphor be taken not solely as a cautionary notion against the hubris of technocrats. Farmers, provincial agricultural extension departments, university researchers, and even bridge engineers have increasingly come to accept that their respective activities depend to varying extents on feedback from other groups. I was repeatedly impressed by the actions of provincial rural development officials, who were usually from the same communities that they served. Every day they engaged in a web of interrelated factors—changing flood levels, changing export prices, changing government policies—directly related to water management decisions. What is perhaps most inspiring, given the long twentieth century, is that today decision making is less autocratic, and access to information easier. Institutions and practices are still far from perfect in the delta, but processes of negotiation and mediation have come a long way from the injustices of the colonial era. For people accustomed to a life mediated by negotiation between changes in their communities and changes in nature, the quagmire metaphor suggests a means for reintegrating stories about nature—actual earth (*đất*) and water (*nước*)— into the core of popular histories that outline the contours of the nation (*đất nước*).

NOTES

INTRODUCTION

1 Trịnh Hoài Đức, *Gia Định Thành Thông Chí*, trans. Đỗ Mộng Khương and Nguyễn Ngọc Tỉnh, ed. Đào Duy Anh (1820; Hà Nội: Giáo Dục, 1998), 19. All translations are my own unless otherwise indicated.

2 J. Rénaud, "Étude sur l'approfondissement du canal de Vinh-té et l'amélioration du port d'Hatien," *Excursions et reconnaissances* 1 (December 1879): 66–73.

3 Ibid., 66.

4 Harvey Meyerson, *Vinh Long* (Boston: Houghton Mifflin, 1970), 38.

5 See, for example, Halberstam's first personal encounter with the delta environment in David Halberstam, *The Making of a Quagmire* (New York: Random House, 1964), 85.

6 Historian Keith Taylor observes this problem with specific attention to Vietnam and suggests that works which reproduce familiar, nationalist narratives not only reinforce an artificial nationalist teleology but also

silence specific experiences that run counter to the national narrative in particular places, moments, and archives. Keith W. Taylor, "Surface Orientations in Vietnam: Beyond Histories of Nation and Region," *Journal of Asian Studies* 57 (November 1998): 954. Also, recent works on Vietnam have begun to pay greater attention to the roles of particular terrains in modern history. See, e.g., Andrew Hardy, *Red Hills: Migrants and the State in the Highlands of Vietnam* (Honolulu: University of Hawai'i Press, 2003).

7   There is a rich literature, with many anthropological and historical works, that critiques such processes as globalization, modernization, and modernism at more theoretical levels. See, e.g., James C. Scott, *Seeing like a State: How Certain Schemes to Improve the Human Condition Have Failed* (New Haven, CT: Yale University Press, 1998).

8   See, e.g., Bruno Latour, *Reassembling the Social: An Introduction to Actor-Network-Theory,* Clarendon Lectures in Management Studies (New York: Oxford University Press, 2005); Donna J. Haraway, *Simians, Cyborgs, and Women: The Reinvention of Nature* (New York: Routledge, 1991); and William Cronon, ed., *Uncommon Ground: Toward Reinventing Nature* (New York: W. W. Norton, 1995).

9   James C. Scott, *Weapons of the Weak: Everyday Forms of Peasant Resistance* (New Haven, CT: Yale University Press, 1987). Also, with regard to the Mekong Delta, see Samuel L. Popkin, *The Rational Peasant: The Political Economy of Rural Society in Vietnam* (Berkeley and Los Angeles: University of California Press, 1979); and James C. Scott, *The Moral Economy of the Peasant: Rebellion and Subsistence in Southeast Asia* (New Haven, CT: Yale University Press, 1977).

10   O. W. Wolters, *History, Culture, and Region in Southeast Asian Perspectives* (Ithaca, NY: Southeast Asia Program Publications, 1999); and John R. W. Smail, "On the Possibility of an Autonomous History of Modern Southeast Asia," *Journal of Southeast Asian History* 2 (1961): 72–102.

11   Thai historian Thongchai Winichakul describes such peripheral areas as interstices where state space yields to more local factors. See Thongchai Winichakul, "Writing at the Interstices: Southeast Asian Historians and Postnational Histories in Southeast Asia," in *New Terrains in Southeast Asian History,* ed. Abu Talib Ahmad and Tan Liok Ee (Singapore: Singapore University Press, 2003), 3–29.

12   Leo Marx, *Machine in the Garden: Technology and the Pastoral Ideal in America* (New York: Oxford University Press, 2000). Rudolf Mrazek extends Marx's interest in the intersections among technology, literature, and place in a study of life in the Dutch Indies. See Rudolf Mrazek, *Engineers of Happy Land: Technology and Nationalism in a Colony* (Princeton, NJ: Princeton University Press, 2002).

13   Sơn Nam is perhaps the most published and most well known Vietnam-

ese author who writes about the Mekong Delta. See, e.g., his *Lịch Sử Khẩn Hoang Miền Nam* (Hồ Chí Minh City: Văn Nghệ, 1994).

14 Pierre Brocheux, *The Mekong Delta: Ecology, Economy, and Revolution, 1860–1960* (Madison, WI: Center for Southeast Asian Studies, 1995), 123. See also Marguerite Duras, *L'amant* (Paris: Prix Goncourt, 1984).

15 David W. P. Elliott, *The Vietnamese War: Revolution and Social Change in the Mekong Delta, 1930–1975,* 2 vols. (Armonk, NY: M. E. Sharpe, 2003); and David Hunt, *Vietnam's Southern Revolution: From Peasant Insurrection to Total War, 1959–1968* (Amherst: University of Massachusetts Press, 2009).

16 Sơn Nam, *Đồng Bằng Sông Cửu Long: Nét Sinh Hoạt Xưa* (Hồ Chí Minh City: Thành Phố Hồ Chí Minh, 1993), 15.

17 Karl A. Wittfogel, *Oriental Despotism: A Comparative Study of Total Power* (New York: Vintage, 1957).

18 Donald Worster, *Rivers of Empire: Water, Aridity, and the Growth of the American West* (New York: Pantheon, 1992); and Michael Adas, *The Burma Delta: Economic Development and Social Change on an Asian Rice Frontier, 1852–1941* (Madison: University of Wisconsin Press, 1974).

19 James Brinkerhoff Jackson, *Discovering the Vernacular Landscape* (New Haven, CT: Yale University Press, 1986).

20 Võ Tòng Xuân and Shigeo Matsui, eds., *Development of Farming Systems in the Mekong Delta of Vietnam* (Hồ Chí Minh City: Hồ Chí Minh City Publishing House, 1998), 18. The total area of the Mekong Delta extending from Kompong Cham in Cambodia to the South China Sea covers about five million hectares.

21 Nguyễn Hữu Chiếm provides an excellent introduction to the (Vietnamese) delta's geologic history in the first chapter of his dissertation. See Nguyễn Hữu Chiếm, "Studies on Agro-ecological Environment and Land Use in the Mekong Delta, Vietnam" (PhD diss., Kyoto University, 1994), 1–17. This dissertation is particularly useful for English-language audiences because it integrates historical sources in English and French on the region's geologic history with more contemporary Vietnamese works.

22 Sơn Nam describes this type of settlement in his book *Văn Minh Miệt Vườn* (Hà Nội: Văn Hoá, 1992).

23 Pierre Paris, "Anciens canaux reconnus sur photographs aeriénnes dans les provinces de Tak Ev et de Châu Đốc," *Bulletin de l'École française de l'Extrême-Orient* 31 (1931): 221–23.

24 One of the most comprehensive descriptions of the ancient material culture in the delta is Louis Malleret, *L'archéologie du delta du Mékong,* 3 vols. (Paris: École française d'Extrême-Orient, 1959). For an excellent discussion of ancient hydraulic infrastructure and pre-Angkor settlements near present-day Châu Đốc and the Vĩnh Tế Canal, see ibid., 1:27–33.

25 Stone inscriptions and Chinese documents suggest that this was the first

"Indianized kingdom" in Southeast Asia and that Indian and Southeast Asian elites traveled from the Gulf of Thailand to India. For a historical description based on epigraphs and Chinese histories, see George Coedès, *The Indianized States of Southeast Asia,* ed. Walter F. Vella, trans. Susan Brown Cowing (Honolulu, HI: East-West Center Press, 1967), 35–80.

26 For a history of early Vietnamese settlement in the late 1600s, see Nguyễn Ngọc Hiền, ed., *Lê Thành Hầu: Nguyễn Hữu Cảnh, 1650-1700* (TP Hồ Chí Minh: Văn Học, 1997). For a record of the 1679 meeting of Fukien Chinese with the Nguyễn Lord at Huế, see *Đại Nam Thực Lục: Quốc Sử Quán Triều Nguyễn* (Hà Nội: Sử Học, 1963), 1:91. For a history of the Chinese city-state at Hà Tiên, see Société des études indo-chinoises, *Géographie physique, économique et historique de la Cochinchine,* fasc. 2, *Monographie de la province d'Hà-Tiên* (Saigon: Imprimerie L. Ménard, 1901), 51.

27 Local scholar Trường Ngọc Tường in Cái Lậy guided me to several historic seats of pre-1800 military and administrative authorities in the vicinity of Đồng Tháp. At all of these sites, the Vietnamese followed the Khmer tradition of building on slight hills atop the ruins of older watchtowers and building foundations. See n. 7 in chapter 1.

28 The occurrence of peat soils in Southeast Asia is still a relatively poorly understood phenomenon. For an excellent summary of peat soil regions in the Mekong Delta and Southeast Asia, see Edward Maltby, C. P. Immirzi, and R. J. Safford, eds., *Tropical Lowland Peatlands of Southeast Asia: Proceedings of a Workshop on Integrated Planning and Management of Tropical Lowland Peatlands Held at Cisarua, Indonesia, 3-8 July 1992* (Gland, Switzerland: IUCN, 1996).

29 The original Khmer names are given in Lê Qúy Đôn, *Phủ Biên Tạp Lục: Quyển 1,* trans. Lê Xuân Giáo (Sài Gòn: Phủ Quốc Vụ Khanh Đặc Trách Văn Hoá, 1972), 108.

30 Sơn Nam, *Lịch Sử An Giang* (Long Xuyên: An Giang, 1986), 3.

31 Phạm Hoàng Hộ, *Cây Cỏ Việt Nam* (Hà Nội: Trẻ, 1999), 3:467.

32 In a case of reverse colonization, snakeheads have recently been introduced in American and European watersheds, where they have gained a reputation as "monsters" for devouring most other aquatic species and even skipping across dry land to colonize adjacent ponds.

1 WATER'S EDGE

1 Giang Minh Đoán, *Nguyễn Trung Trực: Anh Hùng Kháng Chiến Chống Pháp* (Hồ Chí Minh City: Thành Phố Hồ Chí Minh, 1998), 43 (my translation). Trực wrote this poem in classical 7-7 verse (*song thất*).

2 Paulin Vial, "Expedition de Cochinchine," in *Les grands dossiers de*

l'illustration: L'Indochine, ed. Eric Baschet (Paris: Livre de Paris, 1944), 16–18.

3 Nguyễn Khắc Đạm, *Nguyễn Tri Phương: Đánh Pháp* (Hà Nội: Hội Khoa Học Lịch Sử Việt Nam, 1998), 56–58; and Paulin Vial, *Les prèmieres années de la Cochinchine: Colonie française* (Paris: Imprimerie Briez, C. Paillart et Retaux, 1874), 2:90–92.

4 Vial, *Prèmieres années,* 2:144.

5 Ibid., 203–5.

6 Besides Vial's comprehensive accounts of French actions to 1871, there are many Vietnamese histories of these uprisings. On Đồng Tháp, see Nguyễn Hiến Lê, *Bảy Ngày Trong Đồng Tháp Mười: Du Ký và Biên Khảo* (Long An: Long An, 1989). On Nguyễn Trung Trực, see Giang Minh Đoán, *Nguyễn Trung Trực.* On the Bảy Thưa Forest uprisings led by Bửu Sơn Kỳ Hương millenarian Buddhist groups, see Trần Thị Thu Lương and Võ Thành Phương, *Khởi Nghĩa Bảy Thưa (1867–1873)* (Hồ Chí Minh City: Thành Phố Hồ Chí Minh, 1991). See also Nguyễn Văn Hầu, *Đức Cố-Quản: Hay là Cuộc Khởi-Nghĩa Bảy-Thưa* (Sài Gòn: Tân-Sanh, 1956). In addition to these three anticolonial heroes, there were numerous others. People in the delta region spoke of four heroes: these three and Nguyễn Hữu Huân, who led an uprising at Cai Lậy in 1863 and was later caught and exiled to Réunion Island. He was released a few years later and made his way back to Cochinchina, where he led more attacks before being captured and then executed in Mỹ Tho in 1868. Also see "Landscapes: Go Thap," *Nhân Dân,* October 16, 1999.

7 The original tower here was actually a Khmer structure that may have dated to pre-Angkor civilization (300 CE), but its name more likely came from Vietnamese military actions in the early 1800s when the Nguyễn army built new watchtowers here. The most recent work on Oc Eo sites in the Mekong Delta is that of the Mission archéologie du delta du Mékong (1997–2002), conducted by the École française d'Extrême-Orient and the Institute of Social Sciences and Humanities of Southern Vietnam. See Đao Linh Côn, "The Oc Eo Burial Group Recently Excavated at Go Thap (Dong Thap Province, Viêt Nam)," in *Southeast Asian Archaeology 1994: Proceedings of the 5th International Conference of the European Association of Southeast Asian Archaeologists, Paris, October 1994,* ed. Pierre-Yves Manguin (Hull: University of Hull, Centre of Southeast Asian Studies, 1994), 111–17.

8 Nguyễn Hiến Lê, *Bảy Ngày,* 47–49.

9 Vial, *Premières années,* 2:194–95.

10 Giang Minh Đoán, *Nguyễn Trung Trực,* 39–41. Vial includes a translation of Trực's recorded court statement in Sài Gòn in *Premières années,* 2:242–49.

11   Nguyễn Văn Hầu, *Đức Cố-Quản*, 38–41.

12   Hue-Tam Ho Tai, *Millenarianism and Peasant Politics in Vietnam* (Cambridge, MA: Harvard University Press, 1983), 47–48.

13   Ibid., 49.

14   Thongchai Winichakul, *Siam Mapped: A History of the Geo-body of a Nation* (Honolulu: University of Hawai'i Press, 1994). Because Vietnamese and Thai encounters with Europeans were so different in the mid-1800s, their ideas about national and political geography developed along very different lines. The concept of boundaries was also very different in these two cultures, as reflected in Thai and Vietnamese terms, which have very different connotations. The primary reason, however, for a difference in how some people in Cochinchina understood their national space derives from the fact of the delta's radically different physical geography.

15   The first telegraph lines in Cochinchina were laid by the navy in 1863 with over three hundred kilometers of low-grade wire running from Sài Gòn to provincial posts, as well as to Phnom Penh by 1864. The charge for transmitting twenty words in 1863 was five and a half francs. Telegraph offices typically operated in conjunction with post offices; there were nine telegraph offices in 1863. By 1865 the price per twenty words had dropped to two francs, and by 1871 there were nineteen telegraph offices and over one thousand kilometers of lines in operation. On August 1, 1871, the colony contracted with John Pender's China Submarine Telegraph Company to extend its transoceanic cable to create a new link between Hong Kong, Sài Gòn, and Singapore. Four of Pender's private cable ships laid the cable in 1871. See Comité agricole et industriel de la Cochinchine, *La Cochinchine française en 1878* (Paris: Challamel Aîné, 1878), 22–24. See also Cable and Wireless Company, "History of the Atlantic Cable and Submarine Telegraphy," http://atlantic-cable.com/CableCos/CandW/EExt/index.htm. Many people from Alsace-Lorraine serving in the military did not hear about the loss of their home territory to the Prussians until several months later, justifying the extreme need for telegraph service in 1870 and arguing for continued development of telegraph lines to Tonkin to aid ongoing military expeditions there in 1883. See Albert Marie Aristide Boüinais and A. Paulus, *La Cochinchine contemporaine* (Paris: Challamel Aîné, 1884), 481–88.

16   Vial, *Premières années,* 2:292.

17   Direction générale des travaux publics, Gouvernement générale de l'Indochine, *Voies d'eau de la Cochinchine* (Saigon: Imprimerie nouvelle, 1911), 84–85. These seven new canals were Trà Ôn (1876), Chợ Gạo/Duperré (1877), Chét Say (1878), Phu Tuc (1878), Mirador (1879), Boquillon (1875), and Saintard (1879).

18   Jules Brossard de Corbigny, "Notice sur les travaux de canalisation de la Cochinchine française," *Revue maritime et coloniale* 59 (1878): 513.

19 Ibid. The literal translation of *dos d'âne* is "donkey's back" or "hunchback"; the term was used to describe points of constricted flow on canals and more commonly now refers to speed bumps on roads.

20 Direction générale des travaux publics, *Voies d'eau,* 34.

21 Nguyễn Hiến Lê, *Bảy Ngày,* 23–28. Lê's account is a rich memoir of his travels in the Đồng Tháp region as a surveyor for the colonial Department of Public Works. He augmented geographic descriptions with information from historic texts and local history. He also gives a detailed explanation of the ways that *giáp nước* aided development of markets and transport in the delta. The original manuscript was written in the 1930s.

22 The *seize Mai* affair, when President Patrice MacMahon attempted to thwart republican ambitions by replacing the prime minister with a monarchist and dissolving parliament, prompted a shift in colonial policies. But in the general election that followed, republicans won overwhelmingly, and in January 1879 MacMahon resigned from office. William Henry Waddington, the new prime minister, selected Jauréguiberry.

23 Jean Bernard Jauréguiberry, cited in Jean Marie Thévenet-Le Boul, *Les travaux publics et les voies de communication en Cochinchine* (Saigon: Imprimerie nationale, 1880), 1.

24 Alice L. Conklin, *A Mission to Civilize: The Republican Idea of Empire in France and West Africa, 1895–1930* (Stanford, CA: Stanford University Press, 1997); and Michael Adas, *Machines as the Measure of Men: Science, Technology, and Ideologies of Western Dominance* (Ithaca, NY: Cornell University Press, 1989).

25 Charles Le Myre de Vilers, *La politique coloniale française depuis 1830* (Paris: Publication de la nouvelle revue, 1913), 14.

26 Brossard de Corbigny, "Notice sur les travaux," 520.

27 J. Rénaud, "Étude d'un projet de canal entre le Vaico et le Cua-Tieu," *Excursions et reconnaissances* 3 (1880): 317.

28 Cochinchine française, *Les travaux publics et les voies de communication en Cochinchine* (Saigon: Imprimerie nationale, 1880), 144.

29 Charles Combier, "Rapports présentés à S.E. Ministre," p. 3, 1881, record 4/904(3), Social Sciences Information Center, Hanoi.

30 Ibid., 4.

31 Ibid., 9.

32 Ibid., 19.

33 R. Gentilini, *Les voies de communication en Cochinchine* (Paris: Imprimerie Chaix, 1886), 28.

34 Ibid., 42–43.

35 *Messageries fluviales de Cochinchine* (Paris: n.p., 1908), p. 22, file 8°/3811(4), Social Sciences Information Center, Hanoi.

36 Cochinchine française, *Travaux publics,* 143.

37   Gouvernement du Cochinchine, *Contrats pour le service postal des cor-
     respondances fluviales de la Cochinchine et du Cambodge* (Paris: n.p., 1901),
     p. 35, file 8°/3811(3), Social Sciences Information Center, Hanoi.

38   Prosper Cultru, *Histoire de la Cochinchine française des origines à 1883*
     (Paris: Augustin Challamel, 1910), 379.

39   Direction générale des travaux publics, *Voies d'eau*, 39.

40   Ibid., 41.

41   Gilbert Chiếu, "Une bataille intéressante," *Supplement du Nông-Cổ Mín-
     Đàm*, October 23, 1907, 1.

42   Inspection des travaux publics, Gouvernement générale de l'Indochine,
     Dragages de Cochinchine: Canal Rachgia-Hatien (Saigon: n.p., 1930), 20.

43   James Ferguson, *The Anti-politics Machine: "Development," Depoliticiza-
     tion, and Bureaucratic Power in Lesotho* (Cambridge: Cambridge Univer-
     sity Press, 1990).

44   Sơn Nam, *Đồng Bằng Sông Cửu Long*, 136–37.

45   Martin Heidegger, *Vorträge und Aufsätze*, 4th ed. (Pfullingen: Günther
     Neske, 1978), 149, cited in Stuart Elden, *Mapping the Present: Heidegger,
     Foucault and the Project of a Spatial History* (London: Continuum, 2001),
     85.

46   Chantier du canal Bassac Cailon, "Bulletin hebdomadaire du 26 avril au 2
     mai 1908," file IA 13/236(1), Fonds Goucoch, Trung Tâm Lưu Trữ Quốc Gia
     II (hereafter TTLTQG2), Hồ Chí Minh City.

47   Sơn Nam, *Lịch Sử Khẩn Hoang Miền Nam*, 272.

48   Administrator of Can Tho to chief engineer of DPW, February 19, 1908, file
     IA 13/236(3), Fonds Goucoch, TTLTQG2.

49   "Ajudication de travaux de dragages a effectuer en Cochinchine pour
     l'amelioration du réseau des voies de navigation intérieure," January 17,
     1893, file IA 19/174, Fonds Goucoch, TTLTQG2.

50   Direction générale des travaux publics, *Voies d'eau*, 70.

51   "Travaux de dragages en régie," August 1894, file IA 19/174, Fonds Gou-
     coch, TTLTQG2.

52   "Etat au 31 Décembre 1902 des travaux exécutés par l'entreprise de dragages
     Montvenoux et Cie," December 1902, file IA 19/164, Fonds Goucoch,
     TTLTQG2.

53   Service des travaux publics, "Dragages dans les canaux de Cochinchine,"
     1939, file VI-A8/186(31), Fonds Goucoch, TTLTQG2.

54   Direction générale des travaux publics, *Atlas: Les voies d'eau de la Cochin-
     chine* (Saigon: Imprimerie nouvelle, 1911), pl. 14.

55   Direction générale des travaux publics, *Voies d'eau*, 44.

56   J. C. Baurac, *La Cochinchine et ses habitants: Provinces de l'est* (Saigon:
     Imprimerie commerciale Rey, 1899), 332.

57   Ibid., 334.

58 Société des études indo-chinoises, *Géographie physique, économique et historique de la Cochinchine*, fasc. 11, *Monographie de la province de Sóc-Trăng* (Saigon: Imprimerie commerciale Ménard et Rey, 1904), 65–66.

2 WATER GRID

1 P. Régnier, *Nivellement général de la Cochinchine: Rapport du chef du brigade* (Saigon: Imprimerie commerciale M. Rey, 1911), 12–13.

2 Gressier's holdings varied over the years, but by 1940 his firm controlled 140 square kilometers (14,000 hectares) of land and was one of several major companies operating in the delta. The Gressier Estate was originally the Guéry Estate. Administrator Guéry of Rạch Giá Province had petitioned for the concession in 1899. He later flipped the property for a small fortune, selling it to the Gressier Company. See *Plan topographie de la province de Cantho, 1/100.000* (Hanoi: Société geographique de l'Indochine, 1925).

3 Knowledge of the airstrip was gathered from personal trips to the site and examination of aerial photos taken by the U.S. Army in 1945. The airstrip was abandoned after 1954, and the U.S. military later built a military airstrip at the nearby town of Vị Thanh. The mill stood until 2005, when it was demolished, and the Gressier name could still be seen under the paint at the top of the mill.

4 Brocheux, *Mekong Delta*, 133.

5 Ông Diểu, interview with author, April 19, 2002.

6 Ibid.

7 Trịnh Hoài Đức, *Gia Định Thành Thông Chí*, 135 (bk. 3, 79a); Nguyễn Đình Đầu, *Chế Độ Công Điền Công Thổ Trong Lịch Sử Khẩn Hoang Lập ấp ở Nam Kỳ Lục Tỉnh* (Hà Nội: Hội Sử Học Việt Nam, 1992), 58–59. Historical sources from this time typically refer to Khmer provinces as *sóc* and Khmer provincial governors as *óc nha*.

8 *Đại Nam Thực Lục*, 2:133.

9 Lê Văn Năm, "Công Cuộc Khai Phá Trong Nửa Đầu Thế Kỷ XIX," in *Lịch Sử Khai Phá Vùng Đất Nam Bộ*, ed. Huỳnh Lứa (Hồ Chí Minh City: Thành Phố Hồ Chí Minh, 1987), 117.

10 *Đại Nam Thực Lục*, 3:9.

11 Ibid., 329.

12 Lê Văn Năm, "Công Cuộc Khai Phá Trong Nửa Đầu Thế Kỷ XIX," 123.

13 Li Tana, *Nguyễn Cochinchina: Southern Vietnam in the Seventeenth and Eighteenth Centuries* (Ithaca, NY: Southeast Asia Program Publications, 1998), 100–101.

14 Honey gathering was also a major business in the delta's vast forests at the time.

15 Nguyễn Công Bình, Lê Xuân Diệm, and Mạc Đường, *Văn Hoá và Cư Dân Đồng Bằng Sông Cửu Long* (Hồ Chí Minh City: Khoa Học Xã Hội, 1990), 377.

16 Venerating female deities occurred at local and state levels in both Cham and Khmer regions. King Gia Long and King Minh Mạng paid tribute to the Cham deity Thiên-Y-A-Na (a name derived from the Sanskrit *devaraja*), building temples dedicated to her and offering her royal titles. Nguyễn Thế Anh suggests that such actions were attempts to legitimize Vietnamese rule by formally recognizing locally popular deities and giving them official status within the bureaucracy. Nguyễn Thế Anh, "The Vietnamization of the Cham Deity Po Nagar," in *Essays into Vietnamese Pasts*, ed. K. W. Taylor and John K. Whitmore (Ithaca, NY: Southeast Asia Program Publications, 1995), 49. See also Philip Taylor, *Goddess on the Rise: Pilgrimage and Popular Religion in Vietnam* (Honolulu: University of Hawai'i Press, 2004).

17 Sơn Nam, *Lịch Sử Khẩn Hoang Miền Nam*, 62. Sơn Nam notes that Trịnh Hoài Đức (*Gia Định Thành Thông Chí*) does not write directly about the tools used but does describe this land as different from grassland (*thảo điền*). Grass cutting was commonly practiced until 1945; afterward, especially after 1975, continuous rice-cropping cycles prevented regeneration of grasses in fields.

18 Sơn Nam, *Cá Tính Miền Nam* (Hồ Chí Minh City: Trẻ, 1997), 21.

19 Trịnh Hoài Đức, *Gia Định Thành Thông Chí*, 155.

20 Trần Xuân Kiêm, *Nghề Nông Nam Bộ* (Hà Nội: Khoa Học Xã Hội, 1992), 53.

21 Trịnh Hoài Đức, *Gia Định Thành Thông Chí*, 154.

22 Trần Xuân Kiêm, *Nghề Nông Nam Bộ*, 54.

23 Trịnh Hoài Đức, *Gia Định Thành Thông Chí*, 45–46.

24 David P. Chandler, *A History of Cambodia* (Boulder, CO: Westview Press, 1992), 119.

25 Trịnh Hoài Đức, *Gia Định Thành Thông Chí*, 84. For a well-documented biography of Nguyễn Văn Thoại, see Nguyễn Văn Hầu, *Thoại Ngọc Hầu và Những Cuộc Khai Phá Miền Hậu Giang* (Sài Gòn: Hoa Sen, 1972).

26 Nguyễn Văn Hầu, *Thoại Ngọc Hầu*, 159.

27 Trần Nguyện Hành, "Les inscriptions de Thoại Sơn et de Vĩnh Tế," paper presented to the Premier Congress international des études Extrêmes Orientales, Hanoi, 1903. See also Nguyễn Văn Hầu, *Thoại Ngọc Hầu*, 167–79.

28 Trần Nguyện Hành, "Inscriptions de Thoại Sơn et de Vĩnh Tế," 7–9. Hành translated the original inscriptions from Chinese (the written language of the Vietnamese court) to French.

29 Société des études indo-chinoises, *Monographie de la province d'Hà-Tiên*, 10–11. See also Nguyễn Văn Hầu, *Thoại Ngọc Hầu*, 183.

30 Nguyễn Văn Hầu, *Thoại Ngọc Hầu*, 193.

31 Khin Sok, *Le Cambodge entre le Siam et le Viêtnam (de 1775 à 1860)* (Paris: École francaise de l'Extrême-Orient, 1991), 77. See also Chandler, *History of Cambodia,* 120.

32 In light of Vietnamese-Khmer tensions that continued until the Vietnamese military's withdrawal from Cambodia in 1989, Vietnamese histories remain silent on the rebellion and instead focus on the canal's strategic importance to the Vietnamese kingdom. See Nguyễn Văn Hầu, *Thoại Ngọc Hầu,* 193.

33 Sơn Nam, *Lịch Sử An Giang,* 9. See also *Minh Mệnh Chính Yếu: Quốc Sử Quán Triều Nguyễn* (Huế: Thuận Hoà, 1994), 3:152.

34 Sơn Nam, *Lịch Sử Khẩn Hoang Miền Nam,* 83.

35 Ibid., 171.

36 *Minh Mệnh Chính Yếu,* 7:295–307.

37 Trịnh Hoài Đức, *Gia Định Thành Thông Chí,* 80.

38 Nguyễn Đình Đầu, "Remarques préliminaires sur les registres cadastraux (địa bạ) des six provinces de la Cochinchine (Nam Kỳ Lục Tỉnh)," *Bulletin de l'École française d'Extrême-Orient* 78 (1991): 278.

39 This list comes from Nguyễn Đình Đầu's extensive series of projects on the *địa bộ* in the 1990s. In particular, he published six volumes on the six former provinces, discussing in detail examples of complete land entries in the *địa bộ,* area analyses of land cover, and etymologies of place-names from 1836. See Nguyễn Đình Đầu, *Tổng Kết Nghiên Cứu Địa Bộ Nam Kỳ Lục Tỉnh* (Hồ Chí Minh City: Hồ Chí Minh City and Toyota Foundation, 1994), 20–22.

40 Choi Byung Wook, *Southern Vietnam under the Reign of Minh Mạng (1820–1841): Central Policies and Local Response* (Ithaca, NY: Southeast Asia Program Publications, 2004), 195–96.

41 Ngô Vĩnh Long, *Before the Revolution: The Vietnamese Peasants under the French* (New York: Columbia University Press, 1991), 12.

42 Martin J. Murray, *The Development of Capitalism in Colonial Indochina (1870–1940)* (Berkeley and Los Angeles: University of California Press, 1980), 55. Murray and others rely on Yves Henry, *Économie agricole de l'Indochine* (Hanoi: Imprimerie de l'Extrême-Orient, 1932). For more on traditional communal land systems under the Nguyễn, see Nguyễn Đình Đầu, *Chế Độ Công Điền Công Thổ Trong Lịch Sử Khẩn Hoang Lập ấp ở Nam Kỳ Lục Tỉnh.* Sơn Nam's works combine both statistical summaries of land loss and many individual, detailed stories that show how such transfers of land displaced individuals and even entire villages. See Sơn Nam, *Lịch Sử Khẩn Hoang Miền Nam,* 175–90.

43 René Gueyffier, *Essai sur le régime de la terre en Indochine (pays annamites)* (Lyons: Imprimerie BOSC frères and RIOU, 1928), 152.

44 Inspection des travaux publics, *Dragages de Cochinchine,* 25.

45 Ibid., 63.

46 Brocheux, *Mekong Delta,* 123.

47 "Rapport sur l'état de la colonisation agricole europeéne dans les arrondissements depuis la conquête," July 28, 1897, file IA 4/N4(7), Fonds Goucoch, TTLTQG2.

48 "Canton de Đinh Khánh, village de Kế Sách à monsieur le chef de Canton," December 15, 1896, file IB 23/122(1–3), Fonds Goucoch, TTLTQG2.

49 Nguyễn Hiến Lê, *Bảy Ngày,* 69–71.

50 Sơn Nam describes Trần Bá Lộc as one of the three "most efficient" collaborators during the colonial conquest. See Sơn Nam, *Lịch Sử Khẩn Hoang Miền Nam,* 137–41.

51 Nguyễn Hiến Lê, *Bảy Ngày,* 69–71.

52 A. Normandin, *Travaux d'hydraulique agricole à étudier et à entreprendre en Cochinchine: Rapport de mission* (Saigon: Imprimerie commerciale M. Rey, 1913), 32.

53 Nola Cooke, "Water World: Chinese and Vietnamese on the Riverine Water Frontier, from Ca Mau to Tonle Sap (c. 1850–1884)," in *Water Frontier: Commerce and the Chinese in the Lower Mekong Region, 1750–1880,* ed. Nola Cooke and Li Tana (Singapore: Singapore University Press, 2004), 143–44.

54 "Le Service forestier en Indochine," *Bulletin de l'Association amicale des agents forestiers,* no. 11 (1909), file IA 13/308(12), Fonds Goucoch, TTLTQG2.

55 Frédéric Thomas, *Histoire du regime et des services forestiers français en Indochine de 1862 à 1945* (Hà Nội: Thế Giới, 1999), 73.

56 "Nombre de stères de bois à brûler vérifies," March 5, 1904, file IA 13/308(12), Fonds Goucoch, TTLTQG2. Today in the region almost all trees in uncultivated areas are plantations of cajeput or eucalyptus (the latter introduced from Australia).

57 Brière, "Exploration par M. Benoist de la partie déserte comprise entre les inspections de Rach-gia, Cantho et Long-xuyen (Novembre 1871)," *Excursions et reconnaissances* 1 (1879): 44.

58 Ibid., 46. It was named "phantom" rice by Vietnamese settlers because it appeared to float above the water.

59 Ông Mười, interview with author, April 12, 2002.

60 Theodore Porter, *Trust in Numbers: The Pursuit of Objectivity in Science and Public Life* (Princeton, NJ: Princeton University Press, 1995).

61 Société des études indo-chinoises, *Géographie physique, économique et historique de la Cochinchine,* fasc. 10, *Monographie de la province de Cần-Thơ* (Saigon: Imprimerie Ménard et Rey, 1904), 11. Cantons (*tổng*) were roughly equivalent in area to counties in the United States or to districts (*huyện*)

in Vietnam today. A village (*làng*) was the smallest administrative unit located within a canton.

62 Ibid.

63 Nhơn Nghĩa Village Council Head, Định Bảo Canton, May 1901, file IA 13/232(1), Fonds Goucoch, TTLTQG2.

64 Lieutenant-Governor Picanon to administrator of Cantho, July 25, 1901, file IA 13/232(1), Fonds Goucoch, TTLTQG2. In this list of damages, the letter describes average statistics for rice harvests and land at the time: one hectare cost sixty piasters, one hectare produced roughly ninety *giạ* (2700 kilograms) of milled rice, and three thousand kilograms of paddy (unmilled rice) cost fifty piasters. For orchard land, one hectare was worth two hundred piasters.

65 Decision 3378 of governor-general, December 31, 1902, file IA 13/232(1), Fonds Goucoch, TTLTQG2.

66 Ville de Saigon, Commisariat central de la police, May 27, 1914, file IB 25/124, Fonds Goucoch, TTLTQG2.

67 "Le gouverneur generale de l'Indochine à lt-gouv de la Cochinchine," letter 1832, June 14, 1911, file IB 25/124, Fonds Goucoch, TTLTQG2.

68 "M. Charousset, avocat secretaire de M. Thioller, avocat-défenseur à Saigon à M. Le Gouverneur-Generale de l'Indochine," May 22, 1912, file IB 25/124, Fonds Goucoch, TTLTQG2. For later mention of Henri Lachevrotière, see Philip Devillers, *Histoire du Việt-Nam de 1940 à 1952* (Paris: Éditions du Seuil, 1952), 173–74.

69 Ibid.

70 Chief Engineer, Direction générale des travaux publics, 1912, file IB 25/124, Fonds Goucoch, TTLTQG2.

71 Ibid.

72 Tân Bình village head to administrator of Cần Thơ, February 1910, file IA 13/232(5), Fonds Goucoch, TTLTQG2.

73 Benedict R. O. Anderson, *Imagined Communities: Reflections on the Origin and Spread of Nationalism*, 2d ed. (London: Verso, 1991), 374.

74 J. L. Dutreil de Rhins, *Avertissement géographique et orthographique sur la carte de l'Indo-chine orientale suivi d'un vocabulaire des noms géographiques annamites* (Paris: Imprimerie nationale, 1881).

75 Régnier, *Nivellement général de la Cochinchine,* 12–13.

76 Ibid., 11–12.

77 Normandin, *Travaux d'hydraulique agricole,* 6.

78 Ibid., 37–38.

79 "Procès verbaux de réunions de la Commission locale des travaux publics: Cochinchine," file IA 19/182, Fonds Goucoch, TTLTQG2.

80 Georges Lamarre, administrateur de Chaudoc, à monsieur le lieutenant

gouverneur de la Cochinchine (Cabinet) à Saigon, August 8, 1904, file IA 19/244(4), Fonds Goucoch, TTLTQG2.

81   Inspection des travaux publics, *Dragages de Cochinchine,* 5–6.

82   Ibid., 7–8.

83   Ibid., 75.

3   HYDROAGRICULTURAL CRISIS

1   "Commission permanente de 19 Juillet 1927: L'inspection generale du travail," *Tribune indochinoise,* August 24, 1927, 3.

2   Paul Bernard, *Le problème économique indochinois* (Paris: Nouvelles éditions latines, 1934), 123–24.

3   Ibid., 131.

4   Nguyễn Khắc Viên, *Vietnam: A Long History* (Hanoi: Thế Giới Publishers, 1993), 205.

5   Ibid., 207.

6   Brocheux, *Mekong Delta,* 176–78. For more on the Ba Son strike, see Christoph Giebel, *Imagined Ancestries of Vietnamese Communism: Ton Duc Thang and the Politics of History and Memory* (Seattle: University of Washington Press, 2004), 87–126.

7   Pierre Gourou, *Les paysans du delta Tonkinois: Étude de geographie humaine* (Paris: Éditions d'art et d'histoire, 1936).

8   Ngô Vĩnh Long, *Before the Revolution,* 206.

9   M. Combot and Paul Emery, "Étude sur les travaux d'hydraulique agricole dans le Trans-Bassac," October 20, 1942, file H.62/3, Toà Đại Biểu Chính Phủ Nam Việt (hereafter TĐBCPNV), TTLTQG2.

10   Alum (*đất phèn*) refers to aluminum and ferrous silicates (pyrite mottles) found in soils, such as in Đồng Tháp, Long Xuyên, and Phụng Hiệp, that are waterlogged, rich in organic content, and periodically flushed by seawater containing dissolved sulfate. Drainage and drying of the soils causes oxidation of the sulfate and results in severely acidic water. Acidic water itself is not a threat to rice or aquatic ecosystems; but the acidic water may dissolve more toxic ions of aluminum and iron that kill or severely limit rice growth. For a summary of key wetland processes in the Mekong Delta, see BirdLife International, *The Conservation of Key Wetland Sites in the Mekong Delta: Conservation Report Number 12* (Hanoi: Institute of Ecology and Biological Resources, 1999).

11   Normandin, *Travaux d'hydraulique agricole,* 31.

12   *Cây tràm* is still important in the delta as a source of rot-proof wood for construction and for medicinal "tea tree" oil. *Tràm* posts are used as pilings in foundations and for stilt houses. Fishermen used to use leaves and resin

from *cây giá* as a neurotoxin to stun fish; and honey gatherers captured honey from bees that pollinated both species. The name of the coastal city Rạch Giá refers to a creek (*rạch*) bordered by stands of *giá* trees. Cajeput mangroves buffered acidic water, absorbing aluminum and iron ions through their roots. Dr. Đương Văn Ni and others at Cần Thơ University have recently completed studies on the positive effects of cajeput-fish-rice systems for reducing acid sulfate. See Võ Tồng Xuân and Shigeo Matsui, *Development of Farming Systems*, 195.

13 "L'administrateur de Rach Gia a monsieur le gouverneur de la Cochinchine au sujet de la petit colonisation dans le Canton de Kien Hao," December 7, 1932, file IB 23/096(12), Fonds Goucoch, TTLTQG2.

14 "Nicolau, l'ingenieur en chef de la circonscription de HANSI à Mr le directeur des bureaux," August 17, 1943, file H.61/50, Fonds Goucoch divers, TTLTQG2.

15 "Rapport de l'inspecteur des affairs politiques au sujet des inondations dans le province de Chaudoc," September 12, 1923, file H.5/SL 1760, Fonds Goucoch divers, TTLTQG2. See also "Administrateur du mytho a la gouverneur de la Cochinchine," October 3, 1923, file H.5/SL 1760, Fonds Goucoch divers, TTLTQG2.

16 Paul Emery, "Étude sur les travaux d'hydraulique agricole dans le Trans-Bassac," October 20, 1942, file H.62/3, TĐBCPNV, TTLTQG2.

17 Direction générale des travaux publics, *Voies d'eau*, 20–22. Also see Service de la navigation, "Bulletins des crues 1920–21," file IA 2/222(1), Fonds Goucoch, TTLTQG2.

18 "Dossiers divers relatifs aux crues de Mekong," file H.5/HS 2938, Fonds Goucoch divers, TTLTQG2.

19 Bernard, *Problème économique indochinois*, 144–45.

20 M. Bagot, "Malaise agraire dans le Transbassac," April 28, 1939, file M.2/63, TĐBCPNV, TTLTQG2.

21 Ông Mười, interview with author, April 12, 2002.

22 Ông Rì, interview with author, April 12, 2002.

23 Ông Hai, interview with author, April 13, 2002.

24 Lê Quang Liêm, "La vérité sur l'échauffourée de Ninh-Thanh-Loi (Rach-gia)," *Tribune indochinoise*, May 20, 1927, 1–2.

25 Lê Quang Liêm, "La vérité sur l'échauffourée de Ninh-Thanh-Loi (Rach-gia)," *Tribune indochinoise*, May 23, 1927, 1–2.

26 Lê Quang Liêm, "La vérité sur l'échauffourée de Ninh-Thanh-Loi (Rach-gia)," *Tribune indochinoise*, May 25, 1927, 1–2.

27 Ibid.

28 "L'administrateur des Services civils, chef de la province de Rachgia à monsieur le gouverneur de la Cochinchine," December 7, 1932, file IB 23/096(19), Fonds Goucoch, TTLTQG2.

29 Sơn Nam, *Lịch Sử Khẩn Hoang Miên Nam,* 274. Some Javanese workers also came to the Mekong Delta as laborers; more than half of them renewed their contracts. Like the Tonkinese, they came from a rice-growing region of Southeast Asia that was known for both its dense population and its long tradition of rice cultivation. This smaller migration continued until the Dutch restricted labor emigration after World War I. Landowners considered Javanese labor too expensive because of their dietary constraints. See Brocheux, *Mekong Delta,* 27.

30 "De l'emploi la main-d'oeuvre tonkinoise et de la motoculture," *Tribune indochinoise,* April 11, 1927, 1.

31 "Commission permanente de 19 Juillet 1927: L'inspection generale du travail," *Tribune indochinoise,* August 24, 1927, 3.

32 Gourou, *Paysans,* 218.

33 "De l'emploi la main-d'oeuvre tonkinoise et de la motoculture," *Tribune indochinoise,* April 11, 1927, 1.

34 Trần Tử Bình was an *engagé,* and in his memoir he describes meeting such agents at the Phú Riêng Rubber Plantation, where he joined the party and in 1930 helped lead one of the first major labor uprisings. See Trần Tử Bình, *The Red Earth: A Vietnamese Memoir of Life on a Colonial Rubber Plantation,* ed. David Marr, trans. John Spragens Jr., Monographs in International Studies, Southeast Asia Series, no. 66 (Athens: Ohio University Press, 1985).

35 Brocheux, *Mekong Delta,* 177.

36 Paul Vidal de la Blache, *Principles of Human Geography,* trans. M. T. Bingham (New York: Henry Holt, 1926), 328.

37 Karl A. Wittfogel, *Das erwachende China* (Vienna: Agis Verlag, 1926). For a summary biography of Wittfogel, see Richard Peet, "Introduction to the Life and Thought of Karl Wittfogel," *Antipode: A Radical Journal of Geography* 17, no. 1 (1985): 3–20.

38 Gourou, *Paysans.*

39 See Vidal de la Blache, *Principles of Human Geography;* and Vincent Berdoulay's account of the Vidalian legacy in "Place, Meaning, and Discourse in French Language Geography," in *The Power of Place,* ed. John A. Agnew and James S. Duncan (Boston: Unwin Hyman, 1989), 125–28. For a concise biography of Gourou, see Michel Bruneau, "Pierre Gourou (1900–1999): Géographie et civilisations," *L'homme,* no. 153 (2000): 7–26.

40 This period of agricultural research in Indochina influenced many intellectuals who later worked in politics in Vietnam and France. Nguyễn Văn Huyên received his doctorate in 1934 at the Sorbonne and then returned to Vietnam to conduct ethnographic research with the EFEO. In 1944 he published *La civilisation annamite* (Hanoi: Direction de l'instruction publique, 1944), a work that described traditional Vietnamese society. He joined Hồ Chí Minh in 1945 and served as minister of education until 1975.

In his 1944 publication he noted of his French teachers, "We owe a great deal to our teachers, our predecessors and our friends" (8). The French researcher René Dumont was so impressed by his experiences studying agronomy in Tonkin that he voiced his opposition to colonial rule after 1945. He promoted socialist agricultural reforms in Asia and Africa and was pivotal in establishing the Green Party in France. In 1974 he wrote a manifesto for political ecology in his bid for the French presidency. René Dumont, *La culture du riz dans le delta du Tonkin: Étude et propositions d'amélioration des techniques traditionnelles de riziculture tropicale* (1935; Patani: Prince of Songkla University, 1995).

41 Gourou, *Paysans,* 88–89.

42 One of the earliest recorded major projects occurred in 1077, when the Lý dynasty ordered construction of a dike along the Cầu River. See Phan Khánh, ed., *Sơ Thảo Lịch Sử Thủy Lợi Việt Nam,* tập 1 (Hà Nội: Khoa Học Xã Hội, 1981), 32.

43 André Touzet, *L'économie indochinoise et la grand crise universelle* (Paris: Marcel Giard, 1934), 239–40, 241.

44 Normandin, *Travaux d'hydraulique agricole,* 15.

45 See Scott, *Seeing like a State,* 184–85. See also Michael Adas, "From Avoidance to Confrontation: Peasant Protest in Pre-colonial and Colonial Southeast Asia," *Comparative Studies in Society and History* 23, no. 2 (1981): 217–47.

46 Gourou, *Paysans,* 14–15.

47 J. Y. Claeys, "La géographie humaine des pays annamites basée sur des observations aériennes," *Cahiers de l'École française d'Extrême-Orient* 22 (1940): 45.

48 Ibid., 46.

49 Xacat, "Riziculture et hydraulique agricole," August 29, 1944, file H.6/20, TĐBCPNV, TTLTQG2.

50 André Fraisse, "Notes de géographie humaine sur la province de Long-Xuyên," *Extrait du Bulletin de l'Institut indochinois pour l'étude de l'homme* (séance du 26 mai 1942), 140.

51 Paul Emery, "Étude sur les travaux d'hydraulique agricole dans le Trans-Bassac," October 20, 1942, file H.62/3, TĐBCPNV, TTLTQG2.

52 Panivong Norindr, "The Popular Front's Colonial Policies in Indochina: Reassessing the Popular Front's 'Colonisation Altruiste,'" in *French Colonial Empire and the Popular Front: Hope and Disillusion,* ed. Tony Chafer and Amanda Sackur (New York: St. Martin's Press, 1999), 230–32.

53 Administrator of Rạch Giá to governor of Cochinchina, December 7, 1932, file IB 23/096(19), Fonds Goucoch, TTLTQG2.

54 Annual expenditures for dredging from 1930 to 1937 were as follows. 1930: 1.75 million piasters; 1931: 1.75 million piasters; 1932: 1.4 million piasters;

1933: 0.8 million piasters; 1934: 0.4 million piasters; 1935: 0.4 million piasters; 1936: 0.45 million piasters; 1937: 0.4 million piasters. "Dragages dans les canaux de Cochinchine: Concours pour l'exécution de travaux de dragages en Cochinchine pour une période de dix ans," file VIA 8/186(31), Fonds Goucoch, TTLTQG2.

55   Travaux publics, "Amenagements des provinces de Chaudoc, Longxuyen, Rachgia et Hatien en vue d'y recevoir l'immigration tonkinoise: Presentation des avants-projets," file N21/15, TĐBCPNV, TTLTQG2.

56   "Arrêté du 23 November 1937 organisant l'Inspection générale du travail et de la prévoyance sociale," file M1/11, TĐBCPNV, TTLTQG2.

57   M. Bagot, "Malaise agraire dans le Transbassac," April 28, 1939, file M.2/63, TĐBCPNV, TTLTQG2.

58   Shawn F. McHale, *Print and Power: Confucianism, Communism, and Buddhism in the Making of Modern Vietnam* (Honolulu: University of Hawai'i Press, 2003).

59   "La grève des ouvriers et coolies de la Société des dragages à mytho," *La lutte,* April 7, 1938, 4.

60   "La révolte des 'Ta-diên,'" *Tribune indochinoise,* May 6, 1938, 1.

61   Ibid., 4.

62   M. Bagot, "Malaise agraire dans le Transbassac," April 28, 1939, file M.2/63, TĐBCPNV, TTLTQG2.

63   "Surpeuplement du Delta tonkinois," *Tribune indochinoise,* February 9, 1938, 1.

64   "Le president du Partí démocrate indochinois a monsieur le gouverneur de la Cochinchine," April 6, 1938, file VIA 8/207(21), Fonds Goucoch, TTLTQG2.

65   Brocheux, *Mekong Delta,* 185. A prison was located on the island of Poulo Condor (Côn Sòn) from 1861 to 1975.

66   Ông Bảy Long, interview with author, April 20, 2002.

67   Hoeffel, "Le riz," file H.6/20, TĐBCPNV, TTLTQG2.

68   Xacat, "Riziculture et hydraulique agricole," August 29, 1944, file H.6/20, TĐBCPNV, TTLTQG2.

69   Bigorgne, "L'hydraulique agricole en Cochinchine," p. 5, August 25, 1944, file H.6/20, TĐBCPNV, TTLTQG2.

70   Ibid.

71   Decoux to the governor of Cochinchina, September 30, 1942, file H62/10, TĐBCPNV, TTLTQG2.

72   "L'ingenieur en chef de la circonscription d'Hydraulique agricole et de navigation de Sud-Indochine (HANSI) a monsieur le gouverneur de la Cochinchine," September 1, 1943, file BO/3904, TĐBCPNV, TTLTQG2.

73   Eric T. Jennings, *Vichy in the Tropics: Pétain's National Revolution in Madagascar, Guadeloupe, and Indochina, 1940–1944* (Stanford, CA: Stan-

ford University Press, 2001), 170.

74 "L'ingenieur en chef de la circonscription d'Hydraulique agricole et de navigation de Sud-Indochine (HANSI) a monsieur le gouverneur de la Cochinchine," September 1, 1943, file BO/3904, TĐBCPNV, TTLTQG2.

75 "L'administrateur, chef de la province de Rachgia, a monsieur le gouverneur de la Cochinchine," January 22, 1945, file BO/3904, TĐBCPNV, TTLTQG2.

76 "Budget générale: Aménagement de la region Rach-Gia–Ha-Tien," January 25, 1945, file BO/3904, TĐBCPNV, TTLTQG2.

77 The entire collection of "M Project" reports can be found at the Library of Congress and as part of the Henry Field Papers, Collection 72, Otto G. Richter Library Archives and Special Collections Department, University of Miami, Coral Gables, FL. See no. T-109, "Studies of Migration and Settlement: Translation Series—Tonkinese Settlement in Cochinchina, October 20, 1945."

78 P. C. Jammé, "Aménagement de la plaine des Joncs: Avant-projet," July 20, 1943, file H.62/7, TĐBCPNV, TTLTQG2.

79 For a definition of high modernism, see Scott, *Seeing like a State,* 90. Scott repeatedly refers to "villagization" schemes such as "strategic hamlets" in Vietnam as examples of high-modernist reorderings of rural landscapes and rural life, but more fitting examples may be these earlier projects envisioned in the 1940s.

80 Gills Deleuze and Félix Guattari, *Anti-Oedipus: Capitalism and Schizophrenia,* trans. Robert Hurley, Mark Seem, and Helen R. Lane (New York: Viking Press, 1977), 244.

81 For an English translation excerpt from Phi Vân's third book, *Đồng Quê,* see Ngô Vĩnh Long, *Before the Revolution,* 162–75.

82 Deleuze and Guattari, *Anti-Oedipus,* 96–97.

4 BALKANIZATION

1 Jean Leroy, *Un homme dans la rizière* (Paris: Éditions de Paris, 1955), 117.

2 Ông Rõ, interview with author, April 12, 2002.

3 The first French forces to arrive in Sài Gòn included 150 volunteers in the French Expeditionary Corps to the Far East who arrived with General Gracey's British Gurkha Brigade at Tân Sơn Nhất airfield on September 12. Gracey rearmed several hundred French troops who had been imprisoned by the Japanese since March, and fighting broke out almost immediately, with the French soldiers regaining control of key government buildings in downtown Sài Gòn. See Jean Chesneaux, *The Vietnamese Nation: Contribution to a History* (Sydney: Current Book Distributors, 1966), 168; Bernard

Favin-Lévêque, *Souvenirs de mer et d'ailleurs* (Paris: Éditions des 7 vents, 1990), 121.

4 Nguyễn Việt, ed., *Nam Bộ và Nam Phần Trung Bộ Trong Hai Năm Đầu Kháng Chiến (1945-1946)* (Hà Nội: Văn Sử Địa, 1958), 53.

5 Leroy, *Un homme,* 97–98.

6 Elliott's history of the resistance in Mỹ Tho Province suggests that the French attack by river caught Việt Minh leaders by surprise and left both the Communist and non-Communist elements scrambling to evacuate to their bases in Đồng Tháp (Elliott, *Vietnamese War,* 97–98).

7 Chesneaux, *Vietnamese Nation,* 117.

8 Fall includes often-graphic accounts of these killings, using terms such as "blood bath" to describe events in which the actual numbers of those killed and wounded are still widely disputed. See Bernard Fall, "The Political-Religious Sects of Viet-Nam," *Pacific Affairs* 28, no. 3 (September 1955): 246.

9 Jean Mauclère, *Marins dans les arroyos* (Paris: J. Peyronnet, 1950), 129–49.

10 Bùi Văn Thạnh, "Báo Cáo Khái Quát Lịch Sử và Phương Hướng Bảo Tồn, Phát Huy Di Tích Lịch Sử Căn Cứ Địa Cách Mạng U Minh Thượng Kiên Giang," in *Kỷ Yếu Hội Thảo Khoa Học: Di Tích Lịch Sử Căn Cứ Địa Cách Mạng U Minh Thượng Tỉnh Kiến Giang* (Rạch Giá: Sở Văn Hoá Thông Tin—Thể Thao Kiên Giang, 1997), 54–55.

11 Ông Rõ, interview with author, April 12, 2002.

12 Trần Văn Đạt, "Réfection route endommagé près de Rachgoi par les V.M.," August 9, 1950, file H.2/97, TĐBCPNV, TTLTQG2.

13 "L'administrateur, chef de la province de Soctrang à monsieur l'ingenieur principal, chef de l'arrondissement de la navigation," July 29, 1949, file H.O/3, TĐBCPNV, TTLTQG2.

14 Lucien Charles Blanche, *Aperçu sur les opérations amphibies en Cochinchine, 1947-1951* (Paris: Imprimerie nationale, 1951), 17–18.

15 A. M. Savani, *Visage et images du Sud Viet-Nam* (Saigon: Imprimerie française d'Outre-Mer, 1955), 79–80.

16 Tai, *Millenarianism and Peasant Politics,* 135.

17 Savani, *Visage et images,* 87–89. See also Fall, "Political-Religious Sects," 246. Fall claims that on September 8, 1945, 15,000 Hòa Hảo adepts armed with pikes and knives marched on a well-armed Việt Minh garrison at Cần Thơ where several thousand, including Soái's and Số's brothers, had been held prisoner and executed. Pascal Bourdeaux's detailed thesis on Hòa Hảo Buddhism during this era offers three different interpretations of the protests at Cần Thơ, where casualties ranged from a few dozen to several hundred. See Pascal Bourdeaux, "Émergence et constitution de la communauté du Bouddhisme Hòa Hảo: Contribution à l'histoire sociale du delta du Mékong (1933-1955)" (PhD thesis, École practique des hautes études, 2003), 1:299.

18 Interpretations of the nature of the Hòa Hảo–French alliance vary. French sources such as Savani's *Visage et images* and Fall's "Political-Religious Sects" tend to describe the Hòa Hảo forces as opportunist brigands commanded by warlords, while Hòa Hảo sources such as Nguyễn Long Thành Nam's offer much more detailed accounts of the Hòa Hảo negotiating positions and differences. See Nguyễn Long Thành Nam, *Hoa Hao Buddhism in the Course of Vietnam's History* (Hauppage, NY: Nova Science Publishers, 2003), 88–89.

19 Bourdeaux, "Émergence," 2:445.

20 Fall, "Political-Religious Sects," 246.

21 Bùi Văn Thạnh, "Báo Cáo Khái Quát Lịch Sử," 53. Làng Linh was the village founded by Trần Văn Thành, who resisted the French in 1873, and was a center for the Bửu Sơn Kỳ Hương movement in the late 1800s and for the Hòa Hảo forces after 1947. Cán Gáo was a major village along one of the canals bordering the U Minh Forest.

22 Ibid., 52.

23 File H2/78, TĐBCPNV, TTLTQG2. See also Fall, "Political-Religious Sects," 249.

24 Favin-Lévêque, *Souvenirs de mer*, 170.

25 Ibid., 171.

26 Forces franco-vietnamiennes du sud: Zone ouest, "Blocus du Transbassac," Q1/5, TĐBCPNV, TTLTQG2. No explanation is given as to the uses of snakeskin in the liberated zones. However, given the difficulty of raising cattle in the wet, marshy environment, it was likely important as a locally produced leather and might have been a high-revenue-earning local commodity. The U Minh Forest, in particular, was famous for cobras and other snakes.

27 Q1/15, TĐBCPNV, TTLTQG2.

28 F. A., "L'effort de pacification au Sud-Vietnam depuis 1945," *Sud-Est Asiatique* 6 (1949): 45.

29 Michel Foucault, *Discipline and Punish* (Middlesex: Peregrine, 1979), 200.

30 Brocheux, *Mekong Delta*, 202.

31 Elliott, *Vietnamese War*, 126.

32 Lâm Quang Huyền, *Cách mạng ruộng đất ở Miền Nam Việt Nam* (Hà Nội: Khoa Học Xã Hội, 1997), 25. Cited in Brocheux, *Mekong Delta*, 204.

33 The "model" for writing provincial monographs (*địa chí*) predates the colonial series. Trịnh Hoài Đức's *Gia Định Thành Thông Chí* is an example of a Chinese-influenced (possibly also French-influenced) monograph about the southern provinces in 1820. See Trịnh Hoài Đức, *Gia Định Thành Thông Chí*, trans. Đỗ Mộng Khương and Nguyễn Ngọc Tỉnh, ed. Đào Duy Anh (1820; Hà Nội: Giáo Dục, 1998).

34 The 1902–11 monographs were published in installments by the Société des

études indo-chinoises under the title *Géographie physique, économique et historique de la Cochinchine.* In 1936 the Popular Front produced similar monographs but they were internal government reports and were never formally published. They can be found with the 1953 provincial studies in section E02, TĐBCPNV Record Group, TTLTQG2. See also Yves Henry and Maurice de Visme, *Documents de démographie et riziculture en Indochine* (Hanoi: Bulletin économique de l'Indochine, 1928). Henry and de Visme compiled statistics and details about rice cultivation at both the provincial and the district level.

35   President of the Assembly of South Vietnam to the governor of South Vietnam, July 1949, file M2/25, TĐBCPNV, TTLTQG2.

36   See files E02/106 and E02/111, TĐBCPNV, TTLTQG2.

37   File E02/104, TĐBCPNV, TTLTQG2.

38   Mr. Diều, interview with author, April 19, 2002.

39   "People of the U Minh Forest," box 32, CORDS Historical Working Group, U.S. Forces in Southeast Asia, 1950–75, Record Group (hereafter RG) 472, National Archives and Records Administration, Center 2 (hereafter NARA2), College Park, MD.

40   Bùi Văn Thạnh, "Báo Cáo Khái Quát Lịch Sử," 55.

41   File 21487, Phủ Tổng Thống Đệ Nhất Cộng Hoà Miền Nam (hereafter PTT), TTLTQG2.

42   Report 0735–71, Combined Military Interrogation Center, RG 472, NARA2.

43   "Người vợ miền Nam của cố Tổng Bí thư Lê Duẩn," *Tiền Phong Online,* http://www.tienphongonline.com.vn/Tianyon/Index.aspx?ArticleID=51254 &ChannelID=13.

44   Sơn Nam, *Hồi Ký Sơn Nam* (Hồ Chí Minh City: NXP Trẻ, 2003), 125–288.

45   Leroy, *Un homme,* 144.

46   Ibid., 158.

47   Fall, "Political-Religious Sects," 249.

48   Nguyễn Long Thành Nam, *Hoa Hao Buddhism,* 104.

49   Bourdeaux, "Émergence," 549.

50   Devillers, *Histoire du Viêt-Nam,* 173–74. See also Ralph B. Smith, "The Vietnamese Élite of French Cochinchina, 1943," *Modern Asian Studies* 6, no. 4 (1972): 469.

51   Devillers, *Histoire du Viêt-Nam,* 174.

52   *Souverains et notabilités d'Indochine* (Hanoi: Éditions du gouvernement général de l'Indochine, 1943), 78.

53   "R. Schneyder, inspecteur des affaires administratives et du travail, avec monsieur le président du gouvernement provisoire de la République de Cochinchine," February 21, 1947, M2/57, TĐBCPNV, TTLTQG2.

54   M2/63, TĐBCPNV, TTLTQG2.

55 File 9492, PTT, TTLTQG2.

56 "V.P. du Mecredi," January 7, 1953, file 21467, PTT, TTLTQG2.

57 Sơn Nam, *Hai Côi U Minh: Truyện* (Sài Gòn: Hữu Nghị, 1965).

58 Latham suggests that Diệm and his brother Nhu became attracted to British counterinsurgency adviser R. G. K. Thompson's tactics of counterinsurgency in 1961. See Michael E. Latham, *Modernization as Ideology: American Social Science and "Nation Building" in the Kennedy Era* (Chapel Hill: University of North Carolina Press, 2000), 173. Catton draws from Vietnamese sources to suggest that Diệm and Nhu understood that the Vietnamese and Malayan insurgencies were fundamentally different and had already designed their program long before meeting Thompson. See Philip Catton, *Diem's Final Failure: Prelude to America's War in Vietnam* (Lawrence: University of Kansas Press, 2002), 97.

5 MODERNIZATION

1 Wolf Ladejinsky, "South Vietnam Revisited," USOM, Vietnam, Classified Subject Files, RG 469, NARA2.

2 Tổng Giám Đốc Công Chánh Việt Nam k/g Ông Bộ Trưởng Công Chánh và Giao Thông, April 15, 1957, file 1276/1, Bộ Giao Thông Công Chánh (hereafter GTCC), TTLTQG2. Estimates of U.S. dollar figures were obtained by using the official conversion rate of 35 piasters per 1 U.S. dollar set in 1954 and then converting 1954 and 1957 dollars to 2009 values using consumer price index figures.

3 Catton, *Diem's Final Failure,* 97.

4 Graham Greene, *The Quiet American* (New York: Penguin Putnam, 1991).

5 "Ted Gittinger Interview with Keyes Beech, March 22, 1983, Cosmos Club, Washington, D.C.," Oral Histories, 11, Lyndon Baines Johnson Library and Museum, Austin, TX.

6 William J. Lederer and Eugene Burdick, *The Ugly American* (New York: Norton, 1958).

7 Fall, "Political-Religious Sects," 235.

8 A. M. Rosenthal, "Saigon Is Swept by Civil Warfare; Big Area Is Afire," *New York Times,* April 29, 1955, A1.

9 Louis J. Walinsky, ed., *Agrarian Reform as Unfinished Business: The Selected Papers of Wolf Ladejinsky* (New York: Oxford University Press, 1977), 5-7.

10 "Ladejinsky Dispute," *New York Times,* December 26, 1954, E2.

11 Walinsky, *Agrarian Reform,* 217-29.

12 Ibid., 230.

13 Ibid., 261.

14   Wolf Ladejinsky, "South Vietnam Revisited," 48–51, USOM, Vietnam, Classified Subject Files, RG 469, NARA2.

15   Prime minister to the regional delegates, January 8, 1955, file 21467, Phủ Thủ Tướng (Office of the Prime Minister, hereafter PTTg), TTLTQG2.

16   Wolf Ladejinsky, "A Visit with President Ngô Đình Diệm," in Walinsky, *Agrarian Reform,* 240.

17   Ibid., 242.

18   Scott, *Seeing like a State,* 4. For a more thorough retrospective on Scott's ideas about modernism and earlier notions relevant to land reform such as the moral economy, see James C. Scott, "Afterword to *Moral Economies, State Spaces, and Categorical Violence," American Anthropologist* 107 (2005): 395–402.

19   Catton's study on Ngô Đình Diệm and nation-building, *Diem's Final Failure,* especially his chapter "Land Reform, Land Development, and Agrovilles" (51–71), makes a strong case for the crucial role that Third World leaders, many with their own divergent takes on modernist ideas, played in undermining the success or mitigating the failures of American, Soviet, and other internationally driven schemes. Contrary to what the works of Scott and Adas may imply, modernism was not a singular ideology but instead a set of ideas interpreted differently by various local and international actors cooperating on particular projects.

20   Decoux to the governor of Cochinchina, September 30, 1942, file H62/10, TĐBCPNV, TTLTQG2.

21   Catton, *Diem's Final Failure,* 51.

22   Anderson, *Imagined Communities.* In particular, see his often-quoted chapter "Census, Map, Museum," 163–86.

23   "February 1953: War Relief and Rehabilitation," box 13, USOM, Vietnam, Security Classified Files, RG 469, NARA2. Archival records include the script for an American propaganda movie intended to advertise the project as an example of peaceful resistance to Communist advances.

24   Nguyễn Công Viên, *Seeking the Truth: The Inside Story of Viet Nam after the French Defeat by a Man Who Served in Bao Dai's Cabinet* (New York: Vantage Press, 1966), 25–29.

25   "Plan de mise en culture d'une zône de 77.000 Ha. de terre," November 24, 1955, file 21467, PTTg, TTLTQG2.

26   Government of the Socialist Republic of Vietnam, Ministry of Water Resources Planning Institute, *Cai San Water Control Project: Project Summary* (Hanoi, 1979).

27   Report on the works at Cái Sắn, May 4, 1956, box 13, USOM, Vietnam, Security Classified Files, RG 469, NARA2.

28   Robert Alden, "535 Refugees in South Vietnam Turn the Earth in Vital

Project; They Dig Canal That Not Only Will Give Them a New Life, but Also Will Enable Settlement of Foes to Red Penetration," *New York Times*, February 9, 1956, A2. Alden mistakes 535 households, approximately 3,700 people, for 535 refugees.

29 Leland Barrows to D. C. Lavergne, July 23, 1956, Mission to Vietnam: Program and Requirements Division: Research and Statistics Section: Subject Files, 1956, box 6, RG 469, NARA2.

30 Mr. M. H. B. Adler, chief, Field Service, to Ray A. Nichols, field representative, Cần Thơ, August 31, 1956, Mission to Vietnam: Resettlement and Rehabilitation, box 4, RG 469, NARA2.

31 Ibid.

32 John A. Hackett to D. C. Lavergne on Cái Sắn project, February 16, 1956, box 1, Mission to Vietnam: Resettlement and Rehabilitation, RG 469, NARA2.

33 Mr. Leland Barrows to D. C. Lavergne—visit of vice president to Cái Sắn, July 2, 1956, box 1, Mission to Vietnam: Resettlement and Rehabilitation, RG 469, NARA2.

34 "Report of Meeting on October 3, 1956 at 10:00 on Canal," box 3, Mission to Vietnam: Resettlement and Rehabilitation, RG 469, NARA2.

35 "Report on the Initial Results of the Investigation into Graft and Cheating in the Cái Sắn Settlement Zone," October 8, 1956, Nha Giám Đốc Cảnh-Sát và Công-an Nam-Việt, file 10454, PTTg, TTLTQG2. Thanks to Ed Miller for bringing these sources to my attention.

36 For Ladejinsky's interpretation of Ordinance 57, see Wolf Ladejinsky, "Agrarian Reform in the Republic of Vietnam," in Walinsky, *Agrarian Reform*, 299–312.

37 Elliott, *Vietnamese War*, 1:465–67.

38 Bùi Văn Lương, "Báo Cáo về Hoạt Động của Phủ Tổng Ủy Dinh Điền Nhận Dịp Kỷ Niêm Đệ-Tam Chu-Niên Chấp-Chánh của Ngô Tổng Thống Ngày 7.7.1957," file 10807, PTTg, TTLTQG2.

39 Ibid.

40 Trần Lê Quang, Bộ Trưởng Công Chánh và Giáo Thông, "V/v xin nhuợng phi-ảnh vùng Mỹ-Phước Tỉnh Ba-Xuyên," file 1576, GTCC, TTLTQG2.

41 David Biggs, "Reclamation Nations: The U.S. Bureau of Reclamation's Role in Water Management and Nation Building in the Mekong Valley, 1945–1975," *Comparative Technology Transfer and Society* 4, no. 3 (December 2006): 227.

42 "Project for Reconnaissance Survey of Hydroelectric and Irrigation Projects in Underdeveloped Countries Which Might Justify Assistance under the Point IV Program," box 4, RG 115, National Archives and Records Administration, Denver, CO.

43 United Nations Economic and Social Commission for Asia and the Pacific, "History of UNESCAP," http://www.unescap.org/unis/sub_unis/history_ unescap.asp.

44 Eugene R. Black, *Alternatives in Southeast Asia* (New York: Praeger, 1969), 138.

45 "Japanese Technicians for Resettlement Project 030–82–075, July 21, 1956," box 6, Mission to Vietnam: Resettlement and Rehabilitation, RG 469, NARA2.

46 Minister of agriculture to presidential cabinet director, August 20, 1957, file 312, GTCC, TTLTQG2.

47 République du Viêt-Nam, *Les travaux d'hydraulique agricole au Viet-Nam* (Saigon: n.p., 1960), 7.

48 Bùi Văn Lương, general commissioner of land reform, letter to minister of public works, Saigon, November 18, 1957, file C18/1, GTCC, TTLTQG2.

49 John A. Hackett to Randall V. Frakes, field representative, March 14, 1957, box 6, Mission to Vietnam: Resettlement and Rehabilitation, RG 469, NARA2.

50 John A. Hackett to Thomas J. Cockrell, July 24 and March 14, 1957, box 6, Mission to Vietnam: Resettlement and Rehabilitation, RG 469, NARA2.

51 Bùi Văn Lương, "Báo Cáo về Hoạt Động Của Phủ Tổng Ủy Dinh Điền Nhân Dịp Kỷ Niệm Đệ-Tam Chu-Niên Chấp-Chánh của Ngô Tổng Thống Ngay 7.7.1957," file 10807, PTTg, TTLTQG2.

52 "Tờ Trình Của Trưởng Khu Thủy-Nông," November 19, 1957, file C18/1, GTCC, TTLTQG2.

53 M. H. B. Adler to Ray A. Nichols, August 31, 1956, box 6, Mission to Vietnam: Resettlement and Rehabilitation, RG 469, NARA2.

54 Trần Ngọc Cành, "Về Việc Khảo Sát và Đào Các Kinh Nhỏ ở U-Minh và Kinh Ranh Hạt," October 10, 1958, file C18/1, GTCC, TTLTQG2.

55 Hoang Văn Lạc, province administrator of Kiên Giang to minister of public works, October 31, 1958, file C18/1, GTCC, TTLTQG2.

56 "Biên Bản Phiên Nhóm Thảo Luận Về Việc Đào-Vét Kinh Tại Địa-Điểm U Minh," file Q60, GTCC, TTLTQG2.

57 Trần Lê Quang, minister of public works, letter to presidential cabinet minister, Sài Gòn, 12 December 1958, file Q60, GTCC, TTLTQG2.

58 "Biên Bản Phiên Nhóm Thảo Luận Về Việc Đào-Vét Kinh Tại Địa-Điểm U Minh," file Q60, GTCC, TTLTQG2.

59 "L'administrateur de Rach Gia a monsieur le gouverneur de la Cochinchine au sujet de la petit colonisation dans le canton de Kien Hao," 1932, file IB 23/096(12), Fonds Goucoch, TTLTQG2.

60 Jammé, "Amenagement hydraulique des provinces de Rachgia et Baclieu: Regions de U-Minh," file H62/6, TĐBCPNV, TTLTQG2. For more on U Minh and forest management, see David Biggs, "Managing a Rebel Land-

scape: Conservation, Pioneers, and the Revolutionary Past in the U Minh Forest," *Environmental History* 10, no. 3 (July 2005): 448–76.

61 "Security, Hong-Ngu, and My-An, Plaine des Joncs," box 4, Mission to Vietnam: Resettlement and Rehabilitation, RG 469, NARA2.

62 Catton, *Diem's Final Failure,* 58. See also "Báo Cáo về Hoạt Động Của Phủ Tổng Ủy Dinh Điền Nhân Dịp Kỷ Niệm Đệ-Tam Chu-Niên Chấp-Chánh của Ngô Tổng Thống Ngay 7.7.1957," file 10807, PTTg, TTLTQG2.

63 M. Machefaux and M. Walthert, "Rapport de mission d'etudes d'amenagement hydro-agricole au Viet-nam," file 312, GTCC, TTLTQG2. See also Cơ Quan Khai Thác Xáng–Ty Nghiên Cứu và Chương Trình, "Chương Trình Khai Thác Đồng Tháp," 1972, file C1276/2, GTCC, TTLTQG2. In this Vietnamese version of the 1972 Defense Advanced Research Projects Agency (DARPA) study, the Vietnamese date the network of Canals 1–10 and Tổng Đốc Lộc to 1839.

64 "Security, Hong-Ngu, and My-An, plaine des Joncs," box 4, Mission to Vietnam: Resettlement and Rehabilitation, RG 469, NARA2.

65 M. Machefaux and M. Walthert, "Rapport de mission d'etudes d'amenagement hydro-agricole au Viet-nam," 11–12, file 312, GTCC, TTLTQG2.

66 Elliott, *Vietnamese War,* 1:142–43.

67 Daniel, Mann, Johnson, and Mendenhall, "Preliminary Economic and Engineering Study: Dredging Program," contract AID-430–990, file NL504, TTLTQG2.

68 Nguyễn Văn Đình, "V/v đề-nghị mua 2 chiếc xáng Ellicott 12-inch loại Dragon," 1962, file 288/4, GTCC, TTLTQG2.

69 Daniel, Mann, Johnson, and Mendenhall, "Preliminary Economic and Engineering Study," 7, contract AID-430–990, file NL504, TTLTQG2. A dredge foreman working for the Department of Navigation would earn 2,379 VN$ per month, whereas he would earn on average 9,500 VN$ per month working for contractors.

70 Ibid., 38.

71 Gentilini, *Voies de communication en Cochinchine.*

72 Daniel, Mann, Johnson, and Mendenhall, "Preliminary Economic and Engineering Study," 23, contract AID-430–990, file NL504, TTLTQG2.

73 Hà Văn Vương to President Diệm, April 19, 1956, box 1, Mission to Vietnam: Resettlement and Rehabilitation, RG 469, NARA2.

74 "Bộ Công-Chánh k/g Tổng Thống Việt Nam Cộng Hòa," file 55704, GTCC, TTLTQG2.

75 The picture appeared in Ngô Đình Diệm, *Con Đường Chính Nghĩa Độc Lập Dân Chủ* (Sài Gòn: n.p., 1958).

76 "Bộ Công-Chánh k/g Tổng Thống Việt Nam Cộng Hòa," file 55704, GTCC, TTLTQG2.

77 Elliott, *Vietnamese War,* 1:234. In contrast to Elliott's provincial perspective, Young suggests a more conventional understanding of the party's decisions to resume violent struggle. Young describes the southern revolutionary Lê Duẩn, appointed as interim secretary-general of the Politburo in 1957, sanctioning the arming of anti-Diệm propaganda teams in mid-1957, and she suggests that party faithful such as Nguyễn Thị Định of Bến Tre Province raised troops for battle only after having received word first from Hà Nội. Elliott notes that, despite evidence of earlier fighting in Đồng Tháp and smaller incidents elsewhere, official party histories credit the beginning of a "concerted uprising" of revolutionary forces to the actions of Định's followers in Bến Tre because she waited and "played by the rules" as set in resolutions from Hà Nội. See Elliott, *Vietnamese War,* 1:235; Marilyn B. Young, *The Vietnam Wars, 1945-1960* (New York: Harper Perennial, 1991), 64-65.

78 Mr. M. H. B. Adler to J. D. Hanley, "Military Operations in Cao Dai Area, January 27, 1956," box 4, Mission to Vietnam: Resettlement and Rehabilitation, RG 469, NARA2.

79 Marvin E. Gettleman, *Viet Nam: History, Documents and Opinions on a Major World Crisis* (Greenwich, CT: Fawcett Publications, 1965), 256-60. Gettleman's version of Law 10/59 is taken from a North Vietnamese publication: Phạm Văn Bạch, ed., *Fascist Terror in South Vietnam: Law 10/59* (Hanoi: Thế Giới, 1961), 71-77.

80 Nguyễn Thị Định, *No Other Road to Take,* trans. Mai V. Elliott (Ithaca, NY: Southeast Asia Program Publications, 1976), 56-58.

81 King C. Chen, "Hanoi's Three Decisions and the Escalation of the Vietnam War," *Political Science Quarterly* 90, no. 2 (Summer 1975): 246.

82 "V/v phiến loạn đốt phá 4 máy kéo Cormick ở Thổ Sơn Kiên Giang," file 5899, PTT, TTLTQG2.

83 "Việt Cộng phá họai 2 máy cày Dinh Điền Phước Xuyên (Kiến Phong)," file 5899, PTT, TTLTQG2.

84 Catton, *Diem's Final Failure,* 65.

85 Joseph J. Zasloff, "Rural Resettlement in South Viet Nam: The Agroville Program," *Pacific Affairs* 35, no. 4 (1962-63): 330.

86 For a description of agrovilles (1959-61), see ibid., 327-40.

87 Nguyễn Thị Định, *No Other Road to Take,* 59-61.

88 Ibid., 61.

89 Dispatch 426, May 31, 1960, "GVN Agroville Program," Confidential U.S. State Department Central Files: Vietnam 1960-1963, Internal Affairs and Foreign Affairs (Lexis Nexis Microfilm), reel 1, frames 544-57; RG 59: Records of the Department of State, Central Decimal Files, decimal nos. 751K, 851K, and 951K (Vietnam internal affairs); 751G, 851G, and 951G (Indochina [general] internal affairs); 651K and 611.51K (Vietnam for-

eign affairs); and 651G and 611.51G (Indochina [general] foreign affairs), NARA2.

90 Zasloff, "Rural Resettlement in South Viet Nam," 327–28.

91 Tillman Durdin, "Dictatorial Rule in Saigon Charged," *New York Times,* May 1, 1960, 1.

92 "Open Letter to President Ngo Dinh Diem on the Subject of Agrovilles" (English translation dated October 6, 1960), Confidential U.S. State Department Central Files: Vietnam 1960–1963, Internal Affairs and Foreign Affairs (Lexis Nexis Microfilm), reel 2, frames 224–26, NARA2.

93 "Approach to President Diem on Suggested Political Actions," October 14, 1960, Confidential U.S. State Department Central Files: Vietnam 1960–1963, Internal Affairs and Foreign Affairs (Lexis Nexis Microfilm), reel 1, frames 136–44, NARA2.

94 Wolf Ladejinsky, "Agrarian Reform in Vietnam," in Walinsky, *Agrarian Reform,* 299–314.

95 John Ernst, *Forging a Fateful Alliance: Michigan State and the Vietnam War* (East Lansing: Michigan State University Press, 1998), 11.

96 Adrian Jaffe and Milton Taylor, "The Professor-Diplomat: Ann Arbor and Cambridge Were Never Like This," *New Republic* 146 (1962): 28–30.

6 AMERICAN WAR

1 Ông Rỡ, interview with author, April 12, 2002.

2 One notable exception is Elizabeth Kemf, *Month of Pure Light: The Regreening of Vietnam* (London: Women's Press, 1990).

3 Department of the Army, *Vietnam Studies: Base Development, 1965–1970* (Washington, DC: GPO, 1972), 133.

4 Harvey uses the term "compression" in referring to how capitalism causes a "speed-up in the pace of life, while so overcoming spatial barriers that the world sometimes seems to collapse inwards upon us." David Harvey, *The Condition of Postmodernity: An Enquiry into the Origins of Cultural Change* (Oxford: Blackwell, 1989), 240. See David Hunt's recent use of Harvey's ideas with respect to the Vietnam War in *Vietnam's Southern Revolution,* 172.

5 Ông Rỡ, interview with author, April 12, 2002.

6 Meyerson*, Vinh Long,* 58.

7 Alexander S. Cochran Jr., "War in the Delta: US Riverine Operations in Vietnam," *War in Peace* 5, no. 6 (1988): 1195.

8 "Diễn văn của Đại Sứ Hoa Kỳ Frederick Nolting Jr. đọc tại buổi lễ chuyển giao xáng Kim Giang ngày 31 tháng 8 năm 1961," file C15714, GTCC, TTLTQG2.

9 File 55714, GTCC, TTLTQG2.

10   File 55704, GTCC, TTLTQG2.

11   "V/v an ninh các công trường máy xáng 1 June 1962," file 1846/6, GTCC, TTLTQG2.

12   Gardiner to McCauley, "Sabotage and Repair of the Dredge Bac Lieu," July 24, 1959, Bô 218, Records of the Agency for International Development: VN Subject Files 57–63, RG 286, NARA2.

13   Ibid.

14   December 23, 1963, file 21960, PTTg, TTLTQG2.

15   Daniel, Mann, Johnson, and Mendenhall, "Preliminary Economic and Engineering Study," 24.

16   "Report of Dredging Meeting on 7 January 1971," box 37, CORDS Historical Working Group, RG 472, NARA2.

17   "Monthly Historical Summary: March 1967," U.S. Naval Forces, Vietnam Monthly Historical Summaries, 1966–73, Vietnam Archive, Texas Tech University, Lubbock, TX.

18   "Order of Battle Study 66–44: VC Tactical Use of Inland Waterways in South Vietnam," in University Publications of America, *Records of the Military Assistance Command Vietnam, pt. 2, Classified Studies from the Combined Intelligence Center Vietnam, 1965–1973* (Bethesda, MD: University Publications of America, 1988), reel 21, frame 491.

19   Ibid.

20   Frederick Taylor, "Mekong Delta Project Shows the Difficulty of Pacification Effort: Vietcong Murder Government Workers, Raid Outposts; Key Canal Remains Closed," *Wall Street Journal*, June 20, 1967, A1.

21   Meyerson, *Vinh Long*, 91.

22   See Jonathan Rigg, *Southeast Asia, a Region in Transition: A Thematic Human Geography of the ASEAN Region* (London: Unwin Hyman, 1991), 33–56; and Stephen Lansing, *Priests and Programmers: Technologies of Power in the Engineered Landscape of Bali* (Princeton, NJ: Princeton University Press, 1991), 111–26.

23   Robert L. Sansom, *The Economics of Insurgency in the Mekong Delta of Vietnam* (Cambridge, MA: MIT Press, 1970), 167–68.

24   General director of finance and foreign aid to chief of cabinet, May 29, 1958, file 5063, PTT, TTLTQG2.

25   Memo, June 9, 1958, file 5063, PTT, TTLTQG2.

26   Memo, May 28, 1962, file 21491, PTT, TTLTQG2.

27   Sansom, *Economics of Insurgency,* 174.

28   Ông Rõ, interview with author, April 12, 2002.

29   Netherlands Delta Development Team, *Recommendations concerning Agricultural Development with Improved Water Control in the Mekong Delta: Working Paper VI, Irrigation and Drainage* (Bangkok: ECAFE, 1974), 28.

30   Stevenson McIlvaine, "Small Rice Mills in the Mekong Delta," February

6, 1970, Pacification Studies Group, box 22, CORDS Historical Working Group files 1967–73, RG 472, NARA2.

31   Ibid., 4.

32   "Briefing Folder for An Xuyen Province—1967," box 18, Advisory Team 80 (An Xuyen Province): General Records, RG 472, NARA2.

33   James J. Turner, LTC INF, to John P. Vann, February 26, 1971, box 57, Office of Civil Operations for Rural Development Support: Plans, Policy and Programs Directorate, Historical Working Group Files, RG 472, NARA2. For more discussion of Vann, see Neil Sheehan, *A Bright Shining Lie: John Paul Vann and America in Vietnam* (New York: Vintage, 1989).

34   Lyndon B. Johnson, *Public Papers of the Presidents of the United States: Lyndon B. Johnson, 1965,* vol. 1 (Washington, DC: GPO, 1966), 394–99. See also Nguyen Thi Dieu, *The Mekong River and the Struggle for Indochina: Water, War, and Peace* (Westport, CT: Praeger, 1999), 148–96.

35   U.S. Bureau of Reclamation and U.S. Agency for International Development, *To Tame a River* (Washington, DC: USBoR and USAID, 1968), 26.

36   Details of the survey are discussed in Committee for Coordination of Investigations of the Lower Mekong Basin, *Annual Report* (Bangkok: ECAFE, 1965).

37   Peter T. White and W. E. Garrett, "The Mekong: River of Terror and Hope," *National Geographic* 134, no. 6 (December 1968): 748–53. See also David Biggs, "Water Power: Machines, Modernizers, and Meta-commoditization on the Mekong River," in *Taking Southeast Asia to Market: Commodities, Nature, and People in the Neoliberal Age,* ed. Nancy Peluso and Joseph Nevins (Ithaca, NY: Cornell University Press, 2008), 116–19.

38   David Ekbladh, "'Mr. TVA': Grass-Roots Development, David Lilienthal, and the Rise and Fall of the Tennessee Valley Authority as a Symbol for U.S. Overseas Development, 1933–1973," *Diplomatic History* 26, no. 3 (2002): 335–74.

39   David Lilienthal, *The Journals of David E. Lilienthal,* vol. 6, *Creativity and Conflict, 1964–1967* (New York: Harper and Row, 1976), 283.

40   Ibid., 286.

41   Ibid., 373.

42   Ibid., 417–18; Jonathan Nashel, "The Road to Vietnam: Modernization Theory in Fact and Fiction," in *Cold War Constructions: The Political Structure of United States Imperialism, 1945–1966,* ed. Christian G. Appy (Amherst: University of Massachusetts Press, 2000), 152.

43   Lilienthal, *Journals,* 367.

44   Nguyen Thi Dieu, *Mekong River,* 164.

45   Porter, *Trust in Numbers,* 147.

46   "Department of Defense Advanced Research Projects Agency Order No. 1068, Accelerated Development: Plain of Reeds," file NV4730, TTLTQG2.

47 Victor J. Croizat, *The Development of the Plain of Reeds: Some Politico-military Implications* (Santa Monica, CA: Rand, 1969).

48 Richard L. Meier, "Human Ecology in Long Term River Basin Planning—the Mekong Case" (Working Paper 239, University of California—Berkeley Institute of Urban and Regional Development, 1974), 18.

49 Nippon Koei Company, "Design Report on Ngân Rô Barrage Project," October 1966, NL402, TTLTQG2.

50 C. Stuart Callison, "The Land-to-the-Tiller Program and Rural Resource Mobilization in the Mekong Delta of South Vietnam" (Papers in International Studies Southeast Asia Series 34, Ohio University Center for International Studies Southeast Asia Program, 1974), 2.

51 David Elliott, *The Vietnamese War: Revolution and Social Change in the Mekong Delta, 1930–1975,* concise ed. (Armonk, NY: M. E. Sharpe, 2006), 372–73.

52 For more detailed discussion of the PRG and its organization, see Trương Như Tang, *A Viet Cong Memoir* (New York: Vintage, 1985), 218–19.

53 Ông Dang, interview with author, April 19, 2002.

54 Ông Rõ, interview with author, April 12, 2002.

55 Ông Mười, interview with author, April 12, 2002.

56 Ông Bảy Long, interview with author, April 18, 2003.

57 Col. Daniel B. Porter Jr., senior advisor, IV Corps to commanding general, MACV, February 13, 1963, box 2, Headquarters, Military Assistance Command Vietnam, Secretary of the Joint Staff (SJS), Military History Branch, Policy and Precedent Files, RG 472, NARA2.

58 "Bảng Thuyết Trình của Kỷ Sư, Trương Ty Công Chánh Kiến Tường," December 8, 1966, file 1341/03, GTCC, TTLTQG2.

59 "Extortion on VN Waterways," box 22, Office of Civil Operations for Rural Development Support: Plans, Policy and Programs Directorate, CORDS Historical Working Group Files, RG 472, NARA2.

60 William C. McQuilkin, "Operation SEALORDS: A Front in a Frontless War, an Analysis of the Brown-Water Navy in Vietnam" (master's thesis, U.S. Army Command and General Staff College, Fort Leavenworth, KS, 1997), 44–46.

61 Lê Văn Hồng, "U Minh Thượng Trong Cuộc Cách Mạng Giải Phóng Dân Tộc," in *Kỷ Yếu Hội Thảo Khoa Học: Di Tích Lịch Sử Căn Cứ Địa Cách Mạng U Minh Thượng Tỉnh Kiên Giang* (Rạch Giá: Sở Văn Hóa Thông Tin, 1997), 93.

62 Pacification Studies Group, "The People of the U-Minh Forest Region: A Survey of Their Attitudes in the Context of Past and Present VC/GVN Activities," box 32, Office of Civil Operations for Rural Development Support: Plans, Policy and Programs Directorate, CORDS Historical Working Group Files, RG 472, NARA2.

63 Locations of the spraying missions were plotted by botanist Trần Triết and colleagues. See Tran Triet, Le Duc Minh, Mark Cheyne, Dorn Moore, and Jeb Barzen, "Viet Nam, Herbicides and Wetlands: Locating the Hotspots," International Crane Foundation, http://www.savingcranes.org/gis/fedprojects/vietnamherbicide.htm.

64 Pacification Studies Group, "Use of Herbicides," Office of Civil Operations for Rural Development Support: Plans, Policy and Programs Directorate, CORDS Historical Working Group Files, RG 472, NARA2.

65 David K. Shipler, "Vast Aid from U.S. Backs Saigon in Continuing War," *New York Times,* February 25, 1974, A1.

66 Ibid.

67 Joseph B. Treaster, "A Town in Mekong Delta Is Battered as Vietcong Pressure Mounts," *New York Times,* July 20, 1972, A3.

68 Ibid.

EPILOGUE

1 David Biggs, Fiona Miller, Hoanh C. Thai, and François Molle, "The Delta Machine: Water Management in the Vietnamese Mekong Delta in Historical and Contemporary Perspectives," in *Contested Waterscapes in the Mekong Region: Hydropower, Livelihoods and Governance,* ed. François Molle, Tira Foran, and Mira Käkönen (London: Earthscan, 2009), 211.

2 Chu Thai Hoanh, "Livelihood Impacts of Water Policy Changes: Evidence from a Coastal Area of the Mekong River Delta," *Water Policy* 5, no. 6 (2001): 475–88.

3 Chris Baltimore, "Levees Can't Save New Orleans from Floods: Report," Reuters News Service, April 24, 2009, http://www.reuters.com/article/environmentNews/idUSTRE53N4T720090424.

4 "Bridge Collapse: Irregular Numbers," Vietnam Net Bridge, http://english.vietnamnet.vn/reports/2007/09/745835/ (accessed April 16, 2009).

5 "8 giờ sáng 26–9, sập nhịp dẫn cầu Cần Thơ: Thảm họa lớn nhất lịch sử ngành xây dựng Việt Nam," *Sài Gòn Giải Phong,* September 27, 2007, http://www.sggp.org.vn/xahoi/2007/9/122629/ (accessed April 16, 2009).

6 Wayne Arnold, "Clearing the Decks for a Trade Pact's Riches," *New York Times,* August 27, 2000, section 3, 1.

7 David Biggs, "Motor-Powered Mekong: The Vietnamese-'Kohler' Revolution in the Delta," paper presented at the Association for Asian Studies Annual Meeting, San Francisco, April 6–9, 2006.

8 Nola Cooke and Li Tana, eds., *Water Frontier: Commerce and the Chinese in the Lower Mekong Region, 1750–1880* (Singapore: Singapore University Press, 2004).

9   Hữu Ngọc, "Traditional Miscellany: The River Flows Quietly Once Again," Vietnam News Service, May 8, 2005, http://vietnamnews.vnagency.com.vn/ showarticle.php?num=01TRA080505 (accessed January 15, 2008).

10   See, e.g., Human Rights Watch, *On the Margins: Rights Abuses of Ethnic Khmer in Vietnam's Mekong Delta* (New York: Human Rights Watch, 2009).

11   See, e.g., Prime Minister Decrees no. 99 (issued February 9, 1996) and no. 1 (issued January 5, 1998), http://www.asianlii.org/vn/legis/laws/ 0l0atfp019962000fdoitaciraotmrd1368/.

12   B. M. Sanders, *Fire Incident Assessment, U Minh Ha and U Minh Thuong National Park, Ca Mau and Kien Giang Provinces, Vietnam* (Hanoi: J. G. Goldammer/Global Fire Monitoring Center, 2002), 113.

BIBLIOGRAPHY

Adas, Michael. *The Burma Delta: Economic Development and Social Change on an Asian Rice Frontier, 1852–1941.* Madison: University of Wisconsin Press, 1974.

———. "From Avoidance to Confrontation: Peasant Protest in Pre-colonial and Colonial Southeast Asia." *Comparative Studies in Society and History* 23, no. 2 (1981): 217–47.

———. *Machines as the Measure of Men: Science, Technology, and Ideologies of Western Dominance.* Ithaca, NY: Cornell University Press, 1989.

Alden, Robert. "535 Refugees in South Vietnam Turn the Earth in Vital Project; They Dig Canal That Not Only Will Give Them a New Life, but Also Will Enable Settlement of Foes to Red Penetration." *New York Times*, February 9, 1956, A2.

Anderson, Benedict R. O. *Imagined Communities: Reflections on the Origin and Spread of Nationalism.* 2d ed. London: Verso, 1991.

Arnold, Wayne. "Clearing the Decks for a Trade Pact's Riches." *New York Times*, August 27, 2000, section 3, 1.

Baltimore, Chris. "Levees Can't Save New Orleans from Floods: Report." Reuters New Service, April 24, 2009. http://www.reuters.com/article/environmentNews/idUSTRE53N4T720090424.

Bassford, John. "Land Development Policy in Cochinchina under the French." PhD diss., University of Hawai'i, 1984.

Baurac, J. C. *La Cochinchine et ses habitants: Provinces de l'est* [Cochinchina and Its Inhabitants: Eastern Provinces]. Saigon: Imprimerie commerciale Rey, 1899.

———. *La Cochinchine et ses habitants: Provinces de ouest* [Cochinchina and Its Inhabitants: Western Provinces]. Saigon: Imprimerie Rey, Curiol, 1894.

Berdoulay, Vincent. "Place, Meaning, and Discourse in French Language Geography." In *The Power of Place,* edited by John A. Agnew and James S. Duncan, 124–39. Boston: Unwin Hyman, 1989.

Bernard, Paul. *Le problème economique indochinois* [The Indochinese Economic Problem]. Paris: Nouvelles éditions latines, 1934.

Bhabha, Homi K. "The Postcolonial and Postmodern: The Question of Agency." In *The Location of Culture,* 145–74. London: Routledge, 1994.

Biggs, David. "Managing a Rebel Landscape: Conservation, Pioneers, and the Revolutionary Past in the U Minh Forest." *Environmental History* 10, no. 3 (July 2005): 448–76.

———. "Motor-Powered Mekong: The Vietnamese-'Kohler' Revolution in the Delta." Paper presented at the Association for Asian Studies Annual Meeting, San Francisco, April 6–9, 2006.

———. "Problematic Progress: Reading Environmental and Social Change in the Mekong Delta." *Journal of Southeast Asian Studies* 34, no. 1 (February 2003): 77–96.

———. "Reclamation Nations: The U.S. Bureau of Reclamation's Role in Water Management and Nation Building in the Mekong Valley, 1945–1975." *Comparative Technology Transfer and Society* 4, no. 3 (December 2006): 225–46.

———. "Water Power: Machines, Modernizers, and Meta-commoditization on the Mekong River." In *Taking Southeast Asia to Market: Commodities, Nature, and People in the Neoliberal Age,* edited by Nancy Peluso and Joseph Nevins, 108–23. Ithaca, NY: Cornell University Press, 2008.

Biggs, David, Fiona Miller, Hoanh C. Thai, and François Molle. "The Delta Machine: Water Management in the Vietnamese Mekong Delta in Historical and Contemporary Perspectives." In *Contested Waterscapes in the Mekong Region: Hydropower, Livelihoods and Governance,* edited by François Molle, Tira Foran, and Mira Käkönen, 203–26. London: Earthscan, 2009.

BirdLife International. *The Conservation of Key Wetland Sites in the Mekong Delta: Conservation Report Number 12.* Hanoi: Institute of Ecology and Biological Resources, 1999.

Black, Eugene R. *Alternatives in Southeast Asia.* New York: Praeger, 1969.

Blanche, Lucien Charles. *Aperçu sur les opérations amphibies en Cochinchine, 1947–1951* [Overview of Amphibious Operations in Cochinchina]. Paris: Imprimerie nationale, 1951.

Boüinais, Albert Marie Aristide, and A. Paulus. *La Cochinchine contemporaine* [Contemporary Cochinchina]. Paris: Challamel Ainé, 1884.

Bourdeaux, Pascal. "Émergence et constitution de la communauté du Bouddhisme Hoà Hảo: Contribution à l'histoire sociale du delta du Mékong (1933–1955)" [Emergence and Establishment of the Hoa Hao Buddhist Community: Contribution to the Social History of the Mekong Delta]. 2 vols. PhD thesis, École practique des hautes études, 2003.

Brière. "Exploration par M. Benoist de la partie déserte comprise entre les inspections de Rach-gia, Cantho et Long-xuyen (Novembre 1871)" [Mr. Benoist's Explorations of the Barrens between Rach-gia, Cantho, and Long-xuyen Jurisdictions (November 1871)]. *Excursions et reconnaissances* [Tours and Explorations] 1 (1879): 44–47.

Brocheux, Pierre. "Grands propriétaires et fermiers dans l'ouest de la Cochinchine pendant la période coloniale" [Large Landowners and Farmers in the West of Cochinchina during the Colonial Period]. *Revue historique* [Historical Review] 499 (July–September 1971): 59–76.

———. *The Mekong Delta: Ecology, Economy, and Revolution, 1860–1960.* Madison, WI: Center for Southeast Asian Studies, 1995.

Brossard de Corbigny, Jules. "Notice sur les travaux de canalisation de la Cochinchine française" [Notice on Canal Work in French Cochinchina]. *Revue maritime et coloniale* [Naval and Colonial Review] 59 (1878): 512–26.

Bùi Văn Thạnh. "Báo Cáo Khái Quát Lịch Sử và Phương Hướng Bảo Tồn, Phát Huy Di Tích Lịch Sử Căn Cứ Địa Cách Mạng U Minh Thượng Kiên Giang" [Overview Report on the History and Orientation to Conservation and Promoting Historical Sites at U Minh Thượng, Kiến Giang]. In *Kỷ Yếu Hội Thảo Khoa Học: Di Tích Lịch Sử Căn Cứ Địa Cách Mạng U Minh Thượng Tỉnh Kiến Giang* [Symposium Proceedings: Historical Remnants of the U Minh Thượng Revolutionary Base, Kiến Giang Province], 45–82. Rạch Giá: Sở Văn Hoá Thông Tin—Thể Thao Kiên Giang, 1997.

Cable and Wireless Company. "History of the Atlantic Cable and Submarine Telegraphy." http://atlantic-cable.com/CableCos/CandW/EExt/index.htm.

Cadière, L. "Les Français au service de Gia-Long" [The French in the Service of Gia Long]. *Bulletin des amis de vieux Hué* [Bulletin of the Friends of Hué] 13, no. 3 (1926): 359–447.

Callison, C. Stuart. "The Land-to-the-Tiller Program and Rural Resource Mobilization in the Mekong Delta of South Vietnam." Papers in International Studies Southeast Asia Series 34, Ohio University Center for International Studies Southeast Asia Program, 1974.

Carte de la Cochinchine française [Map of French Cochinchina]. Paris: Augustin Challamel, 1901.

Carter, Paul. *Road to Botany Bay: An Essay in Spatial History.* London: Faber and Faber, 1987.

Catton, Philip. *Diem's Final Failure: Prelude to America's War in Vietnam.* Lawrence: University of Kansas Press, 2002.

Chakrabarty, Dipesh. "Postcoloniality and the Artifice of History: Who Speaks for 'Indian' Pasts?" *Representations* 37 (Winter 1992): 1–26.

Chandler, David P. *A History of Cambodia.* Boulder, CO: Westview Press, 1992.

Chatterjee, Partha. "Was There a Hegemonic Project of the Colonial State?" In *Contesting Colonial Hegemony: State and Society in Africa and India,* edited by Dagmar Engels and Shula Marks, 79–84. London: British Academic Press, 1994.

Chen, King C. "Hanoi's Three Decisions and the Escalation of the Vietnam War." *Political Science Quarterly* 90, no. 2 (Summer 1975): 239–59.

Chesneaux, Jean. *The Vietnamese Nation: Contribution to a History.* Sydney: Current Book Distributors, 1966.

Chiếu, Gilbert. "Une bataille intéressante" [An Interesting Battle]. *Supplement du Nông-Cổ Mín-Đàm* [Supplement of Conversations on Agriculture and Commerce over a Cup of Tea], October 23, 1907, 1.

Choi Byung Wook. *Southern Vietnam under the Reign of Minh Mạng (1820–1841): Central Policies and Local Response.* Ithaca, NY: Southeast Asia Program Publications, 2004.

Chu Thai Hoanh. "Livelihood Impacts of Water Policy Changes: Evidence from a Coastal Area of the Mekong River Delta." *Water Policy* 5, no. 6 (2003): 475–88.

Claeys, J. Y. "La géographie humaine des pays annamites basée sur des observations aériennes" [Human Geography of the Annamite Lands Based on Aerial Observations]. *Cahiers de l'École française d'Extrême-Orient* [Notes of the French School of the Far East] 22 (1940): 41–50.

Cochinchine française. *Les travaux publics et les voies de communication en Cochinchine* [Public Works and Lines of Communication in Cochinchina]. Saigon: Imprimerie nationale, 1880.

Coedès, George. *The Indianized States of Southeast Asia.* Edited by Walter F. Vella. Translated by Susan Brown Cowing. Honolulu, HI: East-West Center Press, 1967.

Colby, William E. "William E. Colby Oral History Interview I, 6/2/81." Interview by Ted Gittinger. Lyndon Baines Johnson Library and Museum. Internet copy, http://www.lbjlib.utexas.edu/johnson/archives.hom/oralhistory .hom/Colby/colby-01.pdf.

Combier, Charles. "Rapports présentés à S.E. Ministre" [Reports Presented to His Eminence the Minister]. 1881. Record 4/904(3), Social Sciences Information Center, Hanoi.

Comité agricole et industriel de la Cochinchine. *La Cochinchine française en 1878* [French Cochinchina in 1878]. Paris: Challamel Ainé, 1878.

"Commission permanente de 19 Juillet 1927: L'inspection generale du travail" [Permanent Commission of July 19, 1927: General Inspection of Labor]. *Tribune indochinoise,* August 24, 1927, 3.

Committee for Coordination of Investigations of the Lower Mekong Basin. *Annual Report.* Bangkok: ECAFE, 1965.

Conklin, Alice L. *A Mission to Civilize: The Republican Idea of Empire in France and West Africa, 1895–1930.* Stanford, CA: Stanford University Press, 1997.

Cooke, Nola. "Water World: Chinese and Vietnamese on the Riverine Water Frontier, from Ca Mau to Tonle Sap (c. 1850–1884)." In *Water Frontier: Commerce and the Chinese in the Lower Mekong Region, 1750–1880,* edited by Nola Cooke and Li Tana, 139–58. Singapore: Singapore University Press, 2004.

Cooke, Nola, and Li Tana, eds. *Water Frontier: Commerce and the Chinese in the Lower Mekong Region, 1750–1880.* Singapore: Singapore University Press, 2004.

Corré, A. "Rapport sur des nouvelles recherches relatives a l'Age de la pierre polie et du bronze en Indo-Chine par le docteur A. Corré, médécin de 1re classe de la Marine" [Report on New Research on the Age of Polished Stone and Bronze in Indo-China by Dr. A. Corré, Navy Doctor 1st Class]. *Excursions et reconnaissances* 3 (1880): 361–84.

Crawfurd, John. *Journal of an Embassy to the Courts of Siam and Cochin China.* Kuala Lumpur: Oxford University Press, 1967.

Croizat, Victor J. *The Development of the Plain of Reeds: Some Politico-military Implications.* Santa Monica, CA: Rand, 1969.

Cronon, William, ed. *Uncommon Ground: Toward Reinventing Nature.* New York: W. W. Norton, 1995.

Cultru, Prosper. *Histoire de la Cochinchine française des origines à 1883* [History of French Cochinchina from Its Origins to 1883]. Paris: Augustin Challamel, 1910.

Đại Nam Thực Lục: Quốc Sử Quán Triều Nguyễn [Southern Annals: Official History of the Nguyen Lords]. 38 vols. Hà Nội: Sử Học, 1963.

Đao Linh Côn, "The Oc Eo Burial Group Recently Excavated at Go Thap (Dong Thap Province, Viêt Nam)." In *Southeast Asian Archaeology 1994: Proceedings of the 5th International Conference of the European Association of Southeast Asian Archaeologists, Paris, October 1994,* edited by Pierre-Yves Manguin, 111–17. Hull: University of Hull, Centre of Southeast Asian Studies, 1994.

Deleuze, Gilles, and Félix Guattari. *Anti-Oedipus: Capitalism and Schizophrenia.* Translated by Robert Hurley, Mark Seem, and Helen R. Lane. New York: Viking Press, 1977.

Department of the Army. *Vietnam Studies: Base Development, 1965–1970.* Washington, DC: GPO, 1972.

Devillers, Philip. *Histoire du Viêt-Nam de 1940 à 1952* [History of Vietnam from 1940 to 1952]. Paris: Éditions du Seuil, 1952.

Direction générale des travaux publics, Gouvernement générale de l'Indochine. *Atlas: Les voies d'eau de la Cochinchine* [Atlas: Waterways of Cochinchina]. Saigon: Imprimerie nouvelle, 1911.

———. *Voies d'eau de la Cochinchine* [Waterways of Cochinchina]. Saigon: Imprimerie nouvelle, 1911.

Dumont, René. *La culture du riz dans le delta du Tonkin: Étude et propositions d'amélioration des techniques traditionnelles de riziculture tropicale* [Rice cultivation in the delta of Tonkin: Study and proposals for improvement of traditional techniques of tropical rice culture]. 1935; Patani: Prince of Song-kla University, 1995.

Duras, Marguerite. *L'amant* [The lover]. Paris: Prix Goncourt, 1984.

Durdin, Tillman. "Dictatorial Rule in Saigon Charged." *New York Times,* May 1, 1960, 1.

Dutreil de Rhins, J. L. *Avertissement géographique et orthographique sur la carte de l'Indo-chine orientale suivi d'un vocabulaire des noms géographiques annamites* [Geographic and Orthographic Notice on the Map of Eastern Indo-China Followed by a Vocabulary of Geographical Names in Vietnamese]. Paris: Imprimerie nationale, 1881.

Dutton, George E. "The Tây Son Uprising: Society and Rebellion in Late Eighteenth-Century Viêt Nam, 1771–1802." PhD diss., University of Washington, 2001.

Ekbladh, David. "'Mr. TVA': Grass-Roots Development, David Lilienthal, and the Rise and Fall of the Tennessee Valley Authority as a Symbol for U.S. Overseas Development, 1933–1973." *Diplomatic History* 26, no. 3 (2002): 335–74.

Elden, Stuart. *Mapping the Present: Heidegger, Foucault and the Project of a Spatial History.* London: Continuum, 2001.

Elliott, David W. P. *The Vietnamese War: Revolution and Social Change in the Mekong Delta, 1930–1975.* 2 vols. Armonk, NY: M. E. Sharpe, 2003.

———. *The Vietnamese War: Revolution and Social Change in the Mekong Delta, 1930–1975.* Concise ed. Armonk, NY: M. E. Sharpe, 2006.

Ernst, John. *Forging a Fateful Alliance: Michigan State and the Vietnam War.* East Lansing: Michigan State University Press, 1998.

Fall, Bernard. "The Political-Religious Sects of Viet-Nam." *Pacific Affairs* 28, no. 3 (September 1955): 235–53.

Favin-Lévêque, Bernard. *Souvenirs de mer et d'ailleurs* [Memories of the Sea and Elsewhere]. Paris: Éditions des 7 vents, 1990.

Ferguson, James. *The Anti-politics Machine: "Development," Depoliticization, and Bureaucratic Power in Lesotho.* Cambridge: Cambridge University Press, 1990.

Föreningen, Levande Framtid. "Long Term Consequences of the Việt Nam War: Ecosystems." *Report to the Environmental Conference on Cambodia, Laos, and Việt Nam.* Stockholm, 2002. http://www.nhn.se/environ/ecology.html.

Foucault, Michel. *Discipline and Punish.* Middlesex: Peregrine, 1979.

Fraisse, André. "Notes de géographie humaine sur la province de Long-Xuyên" [Notes on the Human Geography of Long-Xuyên Province]. *Extrait du Bulletin de l'Institut indochinois pour l'étude de l'homme* (séance du 26 mai 1942) [Excerpt of the Bulletin of the Indochinese Institute for the Study of Man (Meeting of May 26, 1942)], 137–44.

Gentilini, R. *Les voies de communication en Cochinchine* [Lines of Communication in Cochinchina]. Paris: Imprimerie Chaix, 1886.

Gettleman, Marvin E. *Viet Nam: History, Documents and Opinions on a Major World Crisis.* Greenwich, CT: Fawcett Publications, 1965.

Giang Minh Đoán. *Nguyễn Trung Trực: Anh Hùng Kháng Chiến Chống Pháp* [Nguyen Trung Truc: Hero of the Uprisings against the French]. Hồ Chí Minh City: Thành Phố Hồ Chí Minh, 1998.

Giebel, Christoph. *Imagined Ancestries of Vietnamese Communism: Ton Duc Thang and the Politics of History and Memory.* Seattle: University of Washington Press, 2004.

Gourou, Pierre. *Les paysans du delta Tonkinois: Étude de geographie humaine* [Peasants of the Tonkin Delta: A Study in Human Geography]. Paris: Éditions d'art et d'histoire, 1936.

Gouvernement du Cochinchine. *Contrats pour le service postal des correspondances fluviales de la Cochinchine et du Cambodge* [Contracts for the postal service of the River Correspondence of Cochinchina and Cambodia]. Paris: n.p., 1901. File 8°/3811(3), Social Sciences Information Center, Hanoi.

Government of the Socialist Republic of Vietnam, Ministry of Water Resources Planning Institute. *Cai San Water Control Project: Project Summary.* Hanoi, 1979.

Greene, Graham. *The Quiet American.* New York: Penguin Putnam, 1991.

Grove, Richard H. *Green Imperialism: Colonial Expansion, Tropical Island Edens, and the Origins of Environmentalism, 1600–1860.* Cambridge, NY: Cambridge University Press, 1995.

Gueyffier, René. *Essai sur le régime de la terre en Indochine (pays annamites)* [Essay on Land Tenure in Indochina (Vietnamese Lands)]. Lyons: Imprimerie BOSC frères and RIOU, 1928.

Halberstam, David. *The Making of a Quagmire.* New York: Random House, 1964.

Haraway, Donna J. *Simians, Cyborgs, and Women: The Reinvention of Nature.* New York: Routledge, 1991.

Hardy, Andrew. *Red Hills: Migrants and the State in the Highlands of Vietnam.* Honolulu: University of Hawai'i Press, 2003.

Harvey, David. *The Condition of Postmodernity: An Enquiry into the Origins of Cultural Change*. Oxford: Blackwell, 1989.

Heidegger, Martin. *Vorträge und Aufsätze* [Lectures and Essays]. 4th ed. Pfullingen: Günther Neske, 1978.

Henry, Yves. *Économie agricole de l'Indochine* [Agricultural Economy of Indochina]. Hanoi: Imprimerie de l'Extrême-Orient, 1932.

Henry, Yves, and Maurice de Visme. *Documents de démographie et riziculture en Indochine* [Documents on Demography and Rice Culture in Indochina]. Hanoi: Bulletin économique de l'Indochine, 1928.

Hồ Sơn Đài. "Có Một Trung Tâm Kháng Chiến Ở Nam Bộ" [One Center of the Resistance in Cochinchina]. In *Gởi Người Đang Sống: Lịch Sử Đồng Tháp Mười* [Note to the Living: A History of Đồng Tháp], edited by Võ Trần Nhã, 53–102. Hồ Chí Minh City: Thành Phố Hồ Chí Minh, 1993.

Human Rights Watch. *On the Margins: Rights Abuses of Ethnic Khmer in Vietnam's Mekong Delta*. New York: Human Rights Watch, 2009.

Hunt, David. *Vietnam's Southern Revolution: From Peasant Insurrection to Total War, 1959–1968*. Amherst: University of Massachusetts Press, 2009.

Huỳnh Lứa, ed. *Lịch Sử Khai Phá Vùng Đất Nam Bộ* [History of Land Reclamation in the South]. Hồ Chí Minh City: Thành Phố Hồ Chí Minh, 1987.

Inspection des travaux publics, Gouvernement générale de l'Indochine. *Dragages de Cochinchine: Canal Rachgia-Hatien* [Dredging in Cochinchina: Rachgia-hatien Canal]. Saigon: n.p., 1930.

Jackson, James Brinkerhoff. *Discovering the Vernacular Landscape*. New Haven, CT: Yale University Press, 1986.

Jaffe, Adrian, and Milton Taylor. "The Professor-Diplomat: Ann Arbor and Cambridge Were Never Like This." *New Republic* 146 (1962): 28–30.

Jennings, Eric T. *Vichy in the Tropics: Pétain's National Revolution in Madagascar, Guadeloupe, and Indochina, 1940–1944*. Stanford, CA: Stanford University Press, 2001.

Johnson, Lyndon B. *Public Papers of the Presidents of the United States: Lyndon B. Johnson, 1965*. Vol. 1. Washington, DC: GPO, 1966.

Kemf, Elizabeth. *Month of Pure Light: The Regreening of Vietnam*. London: Women's Press, 1990.

"Ladejinsky Dispute." *New York Times*, December 26, 1954, E2.

Lâm Quang Huyên. *Cách mạng ruộng đất ở Miền Nam Việt Nam* [Land Revolution in Southern Vietnam]. Hà Nội: Khoa Học Xã Hội, 1997.

"Landscapes: Go Thap." *Nhân Dân*, October 16, 1999.

Lansing, Stephen. *Priests and Programmers: Technologies of Power in the Engineered Landscape of Bali*. Princeton, NJ: Princeton University Press, 1991.

Latham, Michael E. *Modernization as Ideology: American Social Science and "Nation Building" in the Kennedy Era*. Chapel Hill: University of North Carolina Press, 2000.

————. *We Have Never Been Modern*. Translated by Catherine Porter. Cambridge, MA: Harvard University Press, 1993.

Latour, Bruno. *Reassembling the Social: An Introduction to Actor-Network-Theory*. Clarendon Lectures in Management Studies. New York: Oxford University Press, 2005.

Lederer, William J., and Eugene Burdick. *The Ugly American*. New York: Norton, 1958.

Lefebvre, Henri. *The Production of Space*. Translated by Donald Nicholson-Smith. Oxford: Blackwell Publishers, 1994.

Le Myre de Vilers, Charles. *La politique coloniale française depuis 1830* [French Colonial Politics after 1830]. Paris: Publication de la nouvelle revue, 1913.

Lê Quang Liêm. "La vérité sur l'échauffourée de Ninh-Thanh-Loi (Rachgia)" [The Truth about the Scuffle at Ninh-Thanh-Loi]. *Tribune indochinoise*, May 20, 1927, 1–2.

————. "La vérité sur l'échauffourée de Ninh-Thanh-Loi (Rachgia)." *Tribune indochinoise*, May 23, 1927, 1–2.

————. "La vérité sur l'échauffourée de Ninh-Thanh-Loi (Rachgia)." *Tribune indochinoise*, May 25, 1927, 1–2.

Lê Qúy Đôn. *Phủ Biên Tạp Lục: Quyển 1* [Annals of the Southern Frontier: Book 1]. Translated by Lê Xuân Giáo. Sài Gòn: Phủ Quốc Vụ Khanh Đặc Trách Văn Hoá, 1972.

Leroy, Jean. *Un homme dans la rizière* [A Man in the Rice Fields]. Paris: Éditions de Paris, 1955.

Lê Văn Hồng. "U Minh Thượng Trong Cuộc Cách Mạng Giải Phóng Dân Tộc" [U Minh Thuong in the Revolution to Liberate the People]. In *Kỷ Yếu Hội Thảo Khoa Học: Di Tích Lịch Sử Căn Cứ Địa Cách Mạng U Minh Thượng Tỉnh Kiên Giang* [Symposium Proceedings: Historical Remnants of the U Minh Thượng Revolutionary Base, Kiến Giang Province], 89–95. Rạch Giá: Sở Văn Hóa Thông Tin, 1997.

Lê Văn Năm. "Công Cuộc Khai Phá Trong Nửa Đầu Thế Kỷ XIX" [Reclamation Projects in the Early Nineteenth Century]. In *Lịch Sử Khai Phá Vùng Đất Nam Bộ* [History of Reclamation in the Southern Region], edited by Huỳnh Lứa, 94–156. Hồ Chí Minh City: Thành Phố Hồ Chí Minh, 1987.

Lilienthal, David. *The Journals of David E. Lilienthal*. Vol. 6, *Creativity and Conflict, 1964–1967*. New York: Harper and Row, 1976.

Li Tana. *Nguyễn Cochinchina: Southern Vietnam in the Seventeenth and Eighteenth Centuries*. Ithaca, NY: Southeast Asia Program Publications, 1998.

Malleret, Louis. *L'archéologie du delta du Mékong* [The Archaeology of the Mekong Delta]. 3 vols. Paris: École française d'Extrême-Orient, 1959.

————. "Elément d'une monographie de anciennes fortifications et citadelles de Saigon" [An Element of One Monograph on Ancient Fortifications and Citadels of Saigon]. *Bulletin de la Société des études indochinoises* [Bulletin of the Society of Indochinese Studies] 10, no. 4 (October–December 1935): 5–108.

Maltby, Edward, C. P. Immirzi, and R. J. Safford, eds. *Tropical Lowland Peatlands of Southeast Asia: Proceedings of a Workshop on Integrated Planning and Management of Tropical Lowland Peatlands Held at Cisarua, Indonesia, 3–8 July 1992.* Gland, Switzerland: IUCN, 1996.

Mantienne, Frédéric. *Mgr Pierre Pigneaux: Évoque d'Adran, dignitaire de Cochinchine* [Monsignor Pierre Pigneaux: Bishop of Adran, Dignitary of Cochinchina]. Paris: Églises d'Asie, 1999.

Marx, Leo. *Machine in the Garden: Technology and the Pastoral Ideal in America.* New York: Oxford University Press, 2000.

Mauclère, Jean. *Marins dans les arroyos* [Marines in the rice fields]. Paris: J. Peyronnet, 1950.

McHale, Shawn F. *Print and Power: Confucianism, Communism, and Buddhism in the Making of Modern Vietnam.* Honolulu: University of Hawai'i Press, 2003.

McQuilkin, William C. "Operation SEALORDS: A Front in a Frontless War, an Analysis of the Brown-Water Navy in Vietnam." Master's thesis, U.S. Army Command and General Staff College, Fort Leavenworth, KS, 1997.

Meier, Richard L. "Human Ecology in Long Term River Basin Planning—the Mekong Case." Working Paper 239, University of California—Berkeley Institute of Urban and Regional Development, 1974.

Messageries fluviales de Cochinchine [River Couriers of Cochinchina]. Paris: n.p., 1908. File 8°/3811(4), Social Sciences Information Center, Hanoi.

Meyerson, Harvey. *Vinh Long.* Boston: Houghton Mifflin, 1970.

Minh Mệnh Chính Yếu: Quốc Sử Quán Triều Nguyễn [Essential Minh Mang: Official History of the Nguyen Dynasty]. Huế: Thuận Hoà, 1994.

Montgomery, John D. *The Politics of Foreign Aid: American Experience in Southeast Asia.* New York: Praeger, 1962.

Mrazek, Rudolf. *Engineers of Happy Land: Technology and Nationalism in a Colony.* Princeton, NJ: Princeton University Press, 2002.

Murray, Martin J. *The Development of Capitalism in Colonial Indochina (1870–1940).* Berkeley and Los Angeles: University of California Press, 1980.

"Mutual Defense Assistance: Indochina-Agreement between the United States of America and Cambodia, France, Laos and Viet-nam." *American Journal of International Law* 48, no. 3, Supplement: Official Documents (July 1954): 133–37.

Nashel, Jonathan. "The Road to Vietnam: Modernization Theory in Fact and Fiction." In *Cold War Constructions: The Political Structure of United States Imperialism, 1945–1966,* edited by Christian G. Appy, 132–54. Amherst: University of Massachusetts Press, 2000.

Netherlands Delta Development Team. *Recommendations concerning Agricul-*

tural Development with Improved Water Control in the Mekong Delta: Main Report. Bangkok: ECAFE, 1974.

———. *Recommendations concerning Agricultural Development with Improved Water Control in the Mekong Delta: Working Paper VI, Irrigation and Drainage.* Bangkok: ECAFE, 1974.

Ngô Đình Diệm. *Con Đường Chính Nghĩa Độc Lập Dân Chủ.* Sài Gòn: n.p., 1958.

Ngô Vĩnh Long. *Before the Revolution: The Vietnamese Peasants under the French.* New York: Columbia University Press, 1991.

Nguyễn Công Bình, Lê Xuân Diệm, and Mạc Đường. *Văn Hoá và Cư Dân Đồng Bằng Sông Cửu Long* [Culture and Inhabitants of the Mekong Delta]. Hồ Chí Minh City: Khoa Học Xã Hội, 1990.

Nguyễn Công Viên. *Seeking the Truth: The Inside Story of Viet Nam after the French Defeat by a Man Who Served in Bao Dai's Cabinet.* New York: Vantage Press, 1966.

Nguyễn Đình Đầu. *Chế Độ Công Điền Công Thổ Trong Lịch Sử Khẩn Hoang Lập ấp ở Nam Kỳ Lục Tỉnh* [Land Tenure Systems in the History of Settlement of Cochinchina]. Hà Nội: Hội Sử Học Việt Nam, 1992.

———. "Remarques préliminaires sur le registres cadastraux (địa bạ) des six provinces de la Cochinchine (Nam Kỳ Lục Tỉnh)" [Preliminary Remarks on the Cadastral Registers (Dia Bo) of the Six Provinces of Cochinchina (Six Provinces of the South)]. *Bulletin de l'École française d'Extrême-Orient* [Bulletin of the French School of the Far East] 78 (1991): 275–85.

———. *Tổng Kết Nghiên Cứu Địa Bộ Nam Kỳ Lục Tỉnh* [Research Conclusions on the Land Registers of Cochinchina]. Hồ Chí Minh City: Hồ Chí Minh City and Toyota Foundation, 1994.

Nguyễn Du. *The Tale of Kiều: A Bilingual Edition.* Translated by Huỳnh Sanh Thông. New Haven, CT: Yale University Press, 1983.

Nguyễn Hiến Lê. *Bảy Ngày Trong Đồng Tháp Mười: Du Ký và Biên Khảo* [Seven Days in Đồng Tháp: Travel Notes and Explorations]. Long An: Long An, 1989.

Nguyễn Hữu Chiếm. "Studies on Agro-ecological Environment and Land Use in the Mekong Delta, Vietnam." PhD diss., Kyoto University, 1994.

Nguyễn Khắc Đạm. *Nguyễn Tri Phương: Đánh Pháp* [Nguyen Tri Phuong: Fighting the French]. Hà Nội: Hội Khoa Học Lịch Sử Việt Nam, 1998.

Nguyễn Khắc Viện. *Vietnam: A Long History.* Hanoi: Thế Giới Publishers, 1993.

Nguyễn Long Thành Nam. *Hoa Hao Buddhism in the Course of Vietnam's History.* Hauppage, NY: Nova Science Publishers, 2003.

Nguyễn Ngọc Hiền, ed. *Lê Thành Hầu: Nguyễn Hữu Cảnh, 1650–1700* [Le Thanh Hau: Nguyen Huu Canh, 1650–1700]. TP Hồ Chí Minh: Văn Học, 1997.

Nguyễn Thế Anh. "The Vietnamization of the Cham Deity Po Nagar." In *Essays into Vietnamese Pasts,* edited by K. W. Taylor and John K. Whitmore, 42–80. Ithaca, NY: Southeast Asia Program Publications, 1995.

Nguyen Thi Dieu. *The Mekong River and the Struggle for Indochina: Water, War, and Peace*. Westport, CT: Praeger, 1999.

Nguyễn Thị Định. *No Other Road to Take*. Translated by Mai V. Elliott. Ithaca, NY: Southeast Asia Program Publications, 1976.

Nguyễn Văn Hầu. *Đức Cố-Quản: Hay là Cuộc Khởi-Nghĩa Bảy-Thưa* [Saintly Leader: Or the Bảy Thưa Uprising]. Sài Gòn: Tân-Sanh, 1956.

———. *Thoại Ngọc Hầu và Những Cuộc Khai Phá Miền Hậu Giang* [Thoại Ngọc Hầu and the Settlement of the Hậu Giang Region]. Sài Gòn: Hoa Sen, 1972.

Nguyễn Văn Huyên. *La civilization annamite* [Vietnamese Civilization]. Hanoi: Direction de l'instruction publique, 1944.

Nguyễn Việt, ed. *Nam Bộ và Nam Phần Trung Bộ Trong Hai Năm Đầu Kháng Chiến (1945–1946)* [Cochinchina and Southern Annam in the First Two Years of the Resistance (1945–1946)]. Hà Nội: Văn Sử Địa, 1958.

Nguyễn Xuân Lai. "Questions of Agrarian Structures and Agricultural Development in Southern Việt Nam." *Vietnamese Studies*, n.s., 5, no. 75 (1984): 23–63.

Norindr, Panivong. "The Popular Front's Colonial Policies in Indochina: Reassessing the Popular Front's 'Colonisation Altruiste.'" In *French Colonial Empire and the Popular Front: Hope and Disillusion*, edited by Tony Chafer and Amanda Sackur, 230–48. New York: St. Martin's Press, 1999.

Normandin, A. *Travaux d'hydraulique agricole à étudier et à entreprendre en Cochinchine: Rapport de mission* [Irrigated Agriculture under Study and at Work in Cochinchina: Mission Report]. Saigon: Imprimerie commerciale M. Rey, 1913.

Paris, Pierre. "Anciens canaux reconnus sur photographs aeriénnes dans les provinces de Tak Ev et de Châu Đốc" [Ancient Canals Recognized in Aerial Photographs in Tak Ev and Chau Doc Provinces]. *Bulletin de l'École française de l'Extrême-Orient* 31 (1931): 221–23.

Peet, Richard. "Introduction to the Life and Thought of Karl Wittfogel." *Antipode: A Radical Journal of Geography* 17, no. 1 (1985): 3–20.

Phạm Hoàng Hộ. *Cây Cỏ Việt Nam* [Flora of Vietnam]. 3 vols. Hà Nội: Trẻ, 1999.

Phạm Văn Bạch, ed. *Fascist Terror in South Vietnam: Law 10/59*. Hanoi: Thế Giới, 1961.

Phan Đại Đoãn. *Khởi Nghĩa Diệt Nguyễn và Chống Xiêm* [The Rebellion to Destroy the Nguyen and Resist Siam]. Bình Định: Sở Văn Hoá Thông Tin Bình Định, 1993.

Phan Khánh, ed. *Sơ Thảo Lịch Sử Thủy Lợi Việt Nam. Tập 1* [Historical Discussion of Irrigation in Vietnam. Vol. 1]. Hà Nội: Khoa Học Xã Hội, 1981.

Plan du canal du Xano [Chart of Xano Canal]. Saigon: Imprimerie commerciale, 1904. File IA 13/232(1), Fonds Goucoch, Trung Tâm Lưu Trữ Quốc Gia II

[Vietnamese National Archives Center, no. 2]. Hồ Chí Minh City, Việt Nam.

Plan topographie de la province de Cantho, 1/100.000 [Topographic Chart of Cantho Province, 1/100,000]. Hanoi: Société geographique de l'Indochine, 1925.

Popkin, Samuel L. *The Rational Peasant: The Political Economy of Rural Society in Vietnam.* Berkeley and Los Angeles: University of California Press, 1979.

Porter, Theodore. *Trust in Numbers: The Pursuit of Objectivity in Science and Public Life.* Princeton, NJ: Princeton University Press, 1995.

Pratt, Mary Louise. *Imperial Eyes: Travel Writing and Transculturation.* New York: Routledge, 1992.

Régnier, P. *Nivellement général de la Cochinchine: Rapport du chef du brigade* [General Leveling of Cochinchina: Report of the Chief of the Brigade]. Saigon: Imprimerie commerciale M. Rey, 1911.

Rénaud, J. "Étude d'un projet de canal entre le Vaico et le Cua-Tieu" [Study of a Canal Project between Vaico and Cua-Tieu]. *Excursions et reconnaissances* 3 (1880): 315–30.

———. "Étude sur l'approfondissement du canal de Vinh-té et l'amelioration du port d'Hatien" [Study on the Deepening of the Vinh-te Canal and the Improvement of the Hatien Port]. *Excursions et reconnaissances* 1 (December 1879): 65–93.

République du Viêt-Nam. *Les travaux d'hydraulique agricole au Viet-Nam* [Irrigation Works in Vietnam]. Saigon: n.p., 1960.

Rigg, Jonathan. *Southeast Asia, a Region in Transition: A Thematic Human Geography of the ASEAN Region.* London: Unwin Hyman, 1991.

Rosenthal, A. M. "Saigon is Swept by Civil Warfare; Big Area is Afire." *New York Times*, April 29, 1955, A1.

Sakurai, Yumio, and Takako Kitigawa. "Ha Tien or Banteay Mas in the Time of the Fall of Ayutthaya." In *From Japan to Arabia: Ayutthaya's Maritime Relations with Asia,* edited by Kennon Breazeale, 150–220. Bangkok: Foundation for the Promotion of Social Sciences and Humanities Textbooks Project, 1999.

Sanders, B. M. *Fire Incident Assessment, U Minh Ha and U Minh Thuong National Park, Ca Mau and Kien Giang Provinces, Vietnam.* Hanoi: J. G. Goldammer/Global Fire Monitoring Center, 2002.

Sansom, Robert L. *The Economics of Insurgency in the Mekong Delta of Vietnam.* Cambridge, MA: MIT Press, 1970.

Savani, A. M. *Visage et images du Sud Viet-Nam* [Faces and Images of South Vietnam]. Saigon: Imprimerie française d'Outre-Mer, 1955.

Scott, James C. "Afterword to *Moral Economies, State Spaces, and Categorical Violence.*" *American Anthropologist* 107 (2005): 395–402.

———. *The Moral Economy of the Peasant: Rebellion and Subsistence in Southeast Asia.* New Haven, CT: Yale University Press, 1977.

————. *Seeing like a State: How Certain Schemes to Improve the Human Condition Have Failed.* New Haven, CT: Yale University Press, 1998.

————. *Weapons of the Weak: Everyday Forms of Peasant Resistance.* New Haven, CT: Yale University Press, 1987.

Sears, Laurie J. *Shadows of Empire: Colonial Discourse and Javanese Tales.* Durham, NC: Duke University Press, 1996.

Sellers, Nicholas. *The Princes of Hà-tiên, 1682–1867.* Brussels, Belgium: Thanh-Long, 1983.

Sheehan, Neil. *A Bright Shining Lie: John Paul Vann and America in Vietnam.* New York: Vintage, 1989.

Sheehan, Neil, et al. *The Pentagon Papers, as Published by the "New York Times."* New York: Bantam, 1971.

Shipler, David K. "Vast Aid from U.S. Backs Saigon in Continuing War." *New York Times,* February 25, 1974, A1.

Smail, John R. W. "On the Possibility of an Autonomous History of Modern Southeast Asia." *Journal of Southeast Asian History* 2 (1961): 72–102.

Smith, Ralph B. "The Vietnamese Élite of French Cochinchina, 1943." *Modern Asian Studies* 6, no. 4 (1972): 459–82.

Société des études indo-chinoises. *Géographie physique, économique et historique de la Cochinchine* [Physical, Economic, and Historical Geography of Cochinchina]. Fascicle 10, *Monographie de la province de Cần-Thơ* [Installment 10, Monograph of Can-Tho Province]. Saigon: Imprimerie Ménard et Rey, 1904.

————. *Géographie physique, économique et historique de la Cochinchine.* Fascicle 6, *Monographie de la province de Châu-Đốc.* Saigon: Imprimerie L. Ménard, 1902.

————. *Géographie physique, économique et historique de la Cochinchine.* Fascicle 2, *Monographie de la province d'Hà-Tiên.* Saigon: Imprimerie L. Ménard, 1901.

————. *Géographie physique, économique et historique de la Cochinchine.* Fascicle 8, *Monographie de la province de Sa-Déc.* Saigon: Imprimerie L. Ménard, 1903.

————. *Géographie physique, économique et historique de la Cochinchine.* Fascicle 11, *Monographie de la province de Sóc-Trăng.* Saigon: Imprimerie commerciale Ménard et Rey, 1904.

Sok, Khin. *Le Cambodge entre le Siam et le Viêtnam (de 1775 à 1860)* [Cambodia between Siam and Vietnam (from 1775 to 1860)]. Paris: École française de l'Extrême-Orient, 1991.

Sơn Nam. *Cá Tính Miền Nam* [The Character of the South]. Hồ Chí Minh City: Trẻ, 1997.

————. *Đồng Bằng Sông Cửu Long: Nét Sinh Hoạt Xưa* [The Mekong Delta: Features of Life in the Past]. Hồ Chí Minh City: Thành Phố Hồ Chí Minh, 1993.

———. *Hai Cõi U Minh: Truyện* [Two Worlds of U Minh: Stories]. Sài Gòn: Hữu Nghị, 1965.

———. *Hồi Kỳ Sơn Nam* [Memoirs: Son Nam]. Hồ Chí Minh City: NXP Trẻ, 2003.

———. *Lịch Sử An Giang* [History of An Giang]. Long Xuyên: An Giang, 1986.

———. *Lịch Sử Khẩn Hoang Miền Nam* [A History of Settling the South]. Hồ Chí Minh City: Văn Nghệ, 1994.

———. *Văn Minh Miệt Vườn* [Garden Civilization]. Hà Nội: Văn Hoá, 1992.

Souverains et notabilités d'Indochine [Sovereigns and Notables of Indochina]. Hanoi: Éditions du gouvernement général de l'Indochine, 1943.

Stoler, Ann Laura. *Race and the Education of Desire: Foucault's "History of Sexuality" and the Colonial Order of Things.* Durham, NC: Duke University Press, 1995.

Tai, Hue-Tam Ho. *Millenarianism and Peasant Politics in Vietnam.* Cambridge, MA: Harvard University Press, 1983.

Taylor, Frederick. "Mekong Delta Project Shows the Difficulty of Pacification Effort: Vietcong Murder Government Workers, Raid Outposts; Key Canal Remains Closed." *Wall Street Journal,* June 20, 1967, A1.

Taylor, Jean Gelman. *The Social World of Batavia: European and Eurasian in Dutch Asia.* Madison: University of Wisconsin Press, 1983.

Taylor, Keith W. "Surface Orientations in Vietnam: Beyond Histories of Nation and Region." *Journal of Asian Studies* 57 (November 1998): 949–78.

Taylor, Philip. *Goddess on the Rise: Pilgrimage and Popular Religion in Vietnam.* Honolulu: University of Hawai'i Press, 2004.

Thái Văn Kiểm. "Interpretation d'une carte ancienne de Saigon" [Interpretation of an ancient map of Saigon]. *Bulletin de la Societe des études indochinoises* 37, no. 4 (1962): 409–31.

Thayer, Carlyle A. *War by Other Means: National Liberation and Revolution in Viet-Nam, 1954–1960.* Sydney: Allen and Unwin, 1989.

Thévenet-Le Boul, Jean Marie. *Les travaux publics et les voies de communication en Cochinchine* [Public Works and Lines of Communication in Cochinchina]. Saigon: Imprimerie nationale, 1880.

Thomas, Frédéric. *Histoire du regime et des services forestiers français en Indochine de 1862 à 1945* [History of the System of French Forestry in Indochina from 1862 to 1945]. Hà Nội: Thế Giới, 1999.

Thongchai Winichakul. *Siam Mapped: A History of the Geo-body of a Nation.* Honolulu: University of Hawai'i Press, 1994.

———. "Writing at the Interstices: Southeast Asian Historians and Postnational Histories in Southeast Asia." In *New Terrains in Southeast Asian History,* edited by Abu Talib Ahmad and Tan Liok Ee, 3–29. Singapore: Singapore University Press, 2003.

Touzet, André. *L'economie indochinoise et la grand crise universelle* [The Indochinese Economy and the Global Depression]. Paris: Marcel Giard, 1934.

Trần Nguyện Hành. "Les inscriptions de Thoại Sơn et de Vĩnh Tế" [Inscriptions of Thoai Mountain and Vinh Te]. Paper presented to the Premier Congress international des études Extrêmes Orientales. Hanoi, 1903.

Trần Thị Thu Lương and Võ Thành Phương. *Khởi Nghĩa Bảy Thưa (1867–1873)* [The Bay Thua Uprising (1867–1873)]. Hồ Chí Minh City: Thành Phố Hồ Chí Minh, 1991.

Tran Triet, Le Duc Minh, Mark Cheyne, Dorn Moore, and Jeb Barzen. "Viet Nam, Herbicides and Wetlands: Locating the Hotspots." International Crane Foundation. http://www.savingcranes.org/gis/fedprojects/vietnamherbicide.htm.

Trần Tư Bình. *The Red Earth: A Vietnamese Memoir of Life on a Colonial Rubber Plantation.* Edited by David Marr. Translated by John Spragens Jr. Monographs in International Studies, Southeast Asia Series, no. 66. Athens: Ohio University Press, 1985.

Trần Xuân Kiêm. *Nghề Nông Nam Bộ* [Agriculture in the South]. Hà Nội: Khoa Học Xã Hội, 1992.

Treaster, Joseph B. "A Town in Mekong Delta Is Battered as Vietcong Pressure Mounts." *New York Times,* July 20, 1972, A3.

Trịnh Hoài Đức. *Gia Định Thành Thông Chí* [Writings on Gia Định]. Translated by Đỗ Mộng Khương and Nguyễn Ngọc Tỉnh. Edited by Đào Duy Anh. 1820; Hà Nội: Giáo Dục, 1998.

Trương Như Tang. *A Viet Cong Memoir.* New York: Vintage, 1985.

United Nations Economic and Social Commission for Asia and the Pacific. "History of UNESCAP." http://www.unescap.org/unis/sub_unis/history_unescap.asp.

University Publications of America. *Records of the Military Assistance Command Vietnam.* Pt. 2, *Classified Studies from the Combined Intelligence Center Vietnam, 1965–1973.* Bethesda, MD: University Publications of America, 1988.

U.S. Bureau of Reclamation and U.S. Agency for International Development. *To Tame a River.* Washington, DC: USBoR and USAID, 1968.

U.S. Navy. "PACFACTS News: A Glimpse of PACDIV's Remarkable History." http://www.efdpac.navfac.navy.mil/news/0101/linkHistory.htm.

Vial, Paulin. "Expedition de Cochinchine" [Mission to Cochinchina]. In *Les grands dossiers de l'illustration: L'Indochine* [The Great Issues in Illustration: Indochina], edited by Eric Baschet, 16–18. Paris: Livre de Paris, 1944.

———. *Les prèmieres années de la Cochinchine: Colonie française* [The First Years of Cochinchina: A French Colony]. 2 vols. Paris: Imprimerie Briez, C. Paillart et Retaux, 1874.

Vidal de la Blache, Paul. *Principles of Human Geography.* Translated by M. T. Bingham. New York: Henry Holt, 1926.

Võ Tòng Xuân and Shigeo Matsui, eds. *Development of Farming Systems in the Mekong Delta of Vietnam.* Hồ Chí Minh City: Hồ Chí Minh City Publishing House, 1998.

Võ Trần Nhã, ed. *Gởi Người Đang Sống: Lịch Sử Đồng Tháp Mười* [To the Living: History of Đồng Tháp]. Hồ Chí Minh City: TP Hồ Chí Minh, 1993.

Walinsky, Louis J., ed. *Agrarian Reform as Unfinished Business: The Selected Papers of Wolf Ladejinsky.* New York: Oxford University Press, 1977.

Weisberg, Barry. *Ecocide in Indochina: The Ecology of War.* San Francisco: Canfield Press, 1970.

White, Peter T., and W. E. Garrett. "The Mekong: River of Terror and Hope." *National Geographic* 134, no. 6 (December 1968): 737–89.

White, Richard. *The Middle Ground: Indians, Empires, and Republics in the Great Lakes Region, 1650–1815.* New York: Cambridge University Press, 1991.

Wittfogel, Karl A. *Das erwachende China* [The Awakening China]. Vienna: Agis Verlag, 1926.

———. *Oriental Despotism: A Comparative Study of Total Power.* New York: Vintage, 1957.

Wolters, O. W. *History, Culture, and Region in Southeast Asian Perspectives.* Ithaca, NY: Southeast Asia Program Publications, 1999.

Worster, Donald. *Dust Bowl: The Southern Plains in the 1930's.* New York: Oxford University Press, 1979.

———. *Rivers of Empire: Water, Aridity, and the Growth of the American West.* New York: Pantheon, 1992.

Young, Marilyn B. *The Vietnam Wars, 1945–1960.* New York: Harper Perennial, 1991.

Zasloff, Joseph J. "Rural Resettlement in South Viet Nam: The Agroville Program." *Pacific Affairs* 35, no. 4 (1962–63): 327–40.

ARCHIVAL COLLECTIONS

Bộ Giao Thông Công Chánh [Ministry of Communications and Public Works]. Trung Tâm Lưu Trữ Quốc Gia II [Vietnamese National Archives Center, no. 2], Hồ Chí Minh City.

Fonds Goucoch [Records of the Government of Cochinchina]. Trung Tâm Lưu Trữ Quốc Gia II, Hồ Chí Minh City.

Goucoch divers [Miscellaneous Records of the Government of Cochinchina]. Trung Tâm Lưu Trữ Quốc Gia II, Hồ Chí Minh City.

Henry Field Papers. Collection 72. Otto G. Richter Library Archives and Special Collections Department. University of Miami, Coral Gables, FL.

Oral Histories. Lyndon Baines Johnson Library and Museum, Austin, TX.

Phủ Thủ Tướng Ngụy Quyền Miền Nam [Prime Minister's Office: Southern Puppet Regime]. Trung Tâm Lưu Trữ Quốc Gia Số II, Ho Chi Minh City.

Phủ Tổng Thống Đệ Nhất Công Hòa Miền Nam [First Presidential Cabinet]. Trung Tâm Lưu Trữ Quốc Gia II, Hồ Chí Minh City.

Thư Viện Viện Khoa Học Xã Hội [Library of the Institute of Social Sciences and the Humanities], Hồ Chí Minh City.

Toà Đại Biểu Chính Phủ Nam Việt [Southern Delegate of the State of Vietnam]. Trung Tâm Lưu Trữ Quốc Gia II, Hồ Chí Minh City.

Trung Tâm Thông Tin Khoa Học Xã Hội [Social Sciences Information Center], Hà Nội.

U.S. Agency for International Development (USAID). Record Group 286. National Archives and Records Administration, Center 2 (NARA2), College Park, MD.

U.S. Bureau of Reclamation. Record Group 115. National Archives and Records Administration, Denver, CO.

U.S. Department of State. Record Group 59. National Archives and Records Administration, Center 2 (NARA2), College Park, MD.

U.S. Forces in Southeast Asia, 1950–75. Record Group 472. National Archives and Records Administration, Center 2 (NARA2), College Park, MD.

U.S. Naval Forces. Vietnam Monthly Historical Summaries, 1966–73. Vietnam Archive, Texas Tech University, Lubbock, TX.

U.S. Operations Mission, Vietnam. Record Group 469. National Archives and Records Administration, Center 2 (NARA2), College Park, MD.

INDEX

Page numbers in italics refer to captions for maps, figures and tables.

aerial photography: American uses of, 52, 200; in Gourou's research, 105–8, 108; impact on ideas about landscape, 12, 16, 52, 93–95

Agricultural Development Center (Công Trường Khuếch Trương Nông Nghiệp), 170

Agricultural Mechanization Campaign (Quốc-Gia Nông-Cụ Cơ-Giới-Cuộc), 170

agricultural tools: *cây phãng*, 62–63; Chinese imports, 64–65; sickles, 64–65

agroville, 54, 152, 162, 164, *188*, 189–95, 218, 221, 224, 231

alum. See *đất phen*

American War. *See* Second Indochina War

Americans (U.S.): advisers, 151, 153–54, 156, 162–64, 166–70, 174, 180, 190–94, 208–10, 224–25; contractors, 199, 214–16

Anderson, Benedict, 81–82, 163
ấp trù mật. See agroville
arroyo. See *rạch*
Arroyo de la Poste. *See* Bảo Định Canal
Asian Development Bank, 233
Asian regionalism, 211–12, 214, 216
Associated State of Vietnam (1949–55). *See* State of Vietnam
August Revolution, 121, 125, 127, 137

Bà Bèo Canal, 30
Bà Chúa Xứ, 62, 231–32, 246n16
Ba Cụt, 137, 139
Ba Thê Canal, 16, 96, 102, 111
Bạc Liêu (province), 143, 187, 209
Bạc Liêu (town), 100–101, 111, 145, 209
Bãi Xâu, 51, 135
Bảo Đại, King, 134, 140, 154
Bảo Định Canal, 24, 27, 30, 39, 65, 66, 73
barrages. See dams
Barrows, Leland, 166, 194
Bassac River. See Hậu Giang branch
Bassac-Rạch Sỏi Canal, 165
bassin de chasse. See flushing basin
Baurac, J. C., 48, 49, 49–50, 92
Bảy Thưa, 28
Bến Lức River, 27, 30
Bến Tre (province), 128, 146, 187, 189–90, 264n77
Bình Hoa Canal, 80–81
Bình Xuyên, 128–30, 135, 157
blockades: colonial, 24–26; First Indochina War, 134, 139–41
Bonard, Louis-Adolphe, Admiral-Governor, 25–26
Boquillon Canal. *See* Kế Sách Canal
Bordeaux, Pascal, 147
Brocheux, Pierre, 10, 71
Bùi Văn Lương, 169–70

cá lóc, 21
Cà Mau Peninsula, 20, *42,* 58–59, 84, 95, 98, 100, 113–14, 119, 222
Cà Mau (province), 210
Cà Mau (town), 110, *196,* 204
Cái Bè, Rạch (Creek), 41
Cái Bè (town), 72–73
Cái Sắn (settlement), 161–75, 179–80, 184, 190, 195
Cái Sơn Agroville, *152,* 191
Cái Vốn (creek), 137
cajeput *(Malaleuca cajuputi):* clearing, 89; forest fires, 96; and honey production, 74–75; in interior, 3, 70; preserves as a counter-insurgency measure, 175, 177; qualities, 252n12
Callison, C. Stuart, 217
Cambodia, 3, 14–20, 39, 51, 65–68, 102, 178–81, 212, 216, 229, 233, 288. *See also* Khmer (people)
Cần Thơ (province), 99, 146–48
Cần Thơ (town), 76, 81, 103, 110, 136, 137–38, 200, 207, 230–31
Cần Thơ Bridge, 229, 233
canals. *See* waterways
cannonière. See gunships
Cao Đài, 129, 135–36, 138, 148, 179
Carabelli Estate, 72
casier, 94, 106–11, 115–22, 124, 148, 150, 162, 164, 170, 175, 180, *182,* 189, 215, 228
casier tonkinois, 116, 119–22, 162, 164
Catton, Philip, 155, 261n19
Cây Khô Canal, 128
Central Intelligence Agency (CIA), 162, 199, 213, 216
charcoal, 74, 87, 175
Châu Đốc (province), 143, 147
Châu Đốc (town), 18, 20, 68, 85, 97, 136, 138, 147
Chinese (people): enterprises, 10, 32, 50–51, 74, 104, 209–10; immigrant

settlements, 16–17, 20, 56, 59, 61–62, 240n26; in Mekong Delta today, 232; relations with colonial authorities, 69, 129; relations with Hòa Hảo, 147; role in trade of iron tools, 39, 64–65; waterborne commerce, *31*, 35–36

Chợ Gạo Canal, 28, 32–33, 35–36, 41, *42*, 47–48, 128. *See also* waterways

Chợ Lớn, *31*, 31, 39, 59, 157

Choi Byung Wook, 69

cholera, 28, 32, 48–51, 57, 61, 67

Civil Operations for Rural Development Support (CORDS), 209–10, 213, 218,

civilizing mission. See *mission civilisatrice*

Cơ Đỏ Estate, 54, 137. *See also* plantations

Colonial Council, 35–36, 85, 100, 102, 117

Combier, Charles, 36–38, 82, 87, 128, 229

communism, 159–60

Compagnie messageries fluviales, 39–40

công (0.1 hectare), 144

contractors: American, 154, 173, 183–84, 199; colonial-era, 40, 45–47, 242n15; and *corvée*, 35; Doumer's reforms, 47; dredging, 43, 86; labor contracting, 35, 184; military, 224; monopoly, 46, 76, 85, 86; Montvenoux, 46–47, 86; post-1945 Asian, 173; public-private partnerships, 171; Rand Corporation, 216; SFEDTP, 86, 181, 183–84, 208; USAID, 215

creek. See *rạch*

crisis agricole, 87, 97–98, 195

dams: cross-canal, 41, 109, 119, 133; hydroelectric, 171–72, 211–12, 217, 234

đất bỏ hoang, 61, 69, 95–96, 115, 119–20, 150, 162, 164, 189, 218

đất giải phong. *See* liberated zones

đất phèn, 34, 95–96, 250n10

de Lachevrotière, Henri, 79–80, 82, 84, 95, 148

Decoux, Governor-General Jean, 116–17, 119, 121

Department of Public Works (colonial), 31, *42*, 58, 73–74, 76–83, 85, 93, 111–12, 117, 163

Department of Public Works (Republic of Vietnam). *See* Ministry of Public Works and Communication (Bộ Công Chánh và Giao Thông)

địa bộ, 69, 71, 76

địa chí, 18, 57, 42, 240n26, 257n33

Diệm, Ngo Đình. *See* Ngô Đình Diệm

Dinh Điền. *See* Land Settlement General Commission (Tổng-Ủy Phủ Dinh Điền)

Định Tường (province). *See* Tiền Giang (province)

ditch. See *mương*

Đoàn Minh Huyền, 27–28

documentary fiction, 95, 124, 141, 145

đồn điền, 60–61, 69–70, 73, 162

Đồng Quan, 163–64

Đồng Tháp: abandonment of, 85; ancient sites, 16; canalization and diking, *42*, 228; etymology, 18; flooding in, 96–97, 220; resettlement of, 169–71, 174, 179–81, 184–87; Trần Bá Lộc Estate, 72–73; warfare in, 26–28, *31*, 136, 204, 215, 221, 224, 241n6

dos d'âne, 32, 36, 38, 40–41, 43, 47, 135, 205

Doumer, Governor-General Paul, 47

dredges: *Bac Lieu*, 202; *Cần Thơ*, 176; in Châu Đốc, 85; cutter-suction

dredges (*continued*)
(diesel), 181, 183–85, 199, 201–3, 230; *Dredge II*, 42; *Kim Giang*, 202; *Nantes and Loire*, 47; steam-powered, 6, 10, 35, 41–48, 58, 71, 74, 76–78, 111, 122, 135, 174, 179, 181; *U Minh*, 175

dredging: compared with Suez and Panama Canals, 42–43; by conscript labor, *corvée*, 32, 35, 44, 192; ecological and social effects, 43–44; and labor conflicts, 43–46; legal disputes, 76–83; measurement of, 43; Montvenoux, 45; reorganization under Doumer, 47; Société française d'entreprises de dragages et de travaux publics (SFEDTP), 47; spare parts and repair, 45–47, 203; in speeches, 88–90; by steam-powered dredges, 42–44; at U Minh, 174–75; wartime, 201–2

Dubrow, Ambassador Elbridge, 190
Duperré, Victor-Auguste, Admiral-Governor, 30–32
Duperré Canal. *See* Chợ Gạo Canal

Eastern Coastal Zone. 18–20, 26–28, 31
ecological philosophy, 216, 233, 235
Eiffel, Gustave, 38–40, 84, 128. *See also* contractors
Elliott, David, 142, 169, 186
engineering: in colonial expansion, 73, 75–76, 78, 89–91; colonial-era lawsuits, 80–86; contemporary, 229, 235; and equipment problems, 184; and foreign consultants, 171, 172, 215; late-colonial remediation and resettlement, 93–94, 97, 111, 119, 195; in strategic settlements, 170, 174, 176–77, 179–80, 216; during wartime, 121, 135, 176–77, 213, 217
Engineering Agency for Resources Inventories (EARI), 215

engines. *See* motors (boat)
Excursions et Reconnaissances (Rénaud), 5

Fall, Bernard, 130, *131*, 137, 147, 157
famine, 51, 68, 113–14, 141–42, 149
Fascism. *See* Vichy
Father Lộc. *See* Nguyễn Ba Lộc
Ferguson, James, 43
First Indochina War: destruction of infrastructure, 133, 139; *dinnassaus*, 138, 181; enclaves, 130, 139, 144, 157, 179; initial fighting in Mekong Delta, 127–29; role of water environment, 133–35, 138; sectarian fighting, 135–41; Transbassac blockade, 139–41
Fishel, Wesley, 194
flooding: as an annual regime, 15; as a cause of colonial disputes, 41; in Đồng Tháp 1904–07, 73; implications in warfare, 139; in 1923, 96; in 1929, 96–97; in 1937, 98; in 1959, 177; in 1966, 220; in U Minh settlement, 1957, 177
flushing basin, 40–41, 47
forest. *See* cajeput (*Malaleuca cajuputi*)
fortified plantation. See Đồn Điền
Foucault, Michel, 81, 140
French School of the Far East (EFEO), 105, 107
Funan. *See* Oc Eo

garden strips. See *miệt vườn*
gazetteers. See *địa chí*
génie rural. *See* rural engineering corps (Service du génie rural)
geo-body, idea of, 29, 50. *See also* spatial perspectives
ghe tam bản, 2, 10, 27, 71, 126, 129, 135, 200, *201*, 204, 207–8, 214, 222, 231
gịa. *See* rice

Gia Định: 23–24, 59–60, 65, 67–69. *See also* Sài Gòn
Gia Long, King, 59–61, 65–66, 168
giáp nước, 31, 32–34, 135
gleaning, 99
gò (sand hill), 15, 18, 182
Gò Bác Chiên, 182
Gourou, Pierre, 94, 103, 105–8, *108*, 110, 114–15, 123–24
Great Depression, 86, 91–93, 99–100, 102–3, 110, 124, 158
Green Revolution, 94, 154–55, 207
Gressier Estate: aerial view, *52*; agricultural training school, 54; construction and operation of, 53–56, 245n2; scientific management on, 55. *See also* plantations
Gsell, Emile, *2, 33*
gunships: AC-47 "Spooky", 200; brown-water navy (U.S.), 212; *Circe*, 26; *Devastation*, 132; *dinnassaus*, 138–39; *Hache*, 3–4; role in French conquest, 23–24, 26

Hà Tiên (town), 4–5, 17, 18, *60*, 68
Halberstam, David, 7
Hậu Giang branch, 27, 74, 137, 140, 229. *See also* waterways
Hậu Giang region (*Transbassac*), 42, 74–76, 78, 98, 107, 114, 136, 139–40, 148, 150, 225
helicopters, *196*, 198, 205, 219, 221
Henry, Yves, 114
Hòa Hảo Buddhism, 28, 129–31, 135–43, 146–49, 154, 179, 256n17
Hòa Lựu (village), 218
Hồ Chí Minh, President, 149
Hưởng Chủ Chot, 100–102
Huỳnh Phú Sổ, 136–37

Indigo Forest (Rừng Chàm), 180, 182f

Indochinese Communist Party (ICP), 93, 104, 113–14, 122
iron. *See* steel
irrigation: natural, tidal, 14, 34; ditches, 60, 77, 79, 81, 111; mechanical, 56, 156, 159; pollution associated with, 117–18

Jackson, John Brinckerhoff, 13
Jammé, P. C., 121–22, 170–71, 175, 177, 180, *182*, 215
Japanese military occupation (1940–45), 41, 116, 119, 121–22, 124–25, 128–29, 136, 149
Jauréguiberry, Jean Bernard, Minister, 34, 36, 243n22
Jennings, Eric, 119
Johnson, Lyndon Baines, President, 199, 211, 213

Kế Sách Canal, 72
Khmer (people): and agricultural tools, 61–63; ancient sites, 16; contemporary land disputes, 233; correspondence with colonial government, 72; cultural practices, 62–63; former town names, 20; in Ninh Thạnh Lợi protests, 100–102; pre-colonial honey production, 74; rebellions at Vĩnh Tế Canal, 5, 51, 67–68; relations with Nguyễn authorities, 20, 51, 59; resettlement in Long Xuyên Quadrangle, 110–12; resettlement by RVN at U Minh, 174–75
khu trù mật. See agroville
Komer, Robert, 213

La Cochinchine et ses habitants (Baurac), 24, 50, *92*
labor: conditions on colonial estates, 99–100; conscripted (*corvée*), 5,

31–33, *33*, 41, 44, 167, 192; contract
(*engagé*), 103–4, 252n29; strikes and
protests, 93, 113–14; tenant farming
(*tá điền*), 43, 54, 72, 87, 91, 92, 95,
97–103; wage-, 98, 103–4, 110, 112–14,
123, 134, 141, 160, 167–69, 217, 235
Ladejinsky, Wolf, 153, 158–62, 166,
168–69, 193–95
Lagrange Canal, 73, 179–80
Lái Hiếu Canal, 75, 79–81, 84, 87
Lâm Thành Nguyên, 130, 138, 147
land policy: debated during the
First Indochina War, 141, 145,
148–51; dual colonial policies, 70–71,
98–103; contemporary protests for,
230; interest rates, 54, 93, 103, 169;
Land to the Tiller (Thiệu), 217–18;
late colonial debates on, 92–94, 103,
110, 113–15; Ngô Đình Diệm regime,
155, 158–69, 180, 192–95; Nguyễn
dynasty policies, 56–67, 69–70,
247n42; rent ceilings in liberated
zones, 159–60; Việt Minh, 134–45
Land Settlement General Commission
(Tổng-Ủy Phủ Dinh Điền), 169–70
Land to the Tiller Campaign, 93, 141,
169, 217
Láng Hầm (village), *126, 232*
Lansdale, Edward, 162
Law 10/59, 186–87, 189
Lê Duẩn, 144–46
Le Myre de Vilers, Charles, Governor,
34–35, 38, 40
Lê Quang Liêm, 100–102
Lê Văn Hoạch, 148
Lê Văn Khôi, 68
Leroy, Jean, 127–28, 146
Les paysans du delta Tonkinois
(Gourou), 94, 105–8
Li Tana, 61
liberated zones, 130, 135, 139–45, 149,

156, 159–60, 169–70, 174, 181, 192–93,
198, 208, 210, 218, 225
Lilienthal, David, 213–15
literacy, 145, 217
Long Xuyên Quadrangle, *17*, 17–18,
25, 42, 91, 95–96, 99–112, 119, 136,
162–65, 228
Long Xuyên-Rạch Giá Canal, 65–67,
137
lục bình, 4, 20–21, 197, 200

malaise agricole, 94–95, 195
máy kô-le. See under motors (boat)
Mang Thít Canal, 138, 204–6
Mekong Committee, 172–74, 212–14
Mekong Delta: in popular imagination, 9; tourism, 12. *See also* Cà
Mau Peninsula; cajeput (*Malaleuca
cajuputi*); *đất phen*; Đồng Tháp;
Eastern Coastal Zone; Long Xuyên
Quadrangle; *lục bình*; *miệt vườn*;
waterways
Mekong Delta Development Program,
213
Mekong River: etymology, 6; hydrologic characteristics, 14–16; and
mainstream dams, 234. *See also*
waterways
Meyerson, Harvey, 200, 205–6
Michigan State University Group, 191,
194
miệt vườn, 14, 18–22, 34, 50, 70,
109–10, 231
migration: Chinese, 11, 16, 59; cultural
hybridization resulting from, 61–63;
to colonial estates (1920–30), 102–3,
111; between liberated and government zones (1945–75), 143; northern
refugee (1954–75), 121, 130, 140, 144,
153–57, 164–69, 221–22; resettlement
zones, 119–24, 235. See also *nam tiến*

military province. See *trấn*

Military Region 9 (Việt Minh, NLF), 146, 174

millenarianism, 26–29, 136

Minh Mạng, King, 66–69

Ministry of Public Works and Communication (Bộ Công Chánh và Giao Thông), 154, 180, 183–84, 203

Ministry of Water Resources (Bộ Thủy Lợi), 117, 164

mission civilisatrice, 4, 35–37, 40, 49–50, 72, 88–90, 173, 183

modernization: American ideas of, 153–64; colonial ideas of, 35; and high modernism, 161–62; narratives of, 156–57

monographs, provincial. See *địa chí*

Montvenoux, 45–47, 86

motorized pumps. See *under* pumps

motors (boat): Kohler Corporation and, 200–201, 207, 230–31; outboard, 200–201, 214, 227; shrimptail, 199–200, 214. See also pumps

Mr. Dang, 218

Mr. Diều, 53–58, 90, 144

Mr. Hai, 99–100

Mr. Mười, 99, 220

Mr. Rì, 99

Mr. Rỡ, 127, 134, 149, 197, 209

mù u (tree), 64, 116, 220

mương, 34

museums, 82, 121, 163, 200–201, 231, 233

Mỹ An (village), 178–80

Mỹ Tho (province). See Tiền Giang (province)

Mỹ Tho (town): as colonial gateway to the delta, 31–32, 39; in First Indochina War, 133, 140, 169, 186; railroad, 37–38; river steamers, 39–40; in Second Indochina War,

207–9, 224; tourism today, 230

Mỹ Thuận Bridge, 6, 212, 228

Nam Lửa. *See* Trần Văn Soái

nam tiến, 11, 56–58, 60–61, 71, 162

nation building: American narratives of, 154–73; First Indochina War, 148–51; and hybridity, 8; late colonial era, 116; pre-colonial forms of, 67–68; role of nature in, 7; Vietnamization, 214–16

National Liberation Front (NLF), 146, 198–210, 216–25

nationalism: and modernization, 41; response to agricultural problems, 93; and Vichy rule, 119

navigation: blockades and checkpoints, 139–41, 221; colonial-era, 32, 36, 111, 117; Compagnie messageries fluviales, 39; in First Indochina War, 132; insurgent (PLAF) use of waterways, 204; rice convoys, 128, 130, 132, 134–35, 138–40. See also spatial perspectives

Neak Ta (Ông Tà), 62

newspapers: *Courrier de Saïgon*, 72; *la Lutte*, 113–14; *New York Times*, 166, 224, 230; *Nông-Cổ Mín Đàm* [Agricultural Forum], 41; portrayal of rural problems, 113–16; *Tribune indochinoise*, 113–14

Ngô Đình Diệm, 153–70, 174, 177, 180, 182–95, 202, 208

Ngô Đình Nhu, 93

Ngô Đình Nhu, Madame, 156, 167, 193

Ngô Việt Thu, 190

Ngô Vĩnh Long, 70

Nguyễn ánh. *See* Gia Long, King

Nguyễn Ba Lộc, 166–69

Nguyễn dynasty: barracks, 25; cultural assimilation policy, 69; forts in

Nguyễn dynasty (*continued*)
the Mekong Delta, 59–60; reforms,
69; settlement policies of, 17; tax
registers, 63
Nguyễn Hiến Lê, 73, 243n21
Nguyễn Minh Triết, President, 229
Nguyễn Thị Định, 186–87, 189
Nguyễn Thụy Nga, 146
Nguyễn Trị Phương, 24
Nguyễn Trung Trực, 23, 26–27, 136
Nguyễn Văn Tâm, 148, 160
Nguyễn Văn Thiệu, President, 216–18
Nguyễn Văn Thinh, President, 115,
148, 150
Nguyễn Văn Thoại, 65–68, 231
Nguyễn Văn Thơi, 168
Nhơn ái (village), 76–79
Nhơn Nghĩa (village), 76–79, 79,
249n64
Nhu, Madame. *See* Ngô Đình Nhu,
Madame
Nhu, Ngô Đình. *See* Ngô Đình Nhu
Nicolai-Mang Thít Canal. *See* Mang
Thít Canal
Ninh Thạnh Lợi (village), 100–102,
110, 146
Ninth Infantry Division (U.S. Army),
205
Nixon, Richard Milhous, President,
163, 168, 214, 216–17
Nolting, Frederick, U.S. Ambassador,
202
Nông Cổ Mín-Đàm. See under
newspapers

Ô Môn Canal, 137
Oc Eo: 16, 17, 241n7
Ông Vân, Rạch (Creek), 41
opium, 36–37, 87, 128, 155
Ordinance 57, 169–70

Paris, Pierre, 16
Partí constitutionaliste indochinoise,
93, 114, 115
Partí démocrate indochinoise, 115, 148
Pasquier, Pierre, Governor-General,
88–90
peat swamps, 20, 58, 88, 96, 111, 174–75,
177, 234–35, 240n28
Penelope, works of, 37–38, 47, 82, 87,
227
People's Army, 224
People's Army Canal, 138, 145
People's Liberation Armed Forces
(PLAF), 204–9, 221, 224
People's Republic of China, 142
Phạm Hoàng Hộ, 21
Phạm Văn Thành, 208
Phan Quang Đan, 192
Phan Thanh Giản, 25–26
Phi Vân, 124–25, 255n81
Phú Quốc (island), 27
Plain des Joncs. *See* Đồng Tháp
Plain of Reeds. *See* Đồng Tháp
plantations: 43, 47, 54–55, 55, 59,
69–70, 72–76, 92–99, 103–4, 107,
109, 115–16, 124, 129, 132–33, 136–39,
141–42, 148–49, 160, 164, 179, 193.
See also Carabelli Estate; *đồn điền;*
Gressier Estate; Red Flag (*Cờ Đỏ*)
Estate; Trần Bá Lộc Estate
polders. See *casier*
Popular Front (France), 93, 110–14,
116, 125, 141, 145, 150, 162
population: changes during First
Indochina War, 145–47; colonial
census adjustments for, 48–51;
comparative density in Red River
Delta, 252n29; differences between
controlled and non-controlled
territories, 1953, 142–43; growth in
colonial era, 82; growth since 1975,
227–28; increases by province, 56–58

Porter, Theodore, 76, 215

Pouyanne, Albert, 47, 80

protests: Cái Sắn, 167; Caravelle Manifesto, 193–94; contemporary land disputes, 233; Hậu Giang, 114; May Day 1930, 104; Nam Kỳ Uprising, 116; Ninh Thạnh Lợi, 100–102; Thành Thới agroville, 190

provincial monographs. See địa chí

provisional governments. See Associated State of Vietnam (1949–55); Provisional Revolutionary Government; Republic of Cochinchina

Provivisional Revolutionary Government, 218, 224

public works. See Department of Public Works (colonial); Ministry of Public Works and Communication (Bộ Công Chánh và Giao Thông); Ministry of Water Resources (Bộ Thủy Lợi)

pumps: on colonial estates, 55–56; motorized (small), 58, 97, 170, 199, 201, 207–9, 217, 221; stations (large-scale), 53, 119, 122, 163, 174

Quản Lộ-Phụng Hiệp Canal, 42, 95

Quiet American (Greene), 155–56

rạch: 1, 14, 18, 24, 34, 36, 39, 73, 187, 250n12

Rạch Giá (province), 77, 81, 100, 110, 140, 143, 245n2

Rạch Giá (town), 26–28, 41, 66, 88, 96, 133, 165, 250n12

Rạch Giá-Hà Tiên Canal, 42, 44, 88–90, 102

railroads, 34–40, 49–50, 83, 119, 121, 127, 128, 129, 183

Rand Corporation. See under contractors

Ranh Hạt Canal, 175–76, 176

Red Flag (Cờ Đỏ) Estate, 54, 137

Red River Delta (Tonkin), 103–8, 111, 111–15, 121, 124, 163, 167, 192

refugees. See migration

Rénaud, Jacques, 4–5, 35–38, 82, 135, 231–32

Republic Canal, 181, 182, 184, 202

Republic of Cochinchina (1946–47), 147–48

resettlement, Long Xuyên Quadrangle, 101–4, 110–12. See also Long Xuyên Quadrangle; migration

Resistance Canal (Kinh Kháng Chiến), 178

rice: declining values after 1931, 91–92; floating, 63–64, 96, 219; giạ as measure, 98, 100; historical varieties, 63–64; Japanese price quotas, 116; phantom rice, 75, 219; phương as measure, 65; sticky, 64

rice milling: on the Gressier Estate, 54; under the Hòa Hảo, 136–38; Japanese portable units, 209–10

river transport. See navigation

River Transport Company. See Compagnie messageries fluviales

roads, 21, 29, 32, 35, 40, 56, 68, 75, 83, 97, 108, 127–29, 132–35, 140, 166, 173, 179, 185, 227

rural engineering corps (Service du génie rural), 117–19

Sài Gòn, 4, 8, 11, 17, 25, 25–28, 32–33, 37–39, 155–58, 183, 192

Saintard Canal, 41

Saintenoy Canal, 99

Sam Mountain, 5

sampan. See ghe tam bản

Sansom, Robert, 208–9

Sập Mountain, 66–67

Savani, A. M., 156

Scott, James, 161, 255n79, 260n18

Second Indochina War (1959–75): chemicals and, 197–98, 218–19; control of waterways, 205; escalation post-1973, 223–25; wild species and, 219–20

Seven Mountains. *See* Thất Sơn

Sóc Trăng (town): 41, 51, 59, 135, *196*, 216

social science: in colonial approaches to rural poverty, 104–6; French approaches, 104–5, 252n39; Henry Field and the M Project, 121; and Orientalism, 104–5

Socialist Republic of Vietnam, 164

Société française d'entreprises de dragages et de travaux publics (SFEDTP), 47, 85–86, 181–84, 208. *See also* dredging

Société indigènes de crédit agricole et mutuel (SICAM), 97–98

Sơn Nam, 9–11, 43, 146, 150, 238n13, 247n42

Sông Trệm Canal, 176

South East Asia Lake Ocean River Delta Strategy (SEALORDS), 221–22

Southern Regional Committee (Xứ Ủy Nam Bộ), 144–45

southward march. *See nam tiến*

spatial perspectives: bird's-eye versus surface views, 12–13, 108–9; contact zones, 156–57; errors in calculation, 84–85; floating versus surface, 39–40, 139, 200; geo-bodies and topologies, 29–30; hydraulic versus political boundaries, 81; landscape mosaics, 215–16; regional development schemes, 214–15; space-time compression (David Harvey),

265n4; surveying elevation, 82–84; visibility and invisibility, 140–41, 145, 200

State of Vietnam (1949–55), 134, 139, 159–60, 163

steel: scoops on early dredges, 45; span bridges, 38; use in open-air markets, 40; use in Sài Gòn General Post Office, 40

strategic hamlet, 162, *188*, 194

tá điền, 114, 141–50

Tạ Thu Thâu, 113

Tai, Hue-Tam Ho, 28

Tâm, Nguyễn Văn. *See* Nguyễn Văn Tâm

Tân An Bridge, 38

Tân Hiệp (village), 165–68

telegraph, 3, *29*, 30, *31*, 40, 205, 242n15

tenant farming. *See* labor; *tá điền*

Tết Offensive, 198, 212, 215, 217–18

Thành Thới (agroville), *188*, 189, 195

Thắp Mười Canal, 179

Thất Sơn, 18, 130, 136, 143, 147, 157

Thiệu, Nguyễn Văn. *See* Nguyễn Văn Thiệu, President

Thoại Hà. *See* Long Xuyên-Rạch Giá Canal

Thoại Ngọc Hầu. *See* Nguyễn Văn Thoại

Thongchai Winichakul, 29, 238n11, 242n14

Thốt Nốt Canal, 41, 135, 137, 139

Thủ Thừa, *31*, 31–32. See also *giáp nước*

tidal creek. See *rạch*

tides: dual tidal pulses, 14; effects on French canal dredging 32–34; and flushing basins, 40; measurement of, 37, 80; significance during wartime, 204

Tiền Giang (province), 57, 63–65, *66*,

84, 97, 109, 169, 186, 256n6

Tiếp Nhứt (village), 217

Tổng Đốc Lộc. *See* Trần Bá Lộc

Tổng Đốc Lộc Canal, 73, *92*, 132, 180

tools. *See* agricultural tools

tractors, 156, 161, 166–70, 180, 187, 195

tràm. See cajeput (*Malaleuca cajuputi*)

trấn, 18, 65

Trần Bá Lộc, District Chief (Tổng
   Đốc), 27, *55*, 72–73, 248n50

Trần Bá Lộc Estate, 72–73

Trần Chánh Gilbert Chiếu, 41

Trần Văn Soái, 136–39, 147, 256n17

Trần Văn Thành, 26–27, 257n21

Trần Văn Trà, 186

Transbassac. *See* Hậu Giang region
   (*Transbassac*)

Tri Tôn Canal, 102, 111, 120f

Trịnh Hoài Đức, 3

Trương Công Định, 25–26, 28

Trương Ngọc Tường, 64f

Tự Đức, King, 25–27, 63. *See also*
   Nguyễn dynasty

U Minh Forest, 58, 117, 133–34, 136, 138,
   144, 146, 150, 157, 159, 169, 170, 171,
   174–79, *188*, 205, 221–25, 234, 257n21

Ugly American (Lederer and Burdick),
   156, 159

uncultivated land. See *đất bỏ hoang*

United Nations Economic Commission for Asia and the Far East
   (ECAFE). *See* Mekong Committee

Unités mobiles de défense des chrétiens (UMDC), 146. *See also* Leroy,
   Jean

U.S. Agency for International Development (USAID), 207, 209, 215

U.S. Consultants, Inc., 173. *See also*
   contractors

U.S. Operations Mission (USOM),
158–63, 166, 169–73, 177, 180–86, 190,
194, 202, 208

Vàm Cỏ Rivers (East and West), *31*, 32,
   38, 186. *See also* waterways

Vị Thanh (town), 54, 190–92, 218,
   224–25, 231

Vị Thủy, 74–75

Vial, Paulin, 24–26, 241n6

Vichy, 116–25

Việt Minh, 54, 126, 128, *131*, 132–40,
   142–150. *See also* First Indochina
   War; land policy; liberated zones

Vietnam War. *See* Second Indochina
   War (1959–75)

Vĩnh Kim (village), 224

Vinh Long (Meyerson), 205

Vĩnh Long (province), 57, 109, *152*

Vĩnh Long (town), 20, 25, 65, 68, 139

Vĩnh Tế Canal, 3–6, 26–28, 35–37,
   65–68, 231–32

Võ Duy Dương, 26–28, 128

water hyacinth (*Eichhornia crassipes*).
   See *lục bình*

water pumps. *See* pumps

waterways: Bà Bèo Canal, 30; Ba Thê
   Canal, 16, 96, 102, 111; Bảo Định
   Canal, 24, 27, 30, 39, 65, 66, 73;
   Bassac-Rạch Sỏi Canal, *165*; Bến
   Lức River, 27, 30; Bình Hoa Canal,
   80–81; Cái Bè, Rạch (Creek), 41; Cái
   Vồn (creek), 137; Cây Khô Canal,
   128; Chợ Gạo Canal, 28, 32–33,
   35–36, 41, *42*, 47–48, 128; Hậu Giang
   branch, 27, 74, 137, 140, 229; Kế
   Sách Canal, 72; Lagrange Canal, 73,
   179–80; Lái Hiếu Canal, 75, 79–81,
   84, 87; Long Xuyên-Rạch Giá Canal,
   65–67, 137; Mang Thít Canal, 138,
   204–6; Ô Môn Canal, 137; Ông Vân,

waterways (*continued*)

Rạch (Creek), 41; People's Army Canal, 138, 145; Quản Lộ-Phụng Hiệp Canal, *42*, 95; *rạch*: 2, 14, 18, 24, 34, 36, 39, 73, 187, 250n12; Rạch Giá-Hà Tiên Canal, *42*, *44*, 88–90, 102; Ranh Hạt Canal, 175–76, *176*; Republic Canal, 181, *182*, 184, 202; Resistance Canal (Kinh Kháng Chiến), 178; Saintard Canal, 41; Saintenoy Canal, 99; Sông Trệm Canal, 176; Thắp Mười Canal, 179; Thốt Nốt Canal, 41, 135, 137, 139; Tổng Đốc Lộc Canal, 73, *92*, 132, 180; Tri Tôn Canal, 102, 111, *120*; Vàm Cỏ Rivers (East and West), *31*, 32, 38, 186; Vĩnh Tế Canal, 3–6, 26–28, 35–37, 65–68, 231–32; Xà No Canal, *42*, *52*, 53–54, 76–78, *79*, 189. *See also* Mekong Delta; Mekong River

well drilling, 210

White, Peter, 212–13

World Bank, 217, 233

Xà No Canal, *42*, *52*, 53–54, 76–78, *79*, 189

Xáng Canal (Mỹ Tho), 128

Zasloff, Joseph, 191

The Natural History of Puget Sound Country by Arthur R. Kruckeberg

*Forest Dreams, Forest Nightmares: The Paradox of Old Growth
   in the Inland West* by Nancy Langston

Landscapes of Promise: The Oregon Story, 1800–1940 by William G. Robbins

*The Dawn of Conservation Diplomacy: U.S.-Canadian Wildlife Protection
   Treaties in the Progressive Era* by Kurkpatrick Dorsey

Irrigated Eden: The Making of an Agricultural Landscape in the American West
   by Mark Fiege

Making Salmon: An Environmental History of the Northwest Fisheries Crisis
   by Joseph E. Taylor III

George Perkins Marsh, Prophet of Conservation by David Lowenthal

*Driven Wild: How the Fight against Automobiles Launched the Modern
   Wilderness Movement* by Paul S. Sutter

The Rhine: An Eco-Biography, 1815–2000 by Mark Cioc

Where Land and Water Meet: A Western Landscape Transformed
   by Nancy Langston

The Nature of Gold: An Environmental History of the Alaska/Yukon Gold Rush
   by Kathryn Morse

Faith in Nature: Environmentalism as Religious Quest by Thomas R. Dunlap

Landscapes of Conflict: The Oregon Story, 1940–2000 by William G. Robbins

The Lost Wolves of Japan by Brett L. Walker

Wilderness Forever: Howard Zahniser and the Path to the Wilderness Act
   by Mark Harvey

On the Road Again: Montana's Changing Landscape by William Wyckoff

Public Power, Private Dams: The Hells Canyon High Dam Controversy
   by Karl Boyd Brooks

Windshield Wilderness: Cars, Roads, and Nature in Washington's National Parks
   by David Louter

Native Seattle: Histories from the Crossing-Over Place by Coll Thrush

The Country in the City: The Greening of the San Francisco Bay Area
   by Richard A. Walker

Drawing Lines in the Forest: Creating Wilderness Areas in the Pacific Northwest
   by Kevin R. Marsh

Plowed Under: Agriculture and Environment in the Palouse by Andrew P. Duffin

Making Mountains: New York City and the Catskills by David Stradling

The Fishermen's Frontier: People and Salmon in Southeast Alaska
   by David F. Arnold

Shaping the Shoreline: Fisheries and Tourism on the Monterey Coast
by Connie Y. Chiang
Dreaming of Sheep in Navajo Country by Marsha Weisiger
The Toxic Archipelago: A History of Industrial Disease in Japan by Brett L. Walker
Seeking Refuge: Birds and Landscapes of the Pacific Flyway by Robert M. Wilson
Quagmire: Nation-Building and Nature in the Mekong Delta by David Biggs

WEYERHAEUSER ENVIRONMENTAL CLASSICS

The Great Columbia Plain: A Historical Geography, 1805–1910 by D. W. Meinig
*Mountain Gloom and Mountain Glory: The Development of the Aesthetics
    of the Infinite* by Marjorie Hope Nicolson
Tutira: The Story of a New Zealand Sheep Station by Herbert Guthrie-Smith
A Symbol of Wilderness: Echo Park and the American Conservation Movement
    by Mark Harvey
Man and Nature: Or, Physical Geography as Modified by Human Action
    by George Perkins Marsh; edited and annotated by David Lowenthal
Conservation in the Progressive Era: Classic Texts edited by David Stradling
DDT, Silent Spring, and the Rise of Environmentalism: Classic Texts
    edited by Thomas R. Dunlap

CYCLE OF FIRE BY STEPHEN J. PYNE

Fire: A Brief History
World Fire: The Culture of Fire on Earth
*Vestal Fire: An Environmental History, Told through Fire,
    of Europe and Europe's Encounter with the World*
Fire in America: A Cultural History of Wildland and Rural Fire
Burning Bush: A Fire History of Australia
The Ice: A Journey to Antarctica

CPSIA information can be obtained
at www.ICGtesting.com
Printed in the USA
BVHW040800021122
650862BV00002B/166